MONEY, INTEREST RATES AND INFLATION

ECONOMISTS OF THE TWENTIETH CENTURY

General Editors: Mark Perlman, *University Professor of Economics, University of Pittsburgh* and Mark Blaug, *Professor Emeritus, University of London and Visiting Professor, University of Exeter*

This innovative series comprises specially invited collections of articles and papers by economists whose work has made an important contribution to economics in the late twentieth century.

The proliferation of new journals and the ever-increasing number of new articles make it difficult for even the most assiduous economist to keep track of all the important recent advances. By focusing on those economists whose work is generally recognized to be at the forefront of the discipline, the series will be an essential reference point for the different specialisms included.

A list of published and future titles in this series is printed at the end of this volume.

Money, Interest Rates and Inflation

Frederic S. Mishkin

A. Barton Hepburn Professor of Economics
Graduate School of Business, Columbia University
and Research Associate
National Bureau of Economic Research

Edward Elgar

Published by
Edward Elgar Publishing Limited
Gower House
Croft Road
Aldershot
Hants GU11 3HR
England

Edward Elgar Publishing Company
Old Post Road
Brookfield
Vermont 05036
USA

A CIP catalogue record for this book is available from the British Library

Library of Congress Cataloging-in-Publication Data
Mishkin, Frederic S.
Money, interest rates, and inflation/Frederic S. Mishkin.
p. cm. — (Economists of the twentieth century)
1. Interest rates. 2. Inflation (Finance) 3. Monetary policy.
I. Title. II. Series.
HB539.M53 1993
332.4—dc20
93–2700
CIP

ISBN 1 85278 850 X

Printed and Bound in Great Britain by
Hartnolls Limited, Bodmin, Cornwall.

To my Father, who I miss terribly

Contents

Acknowledgements

Research in economics is never done in a vacuum, but requires input from colleagues to reach fruition. Particularly important to developing the line of research laid out in this book have been my coauthors, Robert Cumby of the Stern School of Business, New York University, John Huizinga of the Graduate School of Business, University of Chicago, and Philippe Jorion of the Graduate School of Business, Columbia University. Not only have they contributed directly to this research by being coauthors of several of the studies included in this volume, but they have also contributed indirectly by providing me with valuable comments on my single-authored papers. In addition, they have made the research process far more enjoyable, and I thank them. The research in this book has also benefited from comments made by numerous colleagues, whose names are listed at the beginning of each article. I also wish to thank my wife, Sally, and my children, Matthew and Laura, who provide me with the love and support that makes my work possible.

Introduction

Throughout my career, my research has been driven by the need to understand how monetary policy affects the economy. An integral part of understanding the monetary transmission mechanism is to comprehend the relationship between money, interest rates and inflation, and this is the unifying theme of the 15 articles that make up this volume.

The research in this book is unabashedly empirical. The approach is clearly to lay out the assumptions behind the econometric framework and then to attack the data econometrically from several points of view in order to learn what they have to say about the relationship of money, interest rates and inflation. Indeed, I would characterize my research style in these articles by saying that I have tried to beat the data with a rubber hose until they revealed what they could about the questions posed. This style is not the product of my having watched too many spy movies or by any latent enjoyment of torture on my part, but rather stems from my belief that only by putting the data to a whole battery of tests can we get some sense of what that data may be trying to tell us.

An important motivation for putting all these articles together in one book is that it enables the reader to get a better feel for how the data have been beaten by the rubber hose, since cowing the data into submission often requires several attempts and thus several journal articles. In addition, reading the articles together enables the reader to see the interrelationships between the articles, thereby providing a clearer picture of what they tell us about the economy.

Another common feature of all the articles is that they all pursue a rational expectations approach in conducting the econometric analysis. The rational expectations hypothesis, which indicates that expectations can be modelled as optimal forecasts given all available information, has significant implications for how models should be estimated. Although as Christopher Sims (1980) has pointed out, rational expectations casts doubt on the traditional criteria for identifying and estimating time-series models that make use of exclusion restrictions, the rational expectations approach does provide restrictions of another sort which do allow identification and estimation.

The rational expectations assumption is now a standard one in much of the research in finance and monetary-macroeconomics and understanding its implications for econometric practice is thus very important. The articles here provide valuable insights into rational expectations econometrics because the techniques outlined and developed in the articles now have widespread usage in applied work in both the finance and money-macro areas. Reading these articles together should therefore also provide readers with the additional benefit of adding useful econometric techniques to their tool kits, which can be very useful in empirical research on a broad range of topics, many of which may be very different from the ones treated here.

In order to help the reader see the interactions between the following chapters, it will be beneficial to provide a brief 'road map' for the book, making the journey through it an easier one to follow. There are two additional reasons why I want to supply a quick tour of the book. Firstly, it gives me an opportunity to step back from the articles and give my current perspective on what this body of research tells us about the economy. Secondly, since the investment in reading a book is quite high, I want to convince the reader that his or her time will be well spent. To do this, I want to give the reader an idea of what specifically is to be gained by reading this volume.

Part I Money and interest rates

Part I contains two chapters that look at the empirical relationship between money and interest rates, a hotly debated topic in the literature which continues today. (For example, very recent empirical papers on this topic include Christiano and Eichenbaum (1992), Leeper and Gordon (1992) and Strongin (1991).) According to one view – also a feature of most structural macroeconometric models – an increase in money supply growth leads, at least in the short and medium runs, to a decline in interest rates. The resulting decline in interest rates is seen as a critical element in the transmission mechanism of monetary policy since it is viewed as stimulating investment and consumer spending. In addition, the view that increases in the money supply lead to a decline in interest rates has important implications for what a central bank should do when it wants interest rates to fall. It is the rationale for American government officials' frequent calls on the Federal Reserve to raise the rate of money growth in order to lower interest rates.

An alternative view, which has been championed by Milton Friedman (1968, 1969), indicates that rather than fall when there is an increase in money supply growth, interest rates rise because of higher expected inflation, as well as from the rise in real income and the price level that result from the increase in money growth. Friedman's view thus does not recommend increases in money growth in order to bring interest rates down, but rather suggests that low interest rates can only be achieved in the long run with low rates of money growth. Clearly, the relationship of money supply growth and interest rates is an important one for policy-makers.

The two chapters in Part I use efficient-markets (or, equivalently, rational expectations) models to examine empirically the relationship of money and interest rates. The efficient-markets, rational expectations approach used in this research distinguishes between the effects from unanticipated versus anticipated monetary policy. In the resulting models, cross-equation restrictions implied by rational expectations are of central importance. The advantage of imposing these rational expectations, cross-equation restrictions is that they lead to empirical models that are far easier to interpret; they have the additional benefit of producing more powerful statistical tests of the proposition that increases in money supply growth are correlated with declines in interest rates.

The empirical results in the two Part I chapters uniformly *do not support* the proposition that increases in money growth are correlated with declines in interest rates. Rather than finding a negative relationship between increases in money growth and interest rates, Chapter 1 finds some tendency, although it is weak, for an increase in money growth to lead to a rise in long-term interest rates. Chapter 2 finds much stronger evidence that an increase in money growth results in a rise in short-term interest rates. The results in these chapters thus do not provide support for the common view that central banks should raise the rate of money growth when they want to reduce interest rates.

The econometric techniques outlined in Part I, which make use of rational expectations, cross-equation restrictions and which emphasize the distinction between anticipated and unanticipated effects of policy, have been widely used in the literature since first published in 1981 and 1982. Thus, the chapters in Part I are of interest in their own right for the econometric techniques that they outline.

Part II Real interest rates and inflation

How real interest rates move over time and their relationship with inflation are critical to our understanding of many issues in monetary economics and finance. Movements in real interest rates are a central element in models of the business cycle and in studies of particular business cycle episodes. Real interest rates also have a potentially important role to play in savings-consumption decisions which affect capital formation and productivity, and also in financial decisions which affect investment directly. Modern theories of exchange rate determination also focus on real interest rate movements. Understanding the behaviour of real interest rates is thus central to the design of appropriate monetary policy.

The eight chapters in Part II contain empirical explorations of real interest rate movements in the US and for seven other OECD countries (Canada, the UK, France, Germany, Italy, Switzerland and the Netherlands). These articles look at a set of questions that have repeatedly arisen in the literature. How valid is the hypothesis associated with Eugene Fama (1975) that the real rate of interest is constant? Have short-term bonds been a poor hedge against inflation; that is, have their real interest rates typically declined with increases in expected inflation? What is the relationship of money supply growth and real interest rates? Are cyclical movements in real variables correlated with real interest rate movements? How strong is the so-called Fisher effect in which nominal interest rates primarily reflect changes in expected inflation? Are movements in nominal interest rates a reliable indicator of movements in real interest rates? What is the relationship between real interest rates across countries? What has been the pattern of real interest rate movements over time, and how can we explain why real interest rates have been low in such periods as the 1970s, but very high in the 1980s?

The opening paper in Part II, Chapter 3, lays out the basic econometric methodology for how real interest rates (which are not directly observable) can be measured and how hypothesis tests about their behaviour can be conducted. Chapters 4 and 5, as well as later chapters, expand on this discussion to cover additional econometric issues that arise in the empirical work. The basic econometric methodology employs regressions on the *ex post* real interest rate – the actual realized real return on a one period bond which is directly observable – to make inferences about the real interest rate (more accurately referred to as the *ex ante* real interest rate). Rational expectations supplies the rationale for this procedure because it provides an orthogonality condition for the forecast error of inflation which indicates that it is uncorrelated with any information known at the time the real interest rate is determined. This orthogonality condition is another type of useful restriction derived from rational expectations; like the cross-equation restrictions used in Part I, it is extremely useful in conducting empirical work in the finance and monetary economics areas. Indeed, the type of orthogonality restriction used in the empirical work of Part II, which looks at behaviour of real interest rates (and which is also the linchpin of the research in Part III on the term structure of interest rates), is one of the most common restrictions used in current empirical work in finance and monetary economics. Thus the econometric methodology outlined in Part II of the book is a valuable tool for researchers conducting empirical work in the money and finance areas.

Chapters 3–5 and 7–8 provide measures of real interest rates for the US and other OECD countries and test hypotheses on how real interest rates move over time and with other variables. The conclusions are as follows.

1. The hypothesis that the real interest rate is constant is strongly rejected in the US and in other foreign countries.
2. The real interest rate is found to be negatively correlated with inflation in all countries, thus suggesting that short-term bonds have been a poor inflation hedge.
3. Evidence for longer-term assets indicates that the negative correlation of their real rates with inflation is even stronger, suggesting that long-term assets are the worst inflation hedges of all.
4. Real interest rates are found to decline with higher money growth in all countries although, in the US, the evidence seems to indicate that money growth primarily affects real interest through its effects on inflation.
5. Movements in real interest rates are not found to be significantly correlated with real variables, but the failure to find these correlations likely stems from the small cyclical variations in real interest rates which lead to low power of the econometric tests.
6. The Fisher effect, in which nominal interest rate movements primarily reflect changes in expected inflation, is not a general phenomenon. The Fisher effect was strong in the US, Canada and the UK only in the post-World War II period up until 1979. Before and after this period, the Fisher effect was weak or nonexistent in the US, and even during the pre-1979 period, the Fisher effect was weak for countries such as Germany, Switzerland, France and the Netherlands.
7. Movements in nominal interest rates are frequently found to be unreliable indicators of movements in real interest rates: the correlation of real and nominal interest rates in the US has been negative in most of the post-World War II period with the exception of October 1979 to October 1982 when the Federal Reserve drastically changed its operating procedures. The correlation of real and nominal interest rates was significantly positive in the US from October 1979 to October 1982 and in such countries as France, Germany, Switzerland and the Netherlands even before 1979.
8. In the US, real interest rates were extremely high during the contraction phase of the Great Depression, indicating that money was extremely tight during this period, rather than being loose as might be suggested by the low nominal rates of this period.

9. Real interest rates in the US were frequently negative in the 1940s, were positive in the 1950s and 1960s, turned negative in the 1970s, and then shot up in the early 1980s to levels not seen since the Great Depression.
10. Real interest rates in the other OECD countries do appear to differ from those in the US, but have had similar movements: their real rates declined from the 1960s to the 1970s and then rose to levels unprecedented in the post-World War II period.

As we have seen from the above results, which describe how real interest rates changed over time, there is some indication that these rates may not be equal across countries, although there seems to be a tendency for them to move together. Chapters 6 and 7 perform formal tests as to whether real interest rates are equal across countries and, if they are not, estimate to what extent they move together over time. The empirical evidence in Chapter 6 strongly rejects the equality of real interest rates across countries and also the joint hypothesis of uncovered interest parity and *ex ante* relative PPP (purchasing power parity). Using a somewhat different methodology, Chapter 7 also tests for the equality of real interest rates across countries, in this case by investigating whether real rates in different countries should move one-for-one with each other. It also strongly rejects the equality of real interest rates across countries, but does find that movements elsewhere are significantly linked with the US real interest rate, although the movement is less than one-for-one.

The evidence in both these papers suggests that it is worth studying open economy macroeconomic models which allow the following: (1) domestic real interest rates to differ from world rates, but in which there are linkages between real interest rates across countries, (2) time varying risk premiums in the forward exchange markets, and (3) deviations from *ex ante* relative PPP. The evidence has important policy implications because it suggests that European monetary authorities have some ability to influence domestic economic activity, although there is a strong possibility that the high real interest rates European countries experienced in the 1980s resulted from the high real rates in the US. In addition, the evidence also leaves open the possibility that policies directed at increasing domestic saving can increase the rate of capital formation and hence productivity, since real interest rates can differ across countries.

Another puzzle raised by the results listed above is why real interest rates became so high in the 1980s. Chapter 8 looks at this question and puts forward the answer that disinflationary monetary policy pursued by the Federal Reserve starting in October 1979 was the source of the high real interest rates. The empirical approach in this chapter makes use of the theoretical proposition from modern monetary theory that a change in the monetary policy regime can have an important impact on the stochastic processes of economic variables such as real interest rates. Hence, the empirical analysis examines whether the change in the stochastic process of real interest rates (which resulted in the high real interest rates in the 1980s) occurred when the Federal Reserve changed to a disinflationary monetary policy regime in October 1979. Not only are there significant shifts in the stochastic process of real rates in October 1979 and October 1982 when the Federal Reserve altered the monetary policy regime, but these dates are also found to be the most likely breakpoints for shifts in the real rate process. This evidence, along with similar evidence from a comparable episode of disinflationary monetary policy in the first half of 1920, supports the view that Volcker's change to a disinflationary monetary policy regime was the major factor causing the high real interest rates in the 1980s.

An important feature of the empirical approach of Chapter 8 is that it actually provides identification using historical knowledge to rule out such problems as reverse causation. Because the exact date of a particular historical event (such as the regime change in October 1979) is likely to be exogenous, finding that the behaviour of an economic variable (such as real interest rates) changes immediately thereafter suggests that the direction of causality is from the regime change to the change in real rate behaviour. An historical-econometric approach of the type outlined in Chapter 8 thus provides one method for getting around the basic identification problem in macroeconomics pointed out by Sims (1980): exclusion restrictions – the traditional econometric approach to identification – are not credible when expectations are rational. Not surprisingly, given the persuasiveness of Sims' argument, more researchers are beginning to use historical-econometric approaches to answer basic questions in macroeconomics. This is reflected in research such as Mankiw, Miron and Weil (1987) and Romer and Romer (1989), as well as a resurgent interest in macroeonomic history in the economics profession.

Chapter 9 provides a summary of some of the evidence on real interest rate behaviour for the aggregate economy and then uses the econometric methodology of the previous chapters to look at the behaviour of real interest rates that apply to the agricultural sector. The evidence indicates that real interest rates for the agricultural sector have been extremely high in the 1980s and are linked to real rates for the aggregate economy. Indeed, the burden of the Fed's disinflationary monetary policy fell even more heavily on the agricultural sector than on the rest of the economy since real rates for this sector reached far higher levels than elsewhere.

The final chapter of Part II looks at an alternative approach that does not require rational expectations to make inferences about real interest rate behaviour, but instead uses futures market data. Futures market data can be used to construct own-commodity real interest rates; that is, the *ex ante* real return on a bond in terms of specific commodities. The supposition is that these own-commodity real rates can be used to make inferences about real interest rates derived from aggregate price level data, which are the real interest rates of primary concern to economists. Chapter 10 demonstrates that own-commodity real rates contain information not only about the real interest rate for the aggregate economy, but also about *ex ante* relative price movements for that particular commodity. Empirical evidence indicates that *ex ante* relative price movements (which can be thought of as noise) have so much greater variation than movements in the aggregate real interest rate (the signal), that the noise-to-signal ratio in own-commodity real rates is extremely high. In addition, data on own-commodity real rates are not consistent with several widely accepted facts about the behaviour of aggregate real interest rates. Thus, unfortunately, own-commodity real rates by themselves cannot provide much information about aggregate real interest rates. (However, Hamilton (1992) has shown that futures data may help provide information about aggregate real interest rates if used in a particularly sophisticated way with other information.)

Part III The information in the term structure

Examining the information in the term structure about future interest rates has historically been an important topic of research in the economics profession. This research, which has been receiving increased attention in recent years, has explored to what extent the term structure of interest rates helps predict future movements in interest rates. Research in the early 1980s (Shiller, Campbell and Schoenholtz (1983) and Mankiw and Summers (1984), for example) questioned the value of using the term structure to predict future movement in interest rates. However, since then the pendulum has been swinging the other way, with papers by Fama (1984), Fama and Bliss (1987), and Campbell and Shiller (1987, 1991) resurrecting the view that the term structure does contain information about the future movement of short-term interest rates.

Part III contains five chapters which continue in the tradition of examining the information in the term structure of interest rates. The first paper in Part III (Chapter 11) provides some refinements and updating of Fama's (1984) evidence on the ability of the term structure to forecast future changes in one-month interest rates. It uses econometric techniques that properly correct standard errors for overlapping data and conditional heteroscedasticity, and in addition uses data that have potential advantages over Fama's and which are more recent. The results generally confirm Fama's finding that the term structure helps predict future changes in short-term interest rates for a few months into the future.

The discussion pursued in chapters in Part II suggests that the information in the term structure can be examined from a somewhat different perspective. The evidence in those chapters, as well as in other cited articles, often finds that the level of interest rates helps forecast future inflation (the so-called Fisher effect). When combined with evidence that the term structure of inflation contains information about future interest rate movements, this suggests that the term structure of interest rates might also contain information about the future path of inflation. Looking at the information in the term structure concerning future inflation is an important topic because central banks in most countries are increasingly focusing on the goal of price stability and thus need information on the degree of inflationary pressures in the economy. Indeed, recent testimony by central bank officials indicates that they often adhere to the view that a downward sloping yield curve reflects expectations of a declining rate of inflation.

The final four articles, Chapters 12–15, empirically examine the issue of what the term structure of interest rates tells us about the future path of inflation. An additional payoff to looking at evidence on this question is that it also tells us whether movements in the term structure of *nominal* interest rates (which are directly observable) inform us about movements in the term structure of *real* interest rates (which are not observable). Finding out whether observable data on the nominal term structure reveal information about the real term structure is important for economic analysis since it is the latter which plays an important role in understanding asset-pricing theories and theories of the business cycle.

The findings for the US in Chapters 12 and 13 indicate that for maturities of six months or less, the term structure provides almost no information about the future path of inflation. On the other hand, the short end of the nominal term structure does provide information about the term structure of real interest rates. However, as the maturities lengthen, the term structure contains a great deal of predictive power about future changes in inflation, but little information about the term structure of real interest rates.

The results in Chapters 12 and 13 contrast strongly with those recorded earlier in Part II which find that, for much of the post-World War II period, nominal short-term interest rate movements reflect changes in expected inflation rather than real interest rates. The results in Chapters 12 and 13 also differ dramatically from those in Chapter 8 which indicate that the degree to which the level of nominal interest rates reflects expectations of future inflation significantly decreased with the change in the monetary regime in October 1979. In contrast, Chapters 12 and 13 find no evidence that the amount of information in the term structure about the future path of inflation decreased with the monetary regime shift in October 1979. The nature of the relationship between the term structure and future inflation found in Part III is thus quite different from that found between the overall level of interest rates and future inflation in Part II.

The evidence for the US suggests that the term structure is not a useful guide for assessing inflationary pressures in the economy over the subsequent six months. However, the term structure is capable of providing information about inflationary pressures over longer horizons: when the slope of the term structure steepens at the longer end, it is an indication that the inflation rate will rise over the next several years, while a negative slope indicates a reduction in long-run inflationary pressures. However, some caution is warranted because, as the interpretation in these chapters indicates, changes in the relative variability of expected inflation changes and real term structure slopes (or changes in their correlation) will alter the information in the term structure about future inflation. The results also lend support to the view that the term structure spread between long- and short-term interest rates can be used to assess the credibility of anti-inflation policies: that is, a downward-sloping yield curve is an indication of a credible anti-inflation policy since it reflects expectations that inflation will fall in the future.

Chapters 14 and 15 extend the empirical analysis of the information in the term structure to other countries besides the US. Looking further afield is worthwhile because assessing inflationary pressures is a central concern of central bankers everywhere. Many of these countries have been subjected to very different monetary policy regimes and hence very different inflationary experiences from those found in the US. Thus, results for the US may not be robust across countries, and evidence from outside is needed to assess whether the term structure of interest rates is a good indicator of inflationary pressures in these countries. In addition, the information in the term structure about inflation in the US may be representative of only one type of monetary policy regime; a different monetary regime may well alter the information in the term structure. Thus American policy-makers should not be confident in conclusions generated solely from US data unless they are found to be true for other countries as well.

The results for other countries in Chapters 14 and 15 are generally similar to those found for the US. Evidence for the majority of the countries studied indicates that the shorter maturity term structure does not contain a great deal of information about the future path of inflation, but does embody a lot of information about the term structure of real interest rates. At longer maturities, the opposite conclusion holds, as it does for the US: there is strong evidence that the slope of the term structure has significant forecasting ability for future inflation, but contains little information about the term structure of real interest rates. The evidence suggests that for countries other than the US, the term structure can be used to help assess inflationary pressure, but only for long horizons: a steepening of the slope of the longer-maturity term structure indicates that the inflation rate will rise several years in the future; conversely, a negative slope indicates reduced long-run inflationary pressures.

My hope is that by reading the articles included in this volume together, the reader will obtain a better feel for the interaction of money, interest rates and inflation than can be achieved by reading the articles one at a time. In addition, I hope that the effort put in by the reader of this book will provide him or her with a better appreciation of how rational expectations econometrics of the type practised here can be used to answer other basic questions in the monetary-macroeconomics and finance areas. The hoped-for outcome is that this book will stimulate further research that will add to our understanding of how the economy works.

References

Campbell, John Y. and Shiller, Robert J. (1987), 'Cointegration and Tests of Present Value Models', *Journal of Political Economy*, **95**, 1062–88.

Campbell, John Y. and Shiller, Robert J. (1991), 'Yield Spreads and Interest Rate Movements: A Bird's Eye View', *Review of Economic Studies*, **58**, 495–514.

Christiano, Lawrence J. and Eichenbaum, Martin (1992), 'Liquidity Effects, Monetary Policy and the Business Cycle', Working Paper Series, Federal Reserve Bank of Chicago, WP-92-15.

Fama, Eugene (1975), 'Short Term Interest Rates as Predictors of Inflation', *American Economic Review*, **65**, 269–82.

Fama, Eugene (1984), 'The Information in the Term Structure', *Journal of Financial Economics*, **13**, 509–28.

Fama, Eugene and Bliss, Robert R. (1987), 'The Information in Long-Maturity Forward Rates', *American Economic Review*, **77**, 680–92.

Friedman, Milton (1968), 'The Role of Monetary Policy', *American Economic Review*, **58**, 1–17.

Friedman, Milton (1969), 'Factors Affecting the Level of Interest Rates', *Proceedings of the 1968 Conference on Savings and Residual Financing*, sponsored by the US Savings and Loan League, The League, 11–27.

Hamilton, James (1992), 'Was the Deflation During the Great Depression Anticipated? Evidence from the Commodity Futures Market', *American Economic Review*, **82**, 157–78.

Leeper, Eric M. and Gordon, David B. (1992), 'In Search of the Liquidity Effect', *Journal of Monetary Economics*, **29** (3), 341–70.

Mankiw, N. Gregory, Miron, Jeffrey A. and Weil, David N. (1987), 'The Adjustment of Expectations to a Change in Regime: A Study of the Founding of the Federal Reserve', *American Economic Review*, **77** (3), 358–74.

Mankiw, N. Gregory and Summers, Lawrence H. (1984), 'Do Long-Term Interest Rates Overreact to Short-Term Interest Rates?', *Brookings Papers on Economic Activity*, 223–42.

Romer, Christine and Romer, David (1989), 'Does Monetary Policy Matter? A New Test in the Spirit of Friedman and Schwartz', *NBER Macroeconomics Annual*, 121–70.

Shiller, Robert J., Campbell, John Y. and Schoenholtz, Kermit L. (1983), 'Forward Rates and Future Policy: Interpreting the Term Structure of Interest Rates', *Brookings Papers on Economic Activity*, 173–217.

Sims, Christopher (1980), 'Macroeconomics and Reality', *Econometrica*, **48**, 1–47.

Strongin, Steven (1991), 'The Identification of Monetary Policy Disturbances: Explaining the Liquidity Puzzle', Working Paper Series, Federal Reserve Bank of Chicago, WP-91-24.

PART I

MONEY AND INTEREST RATES

[1]

Journal of Monetary Economics 7 (1981) 29–55. North-Holland Publishing Company

MONETARY POLICY AND LONG-TERM INTEREST RATES

An Efficient Markets Approach

Frederic S. MISHKIN*

University of Chicago, Chicago, IL 60637, USA

This paper is an application of efficient markets theory to analyze empirically the relationship of money supply growth and long-term interest rates. This approach has the advantage over ealier research on this subject in that it imposes a theoretical structure on this relationship that allows easier interpretation of the empirical results as well as more powerful statistical tests. In the interest of ascertaining the robustness of the results, many different empirical tests are carried out in this paper, and they uniformly *do not support* the proposition that increases in the money supply are correlated with declines in long rates.

1. Introduction

The impact of a money stock increase on nominal, long interest rates is an important issue.[1] The most commonly held view — also a feature of most structural macro models — has an increase in the money stock leading, at least in the short and medium runs, to a decline in long interest rates. In these macro models, the long rate decline not only stimulates investment directly, but also has a further expansionary impact on investment and consumer expenditure through its effect on the valuation of capital.[2] This decline in long rates is thus a critical element in the transmission mechanism of monetary policy. In addition, the view that increases in the money stock lead to an immediate decline in long rates has important implications for how the Federal Reserve System should conduct monetary policy when a decline in interest rates is desired. Government officials often warn the Fed that it should not keep the rate of money growth too low because this will encourage an objectionable increase in interest rates.

*I wish to thank the following individuals for their helpful comments: an anonymous referee, Andrew Abel, John Bilson, Eugene Fama, Clive Granger, David Galenson, Robert Lucas, Thomas Mayer, A.R. Nobay, Steven Sheffrin, Gary Skoog and the participants in the Money Workshop at the University of Chicago and in seminars given at the University of California, Davis and San Diego. Research support from the National Science Foundation is gratefully acknowledged.

[1]Unless otherwise noted, whenever the phrase 'interest rates' is used in this paper, it refers to nominal interest rates.

[2]For a survey of the literature on the transmission mechanisms of monetary policy, see Brainard and Cooper (1976) and Modigliani (1974).

Milton Friedman (1968, 1969) has criticized the view above on the grounds that it ignores the dynamic effects of a money stock increase. Friedman concedes that a so-called 'liquidity effect' — where an excess supply of money will create increased demand for securities, a rise in their price, and a resulting fall in interest rates — does work in the direction of a decline in interest rates when the money stock is increased. However, two other effects can counter this liquidity effect. The money stock increase will, over time, have an expansionary effect on both real income and the price level. This 'income and price level effect' will, through the usual arguments in the money demand function, then tend to reverse the decline in interest rates. More importantly for short-run effects on interest rates, increases in the money stock could also influence anticipations of inflation.[3] Higher expected inflation resulting from money stock increases would, through a Fisherian (1930) relation, increase nominal interest rates. This 'price anticipations effect' could thus not only mitigate the decline in interest rates stemming from the liquidity effect, but could also overpower it. That interest rates are highest in countries experiencing rapid rates of monetary growth is casual evidence for this proposition.

There are two lines of empirical work which bear on the issue of whether increases in the money stock lead to a decline versus a rise in long interest rates. 'Keynesian' macro-econometric models impose a fair amount of structure in their estimates of financial market and income-expenditure relationships. In these models, increases in the money stock do lead to a substantial decline in long rates in the short and medium run, as in Modigliani (1974) and the simulation results in section 3 of this paper, for example. This evidence is suspect, however, because these models ignore constraints that should be imposed on the model if financial markets are 'efficient'. Financial market efficiency cannot be ignored because evidence supporting it is quite strong. [See Fama (1970).] Furthermore, recent work [Mishkin (1978)] indicates that a failure to impose financial market efficiency on macro-econometric models can lead to highly misleading results.

An alternative empirical approach to this issue is to estimate reduced form relationships where changes in interest rates are regressed on past changes in the money stock. Evidence using this approach [Gibson (1970)] does not support the view that money stock increases result in a fall in long rates. Unfortunately, this evidence suffers from a problem endemic to reduced form empirical work: interpretation of the empirical results is difficult because the

[3]Early work which discussed the issue of money supply increases and interest rates, such as Cagan (1972), Gibson (1970), and Gibson and Kaufman (1968), tended to stress the 'income and price level effect' more than the 'price anticipations effect' because these researchers believed that adjustments of inflationary expectations proceeded slowly. Recent work on the theory of rational expectations and market efficiency, starting with Muth (1961), indicates that inflationary expectations can adjust quite rapidly. Thus, the 'price anticipations effect' should probably receive more weight in discussions of the effect of money supply increases on interest rates.

theoretical framework behind these results is obscure. Also, the absence of structure when changes in interest rates are regressed on changes in the money stock leads to a large number of parameters being estimated, and this results in statistical tests with low power.

Efficient markets theory suggests an alternative approach for analyzing the relationship of money stock increases to long interest rate movements. This paper develops an efficient markets model of long interest rate determination, and then estimates this model using postwar quarterly data. This approach has the advantage that it imposes a theoretical structure on the problem that allows easier interpretation of the empirical results as well as more powerful statistical tests of the proposition that increases in the money stock are correlated with declines in long rates. In addition, a Keynesian, liquidity preference view of interest rate determination can be embedded in the efficient markets model and tested. Finally, as a side issue, quite attractive tests of bond market efficiency result from the approach used here.

2. The model

Efficient markets theory[4] indicates that securities prices in a capital market should reflect all available information. To be more precise, it implies that the market uses available information correctly in assessing the probability distribution of future prices: i.e.,

$$f_m(p_{1,t+j},\ldots p_{n,t+j} \mid \phi_{t-1}) = f(p_{1,t+j},\ldots, p_{n,t+j} \mid \phi_{t-1}) \quad \text{for all } j \geqq 0, \tag{1}$$

where $p_{i,t}$ is the price of security i at time t, ϕ_{t-1} is the information available at time $t-1$, $f(\ldots \mid \phi_{t-1})$ is the true joint probability density function for the security prices conditional on the available information at $t-1$, and $f_m(\ldots \mid \phi_{t-1})$ is the joint probability density function assessed by the market at time $t-1$.

In order to give this concept empirical content, we must specify the relationship between the probability of future prices and current prices. This requires a model which describes how equilibrium prices at time $t-1$ are determined. Here, the market is assumed to equate expected, one-period, holding returns across securities, allowing for liquidity (risk) premiums which are constant over time. In the case of long-term bonds, which concerns us here, the one-period return is

$$\tilde{BRET}_t = \frac{\tilde{p}_{b,t} - p_{b,t-1} + c_{t-1}}{p_{b,t-1}}, \tag{2}$$

[4]The notation used here is based on Fama (1976a).

where $\tilde{}$ denotes a random variable and $B\tilde{RE}T$ is the one-period (from $t-1$ to t) nominal return from holding long-term bonds — it includes both capital gains plus interest payments, $p_{b,t}$ is the price of the long bond at time t, and c_{t-1} is the coupon (cash payment made during the period) which is known at time $t-1$.

The model of market equilibrium then implies

$$E_m(B\tilde{RE}T_t \mid \phi_{t-1}) = r_{t-1} + \delta, \tag{3}$$

where r_{t-1} is the return on a one-period bond (which of course equals the expected one-period return) — this is just the short-term interest rate, δ is the constant liquidity premium, and $E_m(\ldots \mid \phi_{t-1})$ is the expectation assessed by the market. Market efficiency then implies that

$$E_m(\tilde{p}_{b,t} \mid \phi_{t-1}) = E(\tilde{p}_{b,t} \mid \phi_{t-1}),$$

and hence

$$E(B\tilde{RE}T_t \mid \phi_{t-1}) - E_m(B\tilde{RE}T_t \mid \phi_{t-1})$$

$$= E(B\tilde{RE}T_t - r_{t-1} - \delta \mid \phi_{t-1}) = 0. \tag{4}$$

Eq. (4) above states that $B\tilde{RE}T_t - r_{t-1}$ should be uncorrelated with any past available information or linear combinations of this information. An equivalent characterization of the efficient markets model which satisfies eq. (4) is thus[5]

$$B\tilde{RE}T_t - r_{t-1} = \delta + (X_t - X_t^e)\beta + \varepsilon_t, \tag{5}$$

where an e superscript denotes expected values conditional on all past available information [i.e., an optimal forecast defined as $X_t^e = E(X_t \mid \phi_{t-1})$], and X_t is a variable (or vector of variables) relevant to the pricing of long bonds, β is a coefficient (or vector of coefficients), and ε_t is a serially uncorrelated error process (because $E(\varepsilon_t \mid \phi_{t-1}) = 0$). The efficient markets

[5]It is easy to show that this efficient markets model is consistent with the expectations hypothesis of the term structure where predictions of future short-term interest rates are optimal forecasts. To be more concrete, if the long-term bond is a discount security where the liquidity premium is a constant, δ, the expectations hypothesis of the term structure is approximated by

$$RL_t = \frac{1}{n} E_t(r_t + r_{t+1} + \ldots + r_{t+n-1}) + \delta.$$

When expectations of future short rates in this equation are optimally formed, or equivalently are 'rational' in the sense of Muth (1961), then the expectations hypothesis described by the equation above leads to the same implications as eq. (5) in the text.

model stresses that only when new information hits the market will $BR\tilde{E}T$ differ from $r_{t-1}+\delta$. As eq. (5) makes clear, this is equivalent to the proposition that only unanticipated changes in variables can be correlated with $BRET_t - r_{t-1}$. This distinction between the possible effects from unanticipated versus anticipated changes in variables is indeed an important feature of recent empirical work [for example, Barro (1977, 1978)].

The assumption that the coefficient on r_{t-1} equals one in eq. (5) has been subjected to empirical test both here and in work by Fama and Schwert (1977) and Mishkin (1978), and this model of market equilibrium is not rejected.[6] Furthermore, as is discussed in Fama (1976a), as long as $E_m(BR\tilde{E}T_t \mid \phi_{t-1})$ has small variation relative to other sources of variation in the actual returns — and this appears to be the case for the long-term bonds discussed here[7] — assumptions describing the equilibrium return are not critical to empirical tests of the efficient markets model.[8]

The research question posed in the Introduction suggests that of particular interest is the relationship of money growth and long bond prices displayed in an efficient markets model. Substituting in for X_t in eq. (5) then leads to

$$BR\tilde{E}T_t - r_{t-1} = \delta + \beta_m(MG_t - MG_t^e) + \varepsilon_t, \tag{6}$$

where, MG_t is the money growth rate at time t. Because the long rate (RL) is closely linked to the price of a long bond, over short periods such as a quarter the change in long prices, ΔRL_t, are highly correlated with $BR\tilde{E}T_t - r_{t-1}$. In the 1954–1976 sample period used in the following empirical work, the correlation coefficient of ΔRL_t and $BRET_t - r_{t-1}$ is -0.96. Thus, if unanticipated increases in the money stock are to have a negative correlation with changes in long rates (as might be expected from 'Keynesian' macro-

[6]This assumption was tested using the 1954–1976 sample period used in the empirical work of this paper. The quarterly bond returns series discussed later in the paper was regressed on the beginning-of-period, 90 day treasury bill rate (also at quarterly rates) using weighted least squares to correct for heteroscedasticity. [Mishkin (1978) describes this procedure.] The coefficient on the bill rate was not significantly different from one at the five percent level ($t=0.51$). In a recent paper, Shiller (1979) has found evidence which can be interpreted as implying that the liquidity premium is correlated with the spread between long rates and short rates. To test this proposition for the 1954–1976 sample period, $BRET_t - r_{t-1}$ has been regressed on this spread, again using weighted least squares to correct for heteroscedasticity. The evidence supporting Shiller's proposition is even weaker in this sample period than was true in the regression results reported in Mishkin (1978): the coefficient on the spread variable was not significantly different from zero at even the 10% significance level ($t=1.01$).

[7]For example, using the model of market equilibrium described in the text, over the 1954–1976 period the variation in $E_m(BR\tilde{E}T_t \mid \phi_{t-1})$ is less than 2% of the variation in the actual return stemming from other sources.

[8]A more precise wording of this point would state that, in the case discussed here, tests of hypotheses concerning the equilibrium return would have very low statistical power. This is essentially the same point made by Nelson and Schwert (1977) in their comment on Fama (1975). Note also that more discriminating tests provide evidence that liquidity premiums are not constant over time. See for example, Fama (1976b).

econometric models), this implies that the coefficient on unanticipated money growth should be significantly positive in eq. (6): i.e., $\beta_m > 0$.

An important caveat is in order.[9] The efficient markets model does not guarantee that eq. (5) is a reduced form where $X_t - X_t^e$ is exogenous so that the estimates of β are consistent.[10] It only implies that $BR\tilde{E}T_t - r_{t-1}$ is correlated with only unanticipated movements in variables. Another way of stating this point is to acknowledge that the efficient markets model does not indicate whether a significant β coefficient implies causation from its unanticipated variable to bond prices and hence long interest rates. As far as market efficiency is concerned, causation could just as well run in the other direction, or it could be non-existent as in the case where new information is simultaneously affecting both bond returns and the right-hand side variable. Thus, we must be careful in interpreting empirical results on the β's not to ascribe causation to the results without further identifying information.

The above caveat must be kept in mind especially when we analyze the estimated β_m coefficient. If the money supply process is seen as exogenous — a view that has received some support in the literature,[11] the interpretation of the estimated β_m is straightforward. The finding of a significant positive β_m would then provide evidence supporting the 'Keynesian' position that increased money growth will, at least in the short run, lead to declines in long-term interest rates; and a failure to find this result would cast doubt on this view. However, if the money supply process is not exogenous, which is the position taken by many critics of monetarist analysis, then the estimated β_m coefficient may suffer from simultaneous equation bias and give a misleading impression as to the effect of an increase in the money supply on long-term interest rates. Because the analysis in this paper provides no information on the exogeneity of the money supply process, in the discussion of the empirical results the β_m estimates are viewed as only providing information on the correlations of unanticipated money growth and the change in long rates. Interpretation of these correlations is then deferred to the concluding remarks towards the end of the paper.

The liquidity preference approach to the demand for money suggests other relevant information which might be included in the X-vector of the efficient markets model. In the empirical literature on the demand for money, a common formulation is the following:[12]

[9]A similar caveat applies to the empirical work of Barro (1977).

[10]This issue of the consistency of the β estimates is discussed more formally in Abel and Mishkin (1979).

[11]Sims (1972) contains a discussion of the differing views in the literature on the exogeneity of the money supply process and finds evidence which he interprets as supporting the view that causality runs from money growth to income rather than the other way around. As Jacobs, Leamer and Ward's (1979) and Zellner's (1979) criticisms of these causality tests indicate, however, these tests do not resolve the issue of the exogeneity of the money supply process.

[12]See Goldfeld (1973) and Laidler (1977).

$$\ln(M/P)_t = \alpha_0 + \alpha_1 \ln Y_t - \alpha_2 \ln R_t + u_t, \tag{7}$$

where M_t is the money stock, Y_t is real income, R_t is a representative interest rate (or rates), P_t is the price level, u_t is error term, and α_0, α_1, α_2 are positive coefficients. Solving out for $\ln R_t$ and taking changes in the logs, we have

$$\begin{aligned} \Delta \ln R_t = {} & (\alpha_1/\alpha_2)\Delta \ln Y_t - (1/\alpha_2)\Delta \ln M_t \\ & + (1/\alpha_2)\Delta \ln P_t + (1/\alpha_2)(u_t - u_{t-1}) + (\alpha_0/\alpha_2). \end{aligned} \tag{8}$$

This relationship then indicates that long-term interest rates and bond prices might be related not only to the growth rate in the nominal money stock, as in eq. (6), but also to the growth rate of real income and the price level. Adding this information to the X-vector of the efficient markets model leads to the following:

$$\begin{aligned} BR\tilde{E}T_t - r_{t-1} = {} & \delta + \beta_m(MG_t - MG_t^e) + \beta_y(YG_t - YG_t^e) \\ & + \beta_\pi(\pi_t - \pi_t^e) + \varepsilon_t, \end{aligned} \tag{9}$$

where YG_t is the growth rate of real income, π is the inflation rate, and β_m, β_y, β_π are coefficients. This equation is really an efficient markets analog to the typical money demand relationship found in the literature, as its similarity to eq. (8) indicates. In addition, eq. (9) captures elements of interest rate models of the Feldstein and Eckstein (1970) variety.[13]

The magnitude and sign of the β coefficients in eqs. (6) and (9) depend on the time-series processes of the money supply, real income and the price level, even when the sign and magnitude of these coefficients are assumed to reflect an underlying structural theory such as liquidity preference. If the time-series processes of real income and the price level are such that an unanticipated rise in these variables is not followed by a more than compensating decline in these variables, then a liquidity preference view implies that the coefficients of unanticipated income growth and inflation should be negative in eq. (9): i.e., $\beta_y < 0$, $\beta_\pi < 0$. In this case, an unanticipated increase in income growth would have a negative impact on bond returns, because, ceteris paribus, the rise in income would lead to higher interest rates, currently and in the future. The negative effect of an unanticipated increase in inflation on bond returns follows from the resulting reduction in real money balances which also leads to rising interest rates. The unanticipated inflation effect should be further strengthened if, as in the

[13]Note that if inflation was added as an argument in the money demand model of eq. (7), we would still arrive at an efficient markets equation like (9).

Cagan (1956) adaptive expectations model, expected inflation rises when actual inflation is above its expected value. In this case, an unanticipated rise in inflation promotes a rise in nominal interest rates either through a Fisherian (1930) relationship or because expected inflation is a separate argument in the money demand function as in Friedman (1956).

Note also that the more persistent is the time series process of inflation and income growth — that is, the more an unanticipated increase in these variables leads to further increases, the more powerful are the unanticipated income and inflation effects on interest rates indicated by the theoretical structure discussed above. Thus β_y and β_π might be expected to be even more negative. Clearly, the importance of the 'income and price level' and 'price anticipations' effects also depend on the time-series process of money growth. Thus the β_m coefficient will also not be invariant to changes in the money growth, time-series process.

We now turn to the actual estimation of the efficient markets models of eqs. (6) and (9), with the warning that some caution must be exercised when interpreting results from estimates of these equations because the direction of causation cannot be established in this framework.

3. Empirical results

3.1. The data

The empirical results below use postwar quarterly data over the 1954–1976 sample period. The data sources and definitions of the variables used in these estimates are as follows:

$BRET_t$ = quarterly return from holding a long-term government bond from the beginning to the end of the quarter.

$M1G_t$ = growth rate of $M1$ (quarterly rate) = the first differenced series of the log of the average level of $M1$ in the last month of the quarter.

$M2G_t$ = growth rate of $M2$ (quarterly rate) = the first differenced series of the log of the average level of $M2$ in the last month of the quarter.

IPG_t = growth rate of industrial production (quarterly rate) = the first differenced series of the log of Industrial Production in the last month of the quarter.

π_t = the CPI inflation rate (quarterly rate) = the first differenced series of the log of CPI in the last month of the quarter.

UN_t = unemployment rate in the last month of the quarter — in percent.

RTB_t = the 90 day treasury bill rate, the last trading day in the quarter — in fractions.

r_{t-1} = the beginning of quarter 90 day bill rate at a quarterly rate, equals $RTB_{t-1}/4$.

Unless otherwise noted, all these variables have been constructed from seasonally adjusted data except for the *BRET* and *RTB* variables. The bond return series was obtained from the Center for Research in Security Prices (CRSP) at the University of Chicago and is described in Fisher and Lorie (1977) and Mishkin (1978). The *IPG*, π, and *UN* variables were constructed from data in the Department of Commerce's *Business Statistics* and *Survey of Current Business*. The *M1* and *M2* data were obtained from the Board of Governors of the Federal Reserve, *Banking and Monetary Statistics* and the *Federal Reserve Bulletin*, while the *RTB* data were supplied by the Board of Governors of the Federal Reserve.

Since misleading results can be obtained from efficient markets models using averaged data,[14] the data for bond returns are derived from security prices at particular points in time. In keeping with this, an attempt has been made to derive the other variables used here with data as close to being end of quarter as possible. For this reason, Industrial Production is used as a proxy for real income in estimating eq. (9) rather than a more broadly based National Income Accounts measure. Similarly, the CPI has been used to calculate the inflation variable rather than the GNP deflator. Use of data which is endpoint (or close to it) is necessary in order to unearth significant relationships between bond returns and unanticipated variables. Experiments with quarterly averaged data led to substantially worse fits for equations of the form of (9), fewer significant coefficients and no appreciable differences as to the statistical significance of the β_m coefficients.

3.2. The estimation method

In order to estimate the efficient markets models of eqs. (6) and (9), measures of anticipated money growth, income growth and inflation must be developed. Here, anticipations of variables in the information set X are assumed to be optimal linear forecasts using time-series models of the following form:

$$X_{i,t}=Z_{i,t-1}\gamma_i+u_t, \tag{10}$$

where X_i is *MG*, *IPG*, or π: $Z_{i,t-1}$ is a vector of variables containing information available at time $t-1$ — this includes variables known before $t-1$ as well as at $t-1$; γ_i is a vector of coefficients; and the subscript i refers to either *MG*, *IPG*, or π.

A critical issue in the research strategy used here is the methodology for choosing the specification of the time-series models of (10). It is difficult on theoretical grounds to exclude any particular piece of information available

[14]See Working (1960) for example.

at time $t-1$ as a useful predictor of an $X_{i,t}$ variable. For example, economic theory cannot provide much guidance as to which variables to exclude in a money growth equation. Even though there is no strong theoretical reason for expecting a particular variable to enter the Z-vector, it might be a useful predictor of money growth because the personalities involved in policy making could be such that they react to this variable for their own inscrutable reasons. Thus the theoretical model that a researcher uses to explain this money growth specification might be relatively unimportant in deciding on the validity of his particular specification versus another researcher's.

The discussion above suggests that an atheoretical statistical procedure might be superior to economic theory for deciding on the specification of the time-series models in (10). Furthermore, because theory is less of a useful guide in evaluating the time-series models needed here than is true in other empirical work, it is more important to check for the robustness of results by using several model specifications in estimating the efficient markets model. In keeping with this line of thinking, two procedures for specifying the time-series models of (10) are used in the text, with several additional specifications used in the results discussed in the appendix.

The simplest equations which can be used to describe money growth, industrial production growth and inflation are univariate time-series models of the autoregressive type. Fourth-order autoregressions are usually successful in reducing residuals to white noise and are thus used here. The resulting estimates for *M1G*, *M2G*, *IPG* and π can be found in table 1. Note that there is a fair amount of persistence in the time-series models for money growth and inflation, indicating that 'income and price level' and 'price anticipation' effects of the sort that Friedman (1968, 1969) discusses are potentially important. Although less persistence is evident in the time-series process of industrial production growth, it also has the characteristic that a positive innovation does lead to a permanently higher level of this variable (although not in the rate of growth). Thus, as discussed in the previous section, estimates of eq. (9) might be expected to have negative coefficients on unanticipated inflation and *IPG*.

The univariate time series models of table 1 suffer from the problem of unstable coefficients. Chow (1960) tests where the sample period has been split into equal lengths reject, for all but the inflation equation in table 1, the hypothesis that the coefficients of the univariate models are equal in the two sub-periods.[15] Multivariate time series models have thus been estimated

[15]Note that because lagged dependent variables appear in the time-series models of tables 1 and 2, all the test statistics are only valid asymptotically. The asymptotic F-statistics for the Chow tests of the equations in table 1 are as follows: for 1.1, $F(5,82)=3.50$; for 1.2, $F(5,82)=2.49$; for 1.3, $F(5,82)=2.81$; and for 1.4, $F(5,82)=1.59$. The critical $F(5,82)$ at the 5% level is 2.33.

Table 1

Univariate time-series models.[a]

	Eq. no. (1.1)	(1.2)	(1.3)	(1.4)
Coefficient of	Dependent variable *M1G*	*M2G*	*IPG*	π
Constant term	0.0038 (0.0013)	0.0049 (0.0017)	0.0093 (0.0283)	0.0012 (0.0066)
$M1G(-1)$	0.3777 (0.1078)			
$M1G(-2)$	0.2205 (0.1152)			
$M1G(-3)$	0.0550 (0.1151)			
$M1G(-4)$	−0.0341 (0.1076)			
	$F(4,87) = 9.11$			
$M2G(-1)$		0.6598 (0.1080)		
$M2G(-2)$		−0.0542 (0.1280)		
$M2G(-3)$		0.1736 (0.1286)		
$M2G(-4)$		−0.0758 (0.1094)		
		$F(4,87) = 18.26$		
$IPG(-1)$			0.4254 (0.1003)	
$IPG(-2)$			−0.2346 (0.1091)	
$IPG(-3)$			0.1507 (0.1091)	
$IPG(-4)$			−0.2516 (0.1003)	
			$F(4,87) = 5.95$	
$\pi(-1)$				0.4008 (0.1044)
$\pi(-2)$				0.5520 (0.1112)
$\pi(-3)$				0.1063 (0.1119)
$\pi(-4)$				−0.1837 (0.1033)
				$F(4,87) = 58.96$
R^2	0.2952	0.4563	0.2148	0.7305
Std. error	0.0062	0.0066	0.0237	0.0039
Durbin–Watson	1.97	1.96	2.00	2.03

[a]*Note:* Asymptotic F-statistics test the joint null hypothesis that the coefficients in brackets are equal to zero. Asymptotic standard errors of coefficients are in parentheses.

using the following procedure. Each of the four variables — $M1G$, $M2G$, IPG, and π — was regressed on its own four lagged values as well as on four lagged values of each of the other three variables and four lagged values of each of the following variables: the unemployment rate; the 90 day treasury bill rate; the balance of payments on current account; the growth rate of real federal government expenditure, the high employment budget surplus; and the growth rate of federal government, interest bearing debt, in the hands of the public.[16] (These other variables were selected because a reading of the literature on Federal Reserve reaction functions indicated that they might help explain money growth.[17]) The four lagged values of each variable were retained in the equation only if they were jointly significant at the five percent level or higher. The major advantage of this procedure is that it imposes a discipline on the researcher that prevents his searching for model specifications that confirm his priors.

The resulting multivariate time-series models can be found in table 2,

[16]The source of these variables is the NBER data bank.
[17]See Fair (1978) and the reference therein.

Table 2

Multivariate time-series models.[a]

	Eq. no.						
	(2.1)		(2.2)		(2.3)		(2.4)
	Dependent variable						
Coefficient of	$M1G$		$M2G$		IPG		π
Constant term	−0.0004 (0.0017)		0.0026 (0.0016)		−0.0148 (0.0125)		0.0053 (0.0019)
$M1G(-1)$	0.0906 (0.1655)				0.6904 (0.3938)		
$M1G(-2)$	0.5233 (0.1680)	$F(4,79)$			0.6883 (0.4089)	$F(4,75)$	
$M1G(-3)$	−0.2765 (0.1785)	$=3.10$			1.0207 (0.4200)	$=6.53$	
$M1G(-4)$	−0.1757 (0.1791)				0.2745 (0.4337)		
$M2G(-1)$	0.3590 (0.1618)		0.5050 (0.1119)				
$M2G(-2)$	−0.3972 (0.1754)	$F(4,79)$	0.0985 (0.1266)	$F(4,83)$			
$M2G(-3)$	0.3510 (0.1757)	$=3.98$	0.1517 (0.1167)	$=15.37$			
$M2G(-4)$	0.1396 (0.1645)		−0.0806 (0.1036)				

Table 2 (*continued*)

Multivariate time-series models.[a]

Coefficient of	Eq. no. (2.1) Dependent variable *M1G*		(2.2) *M2G*		(2.3) *IPG*		(2.4) π	
$IPG(-1)$					−0.0947			
					(0.1622)			
$IPG(-2)$					−0.6171			
					(0.1727)	$F(4,75) = 3.71$		
$IPG(-3)$					−0.0902			
					(0.1709)			
$IPG(-4)$					−0.2807			
					(0.1224)			
$\pi(-1)$					−0.5539		0.2245	
					(0.6501)		(0.1079)	
$\pi(-2)$					−0.5186		0.5527	
					(0.6229)	$F(4,75) = 7.61$	(0.1053)	$F(4,83) = 79.32$
$\pi(-3)$					−0.8774		0.2833	
					(0.6533)		(0.1090)	
$\pi(-4)$					−0.7464		−0.0636	
					(0.6533)		(0.1116)	
$UN(-1)$					−0.0904		−0.0036	
					(0.0096)		(0.0009)	
$UN(-2)$					−0.0018		0.0012	
					(0.0120)	$F(4,75) = 3.00$	(0.0016)	$F(4,83) = 6.51$
$UN(-3)$					0.0173		0.0018	
					(0.0114)		(0.0015)	
$UN(-4)$					−0.0001		−0.0004	
					(0.0091)		(0.0095)	
$RTB(-1)$	−0.2647		−0.4966					
	(0.1067)		(0.1000)					
$RTB(-2)$	0.2086		0.4853					
	(0.1305)	$F(4,79) = 2.85$	(0.1373)	$F(4,83) = 9.19$				
$RTB(-3)$	0.1250		0.0332					
	(0.1396)		(0.1472)					
$RTB(-4)$	−0.0277)		0.0519					
	(0.1121)		(0.1132)					
R^2	0.5427		0.6232		0.5159		0.7949	
Std. error	0.0053		0.0056		0.0200		0.0035	
Durbin–Watson	1.97		1.96		2.03		1.96	

[a]*Note:* Asymptotic *F*-statistics test the joint null hypothesis that the coefficients in brackets are equal to zero in the regression model. Asymptotic standard errors of coefficients are in parentheses.

along with asymptotic F-statistics of the joint significance test for whether the four lagged values of each variable should be included in the regression model. These models not only have a better fit than the corresponding univariate models, but also Chow tests now cannot reject stability of the coefficients.[18] Note that these multivatiate time-series models contain some information of independent interest because they make use of Granger's (1969) concept of predictive content.[19] One interesting feature of the multivariate, money growth equations is that, in contrast with Barro's (1977) work, in no case were fiscal policy or unemployment variables found to be statistically significant at the five percent level.[20,21]

One way to proceed in estimating the efficient markets model is to use a two-step procedure outlined in the recent work of Barro (1977, 1978). After estimating the time-series models of tables 1 and 2, the residuals from these regressions can then be used as proxies for the corresponding unanticipated variables in estimating eqs. (6) and (9). Market efficiency tests of whether only unanticipated changes are related to bond returns could then also proceed as in Barro (1977).

Although the empirical results using the above approach are not unreasonable and are similar to those produced here in the text (see the appendix), there is a serious econometric criticism of this approach. As Durbin (1970) and Sims (1977) have shown, using residuals from one regression as variables in another regression, as occurs in the above approach, is econometrically dangerous and has often led to misleading

[18]The asymptotic F-statistics for the Chow tests of the equations in table 2 are as follows: for 2.1, $F(13,66)=1.81$ while the critical F at 5% is 1.88; for 2.2, $F(9,74)=1.60$ while the critical F at 5% is 2.00; for 2.3, $F(17,58)=1.39$ while the critical F at 5% is 1.80; for 2.4, $F(9,74)=1.41$; while the critical F at 5% is 2.00. However, note that the increased number of constraints in these tests may reduce the statistical power of the tests, and this might explain the failure to reject the null hypothesis of unstable coefficients.

[19]I prefer not refer to this as Granger-causality here because this nomenclature has led to much confusion in the literature. For a discussion of this point see Zellner (1979).

[20]The asymptotic F-statistics which tests the null hypothesis that the lagged values of the following variables add no explanatory power to the table 2 regressions are as follows. In the 2.1 regression, the $F(4,75)$ statistics are: 2.04 for π; 0.89 for IPG; 0.77 for UN; 1.54 for the growth rate of real government expenditure; 1.41 for the balance of payments; 0.57 for the high employment surplus; and 0.63 for the growth rate of government debt. In the 2.2 regression, the $F(4, 79)$ statistics are: 1.19 for π; 2.32 for $M1G$; 1.70 for IPG; 0.51 for UN; 0.10 for the growth rate of real government expenditure; 1.04 for the balance of payments on current account; 1.09 for the high employment surplus; and 0.90 for the growth rate of government debt. In the 2.3 regression, the $F(4,71)$ statistics are: 1.95 for RTB; 0.89 for the growth rate in real government expenditure; 0.05 for $M2G$; 1.83 for the balance of payments on current account; 0.54 for the high employment surplus; and 0.36 for the growth rate of government debt. In the 2.4 regression, the $F(4,79)$ statistics are: 1.66 for $M1G$; 0.69 for RTB; 1.08 for IPG; 2.25 for the growth rate in real government expenditure; 2.32 for the balance of payments on current account; 1.57 for the high employment surplus; and 0.57 for the growth rate of government debt.

[21]Sheffrin (1979) also finds that fiscal policy variables do not help explain money growth.

results.[22] The specific problem with this two-step procedure is that the resulting test statistics are unlikely to be consistent. This procedure implicitly assumes that the covariance of the β and γ estimates are zero. If, as would be likely, there are off-diagonal elements in the information matrix of the joint estimates, then ignoring them as is done in the two-step procedure will lead to inconsistent test statistics.[23]

Econometric techniques are available which are less subject to the criticism raised above. One such technique is outlined below and is then used to estimate the efficient markets models of eqs. (6) and (9).[24]

In matrix notation, the efficient markets model can be written as

$$BRET - r_{-1} = \delta + (X - X^e)\beta + \varepsilon, \tag{11}$$

where $BRET = n \times 1$, $r_{-1} = n \times 1$, $\delta = n \times 1$, X and $X_e = n \times k$, $\beta = k \times 1$, $\varepsilon = n \times 1$, n is the number of observations, and k is the number of right-hand side variables in X. The linear time series model for X, whether univariate or multivariate can also be written as

$$X = Z\gamma + U, \tag{12}$$

where Z is an $n \times m$ matrix of lagged variables, where m is the number of variables, γ is an $m \times k$ matrix of coefficients, and U is an $n \times k$ matrix of white noise error terms. The optimal linear forecast of X is then

$$X^e = Z\gamma, \tag{13}$$

and substituting this into (8) we have

$$BRET - r_{-1} = \delta + (X - Z\gamma)\beta + \varepsilon. \tag{14}$$

The system in (12) and (14) can be stacked into one regression system with $n(k+1)$ observations, and it can be estimated by non-linear least squares methods imposing the non-linear constraints that the γ in (12) and (14) are equal. In order to obtain more efficient parameter estimates as well as

[22]See Friedman (1959) and the discussion in Laidler (1977).

[23]As is shown in Abel and Mishkin (1979), tests for market efficiency involve the joint hypothesis that (1) expectations are rational (in the sense of being optimal linear forecasts) and (2) $BRET_t - r_{t-1}$ is correlated with only unanticipated movements in the X variables. A further problem with the two step procedure is that it only tests the second part of the joint hypothesis and is not capable of a test of the full implications of market efficiency.

[24]The technique used here is quite similar in concept to that proposed by Sargent (1979), although it is somewhat easier to execute and notationally is simpler. The empirical results found here are indeed consistent with Sargent's results.

consistent test statistics, corrections must be made for heteroscedasticity both within and across equations in this system.[25]

This procedure is superior to the alternative two-step procedure.[26] More efficient parameter estimates of β and γ will result because both (12) and (14) make use of information from each other in the estimation process. In addition, it generates a very simple test of market efficiency which is similar to recent tests of 'rationality' in the literature that proceed along the lines of Modigliani and Shiller (1973).[27] If the market is efficient, it should behave as if its linear forecasts using the information in Z are no different except by chance, from the optimal linear forecasts using Z. If this were not the case, then a linear combination of the variables in Z could have been used to improve the market forecasts. Thus a test for whether the γ in (12) and (14) are equal is analogous to the usual procedure for testing market efficiency where the one-period return on a security is correlated with past information or linear combinations of past information.[28] The test for market efficiency is then a simple likelihood ratio test for whether the (12) and (14) system satisfies the non-linear constraints implied by the equality of γ in (12) and (14).[29] The likelihood ratio statistic,

$$-2\log(L^c/L^u)$$

is distributed asymptotically as $\chi^2(q)$, where q is the number of non-linear constraints, L^c is the likelihood of the estimated constrained system, and L^u is the likelihood of the estimated unconstrained system. In this non-linear least

[25]The following iterative procedure was used to correct for heteroscedasticity in these estimates. In the first stage estimation of the non-linear system, if Goldfeld–Quandt tests indicated that heteroscedasticity existed within an equation, the variables in this equation were weighted using a time trend procedure outlined by Glesjer (1969). (The *IPG* equation did have a somewhat unusual pattern of residuals which could not be corrected for heteroscedasticity with a single time trend. Here two separate time trend regressions were used for the 1954–1976 period in order to calculate the weighting factors.) Furthermore, the variables in each equation of the system were appropriately weighted so that each equation individually had the same sum of squared residuals. After the first stage estimation, the sum of squared residuals for the two halves of each of the $k+1$ equations were calculated and were then used to weight the variables in each equation so that the sums of squared residuals were the same in all cases. Then the non-linear system was estimated all over again. This resulted in a similar sum of squared residuals in all equations of the (12) and (14) system so that no further iterations were performed. Some experimentation did indicate that no appreciable differences in the results occurred if some modification of this iterative procedure was used which left the sum of squared residuals reasonably equal for all the equations.

[26]See Abel and Mishkin (1979) for a more detailed discussion of the econometric issues in using the joint non-linear procedure.

[27]See Pesando (1975), Sargent (1976), Carlson (1977), Mullineaux (1978) and Friedman (1978).

[28]For examples, see Fama (1970), Mishkin (1978) and Rozeff (1974).

[29]Abel and Mishkin (1979) show that this likelihood ratio test is asymptotically equivalent to the usual procedure for testing market efficiency if the k time-series models include the same set of variables in the Z-vector.

squares system, the likelihood ratio statistic is[30]

$$n(k+1)(\log(SSR^c)-\log(SSR^u)),$$

where SSR^c is the sum of squared residuals from the constrained system, and SSR^u is the sum of squared residuals from the unconstrained system.

3.3. *The results*

Because there is no strong theoretical reason for estimating the efficient markets model with one monetary aggregate versus another, unanticipated growth rates of both *M1* and *M2* are used in estimation. The resulting estimates of the efficient markets model using the non-linear procedure and the seasonally adjusted data discussed above appear in table 3. Panel (A) of this table contains estimates where only univariate models of the form found in table 1 are used in (12), while panel (B) uses the multivariate models of the form found in table 2. The estimates of the γ coefficients are not presented here because they are quite similar to those found in tables 1 and 2.

A basic issue in these results is whether the efficient markets model used here is valid. Previous evidence on the efficiency of the bond market[31] indicates that an efficient markets model of the type used here is a reasonable characterization of bond market data. Furthermore, the likelihood ratio statistics in table 3 provide additional support for this view. They provide tests of the non-linear constraints (and hence market efficiency), and the corresponding *p*-value — also frequently called a marginal significance level — is the probability of obtaining that value of the likelihood ratio statistic or higher, under the null hypothesis that the non-linear constraints are valid. For example, a *p*-value smaller than 0.05 would indicate a significant rejection of the null hypothesis at the 5% level. The results of these efficient market tests indicate that the non-linear constraints cannot be rejected at the 5% level for any of the models of table 3. With this support of the efficient markets framework used here we can now turn to the estimates of the β coefficients in table 3.

The unanticipated *M1G* coefficients in panel (A) do not lend strong support to the view that an unanticipated increase in money growth is correlated with a fall in long bond rates. Although both of these coefficients have a positive sign, they are not significantly different from zero at the 5% level: asymptotic *t*-statistics are less than 0.1. In addition these coefficients are quite small. The β coefficients here denote the percentage point change in

[30]See Goldfeld and Quandt (1972).

[31]For example, see the survey in Fama (1970), and see Mishkin (1978) for more recent tests of bond market efficiency using the same bond returns data used in this paper.

Table 3

Non-linear estimates of the efficient markets model using seasonally adjusted data (asymptotic standard errors of coefficients in parentheses).

Model no.	Coefficients of $(M1G-M1G^e)$	$(M2G-M2G^e)$	$(IPG-IPG^e)$	$(\pi-\pi^e)$	Likelihood ratio test of non-linear constraints	*p*-value
(A) Using univariate models in (12)						
(3.1)	0.0482 (0.5961)				$\chi^2(4)=6.45$	0.1680
(3.2)	0.0501 (0.5517)		-0.4242^b (0.1260)	-1.8482^a (0.8028)	$\chi^2(12)=14.0$	0.3007
(3.3)		0.9174 (0.5459)			$\chi^2(4)=3.20$	0.5249
(3.4)		0.7174 (0.5063)	-0.4077^b (0.1243)	-1.7691^a (0.7880)	$\chi^2(12)=12.43$	0.4118
(B) Using multivariate models in (12)						
(3.5)	−0.2621 (0.7429)				$\chi^2(12)=18.10$	0.1127
(3.6)	0.4108 (0.7164)		-0.5039^b (0.1568)	−1.7529 (0.9552)	$\chi^2(24)=33.81$	0.0881
(3.7)		0.9199 (0.6738)			$\chi^2(8)=10.67$	0.2211
(3.8)		1.0950 (0.6283)	-0.4987^b (0.1492)	−1.8206 (0.9353)	$\chi^2(24)=32.60$	0.1128

[a]Significantly different from zero at the 5 percent level.
[b]Significantly different from zero at the 1 percent level.

the bond return from a 1% error in anticipations. Since in our 1954–1976 sample period, a one percentage point rise in the quarterly bond return series corresponds to approximately a 10 basis point fall in the long bond rate, the *M1G* coefficients in panel (A) indicate that a one percent surprise increase in *M1* is associated with only a 0.5 basis point decline in the long bond rate.[32]

The panel (B) estimates of the *M1G* coefficients indicate that the conclusion on the correlation of unanticipated money growth with the change in long rates is not altered as a result of using multivariate versus univariate time-series models in estimation. Again neither of the unanticipated *M1G* coefficients are significantly different from zero at 5%, and they continue to be small, with the largest of the coefficients indicating that a one percent surprise increase in *M1* leads to only a 4.1 basis point decline in the long bond rate. Furthermore, one of the unanticipated *M1G* coefficients is now negative.

How different are the results found here from those that might be inferred from 'Keynesian', structural macro-econometric models? Using a simulation technique discussed in Mishkin (1979) we can examine the responses of a macro model to a 1% surprise increase in *M1*. Eq. (1.1) was used to trace out the effect on *M1* growth from a 1% innovation. The resulting *M1* numbers were then used in a simulation experiment with the MPS (MIT-Penn-SSRC) Quarterly Econometric Model (1977) in order to derive the response of this model to the 1% *M1* innovation occurring in the 1967-1 quarter. The MPS model indicates that this 1% *M1* innovation would lead to an immediate decline of 18.1 basis points in the long rate. Not only is this long rate decline several times larger than the maximum 4.1 basis point decline implied by the empirical evidence in table 3, but also it is significantly larger at the 5% level for three of the four estimates in table 3 (and is almost significantly larger for the remaining estimate.) Clearly, the coefficients on unanticipated *M1* growth are quite low relative to what might be expected from a structural macroeconometric model.

Although the coefficients on unanticipated *M2* growth in table 3 are more positive than the unanticipated *M1G* coefficients,[33] they also do not lend strong support to the view that unanticipated money growth should be negatively correlated with the change in long rates. They are not significantly different from zero at the 5% level (although in 3.3 the unanticipated *M2G* coefficient is significantly different from zero at the 10% level). Also note that

[32]A basis point is defined as 1/100 of a percentage point. I.e., a one basis point rise in a 5% long rate would denote an increase to 5.01%.

[33]A plausible explanation for this result might run as follows. An unanticipated increase in short rates unrelated to Federal Reserve behavior might lead to disintermediation and thus an unanticipated decline in *M2G* at the same time as this new information would be associated with a decline in bond prices. A more positive correlation between unanticipated *M2G* and *BRET* might thus arise in the data.

the *M2* results in panel (A) versus panel (B) are so similar that it is again clear that the results on unanticipated money growth are not particularly sensitive to the specification of the money growth, time-series model.

The results on the unanticipated inflation and industrial production coefficients in table 3 do conform to our priors. In both the *M1* and *M2* efficient market models, these coefficients are negative and are either significant at the 5% level or are nearly so. The results on the coefficients of unanticipated industrial production are especially strong, with both the panel (A) and panel (B) estimates significantly different from zero at the 1% level. Although the unanticipated inflation coefficients are very similar in both panels, their asymptotic standard errors rise somewhat in going from panel (A) to panel (B). Hence, they are not quite significant at the 5% level in panel (B), while they are significant at this level in panel (A).

The efficient markets model does not specify whether seasonally adjusted rather than seasonally unadjusted data should be used in specifying $X-X^e$. This is essentially an empirical issue that cannot be settled on theoretical grounds. Therefore, the (12) and (14) system has also been estimated with seasonally unadjusted data over the 1954–1976 sample period. The non-linear procedure described above was also used in deriving the estimates appearing in table 4. The likelihood ratio tests again support bond market efficiency when seasonally unadjusted data are used: no significant rejections of the non-linear constraints in the estimated models can be found in table 4. The results on unanticipated industrial production growth and inflation are in accord with the seasonally adjusted data estimates of table 3. Both the unanticipated *IPG* and π coefficients are of the appropriate negative sign and are all significantly different from zero. Indeed, one feature of table 4 is that the unanticipated inflation coefficients now differ from zero at higher significance levels than previously.

The unanticipated money growth coefficients are even less favorable than the previous results to the view that unanticipated increases in the money supply are negatively correlated with changes in long rates. Notice that these coefficients are more often negative using the seasonally unadjusted data than they are positive. In fact, the unanticipated *M1G* coefficients are all negative, and in two cases the coefficients are significantly different from zero. The seasonally unadjusted data, therefore, if anything lend some mild support to the view that unanticipated increases in money growth are correlated with an increase in the long rate.

4. Concluding remarks

A wide range of empirical tests exploring the relationship of money growth and long interest rates has been conducted in this paper and in the appendix. A guiding principle in this research has been the use of many

Table 4

Non-linear estimates of the efficient markets model using seasonally unadjusted data (asymptotic standard errors of coefficients in parentheses).

Model no.	Coefficients of $(M1G-M1G^e)$	$(M2G-M2G^e)$	$(IPG-IPG^e)$	$(\pi-\pi^e)$	Likelihood ratio test of non-linear constraints	p-value
(A) Using univariate models in (12)						
(4.1)	−0.7339[a] (0.3631)				$\chi^2(4)=5.08$	0.2792
(4.2)	−0.5879 (0.3553)		−0.2028[a] (0.0857)	−2.5145[b] (0.6912)	$\chi^2(12)=20.83$	0.0529
(4.3)		0.0001 (0.3610)			$\chi^2(4)=3.27$	0.5137
(4.4)		0.1406 (0.3330)	−0.2420[b] (0.0838)	−2.4438[b] (0.7111)	$\chi^2(12)=19.53$	0.0765
(B) Using multivariate models in (12)						
(4.5)	−1.2781[b] (0.4504)				$\chi^2(12)=12.10$	0.4377
(4.6)	−0.8078 (0.4339)		−0.4105[b] (0.1371)	−2.4472[b] (0.8089)	$\chi^2(24)=28.48$	0.2403
(4.7)		−0.1404 (0.4821)			$\chi^2(8)=7.23$	0.5120
(4.8)		0.1534 (0.4391)	−0.4741[b] (0.1396)	−2.6226[b] (0.8237)	$\chi^2(24)=27.11$	0.2994

[a]Significantly different from zero at the 5 percent level.
[b]Significantly different from zero at the 1 percent level.

different empirical tests of the model in order to provide information on the robustness of the results. The pursuit of this goal has led to model estimation where there have been variations along the following dimensions: (1) the choice of the monetary aggregate, (2) the choice of the relevant variables to include in the X-vector, (3) the use of seasonally adjusted versus seasonally unadjusted data, (4) the specification of the time-series models used to describe expectations formation, (5) the sample period, and (6) the econometric estimation technique. Even though some of these model estimates should be more reliable than others for the reasons discussed earlier, the large number of estimates will provide information on the sensitivity and reliability of the results reported here.

The results uniformly support the following conclusion: *There is little empirical support here for the view that increases in the money stock are negatively correlated with changes in long interest rates.*[34] However there are two aspects of the research methodology used here which raise questions about the general validity of this conclusion.

As has been discussed in the text, the β coefficients in the efficient markets models are not invariant to changes in the time-series processes of the money growth, income growth and inflation variables. Thus, if the time-series processes of MG, IPG and π variables were different in other periods, the conclusions derived from the estimates in this paper only provide information on the relationship of money growth and long rates for the postwar sample period. However, realize that many structural macroeconometric models which display a negative relationship between money growth and long rates have been estimated using a sample period similar to that used here and similar quarterly data as well. Thus the results reported in this paper are certainly of interest in evaluating these models.

A further difficulty with the research methodology followed here is that misspecification of (12), which describes expectations formation, could invalidate the results on the relationship between money growth and long rates. This is possible because misspecification of expectations formation could lead to inconsistent and biased β coefficients. Normally, the possibility of misspecification exists in all empirical work, but in modelling expectations it is a particularly difficult problem. Expectations are probably formed not only with objective data which can be easily incorporated into the Z-matrix of (12), but with subjective information as well. There may be no way to incorporate this subjective information into a time-series model describing such variables as money growth and inflation, with the result that expectations formation will not be properly specified. Unfortunately, there is often no alternative to the approach used here. Empirical work would certainly benefit from the existence of markets which directly provided

[34] I stress this conclusion because it is contrary to my original priors.

information on expectations of importance to that work, yet in most cases these markets do not exist. It is a sad fact that the real world has not been designed to make the tasks of economists easier. Nevertheless, the robustness of this paper's results to different specifications of the time-series models describing expectations provides evidence that this misspecification problem may not be very severe.

Given the conclusion reached above, how should we interpret it? If we are willing to accept exogeneity of the money supply process in the postwar period, the interpretation is clear cut. The evidence here would then cast doubt on the commonly held view that an increase in the money stock will lead, at least in the short run, to a decline in long interest rates. Not only does this suggest that the Federal Reserve cannot lower long interest rates by increasing the rate of money growth, but it also requires some modification of the monetary transmission mechanism embodied in structural macro-econometric models. However, this criticism of these models in no way denies the possible, potent effects of money supply increases on aggregate demand.[35]

As was mentioned in section 2 of the paper, if unanticipated money growth is not exogenous, then the β_m coefficient estimates are inconsistent and can lead to misleading inference. Particularly disturbing in this regard is the case where the Federal Reserve smooths interest rates so that an unanticipated increase in long rates causes a Federal Reserve reaction of an increase in unanticipated money growth. The resulting negative correlation of ε_t and $MG_t - MG_t^e$ would then tend to bias the β_m coefficient downward. Thus, even though the estimated β_m is close to zero or even negative, it is possible that an exogenous unanticipated increase in money growth over a quarter engineered by the Fed does lead to a higher quarterly return on long bonds because of an increase in the bond price. Therefore, the view in structural

[35]Because inflationary expectations adjust so slowly in these models, it is the actual decline in nominal long interest rates that is an important part of the mechanism whereby increases in money growth stimulate aggregate demand. It is plausible that an unanticipated increase in money growth may not induce lower nominal long rates because it leads to an immediate upward revision in expected inflation. Thus although nominal long rates may not fall when there is an increase in money growth, it is plausible that the long real rates may have declined in the short-run, with a resulting expansionary effect on aggregate demand. One piece of evidence supporting this position is that efficient markets tests of stock market behavior find a strong positive correlation of common stock returns with unanticipated money growth [Rozeff (1974)]. The valuation of a common stock can be thought of as expected real profits discounted by the capitalization rate for equity — which is a real interest rate. This positive correlation with unanticipated money growth leads to a decline in this particular real interest rate, and other real interest rates may therefore have declined as well. This evidence is, however, far more casual than we would like. Another possible interpretation for the positive correlation of unanticipated money growth and stock returns is that an increase in money growth is solely associated with higher expected real profits. This may be a less plausible interpretation than one in which the money growth increase leads to a real rate decline, but it is certainly a reasonable interpretation. This leaves us with an unsettled research issue concerning the monetary transmission mechanism.

macroeconometric models that an exogenous increase in money growth leads to a decline in long rates cannot be ruled out despite the empirical results of this paper.

Note however the nature of money growth endogeneity that is required for the above statement to be the case. If money growth is endogenous in the sense that the Federal Reserve modifies money growth within a quarter only in response to past public information available at the start of the quarter, this does not result in $MG_t - MG_t^e$ being correlated with ε_t. Hence the existence of Granger (1969) 'causality' running from interest rates to money growth does not imply that the estimates of β_m will be inconsistent. Tests of the Sims (1972) variety therefore cannot shed light on the consistency of the β_m estimates. If we are not to reject the common view that increases in money growth lead to long interest rate declines, research of a fairly subtle sort is needed to demonstrate that unanticipated money growth is negatively correlated with the contemporaneous error term, ε_t. Hence, as with many studies, this paper demonstrates the need for further research.

Appendix: Estimates of the efficient markets models using the two-step procedure

Table A.1 contains estimates of the efficient markets models using the two-step procedure and seasonally adjusted data over the 1954–1976 period. The coefficient estimates using this procedure are not appreciably different from the table 3 estimates generated by the non-linear procedure of the text. The unanticipated *IPG* and π coefficients in table A.1 have the same sign, are of a similar magnitude and have similar *t*-statistics to those in table 3. The coefficients of unanticipated money growth also do not differ substantially from those in the text. However, they are slightly more favorable to the views that increased money growth is associated with a short-run decline in long interest rates; they are somewhat larger than in table 3 and in one case the unanticipated *M2G* coefficient is positive and significantly different from zero. Market efficiency tests of whether only unanticipated changes are related to bond returns using the Barro (1977) procedure also reveal no violations of market efficiency in the models of table A.1. (However, the significance levels of these market efficiency tests are quite different from those in table 3, as might be expected from the discussion in the text.)

The two-step procedure has been used to gain further information on the robustness of this paper's empirical results. Also used in estimating the efficients markets models were residuals from eighth order autoregressive time-series models, as well as residuals from multivariate models which excluded the four lagged values of a variable only if it was not significant at the ten percent level (rather than the 5% level as in the text). The results were quite close to those in table A.1 and there was no strong evidence

Table A.1

Estimates of the efficient markets models: Using seasonally adjusted data and the two-step procedure. Dependent variable: $BRET_t - r_{t-1}$ (standard errors of coefficients are in parentheses).

Coefficients of						
$(M1G - M1G^e)$	$(M2G - M2G^e)$	$(IPG - IPG^e)$	$(\pi - \pi^e)$	R^2	Standard error	Durbin–Watson
(A) Using residuals from univariate models						
0.3567 (0.5753)				0.0042	0.0335	2.09
0.3658 (0.5460)		−0.4447[b] (0.1412)	−2.136[a] (0.8578)	0.1657	0.0310	2.23
	1.113[a] (0.530)			0.0466	0.0328	2.20
	0.8762 (0.5007)	−0.4265[b] (0.1385)	−1.987[a] (0.8455)	0.1896	0.0305	2.31
(B) Using residuals from multivariate models						
0.2788 (0.7149)				0.0017	0.0335	2.07
0.6262 (0.6958)		−0.5626[b] (0.1863)	−1.997[a] (0.9935)	0.1322	0.0316	2.17
	1.105 (0.6424)			0.0318	0.0330	2.08
	1.194 (0.6076)	−0.5547[b] (0.1795)	−1.973[a] (0.9767)	0.1612	0.0311	2.22

[a]Significantly different from zero at the 5 percent level.
[b]Significantly different from zero at the 1 percent level.

supporting a negative relationship between money growth and changes in long rates.

Because the Federal Reserve seems to have paid more attention to monetary aggregates in the 1970's than it did previously, it is possible that the results reported here do not hold up if the 1970's are excluded from the sample period. The two-step procedure was thus also used to estimate the efficient markets models for the 1954–1969 period. The unanticipated *IPG* and π coefficients continue to be negative although the significance levels of the *t*-statistics are not as high as in table A.1. The unanticipated money growth coefficients are never significantly different from zero and are more often negative when this sample period is used. Similar conclusions about the relationship of money growth and long interest rates thus result from estimates using this shorter sample period.

References

Abel, A. and F.S. Mishkin, 1979, On the econometric testing of rationality and market efficiency, Report 7933, Center for Mathematical Studies in Business and Economics (University of Chicago, Chicago, IL).

Barro, R.J., 1977, Unanticipated money growth and unemployment in the United States, American Economic Review 67, 101–115.

Barro, R.J., 1978, Unanticipated money, output, and the price level in the United States, Journal of Political Economy 86, 549–580.

Brainard, W.C. and R.N. Cooper, 1976. Empirical monetary, macroeconomics: What have we learned in the last 25 years, American Economic Review 65, 167–175.

Cagan, P., 1956, The monetary dynamics of hyperinflation, in: Milton Friedman, ed., Studies in the quantity theory of money (University of Chicago Press, Chicago, IL).

Cagan, P., 1972, The channels of monetary effects on interest rates (National Bureau of Economic Research, New York).

Carlson, J.A., 1977, A study of price forecasts, Annals of Economic and Social Measurement 6, 27–56.

Chow, G.C., 1960, Tests of equality between sets of coefficients in two linear regressions, Econometrica 28, 591–605.

Durbin, J., 1970, Testing for serial correlation in least squares regression when some of the regressions are lagged dependent variables, Econometrica 38, 410–421.

Fair, R., 1978, The sensitivity of fiscal-policy effects to assumptions about the behavior of the federal reserve, Econometrica 46.

Fama, E.F., 1970, Efficient capital markets: A review of theory and empirical work, Journal of Finance 25, 383–417.

Fama, E.F., 1975, Short-term interest rates as predictors of inflation, American Economic Review 65, 269–282.

Fama, E.F., 1976a, Foundations of finance (Basic Books, New York).

Fama, E.F., 1976b, Forward rates as predictors of future spot rates, Journal of Financial Economics 3, 361–377.

Fama, E.F. and G.W. Schwert, 1977. Assets returns and inflation, Journal of Financial Economics.

Feldstein, M.S. and O. Eckstein, 1970. The fundamental determinants of the interest rate, Review of Economics and Statistics 52, 363–375.

Fisher, I., 1930, The theory of interest (Macmillan, New York).

Fisher, L. and J.H. Lorie, 1977, A half century of returns on stocks and bonds, Graduate School of Business (University of Chicago, Chicago, IL).

Friedman, B., 1978, Survey evidence on the 'rationality' of interest rate expectations, National Bureau of Economic Research Working Paper no. 261.

Friedman, M., 1956, The quantity theory of money — A restatement, in: M. Friedman, ed., Studies in the quantity theory of money (University of Chicago Press, Chicago, IL).

Friedman, M., 1959, The demand for money — Some theoretical and empirical results, Journal of Political Economy 67, 327–351.

Friedman, M., 1968, The role of monetary policy, American Economic Review 58, 1–17.

Friedman, M., 1969, Factors affecting the level of interest rates, Proceedings of the 1968 Conference on Savings and Residential Financing, sponsored by the United States Savings and Loan League (The League) 11–27.

Gibson, W.E., 1970, Interest rates and monetary policy, Journal of Political Economy 78, 431–455.

Gibson, W.E. and G.G. Kaufman, 1968, The sensitivity of interest rates to changes in money and income, Journal of Political Economy 76, 472–478.

Glesjer, H., 1969, A new test for heteroscedasticity, Journal of the American Statistical Association.

Goldfeld, S.M., 1973, The demand for money revisited, Brookings Papers on Economic Activity 3, 577–638.

Goldfeld, S.M. and R.E. Quandt, 1965. Some tests for homoscedasticity, Journal of the American Statistical Association 60, 539–547.

Goldfeld, S.M. and R.E. Quandt, 1972, Non-linear methods in econometrics (North-Holland, Amsterdam).

Granger, C.W.J., 1969, Investigating causal relations by econometric models and cross-spectral methods, Econometrica 37, 424–438.

Jacobs, R.L., E.E. Leamer and M.P. Ward, 1979, Difficulties in testing for causation. Economic Inquiry 17, 401–413.

Laidler, D., 1977, The demand for money: Theories and evidence (Dun-Donnelley, New York) 119–152.

Mishkin, F.S., 1978:3, Efficient-markets theory: Implications for monetary policy, Brookings Papers on Economic Activity, 707–752.

Mishkin, F.S., 1979, Simulation methodology in macroeconomics: An innovation technique, Journal of Political Economy 87, 816–836.

MIT-Penn-SSRC, 1977, Quarterly econometric model (Unpublished).

Modigliani, F., 1974, The channels of monetary policy in the FMP econometric model of the U.S. in: G. Renton, ed., Modelling the economy (Heineman Educational Books, New York).

Modigliani, F. and R.J. Shiller, 1973, Inflation, rational expectations, and the term structure of interest rates, Economica 40, 12–43.

Mullineaux, O.J., 1978, On testing for rationality: Another look at the Livingston price expectations data, Journal of Political Economy 86, 329–336.

Muth, J.F., 1961, Rational expectations and the theory of price movements, Econometrica 29, 315–335.

Nelson, C.R. and G.W. Schwert, 1977, Short-term interest rates as predictors of inflation: On testing the hypothesis that the real rate is constant, American Economic Review 67, 478–486.

Pesando, J.E., 1975, A note on the rationality of the Livingston price expectations, Journal of Political Economy 83, 849–858.

Rozeff, M.S., 1974, Money and stock prices: Market efficiency and the lag in the effect of monetary policy, Journal of Financial Economics 1, 245–302.

Sargent, T.J., 1979, A note on maximum likelihood estimation of the rational expectations model of the term structure, Journal of Monetary Economics 5, 133–144.

Sheffrin, S.M., 1979, Unanticipated money growth and output fluctuations, Economic Inquiry 17, 1–13.

Shiller, R.J., 1979, The volatility of long-term interest rates and expectations models of the term structure, Journal of Political Economy 87, 1190–1219.

Sims, C.A., 1972, Money, income, and causality, American Economic Review 62, 540–552.

Sims, C.A., 1977, Comment, Journal of the American Statistical Association 72, 23–24.

Working, H., 1960, Note on the correlation of first differences of averages in a random chain, Econometrica 28, 916–918.

Zellner, A., 1979, Causality and econometrics, in: K. Brunner and A.H. Meltzer, eds., Three aspects of policy and policy making: Knowledge, data and institutions, Carnegie-Rochester Conference Series, Vol. 10 (North-Holland, Amsterdam) 9–54.

THE JOURNAL OF FINANCE · VOL XXXVII, NO. 1 · MARCH 1982

Monetary Policy and Short-term Interest Rates: An Efficient Markets-Rational Expectations Approach

FREDERIC S. MISHKIN*

ABSTRACT

This paper is an application of efficient markets-rational expectations theory to analyze empirically the relationship of money supply growth and short-term interest rates, a hotly debated issue in the literature. This approach has the advantage over earlier research on this subject in that it imposes a theoretical structure that allows easier interpretation of the empirical results as well as more powerful statistical tests. The empirical results uniformly *do not support* the proposition that increases in money growth are correlated with declines in short rates.

THE RELATIONSHIP BETWEEN MONEY supply growth and nominal interest rates is a hotly debated issue in the literature.[1] One view, associated with "Keynesian" structural macromodels, has an increase in money growth leading, at least in the short and medium runs, to a decline in interest rates.[2] An alternative view, associated with Milton Friedman [6, 7], indicates that interest rates might rise in response to higher money growth because there is a rise in inflationary expectations and hence a rise in interest rates through a Fisher [5] effect.

Previous empirical work on this issue has ignored constraints implied by the view that financial markets display rational expectations and are thus "efficient". Financial market efficiency should not be ignored because evidence supporting it is quite strong and recent work indicates that a failure to impose financial market efficiency on macroeconometric models can lead to highly misleading results.[3] In addition, a failure to impose the efficient markets constraints leads to a larger number of parameters to be estimated in this empirical work, and this leads to statistical tests with low power.[4]

The theory of efficient capital markets and rational expectations suggests an alternative approach for analyzing the relationship of money stock increases and

* University of Chicago. A more detailed version of this paper which contains additional results, Mishkin [12], is available as an NBER working paper. I thank James Pesando, Ed Burmeister, Ron Michener, Eugene Fama, and the participants in the Finance Workshop at the University of Chicago and the Money Workshops at the University of Chicago and the University of Virginia for their helpful comments. The National Science Foundation has provided research support. The usual disclaimer applies.

[1] Unless otherwise noted, whenever the phrase "interest rates" is used in this paper, it refers to nominal interest rates.

[2] For example, see Modigliani [15].

[3] See Fama [2] and Mishkin [9].

[4] A more extensive discussion of the previous empirical work on this topic and references to this work can be found in Mishkin [11].

interest rate movements. A previous paper (Mishkin [11]) developed an efficient markets model of long interest rate determination, and then estimated this model using postwar quarterly data. This approach had the advantage of imposing a theoretical structure on the problem, allowing easier interpretation of the empirical results as well as more powerful statistical tests of the proposition that increases in the money stock are correlated with declines in long rates. In addition, a Keynesian, liquidity preference view of interest rate determination was embedded in the efficient markets model and tested.

This paper is a sequel to the earlier paper in that it conducts a similar analysis for short-term interest rates. The next section develops a rational expectations (or, equivalently, efficient markets) model for analyzing movements in short rates, which is estimated in the subsequent section. The paper then concludes with an interpretation of these results.

I. The Model

The theory of rational expectations (or, equivalently, efficient markets theory) indicates that interest rates in a bond market should reflect all available information. More precisely, it implies that the market uses available information correctly in assessing the probability distribution of all future interest rates and hence:

$$E_m(r_t \mid \phi_{t-1}) = E(r_t \mid \phi_{t-1}) \tag{1}$$

where

r_t = short-term (one period) interest rate at time t,

ϕ_{t-1} = information available at time $t-1$,

$E(\cdots \mid \phi_{t-1})$ = the expectation conditional on ϕ_{t-1},

$E_m(\cdots \mid \phi_{t-1})$ = the market's expectations (unbiased forecast) assessed at $t-1$

If we denote the market's one-period-ahead forecast of the short rate of r_t^e (i.e., $r_t^e = E_m(r_t \mid \phi_{t-1})$) then (1) implies

$$E(r_t - r_t^e \mid \phi_{t-1}) = 0 \tag{2}$$

Equation (2) above states that the forecast error for short rates should be uncorrelated with any linear combinations of information in ϕ_{t-1}. An equivalent characterization of the rational expectations model which satisfies (2) is thus:

$$r_t - r_t^e = (X_t - X_t^e)\beta + \epsilon_t \tag{3}$$

where a superscript e continues to denote the market's expectations conditional on all past available information and

X_t = a variable (or vector of variables) of information relevant to the determination of short-term interest rates,

β = a coefficient or vector of coefficients,

ϵ_t = serially uncorrelated error process (because $E(\epsilon_t \mid \phi_{t-1}) = 0$)

The rational expectations model (3) stresses that an unanticipated change[5] in the short rate will occur only when unanticipated information hits the market.

In order to make the rational expectations model above empirically testable we must have a model of market equilibrium. Here we assume, as in Fama [3], that the one-period-ahead forward rate equals the one-period-ahead expected short rate plus a risk (liquidity) premium which varies with the uncertainty in short rate movements. i.e.:

$$ {}_{t-1}F_t = r_t^e + \delta_t \tag{4}$$

and

$$ \delta_t = a_o + a_1 \sigma_t \tag{5}$$

where

${}_{t-1}F_t$ = forward rate for the one-period-rate at time t, implied by the yield curve at $t-1$,[6]

δ_t = risk (liquidity) premium for F_t,

σ_t = measure of uncertainty in short rate movements

Combining the model of market equilibrium with (3), we have the rational expectations model estimated in this paper:

$$ r_t - {}_{t-1}F_t = -a_o - a_1\sigma_t + (X_t - X_t^e)\beta + \epsilon_t \tag{6}$$

The research question posed in the Introduction suggests that the relationship of money growth and unanticipated changes in the short rate in a rational expectations model is of particular interest.[7] Substituting money growth for X_t in Equation (6) leads to[8]:

$$ r_t - {}_{t-1}F_t = -a_o - a_1\sigma_t + \beta_m(MG_t - MG_t^e) + \epsilon_t \tag{7}$$

[5] Since the anticipated change in the short rate equals $r_t^e - r_{t-1}$, $r_t - r_t^e$ is equivalent to the unanticipated change in the short rate.

[6] In the case of 90-day treasury bills which are used here, the forward rate at the end of a quarter is calculated as

$$ {}_{t-1}F_t = 4\left\{1 - \frac{(360 - 180\ rsix_{t-1})}{(360 - 90\ r_{t-1})}\right\}$$

where all rates are in fractions and

$rsix_{t-1}$ = six month (180 day) bill rate at end of previous quarter,

r_{t-1} = 90-day bill rate at end of previous quarter

[7] As has been found in foreign exchange markets (see, for example, Mussa [16]) quarterly changes in the spot rate, in this case the short rate, are primarily attributable to unanticipated movements in the spot rate. Also see Fama [3]. Using the model of the liquidity premium estimated in (9), the correlation of unanticipated short rate movements and the actual change in short rates is high in the 1959–76 sample period used here, being greater than .8. Thus, results obtained in this study for unanticipated changes in short rates also apply to changes in short rates.

[8] Other monetary aggregates are also potential candidates for inclusion in X_t. Of particular interest are such aggregates as unborrowed reserves or the unborrowed base which are under more direct control of the Federal Reserve and are thus possibly more exogenous than the M1 and M2 aggregates.

where

$$MG_t = \text{the money growth rate at time } t$$

The liquidity preference approach to the demand for money indicates that changes in interest rates are related not only to changes in the money stock but also to changes in real income, the price level, and inflation. Hence short-term interest rates might be related not only to the growth rate in the nominal money stock, as in Equation (7), but also to the growth rate of real income and inflation. Adding this information to the X-vector in the Equation (6) model leads to the following:

$$r_t - {}_{t-1}F_t = -a_o - a_1\sigma_t + \beta_m(MG_t - MG_t^e) + \beta_y(YG_t - YG_t^e) + \beta_\pi(\pi_t - \pi_t^e) + \epsilon_t \quad (8)$$

where

$$YG_t = \text{growth rate of real income,}$$

$$\pi_t = \text{inflation rate,}$$

$$\beta_m, \beta_y, \beta_\pi = \text{coefficients}$$

This equation is really a rational expectations analog to the typical money demand relationship found in the literature.

If unanticipated increases in the money stock are to have a negative correlation with unanticipated changes in short rates (as might be expected from "Keynesian" macroeconometric models), the implication is that the coefficient on unanticipated money growth should be significantly negative in Equations (7) and (8): i.e., $\beta_m < 0$. The liquidity preference and Fisher [5] views lead us also to expect both positive income and inflation coefficients: i.e., $\beta_y > 0$ and $\beta_\pi > 0$.

Note that, as is pointed out in Mishkin [11], these coefficients are not invariant to changes in the time-series processes of money growth, income growth, and inflation. However, if, as is found in the sample period used here, these time-series processes display persistence—i.e., an unanticipated rise leads to a higher value in the coming period—then the expected signs are as above. Mishkin [11] also discusses another important caveat. The rational expectations model does not guarantee that Equations (7) and (8) are reduced forms where the right-hand-side unanticipated variables are uncorrelated with the error term, ϵ_t, and therefore the estimates of β are consistent.[9] Because the analysis in this paper cannot demonstrate that Equations (7) and (8) are reduced forms, the β estimates should be viewed only as providing information on the correlations of such variables as unanticipated money growth with the unanticipated change in short rates. Interpretation of these correlations is deferred to the concluding remarks.

We now turn to the actual estimation of the rational expectations models of (7) and (8).

As is discussed later, exogeneity of the monetary aggregate is desirable because interpretation of results is then more clear-cut. Therefore, in future research I plan to estimate the models with these other aggregates.

[9] This issue of the consistency of the β estimates is discussed more extensively in Abel and Mishkin [1].

II. Empirical Results

The Data

Six-month treasury bills were not issued before 1959, and the six-month bill rate is needed to calculate the forward rate used here. Thus, the empirical results below use postwar quarterly data over the 1959–76 sample period. Since misleading results can be obtained from efficient markets models using averaged data,[10] the interest rate data are derived from security prices at particular points in time. In keeping with this, an attempt has been made to derive the other variables used here with data as close to being end-of-quarter as possible. For this reason, Industrial Production is used as a proxy for real income in estimating Equation (8) rather than a more broadly based National Income Accounts measure. Similarly, the CPI rather than the GNP deflator has been used to calculate the inflation variable.[11] A more detailed description of the data is available in a longer version of this paper, Mishkin [12].

The Results

Before turning to the procedures for estimating the rational expectations model, the measure of short rate uncertainty (σ_t) used here requires some discussion. Fama [3] calculates σ_t as the average of the absolute values of the changes in the spot rate during the year before t and during the year following t. Because the risk (liquidity) premium must be set conditional on available information—in this case that known at $t - 1$—allowing σ_t to be calculated from information not available at $t - 1$ poses some conceptual difficulties. An alternative, though similar, measure of σ_t is used in this study. The difference between the forward rate and the spot rate, i.e., $r_t - {}_{t-1}F_t$, was regressed on measures of σ_t, calculated as the average absolute change of the bill rate over a number of previous quarters, where the number of quarters was varied. The best fit was obtained with σ_t calculated from eight previous quarters of changes in the bill rate. The results are as follows

$$r_t - {}_{t-1}F_t = -.0001 - 1.0961\,\sigma_t + \epsilon_t$$

$$\quad\quad\quad\quad (.0017) \quad (.2937)$$

$$R^2 = .1659 \quad \text{Standard Error} = .0068 \quad \text{Durbin-Watson} = 1.90 \tag{9}$$

where

$$\sigma_t = \frac{\sum_{i=1}^{8} |r_{t-i} - r_{t-i-1}|}{8}$$

As in Fama [3], increased uncertainty in short rate movements does lead to an increased risk premium and this effect is statistically significant at the 1% level. In addition, the σ_t measure used here outperforms the Fama measure that is constructed from information unavailable at $t - 1$. The above measure of σ_t is

[10] See Working [19], for example.

[11] In previous work (Mishkin [11]), experiments with quarterly averaged data led to substantially worse fits for equations similar to (7) and (8), fewer significant coefficients and no appreciable differences as to the statistical significance of the β_m coefficients.

used in the empirical tests that follow. However, the specification of the risk premium model is not a critical issue to the outcomes: use of a Fama measure of σ_t or the exclusion altogether of σ_t from the model does not alter the results appreciably.

The (7) and (8) models are estimated jointly with forecasting equations for money growth, industrial production growth and inflation, imposing cross-equation constraints implied by rationality of expectations.[12] The estimation procedure is discussed in Mishkin [11] and [13]. In order to verify the robustness of the results, two methods, rather than one, are used for specification of the forecasting equations, and they are discussed in Mishkin [11]. The simplest specifies these equations as univariate autoregressive time-series models, while the other method involves specifying multivariate models using Granger's [8] concept of predictive content.[13] Because there is no strong theoretical reason for estimating the rational expectations model with one monetary aggregate versus another, unanticipated growth rates of both M1 and M2 are used in estimation. The resulting estimates and test statistics with these data appear in Table I. Panel A of this table contains estimates where the forecasting equations are univariate time-series models, while for Panel B the forecasting equations are multivariate models.

The unanticipated M1G coefficients in Panel A do not support the view that an unanticipated increase in money growth is correlated with an unanticipated fall in short rates.[14] Not only are both of these coefficients in Models 1.1 and 1.2 positive rather than negative, but they are also significantly different from zero at the 1% level. Nor are the coefficients numerically small. They indicate that a 1% surprise increase in M1 is associated with a 25 to 30 basis point unanticipated increase in the bill rate.[15] The Panel B estimates of the M1G coefficients indicate

[12] To be more precise, the nonlinear constraints are generated by two hypotheses: (1) rational expectations, and (2) the model of market equilibrium in Equations (4) and (5). Likelihood ratio tests reported in the longer version of this paper, Mishkin [12], indicate that in over half the models these constraints are rejected at the 5% level. As is argued in Mishkin [12], it is very plausible that these rejections are due to the inadequacy of the model of market equilibrium rather than the nonrationality of expectations. Then it is easily shown that the rational expectations models estimated here are still a valid framework for analyzing the relationship of money growth and short interest rates. Incorrect specification of the model of the risk premium will not lead to inconsistent estimates of the β coefficients. Since the derivation of a better model of the risk premium is not necessary for achieving reliable estimates of the β's if expectations are rational, this tricky research issue, which is beyond the scope of this paper, is left as a subject for further research.

The results in the longer version of this paper do provide some information on the possible direction of this research. Despite Fama's [3] finding that his measure of the risk premium is successful in passing the market efficiency test that forward rates adjusted for this measure outperform a random walk scheme in forecasting interest rates, a more powerful test, such as here, demonstrates that this measure is not adequate. This should not be surprising because there is no obvious utility function that would lead us to this measure. A theoretically more justifiable risk measure would exploit the covariance of treasury bill yields with returns on alternative assets. In addition, these results indicate that the risk premium is possibly related to past money growth and the level of interest rates, while they give no indication that it is related to past inflation, industrial production growth, unemployment or the balance of payments.

[13] The specifications for these equations can be found in Tables 1 and 2 of Mishkin [12].

[14] Urich and Wachtel [18] obtain a similar result using weekly data. Reduction in the unit of observation in the analysis here is therefore likely to leave the findings intact.

[15] A basis point is defined as 1/100 of a percentage point. i.e., a one basis point rise in a 5% short rate would denote an increase to 5.01%.

Table I

Non-Linear Estimates of the Efficient Markets-Rational Expectations Model with Seasonally Unadjusted Data

	Coefficients of					
Model No.	($M1G-M1G^e$)	($M2G-M2G^e$)	($IPG-IPG^e$)	($\pi-\pi^e$)	constant term	σ
	Panel A. Using Univariate Forecasting Equations					
1.1	.3029**				.0003	−1.1255**
	(.0652)				(.0014)	(.2530)
1.2	.2458**		.0274	.4687**	.0001	−1.1267**
	(.0671)		(.0171)	(.1716)	(.0014)	(.2464)
1.3		.1926*			.0003	−1.1468**
		(.0644)			(.0015)	(.2765)
1.4		.1967**	.0440*	.5459**	.0001	−1.1260**
		(.0624)	(.0176)	(.1746)	(.0014)	(.2526)
	Panel B. Using Multivariate Forecasting Equations					
1.5	.3431**				.0007	−1.2403**
	(.0831)				(.0015)	(.2639)
1.6	.2484**		.0386	.5079	.0004	−1.2037**
	(.0956)		(.0376)	(.2623)	(.0016)	(.2861)
1.7		.3285**			−.0007	−.9891**
		(.0918)			(.0015)	(.2841)
1.8		.2011*	.0400	.5788*	−.0003	−1.0791**
		(.0986)	(.0374)	(.2674)	(.0016)	(.3021)

Note: * = significantly different from zero at the 5% level.
** = significantly different from zero at the 1% level.
Asymptotic standard errors of the coefficients are in parentheses.

$M1G-M1G^e$ = unanticipated M1 growth
$M2G-M2G^e$ = unanticipated M2 growth
$IPG-IPG^e$ = unanticipated industrial production growth
$\pi-\pi^e$ = unanticipated inflation
σ = measure of interest rate uncertainty

that the above conclusion on the relationship of short rates and M1 growth is not altered as a result of using multivariate versus univariate time-series models to describe expectations formation. Again both coefficients are positive and significantly different from zero at the 1% level. The coefficients on unanticipated M2 growth tell a similar story. They also display a significant positive correlation of unanticipated money growth and unanticipated bill rate movements.

How different are the results found here from those that might be inferred from "Keynesian" structural macroeconometric models? The response of one such model, the MPS (MIT-Penn-SSRC) Quarterly Econometric Model [14], to a 1% surprise increase in M1 growth has been analyzed with a simulation technique discussed in Mishkin [10].[16] The MPS model indicated that this 1% M1 surprise led to an immediate *decline* of 88 basis points in the bill rate. This strongly contrasts with the finding here that even the least positive M1 coefficient is more than ten standard deviations away from this figure.

The similarity between the money growth as well as other coefficients estimates in going from Panel A to Panel B is encouraging for it gives us confidence that the results found here are robust to changes in the models describing expectations.[17] Note that the asymptotic *t*-statistics for the money growth and inflation coefficients in Panel A tend to be higher than those in Panel B, thus yielding stronger results. This lends some support to the position taken by Feige and Pearce [4] that forecasts from univariate time-series models may be "economically rational" expectations. The results on the unanticipated inflation and industrial production coefficients in Panel A do conform to our priors. In both the M1 and M2 rational expectations models, these coefficients are positive and the inflation coefficients are significantly different from zero at the 1% level while only one of the industrial production coefficients is significantly different from zero at the 5% level. The Panel B results for inflation are similar to those in Panel A, although now only the inflation coefficient in the M2 model is significant.

The rational expectations model does not specify whether the $X - X^e$ variables should be described by seasonally adjusted or seasonally unadjusted data. This is an empirical issue that cannot be settled easily on theoretical grounds because it is not clear whether market participants concentrate on seasonally adjusted versus unadjusted information. For this reason, the rational expectations models have also been estimated using seasonally adjusted data rather than unadjusted data as in Table I. For the sake of brevity, these results are not reported here, but they can be found in Mishkin [12]. The coefficient estimates are very similar, but their standard errors are somewhat larger. We continue to find that all the money growth coefficients are positive with three out of eight statistically significant. The seasonally adjusted data also do not support the view that an unanticipated increase in money growth is associated with an unanticipated fall in short rates. However, they are not quite as strong as the unadjusted data in supporting the opposite view.

[16] More details on this simulation experiment are given in Mishkin [11].

[17] Additional results in the Appendix of Mishkin [12] also support this view. As Feige and Pearce [4] have argued, once past information on the variable to be forecast is used in forecasting, other information might have little incremental predictive power. The similarity of results in Panels A and B gives some credibility to this viewpoint and this issue is discussed more extensively in Mishkin [13].

III. Conclusion

A wide range of empirical tests exploring the relationship of money growth and short-term interest rates have been conducted in this paper and in the longer version, Mishkin [12]. The results uniformly support the following conclusion. There is no empirical support here for the view that unanticipated increases in the money stock are negatively correlated with unanticipated changes in short interest rates. This conclusion is similar to that found in a previous paper, Mishkin [11], which conducts a parallel analysis of long-term interest rate behavior.

Given the conclusion reached above, how should we interpret it? If we are willing to accept exogeneity of the money supply process in the postwar period and a resulting lack of correlation of unanticipated money growth with the error term in the rational expectations model, the interpretation is clear-cut. The evidence here would then cast doubt on the commonly held view that an unanticipated increase in the money stock will lead to an unanticipated decline in short-term interest rates. However, if unanticipated money growth is correlated with the error term, then the β_m coefficient estimates are inconsistent and can result in misleading inference. Particularly disturbing in this regard is the case where the Federal Reserve smooths interest rates so that an unanticipated increase in short rates causes a Federal Reserve reaction of an increase in unanticipated money growth. The resulting positive correlation of ϵ_t and $MG_t - MG_t^e$ would then tend to bias the β_m coefficient upward. Thus, even though the estimated β_m is positive, we cannot rule out the view in structural macroeconometric models that an exogenous increase in money growth leads to a decline in short rates, despite the empirical results of this paper.

Note, however, the nature of money growth endogeneity that is required for the above statement to be the case. If money growth is endogenous in the sense that the Federal Reserve modifies money growth within a quarter only in response to past public information available at the start of the quarter, this does not result in $MG_t - MG_t^e$ being correlated with ϵ_t. Hence the existence of Granger [8] "causality" running from interest rates to money growth does not imply that the estimates of β_m will be inconsistent. Tests of the Sims [17] variety, therefore, cannot shed light on the consistency of the β_m estimates. If we are not to reject the common view that increases in money growth lead to short interest rate declines, research is needed to demonstrate that unanticipated money growth is positively correlated with the contemporaneous error term, ϵ_t. Hence, this issue cannot be resolved without further research.

REFERENCES

1. A. Abel and F. S. Mishkin. "An Integrated View of Tests of Rationality, Market Efficiency and the Short-Run Neutrality of Monetary Policy." Report 8113, Center for Mathematical Studies in Business and Economics, University of Chicago (March 1981).
2. E. F. Fama. "Efficient Capital Markets: A Review of Theory and Empirical Work." *Journal of Finance* 25 (1970), 383–417.
3. ———. "Forward Rates as Predictors of Future Spot Rates." *Journal of Financial Economics* 3 (1976), 361–77.
4. E. L. Feige and D. K. Pearce. "Economically Rational Expectations: Are Innovations in the Rate

of Inflation Independent of Innovations in Measures of Monetary and Fiscal Policy?" *Journal of Political Economy* 84 (June 1976), 499–522.

5. I. Fisher. *The Theory of Interest*. Macmillan (1930).
6. M. Friedman. "The Role of Monetary Policy." *American Economic Review* 58 (1968), 1–17.
7. ———. "Factors Affecting the Level of Interest Rates." *Proceedings of the 1968 Conference on Savings and Residual Financing*, sponsored by the United States Savings and Loan League (The League) (1969), 11–27.
8. C. W. J. Granger. "Investigating Causal Relations by Econometric Models and Cross-Spectral Methods." *Econometrica* 37 (1969), 424–38.
9. F. S. Mishkin. "Efficient-Markets Theory: Implications for Monetary Policy." *Brookings Papers on Economic Activity* 3 (1978), 707–52.
10. ———. "Simulation Methodology in Macroeconomics: An Innovation Technique." *Journal of Political Economy* 87 (1979), 816–36.
11. ———. "Monetary Policy and Long-Term Interest Rates: An Efficient Markets Approach." *Journal of Monetary Economics* (January 1981a), pp. 29–55.
12. ———. "Monetary Policy and Short-Term Interest Rates: An Efficient Markets-Rational Expectations Approach." National Bureau of Economic Research Working Paper (1981b).
13. ———. "Does Anticipated Monetary Policy Matter? An Econometric Investigation." University of Chicago (April 1981c), forthcoming in the *Journal of Political Economy*.
14. MIT-Penn-SSRC. *Quarterly Econometric Model* (unpublished 1977).
15. F. Modigliani. "The Channels of Monetary Policy in the FMP Econometric Model of the U.S." In *Modelling the Economy*, G. Renton, ed. Heineman Educational Books, 1974.
16. M. Mussa. "Empirical Regularities in the Behavior of Exchange Rates and Theories of the Foreign Exchange Market." In *Policies for Employment Prices, and Exchange Rates*, K. Brunner and A. Meltzer, eds. Carnegie-Rochester Conference Series on Public Policy, Volume 11. Amsterdam: North-Holland, (1979), 9–58.
17. C. A. Sims. "Money, Income, and Causality." *American Economic Review* 62 (1972), 540–52.
18. T. Urich and P. Wachtel. "Market Response to the Weekly Money Supply Announcements in the 1970s." Forthcoming in the *Journal of Finance*.
19. H. Working. "Note on the Correlation of First Differences of Averages in a Random Chain." *Econometrica* 28 (1960), 916–18.

PART II

REAL INTEREST RATES AND INFLATION

[3]

Carnegie-Rochester Conference Series on Public Policy 15(1981)151-200
North-Holland Publishing Company

THE REAL INTEREST RATE: AN EMPIRICAL INVESTIGATION

Frederic S. Mishkin*
University of Chicago
and
National Bureau of Economic Research

I. INTRODUCTION

Knowledge of how real interest rates move over time is critical to our understanding of macroeconomics. Movements in the real rate are central both to the discussion of the transmission mechanisms of monetary policy in the standard ISLM paradigm and to modern macroeconometric models.[1] Monetary policy is viewed as affecting the real rate of interest which then affects business and consumers' investment decisions and hence aggregate demand. Real interest rates also play a prominent role in explanations of business cycles and particular business cycle episodes. For example, the apparently unusually high real rates in the early years of the Great Depression are frequently cited as major factors in that business cycle downturn.[2] The impact of real interest rates on savings-consumption decisions has also been the subject of recent work.[3] If saving responds positively to the real return on saving, as some have claimed,[4] then declines in the real interest rate can have an adverse effect on capital formation and hence on productivity, a serious concern of policy-makers. Clearly, the real interest rate deserves careful study.

This paper is an empirical exploration of real interest rate movements in the United States over the last fifty years. It focuses on several questions which have repeatedly arisen in the literature. How valid is the hypothesis

---

*I thank John Huizinga and the participants in the Money Workshop at the University of Chicago and the Carnegie-Rochester Conference for helpful comments, Douglas McTaggart for his competent research assistance, and Eugene Fama for useful discussions and for supplying me with the prewar inflation data. Research support has been provided by the National Science Foundation. I also thank the Center for Research in Security Prices (CRSP) at the University of Chicago, the Board of Governors of the Federal Reserve System, and the Council of Economic Advisors for supplying some of the data used in this study. The usual disclaimer applies.

[1] For example, see Modigliani (1974).

[2] See Mayer (1978) and Meltzer (1976).

[3] Howrey and Hymans (1978), Boskin (1978), and Summers (1978).

[4] Recent empirical results on this issue are quite mixed. For example, Boskin's (1978) study has been strongly challenged by Howrey and Hymans (1978).

associated with Fama (1975) that the real rate of interest is constant? Does the real rate decline with increases in expected inflation? Are cyclical movements in real variables correlated with real rate movements? How reliable is the Fisher (1930) effect where nominal interest rates reflect changes in expected inflation? What kind of variation in real interest rates have we experienced in the last fifty years? Have real rates turned negative in the 1970s, as is commonly believed, and were they unusually high in the initial stages of the Great Depression?

In pursuing these questions, this paper first outlines in section II the methodology and theory used in the empirical analysis. The empirical results then follow in section III, and a final section contains the concluding remarks.

II. THE METHODOLOGY

The real rate of interest for a one-period bond is defined from the Fisher (1930) equation

$$i_t \equiv rr_t + \pi_t^e \tag{1}$$

where,

i_t = the nominal interest rate earned on a one-period bond maturing at time t--i.e., it is the nominal return from holding the one-period bond from t-1 to t.

π_t^e = the rate of inflation from t-1 to t expected by the bond market at time t-1.

rr_t = the one-period real rate of interest expected by the bond market at time t-1 for the bond maturing at time t.

Hence, the real interest rate, rr_t, is just the difference between the nominal rate of interest and the expected rate of inflation:[5] it is the real return from holding the one-period bond from t-1 to t *which is expected at time t-1.* Because the real rate is a return expected at the beginning of the period, it is also frequently referred to as the ex ante real rate. This more precise terminology is used to differentiate it from what is termed the ex post real rate: this is the *actual* real return from holding the one-period bond from t-1 to t. It equals the nominal interest rate minus the *actual* inflation rate from t-1 to t and can be written as

$$eprr_t \equiv i_t - \pi_t \equiv rr_t - (\pi_t - \pi_t^e) \tag{2}$$

[5] **All returns, inflation, and interest rates discussed in this paper are continuously compounded, so that additional second-order terms are not necessary in the Fisher equation (1).**

where,

$eprr_t$ = the one-period ex post real rate for the bond maturing at time t,

π_t = the actual inflation rate from t-1 to t.

Note that the above equations do not allow for taxes. This issue is deferred to a later section of the paper. Note, also, that for expositional convenience, the ex ante real rate is always referred to as the real rate throughout this paper, while the ex post real rate always refers to the variable defined in (2).

One approach to analyzing the movements in the real rate is to calculate them by using a survey measure of inflation expectations, such as the Livingston data, which are then subtracted from nominal interest rates. The resulting survey-based measure of the real rate can then be studied directly, for example, by calculating its correlation with relevant variables.[6] The problem with this approach is that it is only as good as the survey measure of inflation expectations, and there are serious doubts as to the quality of these data.[7] As a result, a different methodology is used in the analysis here which involves correlation and ordinary least squares (OLS) regressions with the ex post real rate.

---

[6]For example, see Gibson (1972), Cargill (1976), Lahiri (1976), Carlson (1977), Levi and Makin (1979), and Tanzi (1980).

[7]One obvious danger with survey data is that there may have been very little incentive for the respondents to answer accurately. A more subtle point that is often unrecognized in the literature is that the behavior of market expectations need not reflect the average expectations of participants in that market. Market expectations are frequently believed to be rational but not because all, most, or even the average market participant is also believed to be rational. Rather, rational expectations are plausible because market expectations can be driven to the rational expectations equilibrium by the elimination of unexploited profit opportunities. This arbitrage view of expectations formation clearly allows the average expectations of market participants to differ from the market's expectations. (Mishkin (1978) and (1981b) discuss this point more extensively.) On theoretical grounds alone then, we should be skeptical of using survey data to measure inflation expectations in a market.

In addition, a recent empirical study of Pearce (1979) raises further doubts about the accuracy, as a measure of bond market expectations, of the survey data most frequently used in this literature, Livingston's. Pearce finds that over the 1959-76 period the Livingston survey data predict inflation substantially worse than a simple (0, 1, 1) ARIMA model estimated only on data available at the time of the forecast. As Pearce notes, this result implies that the Livingston expectations data do not fully exploit information on past inflation rates and are thus inconsistent with rationality. If the bond market is believed to be efficient and hence rational–and there is evidence to support this view–then Pearce's finding suggests that the Livingston data do not accurately measure bond market expectations of inflation. For example, using the sample period closest to Pearce's, 1959-2 to 1976-4, I conducted the same test found in Mishkin (1981b) for the rationality of inflation expectations in the bond market and could not reject rationality: the χ^2 (6) statistic was 3.4, while its critical level at 5% is 12.6. Pearce also regresses nominal interest rates on both the Livingston measure of inflation expectations as well as the ARIMA model measure. Not only is the Livingston measure outperformed by the ARIMA measure in terms of goodness of fit, the Livingston measure also adds no significant additional explanatory power when added to a Fisher equation using the ARIMA measure, while the reverse is not true. Given that a strong Fisher effect (positive correlation) between expected inflation and nominal interest rates is expected in the postwar period, this evidence is also not supportive of using the Livingston data in the Fisher equation (1).

The underlying assumption behind this analysis is the rationality of inflation expectations in the bond market, which implies the following condition:

$$E(\pi_t - \pi_t^e | \phi_{t-1}) = 0 \tag{3}$$

where,

ϕ_{t-1} = information available at time t-1.

This tells us that the forecast error of inflation must be uncorrelated with past available information. A large body of evidence supports this rationality, or equivalently the efficiency of financial markets.[8] Furthermore, tests directed more specifically at the rationality of inflation forecasts in the bond market also support the use of this assumption over long sample periods such as are used here.[9]

If the real rate determined at t-1, rr_t, is correlated with variables, X_{t-1}, which are elements of the available information set ϕ_{t-1}, then we can write

$$rr_t = X_{t-1}\beta + u_t . \tag{4}$$

Note that the error term, u_t, is also determined at t-1. Substituting (4) into (2) and writing the inflation forecast error, $\pi_t - \pi_t^e$, as ϵ_t we get:

$$eprr_t = X_{t-1}\beta + u_t - \epsilon_t \tag{5}$$

where,

$\epsilon_t = \pi_t - \pi_t^e$.

Since data on the ex post real rate, $eprr_t$, are observable, in contrast with data on the real rate, equation (5) can be estimated. The question arises: what will be the relationship between OLS estimates from (5) with those from (4) if it were estimable? To answer this question, several propositions are demonstrated for the simplest case where the X-variables are nonstochastic. With the appropriate assumptions,[10] corresponding asymptotic results can be generated for the case of stochastic X's; but this additional complexity is avoided here.

The first proposition is that the OLS estimates of β from (4) and (5) are equal in expectation for the non-stochastic X case (and with the appropriate

---

[8]See Fama (1970).

[9]See Mishkin (1981b).

[10]For example, an assumption like plim $\frac{X'u}{n} = 0$, where n is the number of observations, performs a similar role in the stochastic X case as the assumption that $E(u) = 0$ (or equivalently $E(X'u) = 0$) performs in the nonstochastic X case.

assumption[11] they will be equal in the probability limit in the stochastic X-case).[12] This proposition is derived as follows. Denote the OLS estimate of β in (4) as $\hat{\beta}_{rr}$ and in (5) as $\hat{\beta}_{eprr}$. Then

$$E(\hat{\beta}_{rr}) = E((X'X)^{-1}X'[X\beta + u]) = \beta + E[(X'X)^{-1}X'u] \tag{6}$$

and

$$\begin{aligned} E(\hat{\beta}_{eprr}) &= E[(X'X)^{-1}X'(X\beta + u - \epsilon)] = \beta + E[(X'X)^{-1}X'u] \\ -E[(X'X)^{-1}X'\epsilon] &= E(\hat{\beta}_{rr}) - E[(X'X)^{-1}X'\epsilon] = E(\hat{\beta}_{rr}) \end{aligned} \tag{7}$$

because the rationality of inflation expectations in (3) implies that $E(X'\epsilon) = 0$. Note that this proposition has been demonstrated without an assumption on the properties of u. Thus, it is valid even if $\hat{\beta}_{rr}$ is a biased (or inconsistent) estimate of β.

This result tells us that although we cannot observe the real rate, rr_t, we can infer information about its relationship to variables known at time t-1 through OLS regressions with the ex post real rate. Note that any problems of inconsistency that might arise in an OLS estimate of (4) because u_t is correlated with X_{t-1} will also exist for the ex post real rate regression. Without the knowledge that X_{t-1} is exogenous, we cannot interpret OLS results as containing information on causation. They can only provide information on movements in the real rates.

We will also be concerned with the variance-covariance matrix of the two estimates. Assume that we have a particularly well-behaved problem where the OLS β-estimates are consistent and serial correlation of either the error term in (4) or the composite error term in (5), $u_t - \epsilon_t$, is ruled out by the following, additional assumptions.[13]

---

[11] i.e., plim $\frac{X'X}{n}$ exists.

[12] If the ex ante real rate is generated by least squares projection on available information, a form of Muthian expectations discussed by Sargent (1979, Chapter 10), then we also find a similar result. This is just an application of the law of iterated projections.

[13] Cumby, Huizinga, and Obstfeld (1980) point out that in a setup of the type discussed here, even if the u's are serially uncorrelated, as are the ϵ's because of rationality, this does not rule out serial correlation in the composite error term $u - \epsilon$. This occurs because rationality does not rule out correlation of the forecast errors with future values of variables such as u. This is why the fifth assumption in (8) is needed. If serial correlation does exist in the composite error term, correcting it with standard techniques leads to inconsistent estimates. For example, see Flood and Garber (1980). An estimator that avoids this problem is discussed in Cumby, Huizinga, and Obstfeld (1980).

$$E(X'u) = 0 \text{ or equivalently } E(u) = 0 \tag{8}$$

$$E(u_t u_{t+s}) = 0 \quad \text{for all } s$$

$$E(u_t^2) = \sigma_u^2 \quad \text{for all } t$$

$$E(\epsilon_t^2) = \sigma_\epsilon^2 \quad \text{for all } t$$

$$E(u_{t+s}\epsilon_t) = 0 \qquad \text{for all } s > 0$$

Then the variance-covariance matrices of $\hat{\beta}_{rr}$ and $\hat{\beta}_{eprr}$ are:

$$E[(\hat{\beta}_{rr} - \beta)(\hat{\beta}_{rr} - \beta)'] = E[(X'X)^{-1}X'uu'X(X'X)^{-1}] = \sigma_u^2(X'X)^{-1} \tag{9}$$

and

$$E[(\hat{\beta}_{eprr} - \beta)(\hat{\beta}_{eprr} - \beta)'] = E[(X'X)^{-1}X'(uu' + \epsilon\epsilon' - \epsilon u' - u\epsilon')X(X'X)^{-1}]$$

$$= \sigma_u^2(X'X)^{-1} + \sigma_\epsilon^2(X'X)^{-1} \tag{10}$$

Note that the derivation of (10) also makes use of the rationality implication in (3), which requires that ϵ_t is serially uncorrelated and uncorrelated with u's dated at t and before.

A comparison of the two variance-covariance matrices above points out the major difficulty with ex post real rate regressions. Although they yield the same expected value of the coefficient estimates as an actual real rate regression (if it were estimable), the variance-covariance matrix of the estimates will be larger by the term $\sigma_\epsilon^2(X'X)^{-1}$. Thus, statistical tests will have lower power. This problem will be particularly severe if $\sigma_\epsilon^2 >> \sigma_u^2$. Unfortunately, as has been pointed out by Nelson and Schwert (1977), the forecast errors for inflation are probably extremely large and are much greater in magnitude than the u's. Because the term $\sigma_\epsilon^2(X'X)^{-1}$ will then be much larger than $\sigma_u^2(X'X)^{-1}$, estimates of β from the ex post regressions will be substantially more imprecise than if they were obtainable from an actual real rate regression. In this case it may be very hard to discern significant β-coefficients in the ex post real rate regressions because the statistical tests will have so little power. This is essentially the point made by Nelson and Schwert in their comment on Fama (1975).[14]

[14] A similar argument to that here is another way to explain the position taken by Fama (1976a) and Mishkin (1978) that when actual returns have large variability relative to expected returns, accurate specification of the model of market equilibrium is not critical to tests of market efficiency.

We can also use the estimated ex post real rate regressions to provide us with information on how the real rate has moved over time. The fitted values from these regressions are an estimate of the real rate and are denoted as $\hat{rr}_t$: i.e.,

$$\hat{rr}_t = X_{t-1}\hat{\beta}_{eprr} \tag{11}$$

This estimate of the real rate has errors for two reasons. First, some variables or nonlinearities which explain real rate movements are probably left out of the regression model, resulting in a non-zero u_t term. Second, the β- coefficient would be estimated with some error in a finite sample. To see this, we just subtract equation (4) from (11) to yield the error,

$$\hat{rr}_t - rr_t = X_{t-1}(\hat{\beta}_{eprr} - \beta) - u_t \tag{12}$$

The variance of the within-sample error is easily derived under the above assumptions as follows:[15,16]

$$\begin{aligned}
\mathrm{Var}(\hat{rr}_t - rr_t) &= E\,(\hat{rr}_t - rr_t)(\hat{rr}_t - rr_t)'] = E\,[(X_{t-1}(X'X)^{-1}X'(u-\epsilon) - u_t) \\
&\qquad (u-\epsilon)'X(X'X)^{-1}X'_{t-1} - u_t)] \qquad (13) \\
&= E\,[X_{t-1}(X'X)^{-1}X'(u-\epsilon)(u-\epsilon)'X(X'X)^{-1}X'_{t-1} + u_t^2 - 2u_t \\
&\qquad (u-\epsilon)'X(X'X)^{-1}X'_{t-1}] \\
&= (\sigma_\epsilon^2 + \sigma_u^2)X_{t-1}(X'X)^{-1}X'_{t-1} + \sigma_u^2 - 2\sigma_u^2 X_{t-1}(X'X)^{-1}X'_{t-1} \\
&= (\sigma_\epsilon^2 - \sigma_u^2)X_{t-1}(X'X)^{-1}X'_{t-1} + \sigma_u^2
\end{aligned}$$

Because we do not know the exact relative size of the σ_ϵ^2 and σ_u^2 which add up to the overall variance of the composite error term $u - \epsilon$, the

[15] Note that this formula is not invalidated if $E(X'u) \neq 0$ as long as u is a linear function of X; i.e., if $u = X\delta + \eta$ where η is also a linear function of X and so on, then $E(\hat{rr}_t - rr_t) = 0$. Consistency of the β estimate is not a necessary condition for the validity of the 95% confidence intervals used in the figures. However, exclusion of relevant variables can invalidate the formula.

[16] The variance of a post sample error would be $(\sigma_\epsilon^2 + \sigma_u^2)X_{t-1}(X'X)^{-1}X'_{t-1} + \sigma_u^2$ which is larger than the within-sample variance in (13). This occurs because the term $E(u_t(u - \epsilon)')$ equals zero in this case. Because the real rate estimates later in the text are all within sample, the within-sample variance, rather than the post-sample variance, is discussed in the text.

formula in (13) cannot be used directly to yield standard errors of $\hat{rr}_t - rr_t$. However, upper and lower bounds for these standard errors can be derived. If the term $X_{t-1}(X'X)^{-1}X'_{t-1}$ is less than one-half, as is always the case in the results of this paper, the lower bound for the standard error of $\hat{rr}_t - rr_t$ is reached when all variation of the composite error term is due totally to the forecast error of inflation.[17] With an estimate of the standard error of the ex post real rate regression, $\hat{\sigma}$, this is the case where it is assumed that $\hat{\sigma}_\epsilon = \hat{\sigma}$ and $\hat{\sigma}_u = 0$. The lower bound estimate of the standard error of $\hat{rr}_t - rr_t$, denoted as $\hat{SE}_\ell(\hat{rr}_t - rr_t)$, is then

$$\hat{SE}_\ell(\hat{rr}_t - rr_t) = \hat{\sigma}\sqrt{X_{t-1}(X'X)^{-1}X'_{t-1}} \tag{14}$$

The upper bound estimate of the standard error, $\hat{SE}_u(\hat{rr}_t - rr_t)$, is reached when all variation of the composite error is due totally to variation in u_t: i.e., $\hat{\sigma}_u = \hat{\sigma}$ and $\hat{\sigma}_\epsilon = 0$.

$$\hat{SE}_u(\hat{rr}_t - rr_t) = \hat{\sigma}\sqrt{1 - X_{t-1}(X'X)^{-1}X'_{t-1}} \tag{15}$$

Because σ_ϵ^2 is likely to exceed σ_u^2 greatly here, the lower bound estimate is likely to be a far more accurate measure of the true standard error than the upper bound estimate. The discussion of the empirical results later in the paper devotes more attention to the lower bound estimate. However, the upper bound estimate will also be reported so those with a different prior can use this information in deriving their estimates of the standard error.

This section has demonstrated that regressions with ex post real rates have many desirable statistical properties. On the other hand, the potential unreliability of survey measures of inflation expectations makes more direct approaches to inference about real rates suspect. Therefore, even though regressions, or equivalent correlations, with ex post real rates may have low statistical power, they are a dependable way of inferring information about real interest rates. This is the method of analysis used here. However, the discussion above issues a warning for interpreting the results that follow. The absence of a variable's significant explanatory power in an ex post real rate regression should not be viewed as evidence that the real rate is unrelated to this variable. An alternative, and equally plausible view, is that the statistical

[17] If we denote $X_{t-1}(X'X)^{-1}X'_{t-1} = Q$ and $\hat{\sigma}_u^2 = a\hat{\sigma}^2$, then the estimated $\hat{VAR}(\hat{rr}_t - rr_t) = [(1-a)\hat{\sigma}^2 - a\hat{\sigma}^2]Q + a\hat{\sigma}^2 \cdot \frac{d\hat{VAR}(\hat{rr}_t - rr_t)}{da} = \hat{\sigma}^2[1-2Q] > 0$ if $Q < ½$. Thus, the lower bound estimate is reached when $a = 0$ and the upper bound estimate when $a = 1$.

tests here just do not have enough power to find this relationship. With this caveat, we now turn to the actual empirical results.

III. THE EMPIRICAL RESULTS

The Data

The empirical analysis here uses quarterly data on the ex post real rate for three-month Treasury bills. These ex post rates are at a quarterly rate and are calculated by subtracting the actual, continuously compounded inflation rate (using the seasonally unadjusted Consumer Price Index (CPI)) from the continuously compounded nominal yield on a three-month bill maturing at the end of the quarter. The bill rate data were obtained from the bond file of the Center for Research in Security Prices (CRSP) at the University of Chicago.[18] As in Fama (1975), the CPI, rather than the Wholesale Price Index (WPI), is used to calculate inflation rates here because only the CPI reflects transaction prices. The dating convention is as follows. The ex post real rate for a quarter is the actual real return on a three-month bill held from the beginning to the end of that quarter. All variables that are growth rates, such as money growth, real GNP growth and inflation, are calculated as the change in the log from the last month of the previous quarter to the current quarter and are thus at quarterly rates. The unemployment rate is for the last month in the quarter, and the investment to capital ratio is constructed comparably to this ratio in Fama and Gibbons (1980) by dividing the investment over the quarter by the capital stock at the end of the quarter. The variables used in the analysis here are discussed in more detail in the Data Appendix.

Monthly data are not used in the analysis for the following reason. The appropriate dating for the CPI in a particular month is not clear since price quotations have been collected over the entire month. Thus, there is no accurate way of matching up the timing of the one-month bills with the dating of the CPI. This problem is somewhat less severe when quarterly data are used. The potential timing error of using the CPI in the last month of the quarter as a match for a three-month bill maturing at the end of the quarter is a smaller fraction of the time to maturity than would be the case if the one-month bill maturing at the end of the month is matched up, as in Fama (1975), with the CPI in that month. As a result, the quarterly ex post real rates should be more accurate than the one-month rates. Furthermore, Fama (1975)

---

[18] The data used here are very similar to that used by Fama (1975). Using his sample period I was able to reproduce very closely his results with quarterly data.

finds only small differences in coefficient estimates with quarterly versus monthly data, and little additional information is contained in the more noisy monthly series, since the standard errors of the coefficients using the monthly data are only slightly smaller than those found with the quarterly data.

The empirical analysis of this paper focuses its main attention on the 1953-1 through 1979-4 sample period as an update to Fama (1975). The 1979-4 quarter was the latest quarter for which the CRSP bill series was available. Fama started his analysis in 1953, as here, because the CPI was substantially upgraded in that year. He ended his sample period at the second quarter of 1971 to avoid any possible distortions that the Nixon price controls might have had on the measurement of the CPI. In preliminary results I excluded the price control period from 1971-3 to 1974-4 from my analysis with little appreciable effect on the coefficient estimates or on the major findings.[19] Since it is not obvious that the Nixon price controls should have severely distorted the CPI, data from this period are included in the analysis.

Results: 1953-1 to 1979-4

Tests with ex post real rates in Fama (1975) could not reject the hypothesis that the real rate was constant over the 1953-71 period. However, later work which frequently used more refined statistical tests did find significant rejections of this hypothesis. Included in this work is not only that of Fama's critics, Carlson (1977), Garbade and Wachtel (1978), Hess and Bicksler (1975), Joines (1977), and Nelson and Schwert (1977) but also that by Fama himself, Fama (1976b) and Fama and Gibbons (1980). Extending Fama's original sample period through the end of the 1970s should yield new insights into the question of the constancy of the real rate, because the 1971-3 to 1979-4 period has been one of unusual economic turbulence by postwar standards. It contains both the worst recession in the postwar period as well as the highest inflation rates. The greater variation in the data that occurred as a result could make statistical relationships more clear-cut.

The null hypothesis of the constancy of the real rate is studied here with two types of tests which are similar to those carried out in Fama (1975). First, we look at the serial correlation structure of the ex post real rate, and then we test whether other variables in the available information set, ϕ_{t-1}, are correlated with the ex post real rate. These tests correspond to the weak form and strong form tests discussed in the efficient markets' literature.[20]

[19] For example, excluding the 1971-3 to 1974-4 quarters from the 1953-79 sample period, the coefficient on $\pi(-1)$ in model 2.1 dropped to -.2469 but remained signficiantly negative with a t-statistic of -4.41. A Chow test of the 2.1 model splitting the 1953-79 sample period into its price control and non-price control periods did not reveal significant changes in the parameter estimates. $F(2,104)$ = 2.36 while the critical F at 5% is approximately 3.1.

[20] See Fama (1970).

Table 1 contains the first twelve autocorrelations of the ex post real rate for the 1953-79 period. These autocorrelations are positive and large, and more than half are more than two standard errors away from zero. The constancy of the real rate implies the null hypothesis that all the autocorrelations equal zero. It is formally tested with the adjusted Q-statistic suggested by Ljung and Box (1978). The $Q(12)$ statistic is distributed approximately as $\chi^2(12)$, and its marginal significance level is the probability of getting that value of the test statistic or higher under the null hypothesis: i.e., a marginal significance level less than .01 indicates a rejection of the null hypothesis at the one percent level. The rejection of the null hypothesis is very strong. The $Q(12)$ statistic exceeds 100 and its corresponding marginal significance level is extremely small. Thus, despite the possible low power of this test discussed by Nelson and Schwert (1977) and the previous section, the additional data added to Fama's (1975) sample period now result in a clear-cut rejection of the constancy of the real rate.

Table 2 contains tests for whether the ex post real rate, and hence the real rate, has been correlated with other variables whose values were known when the real rate was determined. Because heteroscedasticity can have a major impact on results,[21] Goldfeld-Quandt (1965) as well as Glesjer (1969) tests were performed in order to see if corrections for heteroscedasticity were necessary. They uniformly did not reveal the presence of heteroscedasticity for this sample period, and ordinary least squares was used in estimation.[22]

Considering the recurrent discussion of the Mundell-Tobin effect in the literature, the inflation rate is an obvious candidate as a variable that might be correlated with the real rate.[23] Model 2.1 tests for this correlation and the results do exhibit a strong, significant negative correlation of the ex post real rate with the lagged inflation rate: its coefficient of -.3073 has a t-statistic over

---

[21] For example, see the discussion of the Shiller (1979) results in Mishkin (1978) and (1981a).

[22] For example, in model 2.1 a Goldfeld-Quandt (1965) test which excluded 16 observations yielded the $F(44,44)$ statistic of 1.51, while the critical F at the 5% level is approximately 1.7. A Glesjer (1969) test where the absolute value of the residuals in 2.1 was regressed against a time trend yielded a t-statistic on the trend variable of only .94. I also regressed the absolute value of the residuals from the Table 2 model against lagged inflation, because some recent literature has suggested that the variability of inflation forecasting errors, ϵ's, might rise with inflation. The evidence for this was weak. For example, with the 2.1 residuals the t-statistic on lagged inflation was only .72. Furthermore, a heteroscedasticity correction of the type suggested by Glesjer (1969)–i.e., weighting by the fitted values from this regression–has only a slight effect on the results.

[23] A proxy for the expected inflation rate derived from an ARIMA (0, 1, 1) inflation model with a seasonal MA1 term was also used in estimation and the results were very similar. For example, in a model of the form 2.1 when the expected inflation proxy replaced the lagged inflation rate, its coefficient was -.3658 with a t-statistic of -7.03. I preferred not using this proxy variable in the text because the results there clearly indicate that other information besides past inflation rates is used in the bond market to forecast inflation.

TABLE 1

Serial Correlation Structure of the Ex Post Real Rate: 1953-1 to 1979-4

	Lag k												Approximate Standard Error of the Autocorrelations
	1	2	3	4	5	6	7	8	9	10	11	12	
Autocorrelation at Lag k (r_{-k})	.38	.28	.36	.45	.31	.16	.24	.15	.20	.08	.24	.17	.10

Test of $r_1 = r_2 = ,..., = r_{12} = 0$
$Q(12) = 102.33$
Marginal Significance level = 1.94×10^{-16}

NOTES: $Q(12)$ is the adjusted Q-statistic suggested by Ljung and Box (1978) which is distributed approximately as $\chi^2(12) = n(n+2) \sum_{k=1}^{12} (n-k)^{-1} r_{-k}$, where n = number of observations = 108. Marginal significance level is the probability of setting that value of the Q-statistic or higher under the null hypothesis that $r_1 = r_2 = ,..., = r_{12} = 0$.
Approximate standard error = $1/\sqrt{n}$.

TABLE 2

Tests of the Constancy of the Real Rate: 1953-1 to 1979-4

Dependent Variable: Ex Post Real Rate
Estimation Method: Ordinary Least Squares

	Coefficient of										Marginal
Model #	Constant Term	$\pi(-1)$	Time	$Time^2$	$Time^3$	$Time^4$	R^2	*SE*	*DW*	*F*-Statistic	Significance Level
2.1	.0040 (6.26)	-0.3073 (-6.16)					.26	.0045	2.16	38.00	1.30×10^{-8}
2.2	.0331 (2.03)		-0.2195 (-2.13)	.5258 (2.35)	-0.4976 (-2.47)	.1585 (2.48)	.35	.0043	1.85	13.66	5.73×10^{-9}
2.3	.0308 (1.91)	-0.1554 (-1.99)	-0.2024 (-1.99)	.4872 (2.20)	-0.4601 (-2.31)	.1467 (2.32)	.37	.0042	2.18	12.02	3.70×10^{-9}

NOTES: *T*-statistics in parentheses.
SE = standard error of the regression.
DW = Durbin-Watson statistic.
Time = time trend, runs from .01 in 1947-1 to 1.32 in 1979-4, superscript of time variable indicates raised to that power.
$\pi(-1)$ = inflation rate at quarterly rate, lagged one quarter
F = *F*-statistic for null hypothesis that all the coefficients excluding the constant term are zero: distributed as $F(1,106)$ in 2.1, $F(4,103)$ in 2.2 and $F(5,102)$ in 2.3.
Marginal Significance level = probability of getting that value of *F* or higher under the null hypothesis.

six in absolute value with a very low marginal significance level. This result rejecting the constancy of the real rate is consistent with many other studies, such as Lahiri (1976), Carlson (1977), Levi and Makin (1979), and Pearce (1979), which find a significant negative correlation between the real rate and expected inflation.

Since this significant negative relationship between inflation and the real rate is so striking and has such important implications, it deserves further scrutiny and testing for robustness. One question that arises asks: Is this result dependent on the choice of the CPI as the price index in the empirical analysis? The answer appears to be no. Despite the limitations of the WPI because it is not constructed from transaction prices, it is a plausible alternative to the CPI as a price index for use here. When model 2.1 is reestimated with the variables constructed using the WPI rather than CPI, the significant negative correlation of the ex post real rate and inflation continues to hold up. The coefficient on the lagged inflation rate in this WPI regression equals -.3040 and is almost identical to the corresponding coefficient in Table 2. Its *t*-statistic is also highly significant, equaling -4.41.

Another question of robustness is whether the negative relationship of the real rate and inflation is consistent only with data from the last half of the sample period when inflation rates were high. This is a particularly relevant question because Fama (1975) did not find a significant negative correlation of the real rate and inflation, using a sample period that excluded data from the high inflation 1970s. To pursue this question, the sample was split in half and model 2.1 was estimated over both sample periods. The lagged inflation coefficient in the regression for the first half of the sample, 1953-1 to 1966-2, is not significantly negative: it equals -.0067 with a *t*-statistic of only -.05. Note, however, that the standard error of this coefficient is quite large, exceeding .13. In the regression for the last half of the sample, 1966-3 to 1979-4, the lagged inflation coefficient is not far from the value of the corresponding coefficient in Table 2: it equals -.3614 and is statistically significant with a *t*-statistic of -4.23. The discrepancy between these results might occur because, in the early sample period, there is not enough variation in the real rate to discern an inflation effect. A Chow test for the stability of the coefficients of model 2.1 over these two sample periods confirms this conjecture. The $F(2,104)$ statistic equals 2.47 (its critical value at the 5% level is 3.1) and does not reject the equality of the 2.1 coefficients in the two periods. It appears that Fama's (1975) inability to find the significant correlation of inflation with the ex post real rate was due to the peculiar nature of his particular sample period which, as noted by Shiller (1980), has insufficient variation in the real rate. The results here show that the postwar period is more accurately characterized as displaying a negative correlation of the real rate and inflation.

Model 2.2 of Table 2 contains a more mechanical test of the constancy of the real rate by postulating that the real rate moves with a fourth-order polynomial in time. A fourth-order polynomial is used in the tests here because additional variables with higher powers of the time trend did not have significant additional explanatory power.[24] The rejection of the constancy of the real rate is also strong in this case, with an extremely small marginal significance level for the null hypothesis that the coefficients on the time trend variables equal zero. When the trend variables are added to model 2.1, as in model 2.3, there is a significant improvement in explanatory power: $F(4,102) = 4.33$ while the critical F at 5% is approximately 2.5. Here, the marginal significance level that tests the null hypothesis of the constancy of the real rate declines even further.[25]

Table 3 tests whether other variables that have been cited in the literature are correlated with the real rate. The one and four lags of these variables are used in models which either include or exclude the lagged inflation variable. The most striking finding in this Table is that none of the real variables--real GNP growth, the GNP gap which is the percentage difference between potential GNP and real GNP, the unemployment rate and the investment to capital ratio–have significant explanatory power for movements in the ex post real rate.[26] Including lagged inflation in these regressions does not alter this finding. Table 3's lack of success in finding significant correlations should not be viewed

[24] For example, the null hypothesis that when added to model 2.2, the coefficients on four additional powers of time, up to the eighth power, equal zero could not be rejected. $F(4,99) = .95$ while the critical F at 5% is approximately 2.5.

[25] One issue not discussed in the text is the seasonality of the real rate. For a detailed discussion of this issue, see Fama and Schwert (1979) and Shiller (1980). I corroborated both of these studies' findings that seasonality is present in the ex post real rate. For example, a test of whether seasonal dummies entered model 2.1 did reject the null hypothesis that coefficients and seasonal dummies equal zero--($F(3,103) = 5.93$ with a critical value at 5% of 2.7)--yet the results on the coefficient of lagged inflation changed hardly at all. The coefficient on lagged inflation was estimated to be -.3170 with a t-statistic of -6.67. However, more time is not spent on this issue here for two reasons. One is that an extensive treatment of this issue is contained in the two studies mentioned above. Second, as the discussion in Fama and Schwert (1979) indicates, the fact that seasonality exists in the real rate is not evidence against the constancy of the real rate, net of storage costs, and this is the more interesting hypothesis, anyway. In addition, the fixed-weight nature of the CPI may induce some seasonality in the measured ex post real rate that is spurious. When the relative price of a good in the CPI consumption bundle is seasonally high–fruit during the winter is an example–we expect that there will be substitution away from this good. The seasonality in the true price index should be less than in the measured fixed-weight index. In the data here, the seasonality in ex post real rates comes predominantly from the price index. Hence, the seasonality of the measured ex post real rate constructed using the fixed-weight index will be overstated.

[26] An industrial production growth variable as well as other variations of the investment-to-capital-ratio variable suggested by Fama and Gibbons (1980), including one using a new order series for durable goods, were also tested as in Table 3. Again, no significant correlations were found with the ex post real rate.

TABLE 3

Tests for Correlation of Real Rate with Other Variables: 1953-1 to 1979-4

Dependent Variable: Ex Post Real Rate
Estimation Method: Ordinary Least Squares

Model #	Other Explanatory Variable	Coefficient of: Constant Term	$\pi(-1)$	Other Explanatory Variable	R^2	SE	DW	F-test for significant explanatory power of four lags of independent variable when included in this model
3.1	money growth (M1)	.0026 (3.28)		-0.1475 (-2.42)	.05	.0051	1.31	3.34
3.2	money growth (M1)	.0043 (5.62)	-0.2954 (-5.54)	-0.0366 (-0.64)	.27	.0045	2.14	.70
3.3	real GNP growth	.0005 (0.84)		.0699 (1.46)	.02	.0052	1.29	1.52
3.4	real GNP growth	.0040 (4.96)	-0.3064 (-5.90)	.0029 (0.07)	.26	.0045	2.16	.98
3.5	GNP gap	.0012 (1.96)		-0.0061 (-0.33)	.00	.0052	1.21	.79
3.6	GNP gap	.0040 (5.72)	-0.3071 (-6.12)	-0.0010 (-0.06)	.26	.0045	2.16	.61
3.7	unemployment rate	.0042 (2.09)		-0.0593 (-1.60)	.02	.0052	1.25	.82
3.8	unemployment rate	.0050 (2.84)	-0.3010 (-5.90)	-0.0201 (-0.61)	.27	.0045	2.16	.16
3.9	investment to capital ratio	.0042 (0.59)		-0.0321 (-0.44)	.00	.0052	1.21	.41
3.10	investment to capital ratio	.0061 (0.99)	-0.3068 (-6.13)	-0.0219 (-0.35)	.26	.0045	2.16	.08

NOTES: Data definitions are discussed in the Appendix.
T-statistics in parentheses.
F-statistic is distributed as $F(4,103)$ in odd numbered models and $F(4,102)$ in even-numbered models. The critical value of these *F*-statistics at the 5% level is approximately 2.5.

as implying that real factors do not affect the real rate. More plausible is the view that the statistical tests here do not have sufficient power to discern co-movements of real variables and the real rate. Since the real variables used here are meant to capture cyclical effects on the real rate, this might occur because there is not enough cyclical variation in the real rate to be picked up by these tests.[27]

The results with the money growth variable are more interesting. Results with an M2 money growth measure are similar to those found for M1 in Table 3 and are thus not reported.[28] When the lagged inflation rate is excluded from the money growth regressions, the coefficients of the lagged money growth variables are statistically significant and have a negative sum.[29] Thus, an increase in money growth has the usual negative relationship with real rates which we expect from standard monetary theory. However, the 3.2 results indicate that the negative correlation of money growth and the real rate might arise only because of the positive correlation of money growth with inflation: the money growth coefficients are no longer significant when they are added to an ex post real rate regression that includes the lagged inflation rate. Feldstein (1980a) has argued that an increased rate of money growth is non-neutral because it raises inflation and lowers the real return to saving, and this can have an adverse effect on capital formation and productivity. The significant negative correlation of the real rate and money growth found here is in the direction that Feldstein's argument requires, but it can only be taken as evidence supporting

---

[27]Fama (1976b) has suggested that the variability of inflation forecast errors (as measured by the variability of the ex post real rate), as well as the variability of expected inflation (as measured by the variability of the change in nominal *t*-bill rates), might affect risk premiums and hence real rates. Experiments with variables similar to Fama's (1976b) did indicate that the variability of these variables was significantly negatively correlated with ex post real rates. However, when lagged inflation was also included in these regressions, the coefficients of these variables no longer remained significant.

Fama and Gibbons (1980) suggest that expectations of higher returns on investments and, therefore, the investment-capital ratio will be positively correlated with real rates. As Table 3 indicates, experiments with the investment-capital ratio did not yield significant correlations. The failure of this variable could have resulted because it is too loosely correlated with expectations of investment opportunities. One crude variable that might reflect these expectations is the real value of the Standard and Poor's index of stock prices, which measures one component of the valuation of firms. Results with this variable were somewhat, but not strongly, encouraging. One lag of this variable was almost, but not quite, significantly correlated with ex post real rates ($t = 1.95$) and had the expected positive sign. Four lags were significant in a regression that excluded lagged inflation: $F(4,103) = 3.23$, while the critical value at 5% is approximately 2.5. In regressions with lagged inflation included, one lag of this variable was again almost significant ($t = 1.95$) and four lags were not significant ($F(4,102) = 1.97$). The results are encouraging enough that further work on this issue might be worthwhile.

[28]When M2 money growth replaces the M1 measure in 3.1, the coefficient on the M2 growth variable lagged only once is -.1475 with a *t*-statistic of -2.65, and the *F*-statistic on the four lags is 2.89 with the sum of the coefficients equal to -.2155. In the 3.2 result, the coefficient on M2 growth lagged once is -.0571 with a *t*-statistic of -1.11, and the *F*-statistic on the four lags is .66.

[29]In the regression with four lags of the M1 money growth variable, the sum of the M1 money growth coefficients is -.2781.

his position if we are willing to ascribe causation to the results. Because the money growth variables do not have significant explanatory power in addition to lagged inflation, the evidence for a short-run cyclical effect of monetary policy is weak. Again, this might be attributed to the low power of these statistical tests. But it does point out why it might be so difficult to sort out the issue discussed by Shiller (1980) whether the Federal Reserve System can control real interest rates.[30]

To summarize briefly the results in Tables 1-3: The real interest rate has not been constant over the 1953-79 period, and the economic variable most highly correlated with the ex post real rate is the inflation rate. None of the other economic variables add significant explanatory power to the ex post real rate regressions with lagged inflation as an explanatory variable. However, there is something left to explain in real rate movements because time trend variables do add significant explanatory power.

Another approach to understanding these results involves looking at estimates of the real rate derived from fitted values of the most interesting of the regressions. Figure 1 contains the estimates of the real rate derived from the fitted values of the regression with the best fit, #2.3. The inner band surrounding the real rate estimates delimits the region where real rates are within two lower bound standard errors of the estimated real rate (as calculated from (14)). The outer band is the region where real rates are within two upper bound standard errors of the estimated real rate (as calculated from (15)). Because, as discussed previously, it is likely that $\sigma_u^2 << \sigma_\epsilon^2$, the inner band is probably a reasonable characterization of the 95% confidence interval, although it is necessarily an underestimate. Attention will be focused primarily on this inner band when discussing inference in what follows. Yet, the outer band in the figure should warn us to treat such inference with suitable caution.

Figure 1 indicates that the real rate tended to be positive in the first twenty years of the sample period, with a declining trend from 1953-56, an upward trend reaching a maximum in the boom years of the mid-1960s, and a declining trend thereafter. Using the inner band for inference, the estimated

[30]Seasonally unadjusted M1 and M2 data were also used in the 3.1 and 3.2 regressions. In 3.1, the coefficient on the money growth variable lagged only once is insignificantly positive, but the four lagged money growth variables do have significant explanatory power: for M1 $F(4,103) = 5.40$ and for M2, $F(4,103) = 3.35$. Furthermore, the sum of their coefficients is again negative: -.2626 for M1 and -.1276 for M2. In 3.2, the coefficient on M1 lagged only once is significantly positive–it is .0367 with a t-statistic of 2.26–while the coefficient on M2 lagged only once is positive and insignificant. The four lagged M2 variables again do not have significant additional explanatory power–$F(4,102) = 1.87$ with the critical F at 5% equal to 2.5–yet the four lagged M1 variables do–$F(4,102) = 3.85$. However, there is no easily discernible pattern to these coefficients which are both positive and negative and sum to -.0240. This result is intriguing and should be pursued further. Overall then, the evidence with seasonally unadjusted M1 and M2 data is more mixed, although it does continue to support the suggestion that increased money growth is non-neutral because it lowers the real rate by raising inflation.

FIGURE 1

Estimated Real Interest Rate with 95% Confidence Intervals: 1953-1 to 1979-4

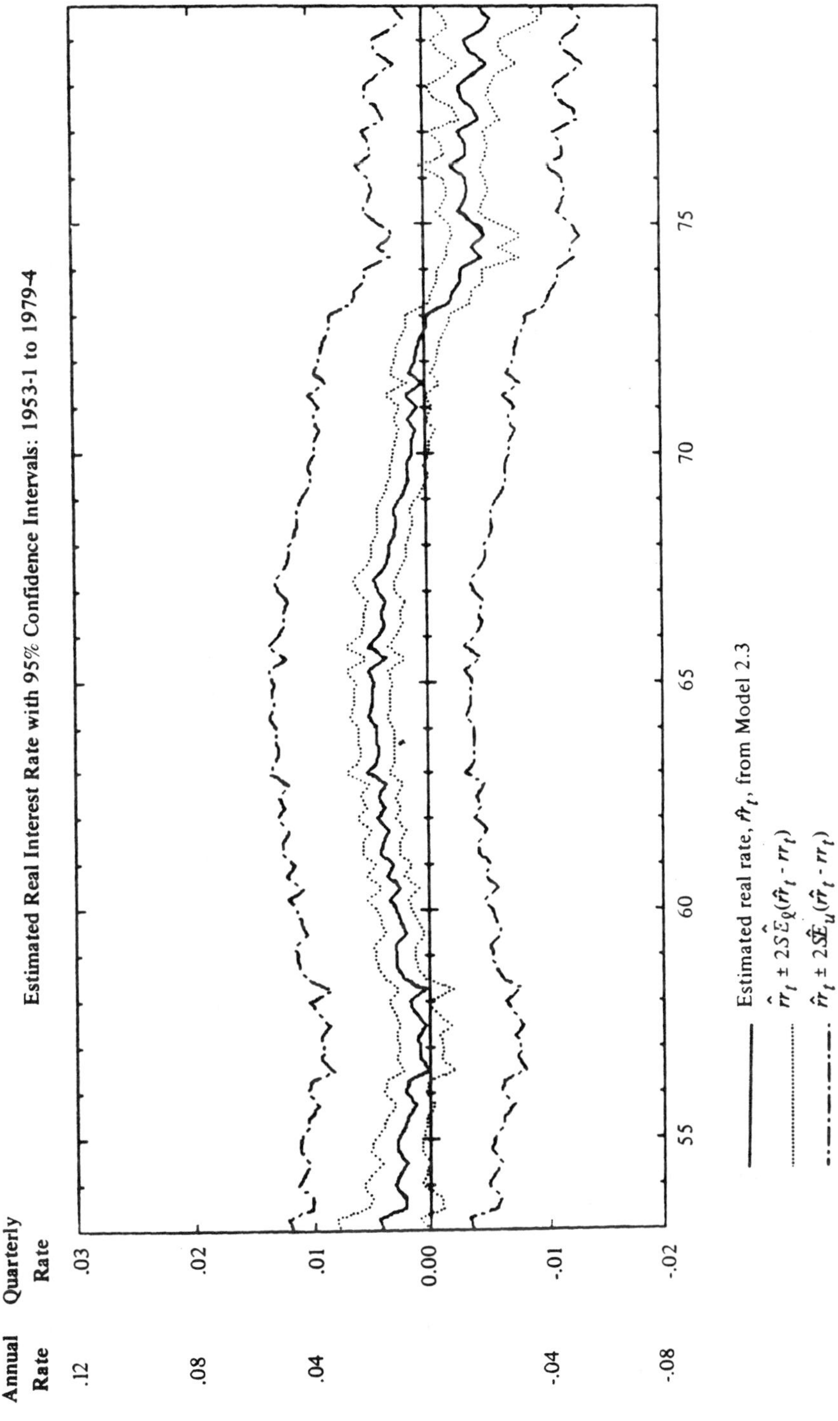

real rates were significantly positive for most of this period, and the peak values of over two percent at an annual rate are more than six of the lower bound standard errors away from zero. The real interest rate appears to turn negative towards the end of 1972 and the downward trend accelerates through the end of 1974, whereupon the real rate stays negative but has no easily discernible trend. Throughout most of the 1973-79 period, the estimated real rates remain significantly negative according to the inner band confidence region, and the most negative estimated real rates, approximately minus two percent at an annual rate, are more than five of the lower bound standard errors away from zero. Thus, as casual inspection of nominal interest rate and inflation data might have led one to suspect, there is strong evidence that real interest rates were positive in the 1950s and 60s but have turned quite negative in the mid- and late 1970s.

One striking feature of these results is their similarity to those of Garbade and Wachtel (1978) and Fama and Gibbons (1980). They also use ex post real rate data but find their results with a very different statistical technique involving variable-parameter regression. Both of these studies assume that the real rate is so highly autocorrelated that its movements over time can be approximated as a random walk. There is somewhat more smoothness in their resulting real rate estimates than is the case here, but the overall magnitudes and peaks and troughs of the series are quite close to those in Figure 1.[31] The corroborating evidence from these studies then lends further support to the results here.

Because time trend variables do contain additional explanatory power over the lagged inflation rate in the ex post real rate regressions, there must be other economic variables left out of the analysis here that help explain real rate movements and are correlated with the trend variables. This leaves us with a puzzle to figure out what these excluded variables might be. One clue comes from a comparison of the estimated real rates from the model which includes only the lagged inflation rate as an explanatory variable with those from the model which includes the time trends as additional explanatory variables. Figure 2 contains one series of estimated real rates derived from the fitted values of model 2.1 while the other series, which has already appeared in Figure 1, is derived from model 2.3. The two series have a roughly similar pattern, but a comparison indicates that the time trend variables make the estimated real rate higher

[31] Garbade and Wachtel (1978) report the standard error of their estimate a_t as the standard error of the estimated real rate. Hence, this standard error is also a lower-bound estimate because implicitly they are assuming that $\sigma_u = 0$. Their standard errors are also similar in magnitude to the lower bound standard errors of Figure 1.

FIGURE 2

Comparison of Estimated Real Rates from Models 2.1 and 2.3: 1953-1 to 1979-4

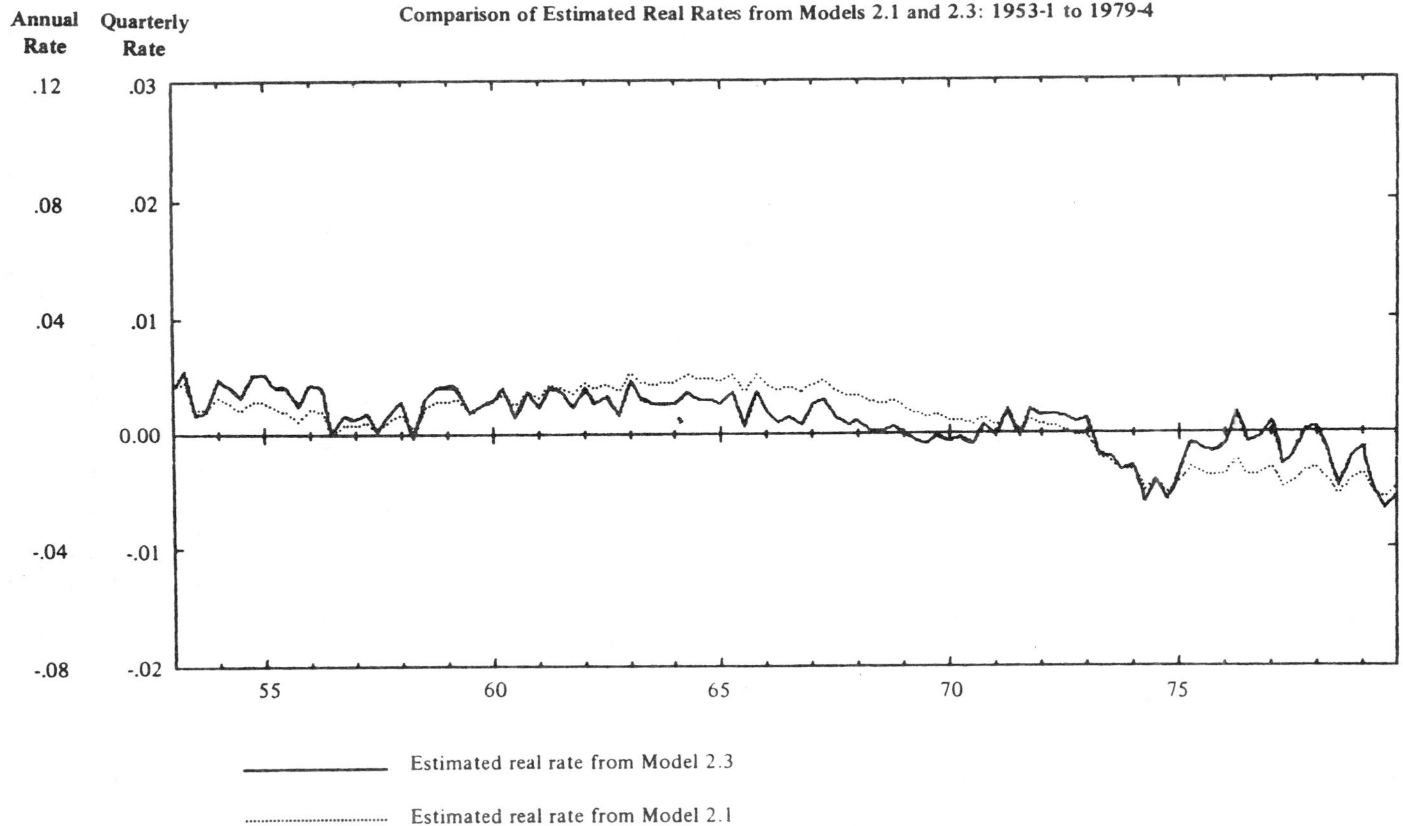

in the 1961-70 period, lower in the 1975-79 period, and lower in the 1954-57 period. We might search for relevant economic variables missing from this analysis by noting that their effect on the real rate should be in a similar direction.

The estimates of the real rate obtained with the approach used here provide another piece of useful information. An estimate of the expected inflation rate, $\hat{\pi}_t^e$, is easily derived by subtracting the estimated real rate, $\hat{rr}_t$, from the nominal interest rate, i_t: i.e.,[32]

$$\hat{\pi}_t^e = i_t - \hat{rr}_t = i_t - X_{t-1}\hat{\beta}_{eprr} \tag{16}$$

This measure of expected inflation has several advantages over those generated from univariate ARIMA time-series models or from surveys, the alternatives most frequently used in the literature. The principal advantage of this measure is that it is a more accurate predictor of inflation. For the prediction error in this sample, the within-sample standard error of the measure derived from an ARIMA (0, 1, 1) model[33] with a seasonal MA1 term is .0047 versus .0042 for the measure derived from model 2.3.[34] Since Pearce (1979) has shown that a similar ARIMA model forecasts inflation better than the Livingston survey measure, it appears as though the approach outlined here will outperform the Livingston measure as well. Because the true expected inflation rate can probably be characterized as rational, the better, and hence more rational, forecasting performance of the $\hat{\pi}_t^e$ discussed here is an indication that it is a more accurate expected inflation measure than the survey or ARIMA alternatives.

In addition, quantitative information on how accurate $\hat{\pi}_t^e$ is as a measure of expected inflation can be calculated, while for the survey or ARIMA measures it cannot. The error in $\hat{\pi}_t^e$ is:

$$\hat{\pi}_t^e - \pi_t^e = (i_t - \hat{rr}_t) - (i_t - rr_t) = -(\hat{rr}_t - rr_t) \tag{17}$$

Since this error is just the negative of the estimated real rate error, its variance is identical to that of the real rate error in (13) and the lower and upper bound standard errors can be calculated with the formulae in (14) and (15).

---

[32] The nominal interest rate adjusted with a constant is one such estimate, if, as in Fama (1975), the real rate is assumed to be constant.

[33] This ARIMA model was identified with the Box-Jenkins (1970) procedure and was subjected to the usual diagnostic checks and found to be adequate. Pearce (1979) also specifies inflation as an ARIMA (0, 1, 1) but does not need to specify any seasonal terms, since he worked with seasonally adjusted data rather than unadjusted data as here.

[34] If seasonal dummies are added to model 2.3, the standard error of the $\hat{\pi}_t^e$ prediction error drops even further to .0039. Therefore, this comparison becomes even more favorable to the $\hat{\pi}_t^e$ estimate.

These standard errors, especially the lower bound which is likely to be more accurate, not only provide confidence intervals for the expected inflation rate but also can be useful in determining how severe the errors-in-variable bias would be when this expected inflation measure is used in other empirical work.

Figure 3 plots the nominal interest rate along with the estimated real rate from Figure 1 and its corresponding estimated expected inflation rate. The most striking feature of this figure is the presence of the Fisher effect. The correlation of the estimated expected inflation rate and the nominal interest rate is .95. Thus, despite the finding here that the real rate is not constant, the basic Fama (1975) position that the Fisher effect is strong in the postwar period is supported. As would be expected from the significant negative correlation of the ex post real rate and lagged inflation, the negative correlation of the estimated expected inflation rate and the estimated real rate is substantial, equaling -.86.

Probably the most important aspect of Figure 3 from the point of view of policy analysis is the negative correlation (-.67) of movements in the nominal interest rate and the estimated real rate. There is an important moral for policy-makers in this negative correlation. Many economists have long warned that increases in nominal interest rates do not necessarily mean that money is tight, because movements in the real rate might not be highly correlated with the nominal rate. Figure 3 indicates something even stronger. It says that an increase in nominal interest rates is associated with a lower real rate rather than the reverse. When nominal rates are high, it is more likely that we are in a period of "easy money" with low real rates than the contrary as has frequently been assumed. Targeting on a nominal interest rate can cause policy to err in the wrong direction. Therefore, it is a highly dangerous policy approach which hopefully has been abandoned by the Fed in the recent revision of its policy procedures in October 1979.

Results: 1931-4 to 1952-4

There are several problems with analysis of ex post real rates in the pre-1953 period. Before the 1953 major revision of the CPI, this price index was not measured that accurately. Particularly troublesome is the fact that prices were often sampled infrequently in constructing the early CPI data, and this could induce spurious correlations with the calculated ex post real rates. Another problem is that for much of this period the nominal interest rate was pegged. From 1937 through 1941 the *t*-bill rate essentially dropped to zero. Since there is an alternative, readily available asset in the economy which has a zero nominal return–i.e., currency–the bill rate could not fall further. It was effectively pegged during this period. Up until the early part of

FIGURE 3

Nominal Interest Rate, Estimated Real Interest Rate and Estimated Expected Inflation: 1953-1 to 1979-4

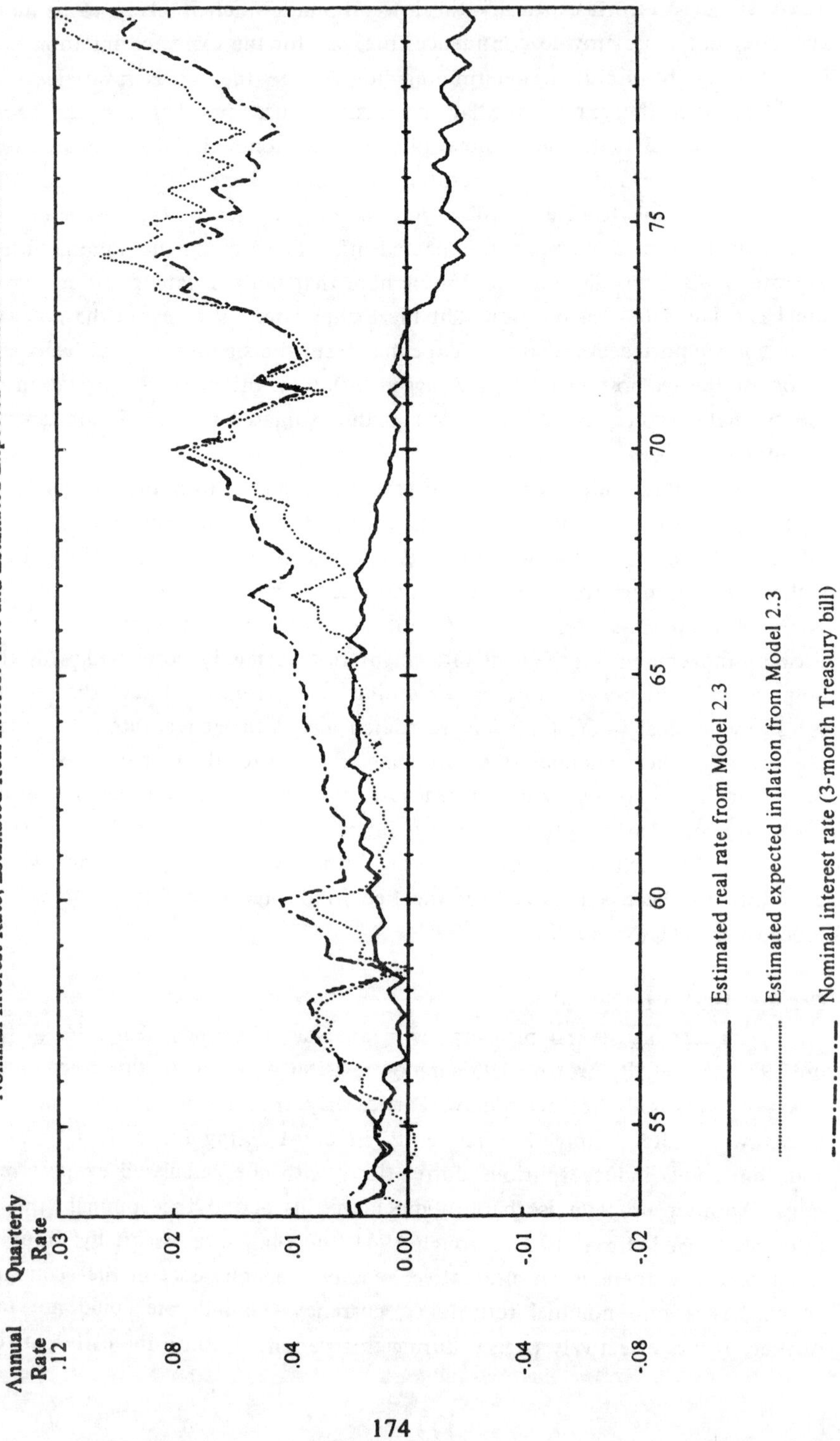

1951, the bill rate was then actually pegged by the Federal Reserve System. As Fama (1975) has noted, we might not expect Fisher relationships to appear in data where nominal interest rates are pegged.

We must, therefore, be cautious when we interpret results using these earlier data. However, it is worthwhile studying these results because they might provide further evidence which corroborates the striking results obtained from the postwar data found in Tables 1 and 2. The sample period analyzed here starts in the fourth quarter of 1931 when *t*-bill data first became available in the CRSP bond file. Goldfeld-Quandt (1965) and Glesjer (1969) tests were again conducted to see if there were heteroscedasticity within the 1931-4 to 1952-4 sample period. No significant heteroscedasticity was found, and estimation again proceeded with ordinary least squares.[35]

Tables 4-5 correspond to Tables 1-2 and again test for the constancy of the real rate, but now for the earlier sample period, 1931-4 to 1952-4. As in the previous results, the ex post real rate from 1931-4 to 1952-4 does display large positive autocorrelations for the first four lags, while the autocorrelations at higher lags are not significantly different from zero. The joint test for the significance of the first twelve autocorrelations in Table 4 also corroborates the previous finding that the ex post real rate is serially correlated. The $Q(12)$ statistic is over 40 with a marginal significance level less than .0001, indicating that the real rate was not constant in the 1931-4 to 1952-4 sample period.

Model 5.1 of Table 5 tests whether the negative relationship between the real rate and lagged inflation also holds up in this earlier sample period. The answer is yes. The coefficient on lagged inflation is again negative and statistically significant: its value of -.4937 is even larger than that found in the postwar data and its *t*-statistic is greater than five in absolute value. Because the nominal bill rate was effectively pegged after 1937, we might wonder if this negative relationship occurs only as a result of the pegging in the later part of the sample period. To explore this, the sample was split at the 1937-4 quarter, and model 5.1 was estimated for the two periods. The coefficient on lagged inflation in the 1931-4 to 1937-4 sample period equals -.4265 and is statistically significant with a *t*-statistic of -2.17. The coefficient on lagged inflation in the 1938-1 to 1952-4 sample period equals -.4654 with a *t*-statistic of -4.04. As would be expected from these results, a Chow test which tests for the stability of the coefficients in 5.1 over the two sample periods cannot reject the null hypothesis

[35]For example, in model 5.1, a Goldfeld-Quandt test which excluded seventeen observations yielded the $F(32,32)$ statistic of 1.21, while the critical F at 5% is approximately 1.8. A Glesjer test where the absolute value of the residuals in 5.1 was regressed against a time trend variable yielded a *t*-statistic on the trend variable of -1.66. A similar test when the absolute value of the residuals was regressed on lagged inflation yielded a *t*-statistic on the lagged inflation coefficient of -.58.

TABLE 4

Serial Correlation Structure of the Ex Post Real Rate: 1931-4 to 1952-4

	Lag k												Approximate Standard Error of the Autocorrelations
	1	2	3	4	5	6	7	8	9	10	11	12	
Autocorrelation at Lag k (r_{-k})	.48	.24	.24	.21	.04	-0.12	-0.02	-0.04	-0.15	-0.10	-0.11	-0.03	.11

Test of $r_1 = r_2 = ,..., = r_{12} = 0$
$Q(12) = 40.80$
Marginal Significance level = 5.29×10^{-5}

NOTES: See Table 1.

TABLE 5

Tests of the Constancy of the Real Rate: 1931-4 to 1952-4

Dependent Variable: Ex Post Real Rate
Estimation Method: Ordinary Least Squares

	Coefficient of								
Model #	Constant Term	$\pi(-1)$	Time	Time^2	R^2	*SE*	*DW*	*F*-Statistic	Marginal Significance Level
5.1	-0.0021 (-1.08)	-0.4937 (-5.13)			.24	.0171	2.00	26.28	1.90×10^{-6}
5.2	.0239 (3.55)		-0.1381 (-4.12)	.1260 (3.55)	.20	.0176	1.25	10.40	9.43×10^{-5}
5.3	.0161 (2.42)	-0.3696 (-3.56)	-0.0938 (-2.78)	.0886 (2.55)	.31	.0165	1.94	12.18	1.18×10^{-6}

NOTES: *T*-statistics in parentheses, R^2, *SE* and *DW*, *F* and marginal significance level are as defined in Table 2 with the *F*'s distributed as $F(1,83)$ for 5.1, $F(2,82)$ for 5.2 and $F(3,81)$ for 5.3. $\pi(-1)$, Time and Time^2 are as defined in Table 2, except that Time runs from .04 in 1931-4 to .88 in 1952-4

that the coefficients are equal: $F(2,81) = 1.16$ with the critical value of F at 5% approximately equal to 3.1.

These results with the earlier sample period provide even more evidence that Fama's (1975) finding that the real rate is constant and is not negatively correlated with inflation is the exception and not the rule. The ex post real rate is found to be significantly negatively correlated with inflation in every sample period except Fama's, and it appears that this is not due to a definite absence of the negative correlation in his sample period but rather to the lack of variation in the data. Indeed, not too surprisingly considering the nature of the pre-1953 data, it appears as though the strong negative association of real rates and inflation found in the postwar data is on the weak side by historical standards. A Chow test, suitably corrected for heteroscedasticity,[36] comparing the coefficients of 2.1 and 5.1, finds that the coefficients are not stable over the 1931-79 sample period: the null hypothesis of equal coefficients is rejected at the one percent level with $F(2,189) = 9.19$, while the critical F at 1% is approximately 4.7.

Model 5.2 conducts the more mechanical test of the constancy of the real rate, assuming that the real rate moves with a second-order polynomial in time. A second-order polynomial is used here because additional variables with time trends raised to a higher power did not add significant explanatory power in both the 5.2 and 5.3 regressions.[37] The null hypothesis that the coefficients of the time trend variables equal zero is rejected with a low marginal significance level. When the time trend variables are added to the model with lagged inflation as an explanatory variable, as in 5.3, they do contain significant, additional explanatory power: $F(2,81) = 4.13$ with the critical F at 5% equal to 3.1. The addition of these variables then leads to an even lower marginal significance level for the null hypothesis implied by the constancy of the real rate. These results again support the postwar findings.

Figure 4 plots the estimate of the real interest rate derived from the fitted values of 5.3. The upper and lower bound 95% confidence bands are derived as for Figure 1 from the formulae in (14) and (15). One interesting feature of this figure is the much greater variability of the estimated real rate in

[36] A comparison of the standard error of 2.1 and 5.1 indicates that the variance of the error term is over fourteen times higher in the pre-1953 than in the 1953-79 sample period. This is a very significant rejection of the null hypothesis that there is homoscedasticity: $F(83,106) = 14.43$ with the critical F at 1% approximately equal to 1.7. The Chow test mentioned above used weighted least squares in estimation where the data for the 1931-52 observations were weighted by the standard error of 5.1 and the 1953-79 observations by the standard error of 2.1.

[37] In the 5.2 model three additional trend variables raised to the third, fourth and fifth power did add significant explanatory power: $F(3,79) = 3.03$ with the critical F at 5% equal to 2.7. However, in the 5.3 model these variables did not add significant explanatory power: $F(3,78) = 1.74$ with the critical F at 5% equal to 2.7. In any case, the same conclusions were reached using either the second-order or the fifth-order polynomial in the above analysis.

this early sample period than in the later, postwar period. (This result is brought out more clearly in Figure A1 in Appendix I, which displays the estimated real rate for both sample periods in one graph.) This might be an indication of the greater economic stability in the later period.

Some economists have challenged the Keynesian position that money was "easy" during the contractionary phase of the Great Depression by stating that real interest rates were probably quite high during this period although nominal interest rates were low.[38] This view is given strong support in Figure 4. The estimated real rates from 1931-4 to 1933-1 range from 6.2% to 10.2% at an annual rate. Using the lower bound standard errors, not only are the estimated real rates significantly higher than zero—sometimes by over four standard errors—but they also appear to be significantly higher than any of the estimated real rates for the postwar period. By the criterion of real rates, the evidence indicates that since 1931 money has never been tighter than in the contraction phase of the Great Depression.

The estimated real rate begins to decline as the economy recovers after 1933-2 and bounces around zero until 1938-2. From then on until 1952-4, the estimated real rate is almost always negative and is significantly so (by the criterion of the lower bound standard errors) for most of this period. Indeed, the estimated real rate is frequently less than -5% and reaches its low point of -16.4% in 1946-4 when it is five of the lower bound standard errors away from zero. Thus, the period where nominal interest rates were pegged also appears to have been a period of negative real rates.

Figure 5 contains the estimated real rates derived from the model with only lagged inflation as an explanatory variable versus those from the model which also includes the time trends as explanatory variables. Because the trend variables do help significantly to explain the ex post real rate, as discussed before, they can provide information on what effect left-out economic variables might have on the real rate. The comparison of the two estimated real rate series in Figure 5 indicates that the left-out variables make the real rate higher in the 1931-37 period and lower thereafter.

Figure 6, which plots the estimated real interest rate from 5.3, its corresponding estimated expected inflation, and the nominal interest rate for the 1931-52 period, is comparable with Figure 3. Here we see some striking differences between the earlier and later sample periods. Again we see the negative correlation of expected inflation and real rates as we might expect, although it is even stronger than before, equaling -.99. However, we no longer find any evidence of the Fisher effect that was so visible in the postwar period. The

---

[38]For example, Meltzer (1976) and Mayer (1978).

FIGURE 4

Estimated Real Interest Rate with 95% Confidence Intervals: 1931-4 to 1952-4

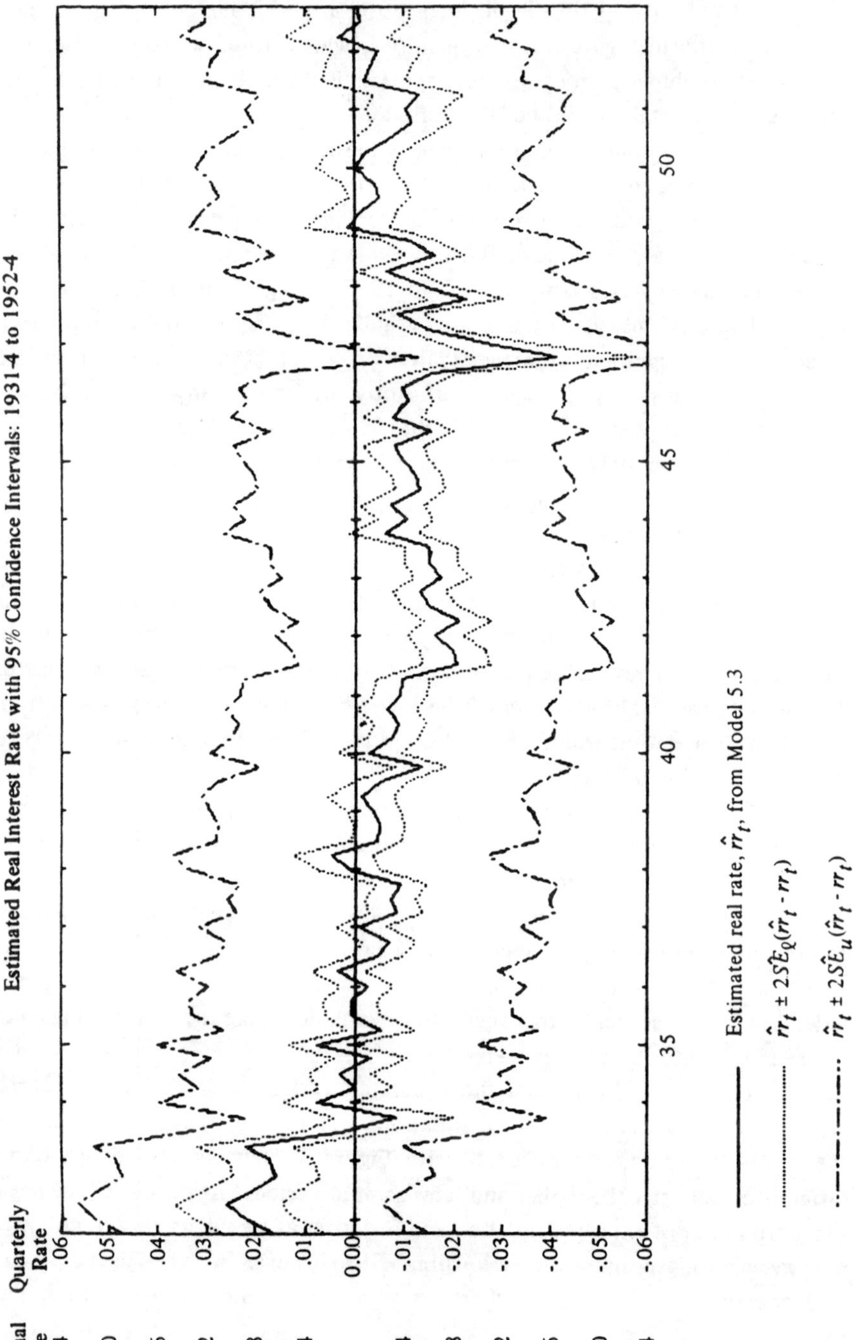

FIGURE 5

Comparison of Estimated Real Rates from Models 5.1 and 5.3: 1931-4 to 1952-4

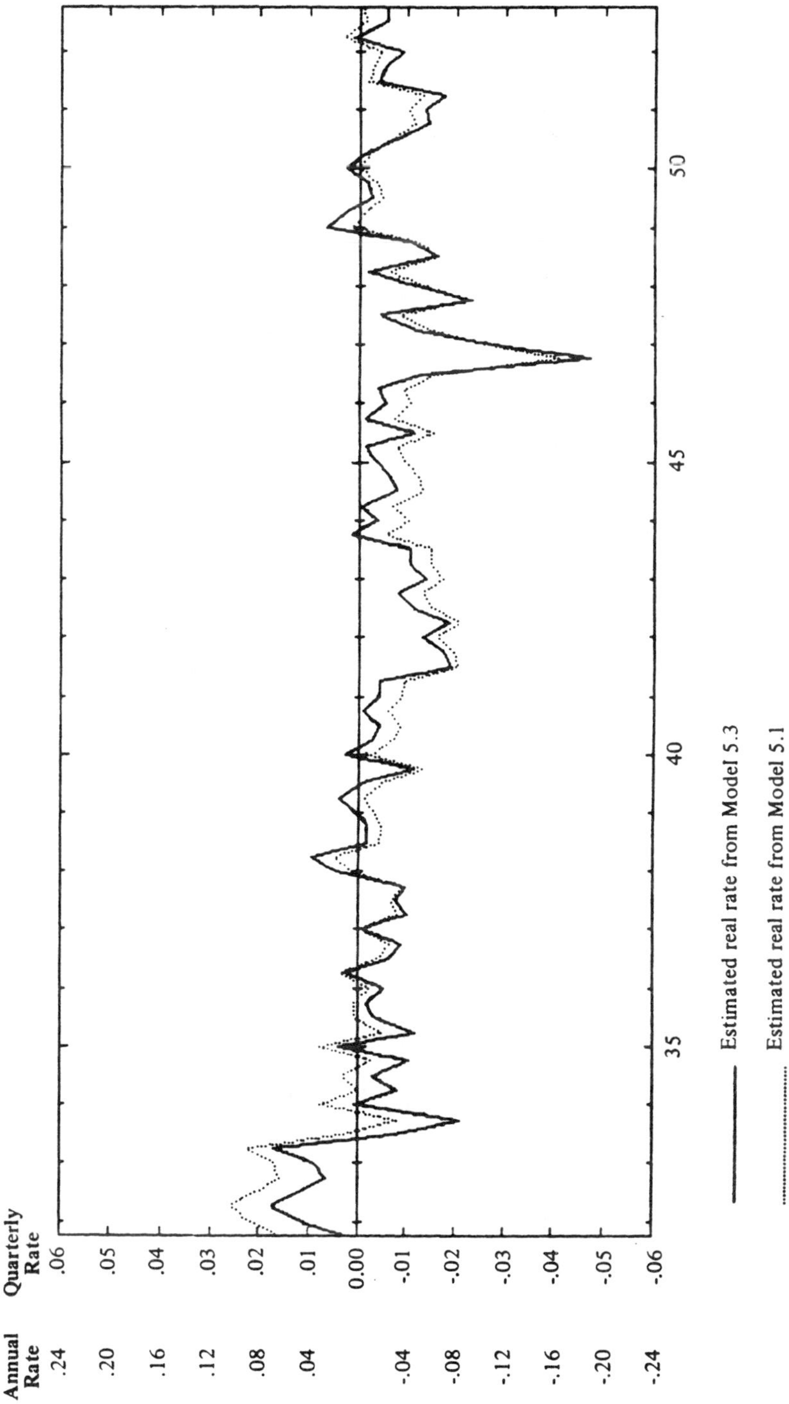

FIGURE 6

Nominal Interest Rate, Estimated Real Interest Rate and Estimated Expected Inflation: 1931-4 to 1952-4

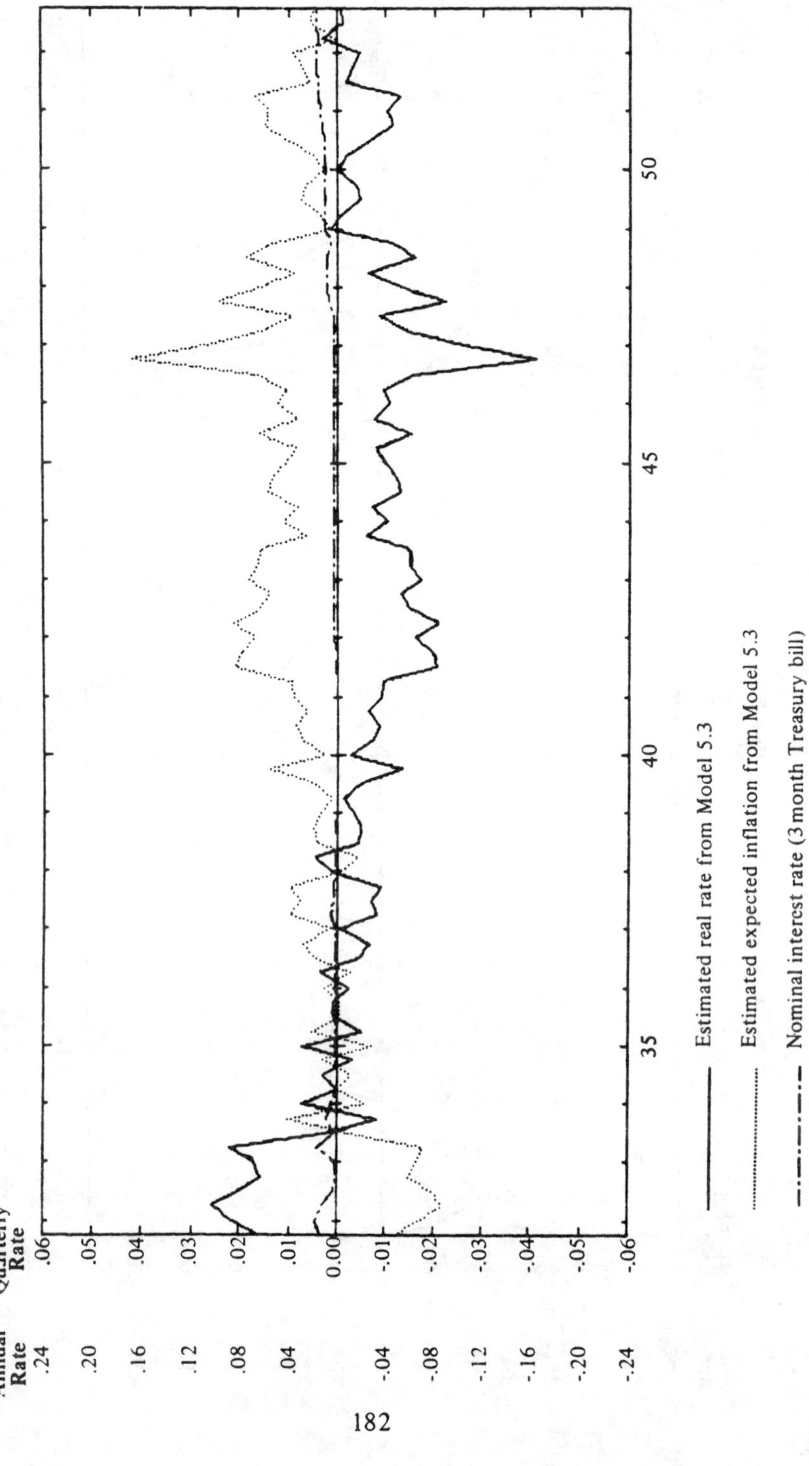

correlation of expected inflation and the nominal interest rates is not even positive in this early sample period: it is quite small and is slightly negative, equaling -.13. None of these results is particularly surprising because, as Figure 6 illustrates, there was very little movement in nominal interest rates in this period. With substantial variation in the expected inflation rate, this must necessarily result in a very strong negative correlation of the real rate and expected inflation as well as the absence of a Fisher effect.

Figure 6 does support the important policy-oriented conclusion of Figure 3. Movements in nominal interest rates contain little information about the movements in real interest rates. In this early sample period, the correlation of the nominal with the real interest rate is only .25. It was just as easy for the monetary authorities in the pre-1953 period to confuse tight versus easy monetary policy as a result of focusing on nominal rather than real interest rates as it was during the more recent period. The policy mistakes of the Fed during the contraction phase of the Great Depression clearly attest to this fact.

Results: Tax Effects On The Real Rate

So far, the consequences of taxes on nominal interest payments have been ignored. As has been emphasized by Darby (1975) and especially Feldstein (1976, 1980a, b) this can be misleading for the postwar period. Clearly, what is relevant to a firm's decision to invest or the consumer's decision to save versus consume is the real *after-tax* interest rate. However, as has been illustrated by Feldstein and Summers (1978) and Shiller (1980), the effective tax rate on interest payments can vary tremendously for different individuals and firms, particularly when they are making different types of decisions. It is easy to find cases where the effective tax rate on interest payments ranges from zero on up to the top marginal tax rate. As a result, it is extremely difficult to know what is the appropriate tax rate on interest payments for the overall economy. This is the primary reason why the analysis in this paper focuses first on real interest rates, ignoring the effect of taxes.

To get a flavor of how taxes might affect the previous results, the empirical analysis in Tables 1-3 has been redone with an *after-tax* ex post real rate which has been calculated under the assumption that the effective marginal tax rate is a third. This tax rate was chosen because it is approximately in the middle of the range of several authors' estimates of the marginal tax rate for interest payments in the postwar period.[39] There is no claim here that this tax rate is an accurate estimate of the effective tax rate on interest, but the results

[39] For example, Wright (1969), Darby (1975), and Tanzi (1980). Note that Levi and Makin (1978) also use this tax rate on interest payments for illustrative purposes.

using it will provide us with a reasonable idea of how important tax effects might be to some of the conclusions reached earlier.

Tables 6-8 contain the estimated results using the after-tax ex post real rate. Because only a crude adjustment has been made here for taxes, these results do not deserve a detailed discussion. A few brief comments should suffice to give us a flavor of how tax effects would affect our views. The tests for the constancy of the after-tax real rate in Tables 6 and 7 reject the null hypothesis at even lower marginal significance levels than in Tables 1 and 2. Adjusting the ex post real rate for taxes increases the variation in this variable, and this is what leads to the even stronger positive serial correlation found in Table 6 and the stronger rejections of the constancy of the after-tax real rate. Because the tax adjustment forces the after-tax real rate to decline as the nominal interest rate rises along with the inflation rate, the coefficient on lagged inflation becomes even more negative and statistically significant. Tax adjustment of the ex post real rate thus generates conclusions similar to and even stronger than those found when it was not adjusted. Clearly, use of a different tax rate would not alter the direction of these results.

Table 8 shows that the conclusions on the correlation of real rates with other variables do not change when a tax adjustment is made. Feldstein (1980a) makes the case that monetary policy will be non-neutral, because even if it leaves the unadjusted real rate unchanged when it causes higher inflation, the *after-tax* real rate will fall. The results in Table 3 indicate that, even without a tax adjustment, the real rate has fallen with faster money growth. However, as the 8.1 and 8.2 results show, when the real rate is adjusted for taxes, this negative correlation is even stronger.

The estimated after-tax real rate derived from the fitted values of 7.3 along with its upper and lower bound 95% confidence intervals is plotted in Figure 7. In the first half of the 1953-79 period, the after-tax real rates appear to be mostly positive, yet even the lower bound confidence interval rarely rejects the hypothesis that the after-tax real rate is zero. In the late 1960s the estimated after-tax real rate turns negative, and from 1969 through the end of the sample period it is significantly negative using the lower bound standard errors. Note that towards the end of the period, even the upper bound standard errors indicate that it is significantly negative. In the 1970s, the estimated after-tax real rate is frequently below -4% at an annual rate and is more than six of the lower bound standard errors away from zero.

Figures 8 and 9 which correspond to 2 and 3 are included in the paper for the sake of completeness. They reveal no surprises. As is evident from Figure 8, the time trend variables play a similar role in altering the estimate of

TABLE 6

Serial Correlation Structure of the After-Tax Ex Post Real Rate: 1953-1 to 1979-4

	Lag k												Approximate Standard Error of the Autocorrelations
	1	2	3	4	5	6	7	8	9	10	11	12	
Autocorrelation at Lag k (r_{-k})	.56	.48	.50	.52	.41	.29	.31	.22	.26	.18	.29	.22	.10

Test of $r_1 = r_2 = ,..., = r_{12} = 0$

$Q(12) = 194.38$

Marginal Significance level = 4.70×10^{-35}

NOTES: See Table 1.
After-tax ex post real rate calculated with tax rate of .33.

TABLE 7

Tests of the Constancy of the After-Tax Real Rate: 1953-1 to 1979-4

Dependent Variable: Ex Post Real Rate, Adjusted for .33 Marginal Tax Rate
Estimation Method: Ordinary Least Squares

	Coefficient of										
Model #	Constant Term	$\pi(-1)$	Time	$Time^2$	$Time^3$	$Time^4$	R^2	*SE*	*DW*	*F*-Statistic	Marginal Significance Level
7.1	.0020 (3.13)	-0.4766 (-9.42)					.46	.0046	2.40	88.79	1.80×10^{-11}
7.2	.0254 (1.49)		-0.1728 (-1.60)	.4106 (1.75)	-0.3917 (-1.85)	.1243 (1.86)	.49	.0045	1.60	24.29	3.58×10^{-14}
7.3	.0216 (1.32)	-0.2564 (-3.23)	-0.1444 (-1.39)	.3469 (1.54)	-0.3297 (-1.63)	.1049 (1.63)	.53	.0043	2.22	23.30	8.00×10^{-12}

NOTES: See Table 2.

TABLE 8

Tests for Correlation of After-Tax Real Rate with Other Variables: 1953-1 to 1979-4

Dependent Variable: Ex Post Real Rate, Adjusted for .33
Marginal Tax Rate
Estimation Method: Ordinary Least Squares

		Coefficient of						
Model #	Independent Variable	Constant Term	$\pi(-1)$	Independent Variable Lagged Once	R^2	*SE*	*DW*	*F*-test for significant explanatory power of four lags of independent variable when included in this model
8.1	money growth (M1)	-0.0001 (-0.15)		-0.2321 (-3.30)	.09	.0058	.99	7.29
8.2	money growth (M1)	.0025 (3.21)	-0.4569 (-8.47)	-0.0605 (-1.04)	.46	.0046	2.37	1.20
8.3	real GNP growth	-0.0032 (-4.30)		.0875 (1.55)	.02	.0061	.90	1.44
8.4	real GNP growth	.0022 (2.75)	-0.4822 (-9.16)	-0.0178 (-0.41)	.46	.0046	2.40	1.08
8.5	GNP gap	-0.0024 (-3.41)		-0.0001 (-0.00)	.00	.0062	.82	.70
8.6	GNP gap	.0019 (2.66)	-0.4778 (-9.40)	.0078 (0.48)	.46	.0046	2.40	.77
8.7	unemployment rate	.0013 (0.55)		-0.0719 (-1.65)	.02	.0061	.86	1.10
8.8	unemployment rate	.0025 (1.42)	-0.4733 (-9.13)	-0.0103 (-0.31)	.46	.0046	2.39	.26
8.9	investment to capital ratio	.0046 (0.54)		-0.0722 (-0.84)	.01	.0062	.82	.82
8.10	investment to capital ratio	.0075 (1.20)	-0.4754 (-9.39)	-0.0564 (-0.88)	.46	.0046	2.41	.27

NOTES: See Table 3.

FIGURE 7

Estimated After-Tax Real Rate with 95% Confidence Intervals: 1953-1 to 1979-4

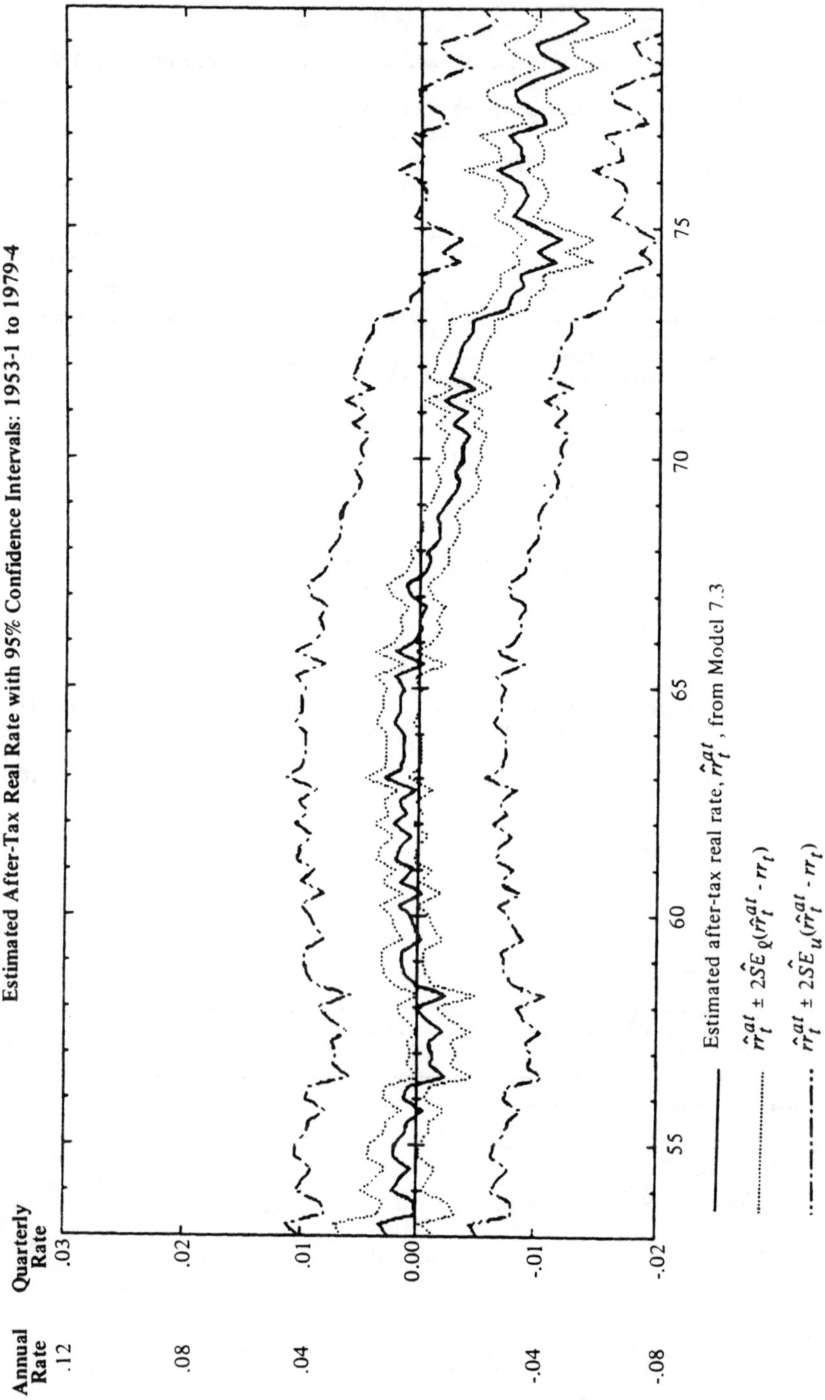

FIGURE 8

Comparison of Estimated After-Tax Rates from Models 7.1 and 7.3: 1953-1 to 1979-4

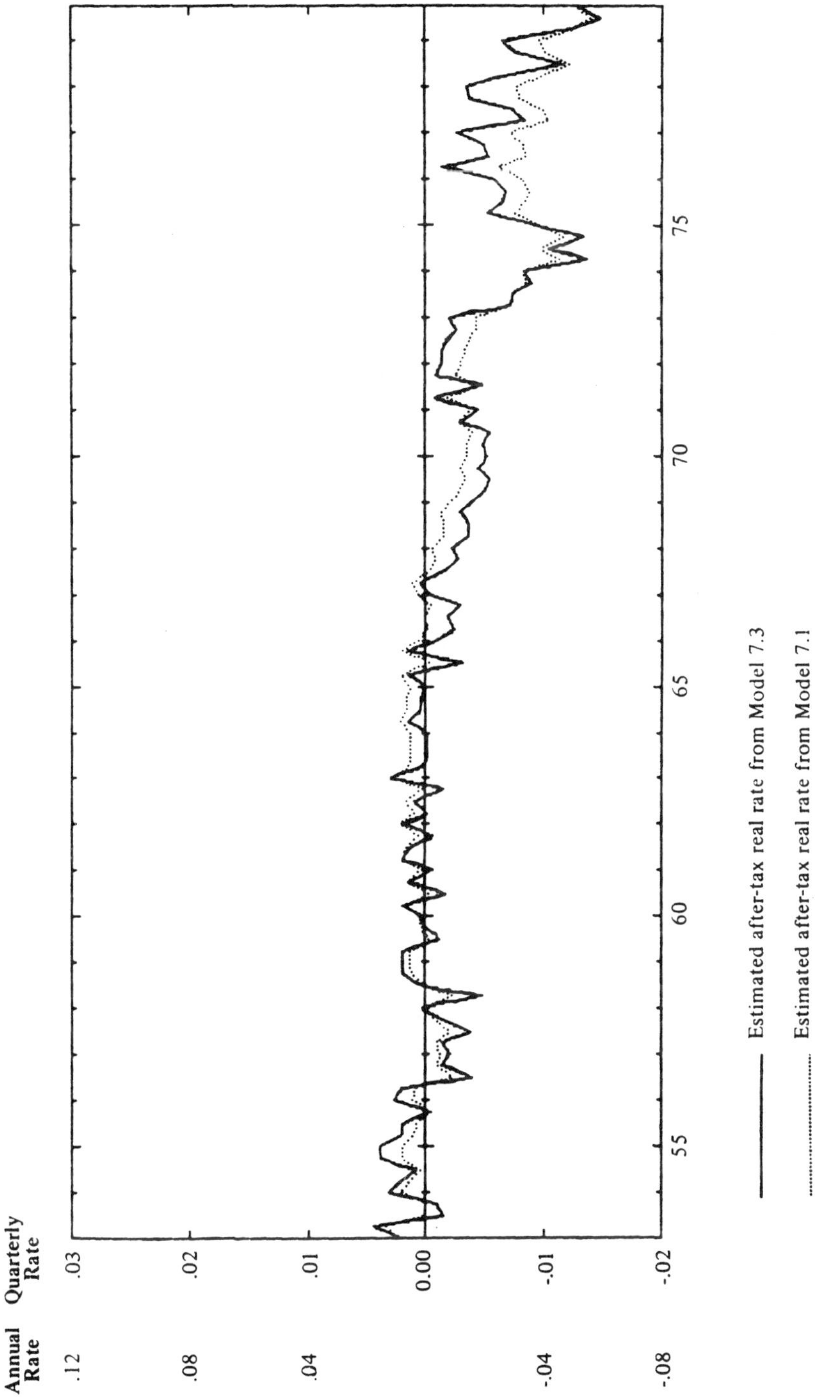

FIGURE 9

Nominal Interest Rate, Estimated After-Tax Real Rate and Estimated Expected Inflation: 1953-1 to 1979-4

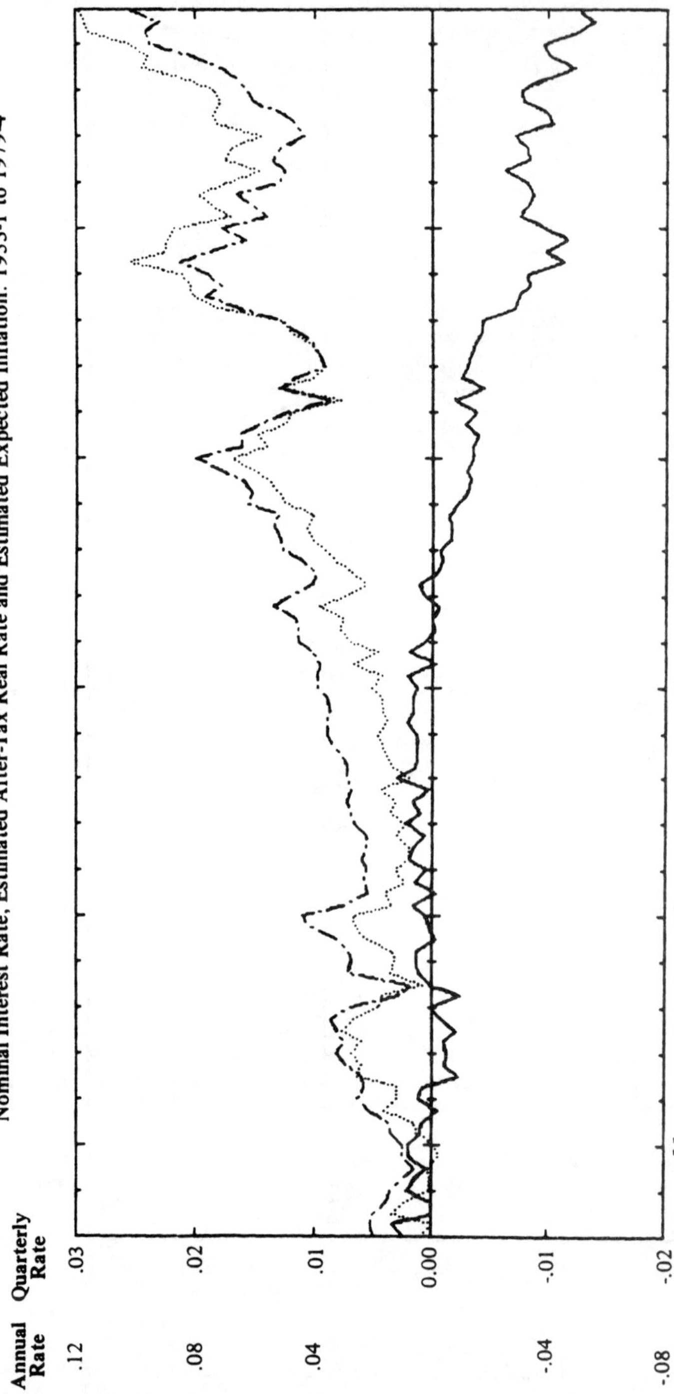

Estimated after-tax real rate from Model 7.3

Estimated expected inflation from Model 7.3

Nominal interest rate (3-month Treasury bill)

190

the after-tax real rate to what they do for the estimate of the real rate unadjusted for taxes. Furthermore, the estimate of expected inflation and its relationship to the nominal interest rate in Figure 9 is similar to that found in Figure 3.[40] Figure 9 does illustrate the expected finding that the correlations of the estimated after-tax real rate with the estimates of expected inflation and the nominal interest rate are even more negative–the respective correlations equal -.96 and -.80–than is the case when the real rate is unadjusted for taxes. The conclusion that the nominal interest rate is a misleading guide to the tightness of monetary policy is then given even greater support when we view the after-tax real rate as the vehicle through which monetary policy is transmitted.

IV. CONCLUSIONS

This paper has analyzed the movements of real interest rates over the 1931-79 period with a statistical methodology that has the advantage of reliability. Despite the low statistical power of the approach used here, many interesting findings have been gleaned from the data. These findings are listed below.

1. The hypothesis that the real rate is constant is strongly rejected both for the 1953-79 period and the 1931-52 period. Fama's (1975) finding that the constancy of the real rate could not be rejected is the exception and not the rule. His result seems to stem from the lack of variation in the real rate for his sample period. The adjustment of the real rate for taxes lends even stronger support to the position that the after-tax real rate, which is probably more relevant to economic decisions, is not constant.
2. The real rate, whether adjusted or unadjusted for taxes, is negatively correlated with inflation. This result is found for both the 1953-79 and 1931-52 sample period, and again Fama's (1975) failure to find this result appears to be due to a lack of variation in the real rate data.

[40]Once lagged inflation, which is highly correlated with the lagged nominal interest rate, is included as an explanatory variable in a real rate regression, the results for additional explanatory variables are expected to be very similar, regardless of whether the real rate is adjusted or unadjusted for taxes. To see this, just realize that if the lagged nominal interest rate were an explanatory variable, then a regression with the after-tax real rate as the dependent variable is just a linear transformation of the regression with the unadjusted real rate as the dependent variable. In this case, the results on additional explanatory variables would be identical in either regression. They should, therefore, be quite similar if the lagged nominal interest rate is replaced by the lagged inflation rate. This same point explains why the estimates of expected inflation from the after-tax versus unadjusted real rate models 2.3 and 7.3 are also so similar.

3. Movements in real variables are not significantly correlated with ex post real rates, whether adjusted or unadjusted for taxes. The failure to find these correlations is more likely the result of small cyclical variations in real rates rather than the absence of relationships between real variables and real rates.
4. Increased money growth is associated with a decline in real rates. This non-neutrality result is even stronger when the real rate is adjusted for taxes. Little evidence was found that money growth affects real rates other than through its effect on inflation, but again this could be due to the low power of the statistical tests used here.
5. The real interest rate appears to have been positive in the 1950s and 1960s but has since turned negative in the mid- and late 1970s. When the real rate is adjusted for taxes, there is less evidence that it has been positive in the post-war period, and there is strong evidence that it has been negative since 1969.
6. Real rates were extremely high during the contraction phase of the Great Depression and have never been as high since. From the perspective of real interest rates, money has never been tighter than during this period.
7. The period where nominal interest rates were effectively pegged from 1938-1951 was a period where real interest rates were negative.
8. Estimates of expected inflation rates have been derived from models of the real rate, and these estimates have several advantages over those obtained from surveys or Box-Jenkins' ARIMA models. The estimates of expected inflation confirm Fama's (1975) view that in the postwar period there is a strong Fisher effect where expected inflation and nominal interest rates move together. However, no Fisher effect is evident in the pre-1953 sample period.
9. Movements in nominal interest rates are not a reliable indicator of movements in real rates, whether adjusted for taxes or not. This is true of both the 1931-52 and 1953-79 sample periods. The correlation of estimated real rates and nominal interest rates is low in the 1931-52 sample period and is even negative in the postwar period.

The most important policy implication from these results is the recommendation that policymakers, politicians, and the public should not focus on nominal interest rates as indicating the tightness of monetary policy. Not only do the results here indicate that nominal interest rates contain little information on real interest rates and hence on the tightness of monetary policy; they also indicate that nominal interest rates have been a highly misleading indicator of monetary tightness during some crucial business cycle episodes. For example, real interest rates appear to have been extremely high during the Great Depression downturn, and yet, by the criterion of low nominal interest rates, this period appears to have been one of "easy money" rather than the reverse. Knowledge of the true state of monetary tightness might have led the Fed to take more appropriate policy actions. Similarly, the period of the 1970s appeared to be one of "tight money" by the nominal interest rate criterion, yet real rates appear to have been quite low. Knowledge of how "easy" money truly was might have encouraged a less expansionary monetary policy, resulting in less inflation.

FIGURE A1

Estimated Ex Post and Ex Ante Real Rates: 1931-4 to 1979-4

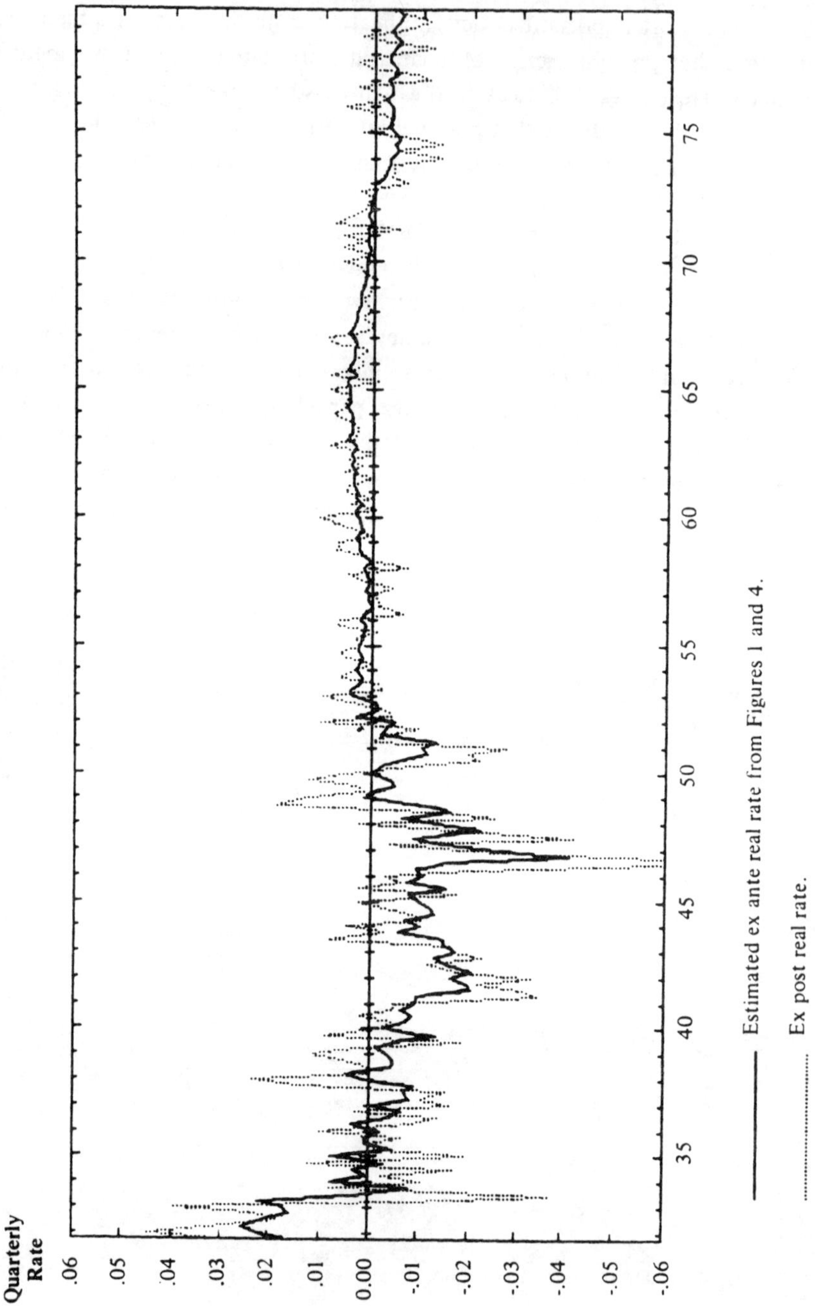

DATA APPENDIX

Variables And Sources Of Data

π_t = inflation rate (at quarterly rate) = $\log(CPI_t/CPI_{t-1})$.

CPI_t = seasonally unadjusted consumer price index for the last month of quarter t: postwar data obtained from the *Survey of Current Business* and *Business Statistics*; prewar data obtained from the BLS.

i_t = the nominal return (at a quarterly rate) over the quarter of a 3-month Treasury Bill maturing at the end of the quarter = log $(100/PB_t)$.

PB_t = the average of the bid and asked price at the beginning of the quarter for the 3-month bill maturing at the end of quarter t: obtained from the Center for Research in Security Prices (CRSP) bond file.

$eprr_t$ = the ex post real rate for the 3-month bill maturing at the end of quarter $t = i_t - \pi_t$.

money growth $(M1)_t$ = the log of M1 for the last month of quarter t minus the log of M1 for the last month of quarter t-1: data obtained from *Business Statistics* and the *Survey of Current Business.*

real *GNP* growth$_t$ = the log of real *GNP* for quarter t (GNP_t) minus the log of real *GNP* for quarter t-1: data obtained from *Business Statistics* and the *Survey of Current Business.*

$GNP\ gap_t$ = $\dfrac{POTGNP_t - GNP_t}{POTGNP_t}$: $POTGNP_t$ is potential *GNP* for quarter t, estimated by the Council of Economic Advisors and obtained from them.

unemployment rate$_t$ = the unemployment rate for the last month of the quarter t: obtained from *Business Statistics* and the *Survey of Current Business.*

investment to capital ratio$_t$ = expenditures on housing and business fixed investment in plant and durable equipment in quarter t, divided by the stock of residential, plant and durable equipment capital at the end of the quarter t: data obtained from the (MPS) Quarterly Econometric Model data bank at the Board of Governors of the Federal Reserve.

References

Boskin, M.J.
(1978) Taxation, Saving and the Rate of Interest. *Journal of Political Economy*, **86**, #2: S3-S27.

Box, G.E.P. and Jenkins, G.M.
(1970) *Time Series Analysis, Forecasting and Control.* San Francisco: Holden Day.

Cargill, T.F.
(1976) Anticipated Price Changes and Nominal Interest Rates in the 1950s. *Review of Economics and Statistics,* **58**: 364-67.

Carlson, J.A.
(1977) Short-Term Interest Rates as Predictors of Inflation: Comment. *American Economic Review,* **67**: 469-75.

Cumby, R., Huizinga, J., and Obstfeld, M.
(1980) Two-Step, Two-Stage Least Squares Estimation in Models with Rational Expectations. Discussion Paper Series #71, Columbia University, Department of Economics.

Darby, M.R.
(1975) The Financial and Tax Effects of Monetary Policy on Interest Rates. *Economic Inquiry,* **12**: 266-76.

Fama, E.F.
(1970) Efficient Capital Markets: A Review of Theory and Empirical Work. *Journal of Finance,* **25**: 383-417.

____
(1975) Short-Term Interest Rates as Predictors of Inflation. *American Economic Review,* **65**: 269-82.

____
(1976a) *Foundations of Finance.* New York: Basic Books.

Fama, E.F.

(1976b) Inflation Uncertainty and Expected Returns on Treasury Bills. *Journal of Political Economy*, **84**: 427-48.

——— and Gibbons, M.R.

(1980) Inflation, Real Returns and Capital Investment, Graduate School of Business, University of Chicago. Unpublished paper.

——— and Schwert, G.W.

(1979) Inflation, Interest, and Relative Prices. *Journal of Business*, **52**: 183-209.

Feldstein, M.

(1976) Inflation, Income Taxes and the Rate of Interest: A Theoretical Analysis. *American Economic Review*, **66**: 809-20.

———

(1980a) Tax Rules and the Mismanagement of Monetary Policy. *American Economic Review*, **70**: 182-86.

———

(1980b) Comment on Shiller in *Rational Expectations and Economic Policy*. S. Fischer, ed. Chicago: University of Chicago Press: 163-4.

——— and Summers, L.

(1978) Inflation, Tax Rules and the Long-Term Interest Rate. *Brookings Papers on Economic Activity*, **1**: 61-100.

Fisher, I.

(1930) *The Theory of Interest*. New York: Macmillan.

Flood, R.P. and Garber, P.M.

(1980) A Pitfall in Estimation of Models with Rational Expectations. *Journal of Monetary Economics*, **6**: 433-35.

Garbade, K. and Wachtel, P.

(1978) Time Variation in the Relationship Between Inflation and Interest Rates. *Journal of Monetary Economics*, **4**: 755-65.

Gibson, W.E.
(1972) Interest Rates and Inflationary Expectations: New Evidence. *American Economic Review*, **62**: 834-65.

Glesjer, H.
(1969) A New Test for Heteroscedasticity. *Journal of the American Statistical Association*, **64**: 316-23.

Goldfeld, S. and Quandt, R.E.
(1965) Some Tests for Homoscedasticity. *Journal of the American Statistical Association*, **60**: 539-47.

Hess, P.J. and Bicksler, J.L.
(1975) Capital Asset Prices Versus Time Series Models as Predictors of Inflation: The Expected Real Rate of Interest and Market Efficiency. *Journal of Financial Economics*, 2: 341-60.

Howrey, R.P. and Hymans, S.H.
(1978) The Measurement and Determination of Loanable-Funds Saving. *Brookings Papers on Economic Activity*, 3: 655-85.

Joines, D.
(1977) Short-Term Interest Rates as Predictors of Inflation: Comment. *American Economic Review*, **67**: 476-7.

Lahiri, K.
(1976) Inflationary Expectations: Their Formation and Interest Rate Effects. *American Economic Review*, **66**: 124-31.

Levi, M.D. and Makin, J.H.
(1978) Anticipated Inflation and Interest Rates. *American Economic Review*, **68**: 801-12.

———
(1979) Fisher, Phillips, Friedman and the Measured Impact of Inflation on Interest. *Journal of Finance*, **34**: 35-52.

Ljung, C.M. and Box, G.E.P.
(1978) On a Measure of Lack of Fit in Time Series Models. *Biometrika*, **65**: 297-303.

Mayer, T.

(1978) Money and the Great Depression: A Critique of Professor Temin's Thesis. *Explorations in Economic History*, **15**: 127-45.

Meltzer, A.

(1976) Monetary and Other Explanations of the Great Depression. *Journal of Monetary Economics*, **2**: 455-71.

Mishkin, F.S.

(1978) Efficient Markets Theory: Implications for Monetary Policy. *Brookings Papers on Economic Acitvity*, **3**: 707-52.

———

(1981a) Monetary Policy and Long-Term Interest Rates: An Efficient Markets Approach, *Journal of Monetary Economics*, **7**: 29-55.

———

(1981b) Are Market Forecasts Rational? *American Economic Review*, **71**.

Modigliani, F.

(1974) The Channels of Monetary Policy in the FMP Econometric Model of the U.S., G. Renton, ed. *Modelling the Economy*. Heineman Educational Books.

Nelson, C.R. and Schwert, G.W.

(1977) Short-Term Interest Rates as Predictors of Inflation: On Testing the Hypothesis that the Real Rate of Interest is Constant. *American Economic Review*, **67**: 478-86.

Pearce, D.K.

(1979) Comparing Survey and Rational Measures of Expected Inflation: Forecast Performance and Interest Rate Effects. *Journal of Money, Credit and Banking*, **11**: 447-56.

Sargent, T.

(1979) *Macroeconomics*. New York: Academic Press.

Shiller, R.J.
(1979) The Volatility of Long-Term Interest Rates and Expectations Models of the Term Structure. *Journal of Political Economy,* **87**: 1190-1219.

———
(1980) Can the Fed Control Real Interest Rates? S. Fischer, ed., *Rational Expectations and Economic Policy.* Chicago: University of Chicago Press: 117-56.

Summers, L.H.
(1978) Tax Policy in a Life Cycle Model. National Bureau of Economic Research Working Paper #302, Cambridge, Mass.

Tanzi, V.
(1980) Inflationary Expectations, Economic Activity, Taxes and Interest Rates. *American Economic Review,* **70**: 12-21.

Wright, C.
(1969) Saving and the Rate of Interest. *The Taxation of ncome From Capital.* Harberger, ed. The Brookings Institution: 275-300.

[4]

THE JOURNAL OF FINANCE • VOL. XXXIX, NO. 3 • JULY 1984

Inflation and Real Interest Rates on Assets with Different Risk Characteristics

JOHN HUIZINGA* and FREDERIC S. MISHKIN**

GIVEN THE IMPORTANCE of ex ante real interest rates to economic decision making, it is no surprise that much empirical research focuses on them.[1] Several recent studies find that the ex ante real returns for short-term U.S. Treasury securities are not constant and are negatively correlated both with inflation and with nominal interest rates. This paper examines the extent to which these findings hold for assets of longer maturity, are robust with respect to the choice of price index, and are stable over time.

We expand the set of assets studied to include those of longer maturity, both publicly and privately issued, for two reasons. First, their ex ante real returns may differ substantially from that of a short-term nominally riskless security. Second, because longer-maturity assets have risk characteristics closer to capital, their ex ante real returns are potentially more relevant for investment and savings decisions. We explore the use of various price indices because the index used in most studies, the Consumer Price Index, severely overstates inflation during the 1970s as a result of its inappropriate treatment of residential housing costs.[2] This overstatement casts doubt on an important finding of previous studies—that there are long stretches of time during the 1970s when ex ante real rates are significantly negative. Given the existence of holding costs for the goods relevant to most price indices and the absence of a riskless real return, no arbitrage conditions are violated by a negative ex ante real rate. However, its persistence is problematical because asset holders are typically assumed to have a positive rate of time preference, which ensures a positive ex ante real rate in the long run.

We find that before 1979 a negative relationship of ex ante real rates both with inflation and with nominal interest rates appears for the longer maturity assets as well as the short-term nominally riskless asset; indeed the relationship grows

* University of Chicago, Graduate School of Business and National Bureau of Economic Research.

** Columbia University, Graduate School of Business and National Bureau of Economic Research.

We thank Robert Dennis, Gene Fama, Larry Fisher, Bob Holthausen, Roger Ibbotson, Steve LeRoy and participants in seminars at the University of Chicago, Northwestern University, University of California at Berkeley, Stanford University, University of California at Santa Barbara, North Carolina State University, the Congressional Budget Office and the Federal Reserve Bank of Philadelphia for their helpful comments. Randy Picker and Dan Goldman provided valuable research assistance. This research has been financed by the National Science Foundation and the Sloan Foundation. It is part of the National Bureau of Economic Research's Program in Economic Fluctuations.

[1] See Litterman and Weiss (1982), Barro (1982), Fama and Gibbons (1982), Summers (1982), Mishkin (1981b, 1982, 1984) and Huizinga and Mishkin (1983). More detailed references on earlier work can be found in Mishkin (1981b).

[2] See Blinder (1980).

monotonically with the maturity of the asset. This suggests that although short-term U.S. Treasury bills are, of all the assets we study, the best hedge against expected inflation, none of the assets are perfect hedges.[3] Our results also indicate that nominal interest rates are not a reliable indicator of the tightness of credit markets, since they are negatively correlated with ex ante real returns on all assets examined.

The use of a more accurate price index than the Consumer Price Index results in noticeably different estimates of ex ante real rates—rates that are generally higher and statistically significantly negative for far shorter periods of time. Our findings on the relationship of ex ante real interest rates with inflation and nominal interest rates are, however, robust to the choice of price index.

When we examine the behavior of financial markets since October 1979, we find a statistically significant change in the stochastic process of ex ante real returns on bonds. In contrast to the earlier period, after October 1979 nominal interest rates are *positively* correlated with ex ante real returns. However, this change in the stochastic process appears only for bonds and not for common stocks. Given the small amount of data since 1979, we clearly consider these results tentative; nonetheless they suggest topics for future research.

I. Methodology

Following Fisher (1930), at each time t the ex ante, or expected, real return earned from holding an asset for j periods can be decomposed into an expected nominal return and an expected inflation rate:

$$rr_{t,j} = i^e_{t,j} - \pi^e_{t,j}, \tag{1}$$

where $rr_{t,j}$ is the expectation at time t of the real return earned by holding an asset from time t to time $t + j$, $i^e_{t,j}$ is the expectation at time t of the nominal return earned by holding an asset from time t to time $t + j$, and $\pi^e_{t,j}$ is the expectation at time t of the inflation rate from time t to time $t + j$. Similarly, the ex post, or realized, real return can be decomposed into an ex post nominal return and ex post inflation rate:

$$eprr_{t,j} = i_{t,j} - \pi_{t,j}, \tag{2}$$

where $eprr_{t,j}$ is the realized real return earned by holding an asset from time t to time $t + j$, $i_{t,j}$ is the realized nominal return earned by holding an asset from time t to time $t + j$, and $\pi_{t,j}$ is the realized inflation rate from time t to time $t + j$. Given equations (1) and (2), the ex post real return can be expressed as

$$eprr_{t,j} = rr_{t,j} + \varepsilon 1_{t,j} - \varepsilon 2_{t,j}, \tag{3}$$

where $\varepsilon 1_{t,j} = i_{t,j} - i^e_{t,j}$ and $\varepsilon 2_{t,j} = \pi_{t,j} - \pi^e_{t,j}$. From equation (3) it is clear that ex ante and ex post real returns will diverge when either the nominal return on the asset or the inflation rate is uncertain. It is also clear that if the nominal interest

[3] The notion of a hedge against expected inflation was suggested in Fama and Schwert (1977). It is not a standard use of the term because the holder of the asset is not protected against an unanticipated event. Nevertheless, the meaning of hedge as used here should be clear.

rate and inflation surprises are observable, the ex ante real interest rate is observable. Much measurement of ex ante returns is based on equation (3), with survey data used to construct $\varepsilon 2_{t,j}$ and j-period default free bond that ensures $\varepsilon 1_{t,j} = 0$.

We use an alternative procedure to estimate ex ante real interest rates. The procedure does not require survey measures of inflation,[4] allows for estimation of the ex ante real return on all assets—not just j-period default-free bonds—and simultaneously allows us to measure the correlation of ex ante real rates with variables that are observable at time t. The critical assumption underlying the methodology is rationality of expectations; this assumption ensures that forecast errors are uncorrelated with past information. Specifically,

$$E(\varepsilon 1_{t,j} \mid \psi_t) = E(\varepsilon 2_{t,j} \mid \psi_t) = 0, \tag{4}$$

where ψ_t represents all the information available to agents in the economy at time t and $E(\mid \psi_t)$ is the mathematical expectations operator, conditional on ψ_t. While ψ_t is the information set used by economic agents to form their ex ante real returns, we assume that as econometricians we can observe only a subset of ψ_t, X_t. Since any estimate of ex ante real returns must be based solely on X_t, a logical choice is the best linear predictor of $rr_{t,j}$ given X_t, which we represent as

$$P(rr_{t,j} \mid X_t) = X_t\beta. \tag{5}$$

Note that when the ex ante real interest rate is constant, $\beta = 0$ for all regressors except a constant term.

Obviously $P(rr_{t,j} \mid X_t)$ cannot be used directly, because β is unknown, and so we use

$$\hat{rr}_{t,j} = X_t\hat{\beta}, \tag{6}$$

where $\hat{\beta}$ is an estimate of the unknown parameter β. To obtain $\hat{\beta}$, we estimate the equation

$$eprr_{t,j} = X_t\beta + \eta_{t,j}, \tag{7}$$

by ordinary least squares where $u_{t,j} = rr_{t,j} - P(rr_{t,j} \mid X_{t,j})$ and $\eta_{t,j} = u_{t,j} + \varepsilon 1_{t,j} - \varepsilon 2_{t,j}$. A separate equation is estimated for each of the seven assets we study.

There are several important econometric issues concerning this estimation strategy that need to discussed. Formal demonstration of the following points can be found in Mishkin (1981b, 1982, 1984) and Cumby, Huizinga and Obstfeld (1983).

1. Given the rationality of expectations, $\hat{\beta}$ will be a consistent estimate of β. That is, using ex post real rates will asymptotically yield the same estimate of β as a regression using ex ante real rates. Although we cannot observe the ex ante real rate, we can estimate it and can infer information about its relationship with other variables known at time t via ex post real rate regressions.

[4] As is indicated in Mishkin (1981a), survey data on expected inflation may not be a reliable guide to the bond market's rate of expected inflation.

2. We do lose information by using ex post real interest rates in the regression rather than ex ante rates. The presence of the forecast errors $\varepsilon_{t,j}$ and $\varepsilon2_{t,j}$ in equation (7) means that β will be estimated less precisely; that is, the standard errors of the estimated parameters will be larger. In addition, as the maturity of the asset lengthens we expect more volatility in the asset price, so the variance of the holding period return should increase, increasing the variance of $\varepsilon1_{t,j}$. We thus expect less precise estimates of β for common stocks and long-term bonds than for short-term bills.
3. The coefficient β, and hence its estimate $\hat{\beta}$, does not imply that X_t causes the ex ante real interest rate, only that X_t helps to predict it. Without further information, β should be interpreted only as measuring the correlation between X_t and ex ante real returns.
4. For the case $j > 1$ that we consider here, the data is overlapping; that is, the holding period is longer than the observation interval. In this case, estimated standard errors of the parameters reported by typical regression packages will generally be inconsistent. The problem stems from the fact that when $j > 1$, $\varepsilon1_{t-1,j}$ and $\varepsilon2_{t-1,j}$ are not in the information set ψ_t because they are not known until time $t + j - 1 > t$. Thus, in contrast to the nonoverlapping case of $j = 1$ where the rational expectations conditions of equation (4) imply that $\varepsilon1_{t,j}$ and $\varepsilon2_{t,j}$ are serially uncorrelated, $\varepsilon1_{t,j}$, $\varepsilon2_{t,j}$ and therefore $\eta_{t,j}$ are likely to be serially correlated. In this case, consistent estimates of the standard errors for $\hat{\beta}$ can be computed with methods outlined by Hansen (1982) or Cumby, Huizinga and Obstfeld (1983). The estimates used here are similar to those used by Hansen and Hodrick (1980) but are more general because they allow for conditional heteroscedasticity of the regression residuals. Tests of the null hypothesis that the residuals were conditionally homoscedastic indicated rejection in our sample.[5]
5. With respect to testing hypotheses such as the constancy of ex ante real returns, tests that are joint for all assets together will have increased power even though the equation for each asset is efficiently estimated in isolation. In doing a joint test, however, the correlation of the $\hat{\beta}$ estimates obtained from regression equations for different assets must not be ignored. One reason this correlation can be expected to be nonnegligible is that all regression errors contain the common element $\varepsilon2_{t,j}$, unexpected inflation.

II. Data

This paper analyzes monthly data from 1959 to 1981 on real returns over a three month holding period for the following seven securities: (1) three month U.S.

[5] Conditional heteroscedasticity in the error term is heteroscedasticity that can be explained by movements in the regressors. We test for this by regressing the squared residuals from our estimated equations on the squared regressors. Significant coefficients on any variable except the constant term is evidence of conditional heteroscedasticity. Space does not permit us to report the results of all these tests. However, for the regressions where the CPIX price index is used, the t-statistics on the squared values of inflation (in a regression of the squared residual on a constant and squared inflation) are TBILL3: 1.51, TBILL6: 1.17, TBILL12: 2.01, INTBOND: 2.56, LONGBOND: 2.23, CORPBOND: 3.36, and STOCK: 1.79. It should be noted that the method of correcting the estimated parameter standard errors used here does not require a parameterization of how the variance of the error is related to the regressors.

Treasury bills (TBILL3), (2) six month U.S. Treasury bills (TBILL6), (3) twelve month U.S. Treasury bills (TBILL12), (4) intermediate-term (5–10 years maturity) U.S. Treasury bonds (INTBOND) (5) long-term U.S. Treasury bonds (over 10 years maturity) (LONGBOND), (6) long-term corporate bonds (CORPBOND), (7) common stocks (STOCK). The nominal return data is obtained from the Center for Research in Security Prices (CRSP) at the University of Chicago. Because there are no U.S. Treasury bills with more than three months of maturity until 1959, the data for the six- and twelve-month bills cannot be collected before this date. In fact, twelve month bond data are not available until late 1963. The bonds chosen for the intermediate-term bond returns are an update (supplied to us by Lawrence Fisher) of the same securities used in Fisher and Lorie (1977). The bonds chosen for the long-term bond returns are an update (supplied by Roger Ibbotson) of those used in the Ibbotson and Sinquefeld (1976) long-term Treasury bond return index. The corporate bond data are derived from the Ibbotson-Sinquefeld corporate bond returns index and the CRSP NYSE value-weighted index, is used to calculate the stock returns.

The three month holding period has been chosen because a shorter holding period would increase timing problems created by the sampling methods used to construct the price indices. The problem is that the price components in the indices are sampled at different times over the course of the month. Thus it is not clear what is the appropriate dating for the price index. With monthly holding periods, the dating can easily be off by as much as half of the holding period. With three month holding periods, the dating can be off by only one-sixth.

Four price indices are used here to construct inflation and real interest rates. The first is the CPI, the price index most frequently used in empirical research on real rates. In January of 1983 the Bureau of Labor Statistics began calculating the official CPI using a new "rental equivalence" measure for the residential housing component. Our second price index, denoted CPIX, reconstructs the CPI from 1959 to 1981 using this new procedure.[6] This is likely to be the most accurate of our four price indices and its use should lead to the most reliable measures of inflation and real rates. The third price index is the Personal Consumption Expenditure Deflator, denoted PCED, which comes from the National Income and Product Accounts but is available monthly. The index, like the CPIX, does not suffer from the inappropriate treatment of housing found in the CPI, but it differs from the CPIX in being a variable weight index. The PCED is not without problems for our study; unlike other indices, it is available only in seasonally adjusted form and, more important, it uses more interpolation of prices than the other indices do. Finally, we use the Producer Price Index,

[6] The rental equivalence measure, first announced in October 1981, became the official residential housing component for the CPI for All Urban Consumers in January 1983. The CPI for Urban Wage Earners and Clerical Workers will continue to use the old home-ownership method until January 1985. A detailed description of the new rental equivalence measure can be found in the CPI Detailed Report, January 1983 issue. The CPIX should be a better index than the CPI less home mortgage interest costs, a series often used to minimize the mismeasurement of prices by the CPI, because this latter index still includes a large interest rate component via its inclusion of the purchase price for new homes. We thank Robert Dennis of the Congressional Budget Office for providing us with the CPIX data back to 1959.

Table 1

Relationship of Ex Ante Real Rates with Inflation and Nominal Interest Rates 1959:5 to 1979:10
Estimation of β in $eprr = \alpha + \beta X$

X	Inflation				Nominal Three Month Bill Rate			
Price Index[a]	CPI	CPIX	PCED	PPI	CPI	CPIX	PCED	PPI
ASSET								
TBILL3	−.349**	−.280**	−.242**	−.309**	−.562**	−.319**	−.206*	−1.015**
	(.047)	(.050)	(.060)	(.096)	(.101)	(.103)	(.097)	(.310)
TBILL6	−.354**	−.282**	−.240**	−.312**	−.556**	−.313**	−200	−1.009**
	(.062)	(.062)	(.082)	(.105)	(.118)	(.112)	(.113)	(.322)
TBILL12	−.433**	−.379**	−.338	−.312*	−.627*	−.343	−.216	−.977*
	(.145)	(.144)	(.190)	(.149)	(.273)	(.264)	(.274)	(.492)
INTBOND	−.746*	−.701	−.809	−.478	−1.432*	−1.189*	−1.077	−1.886*
	(.376)	(.390)	(.440)	(.264)	(.606)	(.597)	(.613)	(.732)
LONGBOND	−.777	−.648	−.774	−.374	−1.711*	−1.468	−1.355	−2.164*
	(.518)	(.538)	(.616)	(.350)	(.795)	(.787)	(.809)	(.912)
CORPBOND	−.971	−.878	−1.060	−.540	−2.153*	−1.910*	−1.797	−2.606*
	(.638)	(.677)	(.783)	(.430)	(.971)	(.962)	(.983)	(1.102)
STOCK	−1.793	−1.924	−2.095	−1.390*	−3.645	−3.402	−3.289	−4.098*
	(1.126)	(1.240)	(1.444)	(.552)	(1.878)	(1.883)	(1.900)	(2.008)
χ^2 value[b]	71.85	46.75	35.93	25.37	48.16	23.56	16.86	23.90
Marginal significance level	$<10^{-10}$	6×10^{-8}	7×10^{-6}	7×10^{-4}	3×10^{-8}	1×10^{-3}	2×10^{-2}	1×10^{-3}

Notes: Numbers in parentheses are estimated standard errors.
* denotes significantly different from zero at the 5% level.
** denotes significantly different from zero at the 1% level.
[a] price index used to construct *eprr* and, for the first four columns, the regressor X.
[b] distributed according to the χ^2 distribution with seven degrees of freedom under the null hypothesis that all coefficients in the column are zero.

denoted PPI. It does not include residential housing in any manner but has the drawback that it is constructed with list prices rather than transactions prices.

III. Empirical Results

A. *Results for the Pre-October 1979 Period*

The relationship of real rates with inflation and nominal interest rates for the 1959:5 to 1979:10 sample period is described in Table 1. The post 1979:10 period is dealt with later in the paper because, as we shall see, the stochastic process of real rates undergoes a major shift near the end of 1979. The inflation coefficients are generated from regressions where the X_t variables include a constant term and the inflation rate for the past three months. The nominal three-month bill coefficients are obtained from regressions where the X_t variables include a constant term and the nominal rate on three-month U.S. Treasury bills known at time t. The timing of both the inflation rate and the nominal bill rate clearly reflects that X_t must be a subset of ψ_t, the information set agents have available to form their ex ante real rates for period t.[7]

The inflation coefficients tell us that ex ante real rates on all seven assets are negatively correlated with inflation. Regardless of the price index used, all the inflation coefficients are negative, many of them significantly so.[8] An extremely interesting finding is that as maturity length increases, and the asset gets closer in its risk characteristics to capital, an increase in inflation is associated with an even larger decrease in the ex ante real return. For example, the CPIX results

[7] Our sample period starts in 1959:5 because the PCED price index is not available until 1959. The dating of the real returns follows the convention described in Section I, so that a time period 1959:5 to 1979:10 has the return from May 1, 1959 to July 31, 1959 as its first observation and the return from October 1, 1979 to December 31, 1979 as its last. The first observation for the inflation rate regressor is constructed using the January and April 1959 price indices. By using the April index to explain the real return from May to August, we are assuming that agents know the April price index on April 30. In fact, the April index will not be announced until sometime in May. However, replacing the January–April inflation rate with the December–March rate does not change our results appreciably. See Huberman and Schwert (1983) for evidence on this issue in the Israeli bond market. The nominal three-month bill rate used as a regressor for the first observation is the rate on April 30, 1959. There is no seasonal adjustment of any data, except for PCED which we could only get in seasonally adjusted form. We have constructed tests where all data except PCED are seasonally adjusted with Box-Jenkins (1976) seasonal models and the results are essentially the same.

[8] In computing the standard errors reported in Table 1, the error terms of the regressions are assumed to have nonzero autocorrelations at lags one and two. This is based on examination of the sample residuals. For example, when using CPIX, the first twelve autocorrelations of the residuals from a regression of the ex post real rate for TBILL3 on a constant and the inflation rate are .68, .35, −.03, −.07, −.08, −.02, −.01, .04, .12, .22, .25 and .25. The non-zero autocorrelations at lags one and two are exactly what one should expect given the quarterly real rates and monthly data. Since lagged real rates do not appear as regressors the u_t component of the error term, and hence the entire error term, can display autocorrelation at any lag without violating our assumptions of rational expectations. The rise in the autocorrelations near lag twelve can be interpreted as a mild seasonal fluctuation in the ex ante real rate that is not captured by the inflation rate. Sample residuals from other equations display essentially the same pattern of autocorrelations, though for the bonds and stock equations there is no evidence of a seasonal. This is not surprising since the larger variance of the forecast errors $\varepsilon 1_{t,j}$ and $\varepsilon 2_{t,j}$ in the equations for the longer maturity assets should make a seasonal harder to find.

indicate that a one-percentage-point increase in the inflation rate is associated with a 28-basis-point drop (a basis point is 1/100 of a percentage point) in the ex ante real rate on three month U.S. Treasury bills, a 65-basis-point decline in the ex ante real rate on long-term U.S. Treasury bonds, and a 192-basis-point decline in the ex ante real rate on common stocks.[9]

The χ^2 statistic at the bottom of each column tests the null hypothesis that all seven coefficients in the column equal zero.[10] This is a joint test of the constancy of ex ante real rates on all seven assets. The low values of the marginal significance levels indicate that the null hypothesis can always be rejected at the 1% level. As the asterisks indicate, constancy of ex ante real rates is rejected less frequently for the longer maturity assets. Despite their more negative coefficients, there is less statistical significance because the standard errors increase. As described earlier, this is exactly what we expect since the forecast error of the nominal return, $\varepsilon 1_{t,j}$, should become more variable with lengthening maturity. Both because of this and because of the consistent pattern of the coefficients, our view is that an appropriate interpretation of the Table 1 results is that ex ante real returns on intermediate term bonds, long-term bonds, and common stocks are negatively associated with inflation. The absence of statistical significance is a reflection of the low power of the tests.[11]

The nominal three month bill rate coefficients follow a pattern similar to that of the inflation coefficients. They are all negative, many are significantly so, and they increase as we go to the longer maturity assets. Again, constancy of the ex ante return for all seven assets is soundly rejected by the χ^2 values. Rejection is widely spread across the seven assets. The negative coefficients indicate that a nominal interest rate, such as that on three month U.S. Treasury bills, is a poor indicator of the tightness of credit markets. When we use the nominal yield to maturity for each asset as the explanatory variable in the regression for that asset, the findings are similar. During times of high nominal rates, credit market conditions are not tight; rather the contrary is true, with low ex ante real rates on all assets.[12]

For the sample period studied here, previous evidence has found that movements in the nominal three month bill rate primarily reflects movements in

[9] When the coefficients in Table 1 differ significantly from equation to equation, it is evidence of a risk premium in the returns. This issue is formally addressed in Huizinga and Mishkin (1983).

[10] The test statistic at the bottom of each column is distributed as a χ^2 random variable with seven degrees of freedom under the null hypothesis that all seven coefficients in the column are zero. Its marginal significance level is the probability, when the null hypothesis is true, of getting a test statistic as high as, or higher than, the one observed. Thus a marginal significance level smaller than .01 indicates rejection of the null hypothesis at the 1% level.

[11] When we test the null hypothesis that there is no relationship between inflation and the ex ante real return on the four long-term assets—i.e. jointly test that the coefficient of inflation is zero for the INTBOND, LONGBOND, CORPBOND, and STOCK equations—we get χ^2_4 values of 13.90 for CPI, 14.69 for CPIX, 11.68 for PCED, and 18.74 for PPI. This indicates rejection of the null hypothesis at the 1% level for CPI, CPIX, and PPI and rejection at the 5% level for PCED. Thus our tests do have some power to reject the hypothesis that inflation is uncorrelated with the ex ante real return for long-term assets.

[12] When we included both the yields to maturity and the three month bill rates as regressors, the coefficients for the yield variables generally were insignificantly different from zero.

expected inflation.[13] Since inflation is a highly positively autocorrelated series, the inflation rate over the past three months should also be highly positively correlated with the expected inflation rate. Thus the inflation and interest rate coefficients of Table 1 convey information about how ex ante real rates are correlated with expected inflation. They suggest that, while of all the assets we study three month U.S. Treasury bills are the best hedge against expected inflation, all assets are an imperfect hedge. Additional evidence supporting this proposition is presented in Huizinga and Mishkin (1983). Our results are in general agreement with those of Fama and Schwert (1977), who also find that as assets lengthen in maturity and become more like equity, they become worse inflation hedges. However Fama and Schwert's conclusion that U.S. Treasury bills and bonds of five-year maturity or less are reasonably good hedges against expected inflation is not supported here. The main reason for the difference is that our sample includes the high inflation sample period after 1971 while Fama and Schwert's does not. As has been documented in Nelson and Schwert (1977), Mishkin (1981b), and Fama and Gibbons (1982), the period before 1971 is one with little variation in ex ante real rates and inflation. This makes it difficult to detect a negative relationship between ex ante real rates and expected inflation. However, with the addition of the highly variable data after 1971, the negative association clearly emerges.

The conclusions described above are robust to the use of different price indices—a comforting finding. We should still be concerned, however, that the overstatement of inflation by the CPI in the 1970s may lead to misleadingly low estimates of ex ante real interest rates. To see how severe the bias is from using the CPI, we plot in Figure 1 the estimated ex ante real return for three month U.S. Treasury bills using both the CPI, the broken line, and CPIX, the solid line. We use the CPIX because we consider it to be the most reliable of our price indices. Although it is not reported here, the effect of choosing the CPIX instead of the CPI is similar for the other six assets. As described in Section II, the estimated ex ante real rates are the fitted values from regressions of the ex post real rates on information available at the beginning of the period. Our regressors were a constant term, the inflation rate over the past three months, the current nominal interest rate on three-month U.S. Treasury bills and a fourth order polynomial in time that proxies for economic variables left out of the specification.

The comparison of the two measures is quite illuminating. Both measures show that ex ante real interest rates were higher in the 1960s than in the 1970s. However, from 1964 onward, estimated real rates using CPIX are almost always above those using CPI, expecially so during 1968–71, 1973–75, and 1977–79. These are all periods of rising inflation and nominal interest rates, periods when the CPI is most likely to overstate inflation.

Although both estimated ex ante real returns turn negative in mid 1972, those based on CPIX are significantly negative only during the short period from late 1975 to 1977, while those using the CPI are continuously significantly negative from 1974 onward. This is easily seen because, as an approximation, only rates

[13] See Fama (1975), Mishkin (1981b), Fama and Gibbons (1982), and Huizinga and Mishkin (1983).

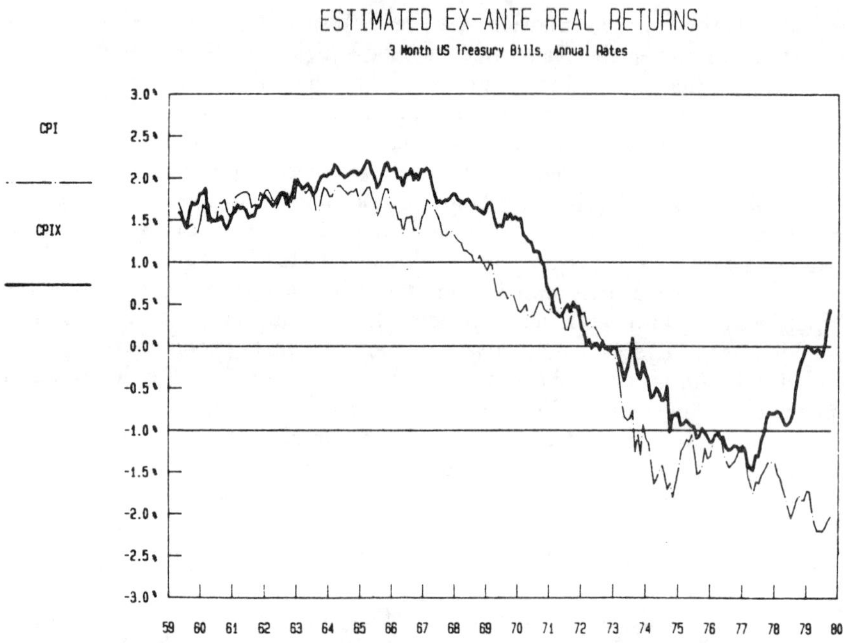

Figure 1. Estimated Ex Ante Real Returns, 3 Month U.S. Treasury Bills, Annual Rates

that lie outside the range ±1% are significantly different from zero at the 5% level of significance.[14] Previous findings of significantly negative ex ante real interest rates for long periods of time have apparently been spurious, a result of the CPI's mismeasurement of inflation.

B. *Stability of the Stochastic Process of Real Rates*

Casual observation of nominal interest rates and inflation makes it obvious that real rates have undergone a major shift in the 1980s. We look at this phenomenon with a standard test for the stability of the coefficients in the CPIX regressions of Table 1, testing for a stable relationship of ex ante real rates with inflation and with nominal rates. We use 1959:5 to 1979:10 as one time period and 1979:11 to 1981:10 as the other. The breakpoint was chosen to coincide with the shift in the Federal Reserve policy regime towards a monetary aggregates target and away from interest rate targets. The choice of this breakpoint is somewhat arbitrary and we are by no means sure that the shift in the stochastic process for real rates occurred at this time. We intend to pursue a statistically based approach to the dating of the breakpoint in future research. Nevertheless, the advent of the new Federal Reserve policy has seemed to coincide with major changes in the behavior of U.S. financial markets.

[14] The standard errors of the estimated real rates are calculated under the assumption that unexpected inflation is the major component of the error term. These standard errors do show some variation over time but do not differ greatly from .5%. The calculations used are described in Mishkin (1981a).

Table 2
Stability Tests and Coefficient Estimates for $eprr = \alpha + \beta X$ Using the CPIX Price Index

	PANEL A 1959:5 to 1979:10 vs. 1979:11 to 1981:10 Stability Test for β		PANEL B Estimates of β for 1979:11 to 1981:10	
X	Inflation	Nominal Bill Rate	Inflation	Nominal Bill Rate
ASSET				
TBILL3	0.67	40.91**	.014	1.160**
TBILL6	1.69	33.19*	.722	1.898**
TBILL12	3.43	23.08*	2.452	3.181**
INTBOND	5.97	13.13	7.649	5.926
LONGBOND	10.99	11.91	12.711	7.984
CORPBOND	10.72	12.37	12.217	7.166
STOCK	11.37	2.11	6.990	−6.810*

Notes: The stability tests of Panel A are standard Wald tests. Under the null hypothesis of coefficient stability, the statistics are asymptotically distributed as a χ^2 random variable with one degree of freedom. The α's were not constrained to be equal in the two periods.

A * in Panel A denotes rejection of the null hypothesis of coefficient stability at the 5% level of significance, ** represents rejection at the 1% level. In Panel B * denotes a coefficient which is significantly different from zero at the 5% level of significance and ** significantly different at the 1% level. Significance values were determined using the Monte Carlo simulation described in footnote 15.

Table 2 contains the χ^2 values for testing coefficient stability and the coefficients estimated for the 1979:11 to 1981:10 period. Because there are only twenty four highly autocorrelated observations for this latter period, a serious question arises as to whether using asymptotic distribution theory to test coefficient stability is appropriate. A set of Monte Carlo simulations[15] indicates that the small sample distribution of the test statistics is quite different from the asymptotic. For example, in the case of using CPIX in the nominal bill rate regression for TBILL3, the real probability of rejecting the null hypothesis of coefficient stability when it is true, using a 5% significance level and the asymptotically valid χ^2 distribution, is 26.1%. Using the asymptotic distribution can, therefore, lead to rejecting the null hypothesis far too often. For this reason, the significance levels calculated by the Monte Carlo simulation are used for both the tests of coefficient stability in Panel A and tests of coefficients equal to zero in Panel B.

The results of Panel A indicate that for the nominal bill rate regressions, the equality of coefficients in the pre- and post-October 1979 periods is strongly rejected for the short-term assets. However, there are no rejections for any assets

[15] To do the Monte Carlo simulations, the inflation rate, nominal interest rate on three month U.S. Treasury bills and residuals from each of the fourteen CPIX regressions reported in Table 1 were fit to a univariate time series process. Using the estimated time series representation, including the estimated correlation of the innovations in the series, two thousand replications of each of the fourteen regressions were run. A replication consisted of generating a new regressor, generating a new residual, generating a new dependent variable from the regressor, the residual and the coefficients reported in Table 1 and finally, estimating the equation.

with the inflation coefficients. Although we do not report them here, we also performed stability tests where the 1959:5 to 1979:10 period was split in half. These tests rarely reveal a rejection of coefficient stability; the shift in the stochastic process of real rates after 1979:10 is more noticeable than any shift we have detected before this date.

A deeper understanding of why stability of the nominal bill rate coefficients is rejected is provided by Panel B of Table 2. The coefficients for the latter period three month U.S. Treasury bills were negatively correlated, in the latter period an increase in the nominal rate reflects a one-for-one increase in the ex ante real rate. That is, the nominal bill rate coefficient in the TBILL3 regression is not statistically different from one using CPIX. Furthermore, with the exception of tell a very different story than those for the earlier one. After 1979:10 an increase in the nominal interest rate on three month U.S. Treasury bills is associated with a rise in the ex ante real return on all assets except common stock. In contrast to the pre 1979:10 period, when the nominal and ex ante real rates on stocks, the magnification effect found in the earlier period is still present; but it now indicates that high short-term nominal rates are associated with higher real rates on longer maturity assets relative to those on short-maturity assets. The inflation coefficients in Panel B also undergo a large shift from their pre-October 1979 levels. However, this shift is not statistically significant because, despite some large coefficients, the relationship between real rates and inflation is not statistically significant in the latter period.

Taken together, the combined results of Tables 1 and 2 can be characterized by the following relationship among ex ante real rates, expected inflation, and the nominal interest rate on three-month U.S. Treasury bills. In the pre-October 1979 period, the ex ante real return on all seven assets studied here is negatively related to expected inflation, and given the positive autocorrelation of inflation, negatively related to actual inflation. Further, although the ex real rate on three-month U.S. Treasury bills is not constant, their movement is sufficiently small, as is demonstrated by Fama and Gibbons (1982) and Huizinga and Mishkin (1983), so that nominal three month bill rate movements mainly reflect changes in expected inflation. This, when combined with the negative correlation between real rates and expected inflation, accounts for the negative correlation between the nominal bill rate and the seven ex ante real rates displayed in Table 1.

In the post-October 1979 period, movements in the ex ante real rates appear to have been highly variable and uncorrelated with expected inflation, thereby breaking the link between ex ante real rates and actual inflation. Because of the high variability in the ex ante real rate on three month U.S. Treasury bills, movements of their nominal rate no longer primarily reflect changes in expected inflation but rather movement of the real rate. The result for CPIX and TBILL3 presented in Panel B of Table 2 emphasizes this result, because it implies that in the post-October 1979 period a regression of inflation on a constant and the nominal three-month bill rate yields a coefficient on the bill rate of −.16. This is significantly different from one, the value we should get if the nominal rate is primarily reflecting expected inflation. The positive correlation of the nominal bill rate and the ex ante real rates on all assets except stock displayed in Panel B of Table 2 then means that the real rates on bills and bonds have been positively correlated in this latter period. The negative relationship between the nominal rate on three-month bills and the ex ante real return on common stock indicates a divergence of the real rate on stock from that on other assets. This result is certainly one that merits further investigation.

IV. Conclusions

This paper discusses a methodology for measuring ex ante real interest rates and assets with different risk characteristics and for examining their correlation with inflation and nominal interest rates. It is applied to the 1959–1981 time period for the following seven assets: (1) three-month U.S. Treasury bills, (2) six-month U.S. Treasury bills, (3) twelve-month U.S. Treasury bills, (4) intermediate-term (5–10 years maturity) U.S. Treasury bonds, (5) long-term (10–20 years maturity) U.S. Treasury bonds, (6) long-term corporate bonds, and (7) common stock. The importance of choosing a price index for constructing inflation and real rates is also examined. The major findings are as follows:

1. Pre-October 1979, the negative association between ex ante real rates on both inflation and nominal interest rates, which was previously found for short-term U.S. Treasury bills, appears for all the assets in this study. Indeed, the negative association is even larger for the longer-maturity assets. This suggests that all seven assets have been poor hedges against expected inflation, and that the longer-maturity assets have been the worst hedges.
2. The results described above are robust with respect to the use of price indices other than the Consumer Price Index (CPI). The puzzling finding of previous research that ex ante real returns on short-term U.S. Treasury securities were persistently significantly negative in the 1970s, however, appears spurious and due to the CPI's mismeasurement of inflation. A more reliable estimate of ex ante real returns, one that uses a more accurate price index, finds statistically significant ex ante real rates for far shorter periods of time.
3. A statistically significant shift in the stochastic process of real rates does occur sometime around the October 1979 change in the Federal Reserve's policy regime. In contrast to the pre-October 1979 period where ex ante real rates and nominal rates are negatively correlated, the post-October 1979 period has real and nominal rates moving together. In particular, movements in the nominal interest rate on three-month U.S. Treasury bills no longer primarily indicate changes in expected inflation, but rather the movement of the ex ante real return. There also seems to be a change in the relationship between the ex ante real returns on stock and the ex ante real return on bills and bonds near the end of 1979.

REFERENCES

Barro, R. J. (1981), Intertemporal Substitution and the Business Cycle, Supply Shocks, Incentives and National Wealth, *The Carnegie-Rochester Conference Series on Public Policy* 14: 237–268.

Blinder, A. (1980), The Consumer Price Index and the Measurement of Recent Inflation, *Brookings Papers on Economics Activity* 2, 539–566.

Box, G. E. P. and G. M. Jenkins (1976), *Time Series Analysis: Forecasting and Control*, Holden Day, San Francisco.

Cumby, R., J. Huizinga and M. Obstfeld (1983), Two-Step, Two-Stage Least Squares Estimation in Models with Rational Expectations, *Journal of Econometrics* 21: 333–355.

Fama, E. F. (1975), Short-Term Interest Rates as Predictors of Inflation, *American Economic Review* 65: 269–82.

——— and M. R. Gibbons (1982), Inflation, Real Returns and Capital Investment, *Journal of Monetary Economics* 9(3): 297–324.

——— and G. W. Schwert (1977), Asset Returns and Inflation, *Journal of Financial Economics* 5(2): 115–146.

Fisher, I. (1930), *The Theory of Interest*, New York: Macmillan.

Fisher, L. and Lorie, J. H. (1977), *A Half Century of Returns on Stocks and Bonds: Rates of Return on Investment in Common Stock and U.S. Treasury Securities, 1926–1976*, University of Chicago, Graduate School of Business.

Hansen, L. P. (1982), Large Sample Properties of Generalized Method of Moments Estimators, *Econometrica* 50(4): 1029–1054.

——— and R. J. Hodrick (1980), Forward Exchange Rates as Optimal Predictors of Future Spot Rates: An Econometric Analysis, *Journal of Political Economy* 88: 829–853.

Huberman, G. and G. W. Schwert (1983), Information Aggregation, Inflation and the Pricing of Indexed Bonds, CRSP Working Paper #105.

Huizinga, J. and F. S. Mishkin (1983), The Measurement of Short-Term Real Interest Rates on Assets with Different Risk Characteristics, CRSP Working Paper #95.

Ibbotson, R. G. and Sinquefeld, R. A. (1976), Stocks, Bonds, Bills and Inflation: Year by Year Historical Returns (1926–1974), *Journal of Business* 42(1): 11–47.

Litterman, R. and L. Weiss (1982), Money, Real Interest Rates, and Output: A Reinterpretation of Postwar U.S. Data, NBER Working Paper #1077.

Mishkin, F. S. (1981a), Are Market Forecast Rational? *American Economic Review* 71(3): 295–306.

——— (1981b), The Real Rate of Interest: An Empirical Investigation, *The Cost and Consequences of Inflation, Carnegie-Rochester Conference Series on Public Policy* 15: 151–200.

——— (1982), Are Real Interest Rates Equal Across Countries? An Empirical Investigation of International Parity Conditions, NBER Working Paper #1048 (December).

——— (1984), The Real Interest Rate: A Multi-Country Empirical Study. Forthcoming in *The Canadian Journal of Economics.*

Nelson, C. R. and G. W. Schwert (1977), Short-Term Interest Rates as Predictors of Inflation: On Testing the Hypothesis that the Real Rate of Interest is Constant, *American Economic Review* 67(3): 478–86.

Summers, L. H. (1982), The Non-Adjustment of Nominal Interest Rates: A Study of the Fisher Effect, NBER Working Paper #836.

[5]

The real interest rate: a multi-country empirical study

FREDERIC S. MISHKIN / Columbia University and National Bureau of Economic Research

Abstract. How real interest rates behave over time is critical to our understanding of many macro-economic issues, and much recent research has pursued this question. Very little of the research, however, has focused on real interest rates outside the United States. This paper is an empirical exploration of real interest rate movements in seven OECD countries from 1967–II to 1979–II. Further research is needed on real rates in other countries for several reasons. Not only are measures of foreign real rates of interest in their own right, but extending an analysis of real rates to other countries also has the following benefits: it can generate more powerful statistical tests of propositions previously tested on U.S. data and yield information on whether results found for the United States hold up in other countries.

This study pursues several questions that have arisen naturally from this earlier work. Is the hypothesis that the real rate is constant rejected when the analysis is extended to other countries? Does the real rate decline with increased inflation and money growth in other countries besides the United States? How reliable is the Fisher effect, in which nominal interest rates reflect changes in expected inflation? Are movements in nominal interest rates a reliable indicator of movements in real rates? What kind of variations in real interest rates are there in different countries? Have real rates declined from the 1960s to the 1970s for other countries besides the United States?

Le taux d'intérêt réel: une analyse empirique de plusieurs pays. Pour comprendre plusieurs problèmes macroéconomiques importants, il faut comprendre comment se comportent les taux d'intérêt réels dans le temps. On a fait beaucoup de recherche sur cette question récemment mais peu de travaux ont porté sur les taux d'intérêt réels en dehors des Etats-Unis. Ce mémoire examine les mouvements du taux d'intérêt réel dans sept pays de l'OCDE de 1967(II) à 1979(II). On a besoin de recherches additionnelles non seulement parce qu'une meilleure connaissance du comportement des taux d'intérêt réels dans ces autres pays est intéressante en

I thank for their helpful comments: Andrew Abel, Russel Boyer, Reuven and Gabrielle Brenner, Ed Burmeister, Benjamin Eden, Robert Gordon, Craig Hakkio, Robert Hall, John Huizinga, Jan Kmenta, Bennet McCallum, Donald McCloskey, Marjorie McElroy, Michael Mussa, Christopher Sims, and the participants in the NBER Summer Institute for Economic Fluctuations and the International and Finance Workshops at the University of Chicago, and workshops at the University of California, Los Angeles, University of Maryland, University of Iowa, University of Liverpool Seminar in Open Economy Macroeconomics, University of Michigan, Université de Montréal, University of Western Ontario, Virginia Polytechnic Institute, Northwestern University, and the Kansas City Federal Reserve Bank. This research is part of the National Bureau of Economic Research's Program in Economic Fluctuations. The National Science Foundation and The Sloan Foundation have provided research support. The usual disclaimer applies.

Canadian Journal of Economics / Revue canadienne d'Economique XVII, No. 2
May / mai 1984. Printed in Canada / Imprimé au Canada

0008-4085 / 84 / 283–311 $01.50

soi, mais aussi parce que ces études vont permettre de vérifier d'une manière encore plus robuste certaines propositions vérifiées à partir de données américaines afin d'établir si ces propositions tiennent aussi pour ces autres pays.

Est-ce que l'hypothèse que le taux d'intérêt réel est constant est rejetée quand on l'applique à d'autres pays que les Etats-Unis? Est-ce que le taux réel chute quand l'inflation et la croissance monétaire prennent leur essor comme c'est le cas aux Etats-Unis? Est-ce que l'effet de Fisher est une base robuste de prévision? (i.e. est-ce que les taux d'intérêt nominaux reflètent les changements dans le taux d'inflation anticipée?) Est-ce que les mouvements dans les taux d'intérêt nominaux sont un indicateur fiable des mouvements dans les taux d'intérêt réels? Quelles familles de variations dans le taux d'intérêt réel a-t-on observées dans les divers pays? Est-ce que les taux d'intérêt réels ont chuté des années 1960 aux années 1970 ailleurs qu'aux Etats-Unis?

INTRODUCTION

How real interest rates – to be more precise, ex ante real interest rates – move over time is critical to our understanding of many issues in monetary economics. Movements in the real rate are a central element in models of the business cycle[1] and contain valuable information for the design of appropriate stabilization policies.[2] Current investigations indicate that real interest rates may play an important role in the savings-consumption decision and hence on the formation of the capital stock and productivity. (See Boskin, 1978; Howrey and Hymans, 1978; Summers, 1978; and Feldstein, 1980a, b.) Open economy macro-economics and modern theories of exchange rate determination also focus on real rate movements. (See Dornbusch, 1976; Frenkel, 1979; and Mussa, 1982.)

It is not surprising, given the importance of real interest rates, that much recent research analyses how they have moved over time.[3] Very little of this research, however, has focused on real rates outside the United States.[4] More research on real interest rates in other countries is needed, because analysing foreign real rates can enhance our understanding of open economies. Extending an analysis to other countries can, in addition, provide information about the robustness of results previously found for the United States and can yield more powerful statistical tests.

This paper is an empirical exploration of short-term real interest rates in the euro market for seven OECD countries (the United States, Canada, the United Kingdom, France, Germany, the Netherlands, and Switzerland) from 1967–II to 1979–II. It pursues several questions that have arisen naturally from earlier work.

Recent U.S. data now reject the hypothesis associated with Fama (1975) that the real interest rate is constant. (See Mishkin, 1981 and Fama and Gibbons, 1982.) Is

1 Not only is this true for traditional IS-LM approaches described in current macro-economics text-books, but it is also true in equilibrium models focusing on intertemporal substitution, such as Lucas and Rapping (1969), Lucas (1975), Barro (1980), and Grossman and Weiss (1982).

2 For example, policy discussions have recently focused on whether the Fed should target on real interest rates. See Hester (1981) and Goldfeld's discussion (Goldfeld and Quandt, 1965).

3 For example, Aliber (1980), Cargill (1976), Carlson (1977), Fama (1975, 1976), Fama and Gibbons (1982), Fama and Schwert (1979), Garbade and Wachtel (1978), Gibson (1972), Hess and Bicksler (1975), Hodrick (1980), Joines (1977), Lahiri (1976), Mishkin (1981), Nelson and Schwert (1977), Pearce (1979), Roll (1979), Schiller (1980), and Summers (1982).

4 Aliber (1980), Cumby and Obstfeld (1982), Hodrick (1980), and Roll (1979) are exceptions, but they pursue a more limited set of issues than is analysed here and in a companion piece Mishkin (1982b).

this hypothesis rejected when the analysis is extended to other countries? The evidence produced here strongly confirms the U.S. finding: the constancy of the real rate in these seven OECD countries is jointly rejected at extremely low marginal significance levels. As had been found previously for the United States, real rates in these countries are higher in the 1960s than in the 1970s, declining with higher domestic inflation and money growth.

In the United States, short-term bonds have been a poor hedge against inflation, even in an ex ante sense; that is, their real interest rates have been significantly, negatively correlated with expected inflation.[5] Is this also true for other countries? The empirical evidence seems to indicate that the answer is yes. The real interest rates for all the countries studied here are negatively correlated with expected inflation.

The bulk of the movement in short-term, nominal interest rates in the post-war United States reflects changes in expected inflation. The presence of this so-called Fisher effect, in which higher nominal interest rates are associated with higher expected inflation, will usually result in nominal interest rates' being an unreliable indicator of real rate movements and hence of the tightness of financial market conditions. As is documented in Mishkin (1981), nominal rate movements in the United States are not highly correlated with those of real rates. A fascinating finding of the present study is that the Fisher effect does not generalize to all countries. Although the evidence here supports the existence of a strong Fisher effect and a weak association of nominal rates with real rates for Canada, the United Kingdom, and the United States, the Fisher effect is weak for France, Germany, the Netherlands, and Switzerland. Not only do these four countries exhibit a close association between nominal and real rate movements, but the hypothesis that movements in the nominal rate reflect a one-for-one movement in the real rate cannot be rejected. Thus, in these countries, unlike the United States, nominal interest rates have revealed accurate information about financial market conditions.

Before proceeding to the empirical evidence summarized above, we turn to the statistical methodology of this study, outlined in the next section.

METHODOLOGY

Each country's real rate of interest for a one-period bond is defined from the Fisher (1930) equation,[6]

$$i_t \equiv rr_t + \pi_t^e, \tag{1}$$

5 For example, again see Mishkin (1981), Fama and Gibbons (1982), and Summers (1982). Fama and Schwert (1979) did not find this result, because the 1953–71 sample period of their study did not have enough variation to allow them to unearth this finding. See Mishkin (1981) for a discussion of this point.

6 All returns, inflation and interest rates in the empirical work are assumed to be continuously compounded so that the usual additional second-order term is not necessary in the Fisher equation (1). Note that if holding period real returns rather than continuously compounded returns are used in the empirical work here, there is almost no change in the results. Note also that the definition ignores the taxation of nominal interest rates. As pointed out in Mishkin (1981), it is extremely difficult to know what the appropriate marginal tax rate is for holders of these one-period bonds, and this is even more true for the euro market. However, to the extent that the effective marginal tax rate is above zero, it will just strengthen some of the results found here, such as the negative correlation of real rates and inflation.

where

i_t = the nominal interest rate earned on a one-period bond maturing at time t, that is, the nominal return from holding the one-period bond from $t-1$ to t,
π_t^e = the rate of inflation from $t-1$ to t, expected at time $t-1$; and
rr_t = the one-period real rate of interest expected for the bond maturing at time t.

Hence, the real interest rate, rr_t, is just the difference between the nominal rate of interest and the expected rate of inflation; it is the real return from holding the one-period bond from $t-1$ to *t that is expected at time* $t-1$. Because the real rate is a return expected at the beginning of the period, it is also frequently referred to as the ex ante real rate. The more precise terminology is used to differentiate it from the ex post real rate, namely, the *actual* real return from holding the one-period bond from $t-1$ to t. It equals the nominal interest rate minus the *actual* inflation rate from $t-1$ to t and can be written as

$$eprr_t \equiv i_t - \pi_t \equiv rr_t - (\pi_t - \pi_t^e) \equiv rr_t - \epsilon_t, \tag{2}$$

where $eprr_t$ = the one-period ex post real rate for the bond maturing at time t; π_t = the actual inflation rate from $t-1$ to t; and $\epsilon_t = \pi_t - \pi_t^e$ = the forecast error for inflation. Note that for expositional convenience the ex ante real rate is always referred to as the real rate throughout this paper, while the ex post real rate always refers to the variable defined in (2).

The assumption underlying the methodology used here is rationality of inflation expectations in the bond market, which yields the condition[7]

$$\pi_t^e = E(\pi_t|\phi_{t-1}) \tag{3}$$

and hence

$$E(\epsilon_t|\phi_{t-1}) = 0, \tag{4}$$

where ϕ_{t-1} = all available information at time $t-1$. Note that the rationality of inflation expectations is necessary and sufficient for the rationality of the ex ante real rate, implying that the ex ante real rate equals the expected real return on the one-period bond, conditional on available information; that is,

$$rr_t = E(eprr_t|\phi_{t-1}) \tag{5}$$

A large body of evidence supports this rationality, or equivalently the efficiency of financial markets, and tests directed more specifically at the rationality of inflation forecasts in the bond market also support the use of this assumption over long sample periods such as those used here. (See Mishkin, 1983.)

If the real rate determined at $t-1$, rr_t, is correlated with observable variables, X_{t-1}, which are elements of the available information set ϕ_{t-1}, then we can write the optimal linear prediction of rr_t given X_{t-1} as the linear projection of rr_t into X_{t-1}:

$$P(rr_t|X_{t-1}) = X_{t-1}\beta \tag{6}$$

7 An alternative methodology would involve using survey data to measure inflationary expectations in order to construct real rates. Mishkin (1981) discusses why the methodology used here should be more reliable.

and then

$$rr_t = X_{t-1}\beta + u_t, \tag{7}$$

where by definition,

$$u_t = rr_t - P(rr_t | X_{t-1}).$$

Note that $P(u_t | X_{t-1}) = 0$ by the law of iterated projections,[8] and so u_t is orthogonal to X_{t-1}. Furthermore, u_t is also in the information set ϕ_{t-1}, because economic agents observe the ex ante real rate even if the econometrician cannot. Equation (6) cannot be estimated, because rr_t is not observable. However, substituting (7) into (2), we get

$$eprr_t = X_{t-1}\beta + u_t - e_t. \tag{8}$$

Because data on the ex post real rate are observable, the equation above can be estimated for each country with ordinary least squares (OLS). The resulting estimates of β, $\hat{\beta}_{\mathrm{OLS}}$ can then be used to construct estimates of the ex ante real rate, $\hat{rr}_t$, and expected inflation, $\hat{\pi}_t^e$, as follows:

$$\hat{rr}_t = X_{t-1}\hat{\beta}_{\mathrm{OLS}} \tag{9}$$

and

$$\hat{\pi}_t^e = i_t - \hat{rr}_t = i_t - X_{t-1}\hat{\beta}_{\mathrm{OLS}}. \tag{10}$$

Several econometric issues need to be emphasized in order for the following empirical results to be comprehensible; formal demonstrations of the points discussed below can be found in Mishkin (1981) and in the appendix to this paper.

1. Because u_t is by definition orthogonal to X_{t-1}, as is ϵ_t by the assumption of rational expectations, the resulting $\hat{\beta}_{\mathrm{OLS}}$ estimate is a consistent estimate of the projection equation β in (7). That is, using ex post real rates will asymptotically yield the same estimates of β as a regression using ex ante real rates. Thus, we can make inferences about the relationship of the ex ante real rate with variables known at time $t - 1$ via ex post real rate regressions, even though the ex ante real rate is unobservable.
2. However, we do lose information by using ex post real rates in a regression, rather than ex ante real rates. The appearance of the error term ϵ_t in the regression equation (8) means that $\hat{\beta}_{\mathrm{OLS}}$ will have higher standard errors and will be measured less precisely.
3. The projection coefficient β and its consistent estimate $\hat{\beta}_{\mathrm{OLS}}$ do not imply causation from X_{t-1} to the real rate, because (a) the X_{t-1} variables are not necessarily exogenous and (b) information relevant to real rates that is correlated with X_{t-1} may have been excluded from the explanatory variables of the regression equation. Without further identifying information, the $\hat{\beta}_{\mathrm{OLS}}$ can be interpreted only as reflecting the correlation of ex ante real rates with the X_{t-1} variables.
4. One advantage of using data from several countries is that we can conduct joint tests for several countries at once. The result can be more powerful statistical tests

8 See Sargent (1981) for an excellent exposition of linear projection and the law of iterated projections.

of propositions such as the constancy of real rates, because we can exploit more data. One pitfall is that these joint tests cannot be conducted by estimating each country's OLS constrained and unconstrained regressions separately, adding up their sum of squares, and then carrying out the usual comparison to construct the F-test.[9] The covariance of the $\hat{\beta}_{OLS}$, estimates across the regression equations for different countries must not be ignored when the test statistics are generated, if they are to be reliable.[10]

5. In order to yield correct standard errors of $\hat{\beta}_{OLS}$, the regression residuals must satisfy the conditions for the Gauss-Markov Theorem. Tests of the residuals do not reveal heteroscedasticity or serial correlation, and so these Gauss-Markov conditions are satisfied.[11]
6. The absence of serial correlation of the residuals is no accident. An important element of the methodology in this paper is the use of non-overlapping data – that is, when the forecast horizon is never longer than the observation interval.[12] With non-overlapping data, rational expectations implies that ϵ_t is serially uncorrelated. If the variance of u_t is much smaller than the variance of ϵ_t, then even if u_t is serially correlated or is correlated with past ϵ_t, the amount of serial correlation in the composite error term $u_t - \epsilon_t$ will necessarily be small. Because there is no reason to suspect that u_t should be serially uncorrelated if we do not include lagged

9 This is equivalent to generating the test statistics using a standard seemingly unrelated regression package where the variance-covariance matrix of the residuals is specified to be diagonal.

10 Since we must allow for covariance of the residuals and the parameter estimates in order to generate correct F-statistics, why are the models estimated here with OLS rather than with a GLS seemingly unrelated regressions technique? Using OLS was, in fact, far more costly in time and effort than GLS, because standard econometric packages (such as SAS or TSP) are not easily set up to calculate the F-statistic decribed in the appendix. There are two main reasons that OLS is preferred. First, one sensible view of results from ex post real rate regressions is that they are nothing more than useful summary statistics when OLS is used. The OLS results are easy to interpret in terms of the comprehensible concept of correlation. If the regressions are not viewed as reduced forms, however, then GLS results have no interpretation. Second, when GLS is used in estimation, the parameter estimates from ex post regressions no longer have the desirable property that they are equal in the expectation (or in the probability limit) to those obtained from ex ante real rate regressions. It is easy to demonstrate that they will be equal only if the variance-covariance matrix of ϵ is proportional to the variance-covariance matrix of u. The use of OLS rather than GLS does not appreciably affect the results in this paper. The GLS standard errors are slightly smaller and test statistics slightly higher, as we might expect, while the parameter estimates are quite close to those reported in the text.

11 For example, in the regressions used to generate the estimated real rates in figures 1 through 7, the residual autocorrelations do not display any evidence of serial correlation. The Durbin-Watson statistics range from 1.74 to 2.36, and none of them indicates the presence of first-order serial correlations. None of the Ljung and Box (1978) $Q(12)$ statistics rejects the null hypothesis that the first twelve residual autocorrelations all equal zero: the $Q(12)$ statistics range from 5.23 to 17.88, while the critical value at the 5 per cent level is 21.0. In regressions with fewer explanatory variables there are a few cases where Durbin-Watson statistics sometimes fall below 1.6, but never below 1.0. However, such cases are unusual. Goldfeld and Quandt (1965) tests also did not indicate that the homoscedasticity assumption is strongly violated. For example in the regressions used to generate figures 1 through 7 there was only one rejection of homoscedasticity in the seven CPI regressions and one in the seven WPI regressions. These rejections were not, however, for the same country and there was no consistent pattern of the variance of the residuals having a similar upward or downward trend in all the countries.

12 See Huizinga and Mishkin (1983) for an example of how the empirical analysis can be conducted when the data are overlapping.

dependent variables in X_{t-1}, the finding in the empirical work here – that the residuals do not display serial correlation – provides some indication that the size of the u_t error term is probably not very large.

7. The $\hat{rr}_t$ and $\hat{\pi}_t^e$ estimates will be good estimates of real rates and expected inflation only if the variance of the u_t error terms are small. This will be the case if no relevant information is excluded from the regressions or if the relevant information left out is highly correlated with X_{t-1}. As should be clear from the preceding paragraph, one piece of supporting evidence for the value of the $\hat{rr}_t$ and $\hat{\pi}_t^e$ estimates provided in this paper is the absence of serial correlation in the regression residuals.
8. Bounds for the standard errors of the measurement error for $\hat{rr}_t$ (which will be equal to that for $\hat{\pi}_t^e$) can be derived from the two extreme cases where var $(\epsilon_t) \gg$ var (u_t) and var $(u_t) \gg$ var (ϵ_t). These can then be used to construct bounds on the confidence intervals for the true real rate. The standard error bound when var (ϵ_t) $\gg$ var (u_t) is likely to be closer to the true standard error of $\hat{rr}_t$, because the regression results do not reveal serial correlation of the composite error term $u_t - \epsilon_t$, and because, as Nelson and Schwert (1977) point out, the variance of the forecast error of inflation, ϵ_t, is likely to be very large. Note that even in the unlikely case where var $(u_t) \gg$ var (ϵ_t) and thus the $\hat{rr}_t$ estimate is not a good estimate of the real rate, the confidence interval constructed assuming var $(u_t) \gg$ var (ϵ_t) yields appropriate inference about the location of the real rate.[13] Both confidence intervals are reported in the figures that follow so that someone with a different prior than the author's can see how this might affect inference.

EMPIRICAL RESULTS

The data

Obviously, there is no unique real interest rate. The magnitude of a real rate depends not only on the risk characteristics of the security being studied, but also on the price index used to calculate real returns. What the appropriate price index is depends on what economic decision is being analysed. If we are interested, for example, in the savings consumption decision, a price index based on a commodity bundle of consumption goods, such as the CPI, is appropriate. If, on the other hand, we are interested in decisions to trade among countries, then a price index with tradable goods a larger proportion of its commodity bundle, such as the WPI, is more appropriate.

This study analyses real interest rates in the euro deposit market in the 1967–II to 1979–II period for the following OECD countries: the United States, Canada, the United Kingdom, France, West Germany, the Netherlands, and Switzerland. Quarterly data on three-month euro rates obtained from the Harris Bank tape are used

13 This result requires that u as well as ϵ be serially uncorrelated, which can be achieved by including lags of the ex post real rate in X_{t-1}. It is not necessary to do this in the models used to derive $\hat{rr}_t$ in figures 1 through 7, because they do not display any serial correlation in the residuals (see fn. 11) and four lagged values of the ex post real rate do not add significant explanatory power to these models.

in this study for several reasons.[14] High quality data for domestic, short-term interest rates are not as readily available for other countries as for the United States and Canada. Unlike the United States and Canada, other countries' Treasury bill rates are not market clearing, so that these data, although available, do not reflect the true cost of credit. Euro rates, however, are market clearing. In addition, euro deposits denominated in different countries' currencies are issued by banks that have similar default risks,[15] and they are not subject to capital controls, because they are offshore securities. Hence a comparison of real euro rates across countries will not have to be adjusted for differing default risks or non-comparability because of capital market controls. Quarterly data on three-month rates have the advantage that the data are non-overlapping and timing problems that would arise with monthly data are avoided. (See Mishkin, 1981.) The dating convention is as follows. The ex post real rate for a quarter is the actual real return on a three-month euro deposit held from the beginning to the end of that quarter, continuously compounded. The ex post real rate for each country is constructed by substracting the continuously compounded inflation rate for that country from the continuously compounded nominal return on the euro deposit denominated in that country's currency.[16]

Both the CPI and WPI have been used in the empirical analysis to calculate inflation rates for the reasons discussed above. However, because the WPI results are usually quite similar to those found using the CPI, to conserve space only the CPI results are reported in the tables in this paper. The WPI results are discussed only when they exhibit an interesting difference from the CPI results. The interested reader can find the WPI results in a longer version of this paper (Mishkin, 1982a). The money growth and inflation variables are calculated as the change in the log of the money stock or price level, from the last month of the previous quarter to the current quarter, and are at quarterly rates. The euro rate and U.S. Treasury bill data were obtained from the

14 Only seven of the ten countries' data available in the tape are used here, because three of the countries – Italy, Belgium, and Japan – either had a high proportion of the data missing or did not satisfy interest parity because of two-tiered exchange rates. In the few cases where euro rate data were missing for the seven countries the euro rate was calculated from the interest parity condition. The rest of the data were checked by verifying that there were no large deviations from interest parity. Several obvious errors in the tape were found in this manner and were corrected.

15 The euro deposit rates are collected from quotes by the Harris bank in the case of euro dollars and by other banks that specialize in issuing euro deposits in other currencies. The fact that interest parity conditions hold fairly tightly in the data here indicates that the risk premiums are very similar for the different banks quoting the euro deposit rates.

16 These real rates seem to be the most natural to study, but matching up the country's price index with the euro deposit rate denominated in its currency is somewhat arbitrary. Clearly a Frenchman might also be interested in his real return from holding a U.S.-dollar-denominated euro deposit, even though the price index relevant to him is, say, the French CPI. If uncovered interest parity holds, which will be the case when the forward exchange rate is an unbiased forecast of the spot exchange rate, since interest parity in euro rates is a pure arbitrage condition, then the real euro rate for a Frenchman will be the same, regardless of the denomination of the euro deposit. In this case only the real euro rates analysed in the present paper need to be studied. However, recent evidence does not support the unbiasedness of the forward rate prediction or uncovered interest parity (e.g., see Cumby and Obstfeld, 1981, 1982; Hansen and Hodrick, 1980; and Mishkin, 1982b). Thus it is potentially worth studying real rates where the currency denomination of the euro rate is not matched up to the price index for that country. This is not done here because it would make this already long paper unwieldly.

Harris Bank tape maintained at the University of Chicago; the CPI, WPI, and money stock data were obtained from the International Financial Statistics (IFS) tape maintained by the International Monetary Fund.

The measures of ex ante real rates

Figures 1 through 7 contain measures of real rates generated from regressions for each country, where the X_{t-1} variables include four lags of the domestic inflation rate, one lag of domestic money growth ($M1$), the nominal euro rate and a fourth order polynomial in time.[17] These are featured in the empirical analysis here for several reasons. Recent research (see fn. 5) is interested in the relation of real rates to inflation and nominal interest rates, because these variables are usually correlated with expected inflation. Their coefficient estimates thus provide information about whether real rates are constant and whether assets are good inflation hedges. In addition, the coefficients on the nominal euro rates indicate whether movements in nominal interest rates reflect movements in real rates. The relation of real rates and money growth is also of interest, since a link might be expected from standard monetary theory. The fourth-order polynomial in time is included in the specification of the real rate regression, because it has significant additional explanatory power[18] and it potentially proxies for economic variables left out of the specification (see the appendix), of which one important possibility is world-wide economic factors that are related to the real rate movements in all the countries.

The solid line in the figures displays the estimated ex ante real rates. The dotted lines show the 95 per cent confidence interval for the location of the true real rate under the assumption that var $(\epsilon_t) \gg$ var (u_t). The dashed lines show the 95 per cent confidence interval for the case where var $(u_t) \gg$ var (ϵ_t). Here, the discussion of inference will focus on the dotted-lines confidence interval, because, as argued in the previous section, it is likely to be closer to the true confidence interval.

The U.S. results in figure 1 are qualitatively similar to those found with Treasury bill data in Mishkin (1981). In the period of the 1960s the real euro dollar rate is positive, frequently significantly so. In the 1970s the real rate has fallen and fluctuates around zero. However, significantly negative real rates for U.S. Treasury bills in the 1970s rarely appear in the euro market. This result illustrates the important point that real rates for securities with different risk characteristics need not move together. The U.S. Treasury bill is a riskless asset in nominal terms, whereas the euro deposit bears risk. Since the risk premium for the three-month euro dollar rate, plotted in figure 8, averages 2 per cent over the Treasury bill rate in this period, its estimated real rate is now less frequently below zero.

17 Even though all variables in the empirical work are calculated as quarterly rates, the figures report the real rates as annual rates.

18 The F-statistic that jointly tests the null hypothesis that the coefficients on the time variables are zero in the regressions for all seven countries is $F(28,266) = 3.05$ with a marginal significance level of 1.57×10^{-6}. Note that previous research (Mishkin, 1981) did not reveal significant explanatory power from real variables such as unemployment and industrial production growth, which is why they are not included in this analysis. Clearly some real variables might influence real rates and the time variables might proxy to some extent for their effect.

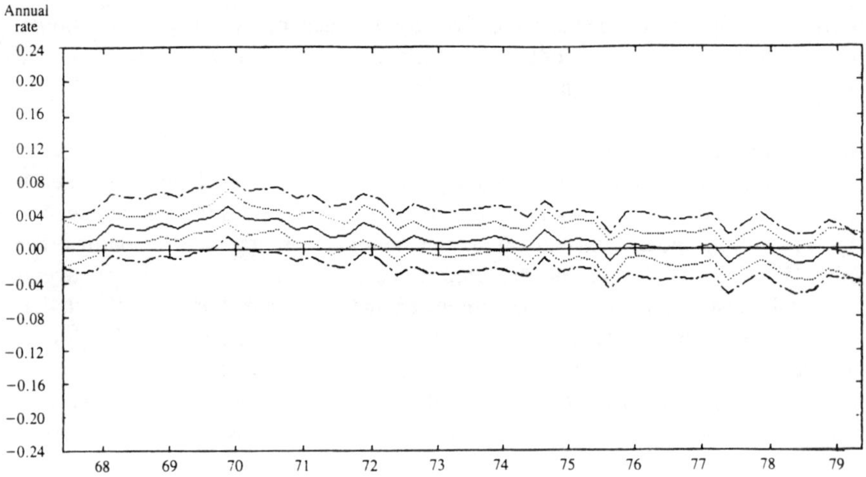

Key for figures 1–7

———— estimated real rate, $\hat{rr}_t$

.... confidence interval for $\hat{rr}_t$ if var (ε_t) $\gg$ var (u_t)

– – – – confidence interval for $\hat{rr}_t$ if var (u_t) $\gg$ var (ε_t)

FIGURE 1 U.S. dollar; estimated real euro rate with 95 per cent confidence intervals

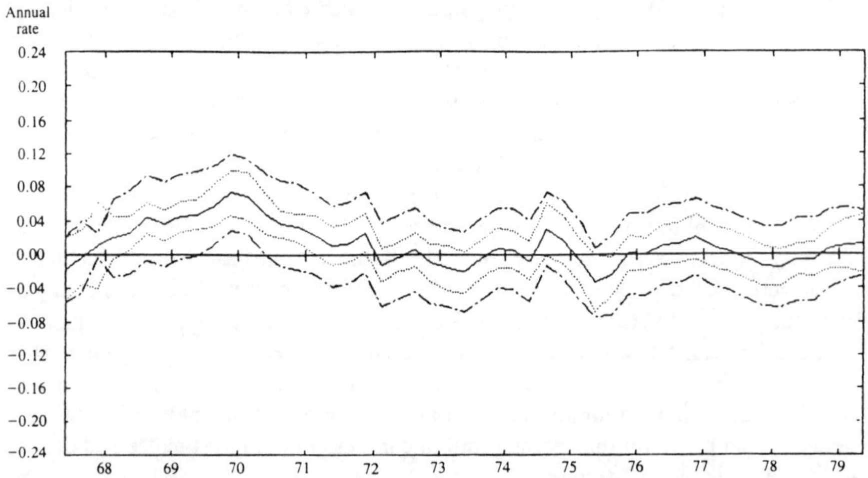

FIGURE 2 Canadian dollar: estimated real euro rate with 95 per cent confidence intervals

Canada's real rates are very close to those of the United States, as might be expected, while the British real euro rates fluctuate more widely, with significantly negative estimated real rates appearing in 1975 and 1976. The greater fluctuation in British real rates is not surprising, considering the greater fluctuations in British inflation rates. The French real rates reach the highest levels for any country; during the exchange rate crises of 1968 and 1969 they are above 10 per cent at an annual rate.

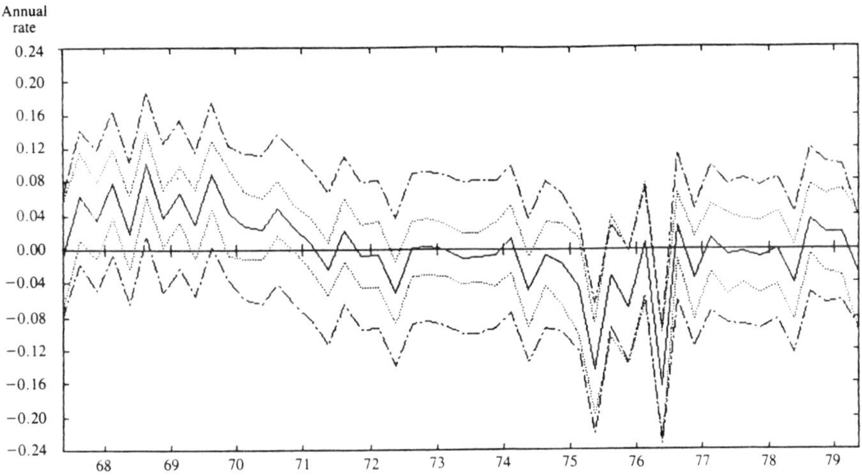

FIGURE 3 United Kingdom pound sterling; estimated real euro rate with 95 per cent confidence intervals

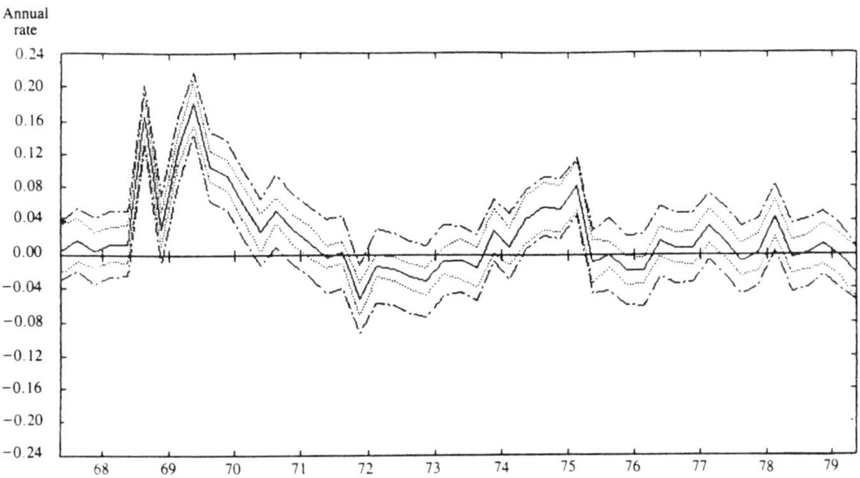

FIGURE 4 French franc; estimated real euro rate with 95 per cent confidence intervals

They then decline to levels more prevalent in the other OECD countries. Significantly positive French real rates appear again in the 1974–75 period, then sink back to the near zero level. The German, Dutch, and Swiss estimated real rates are also positive in the late 1960s, sometimes significantly so; they decline somewhat until 1974, rise and then fall in 1974, and fluctuate around zero thereafter.

The estimated real rates in figures 1 through 7 do have substantially different values in the seven OECD countries – real-rate differentials of over 10 per cent are not uncommon – but there are also some similarities. The real euro rates are positive for most countries in the late 1960s, decline thereafter, rise in 1974, and then fall back

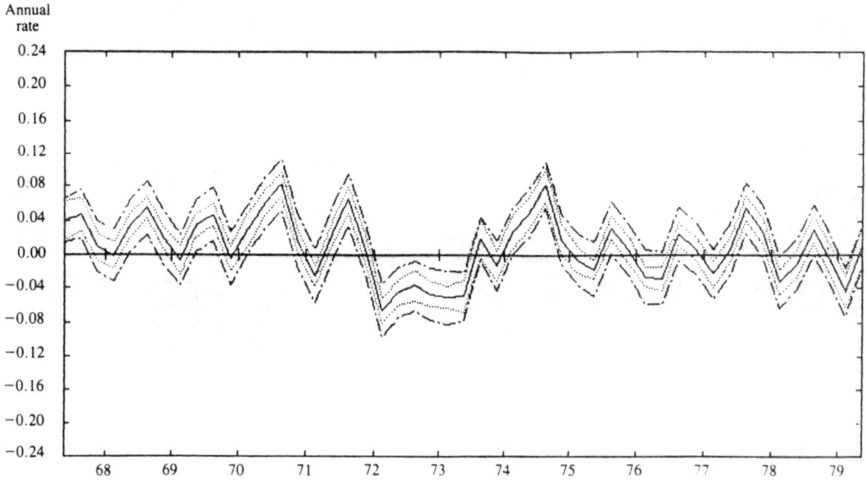

FIGURE 5 West Germany Deutschmark; estimated real euro rate with 95 per cent confidence intervals

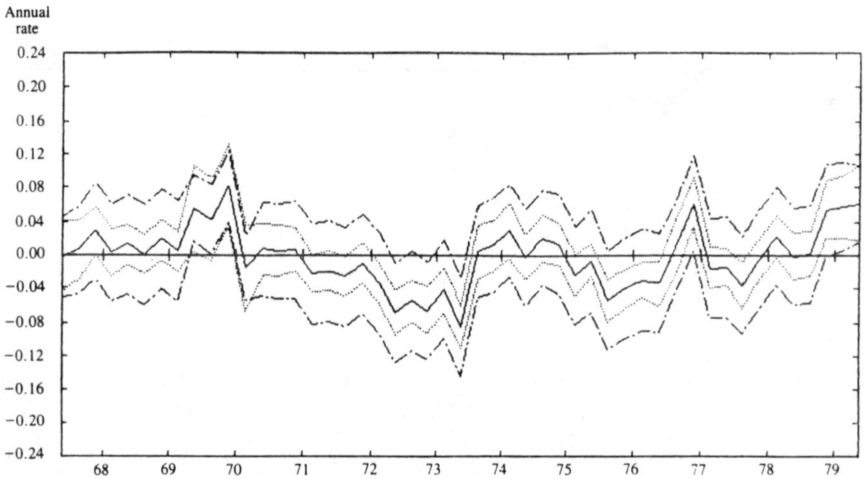

FIGURE 6 Dutch guilder; estimated real euro rate with 95 per cent confidence intervals

again to the near zero level. More formal tests of the relations of these real rates across countries can be found in Mishkin (1982b).

Results using the WPI to calculate the inflation rate, rather than the CPI as in figures 1 to 7, give a similar picture as to movements of real rates in these countries, with one notable exception: France. The two real rates calculated using either the CPI or the WPI price indices rise substantially in 1974, but the WPI real rate reaches the astronomical level of 33 per cent annual rate, while the CPI real rate rises to only 8 per cent. This sharp difference in the French CPI and WPI real rates is the result of widely diverging

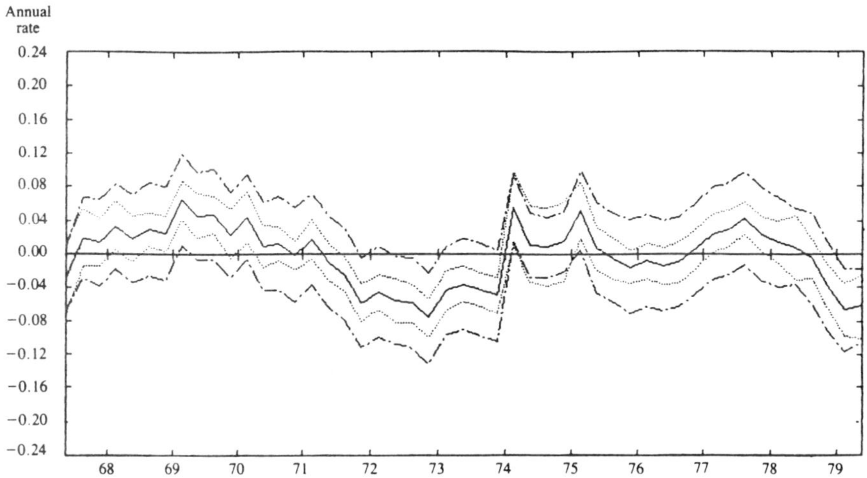

FIGURE 7 Swiss franc; estimated real euro rate with 95 per cent confidence intervals

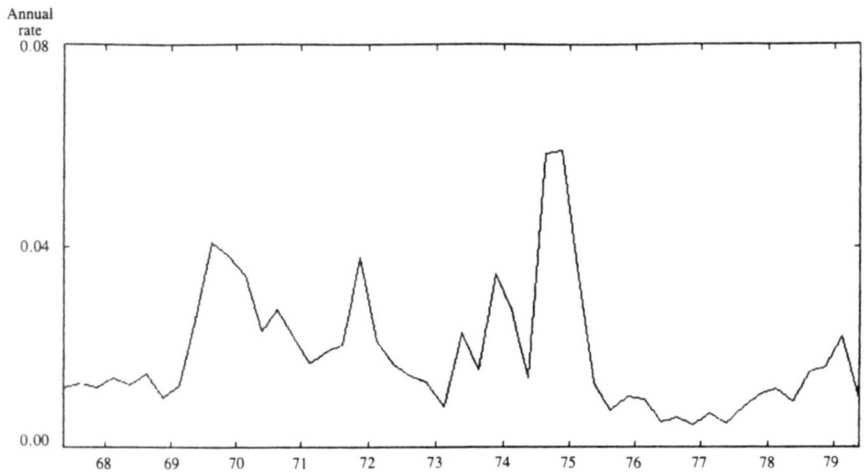

FIGURE 8 Premium of three-month euro dollar rate over three-month U.S. Treasury bill rate

patterns of CPI and WPI inflation for France. (See Frenkel, 1981.) Particularily striking is the fact that the French WPI actually declines in 1974, while the CPI inflation rate is substantial. This deflation of the WPI when the nominal French euro rate was high is the source of the unusually high WPI real rate in 1974.

The ex post real rates are constructed from seasonally unadjusted data, so it is not surprising that figures 1 through 7 display seasonality in the estimated real rates. This seasonality is especially strong for Germany and the United Kingdom and it emerges from the strong seasonality of their CPIs. All the empirical results in this paper have been generated also from CPI data seasonally adjusted with the multiplicative seasonal model outlined in Box and Jenkins (1970).[19] The results from adjusted and unadjusted data do not differ appreciably, and none of the conclusions of the paper is changed. The most noticeable difference is that the estimated real rates for the United Kingdom and, especially, Germany have the same general movements but no longer display the jagged saw-tooth pattern exhibited in figures 3 and 5.

Real rates, nominal rates, and expected inflation

Figures 9 through 15 show the relationships among each country's estimated expected inflation, real rates, and nominal interest rates.[20] Table 1 provides the correlations of these variables for each country. Because there may be non-stationarity in the variables, we must be somewhat cautious in drawing inferences from the correlations. They are useful, however, as summary statistics that can help us pick out the co-movements in the figures.

The one result that appears in all the figures and is also obtained with the WPI is a negative correlation of the real rate with expected inflation.[21] In none of these countries has the short-term euro asset been a good inflation hedge, even in an ex ante sense. These results are consistent with previous findings for the United States that short-term Treasury bills have also been a poor hedge against inflation. That short-term bonds are a poor inflation hedge is a surprisingly robust result; not only is it found for many countries, as here, but it has also been found for other sample periods in which the experience has ranged from inflation to deflation (see Mishkin, 1981).

Despite the negative association of real rates and expected inflation, there is still a close association between movements of the nominal interest rate and expected inflation for the United Kingdom and Canada, as well as in the United States. This so-called Fisher effect, which has been found in the post-war U.S. Treasury bill data by Fama (1975) and others, however, is not robust either to changes in sample period as in Mishkin (1981) or to the choice of different countries. Germany, the Netherlands, and Switzerland display a much weaker Fisher effect.[22]

An important question for the conduct of monetary policy is whether movements in nominal interest rates provide information about the tightness of financial market conditions. One way of answering this question is to explore the question of whether nominal interest rates are highly correlated with real rates. As is evident in figures 9 through 15, nominal and real rates are not tightly linked for the United States,

19 This method of seasonal adjustment was chosen rather than the Census $X-11$ method because, as is well known, $X-11$ does not remove seasonal frequencies from the data. Also $X-11$ makes use of both leads and lags in its calculations, thus making the adjusted data less 'clean' for the rational expectations model estimated here.

20 The nominal euro rate plotted in these figures is the continuously compounded rate rather than the rate reported in the Harris Bank tape.

21 These correlations tend to be even more strongly negative when WPI inflation data are used. This is especially true of France, where the correlation using the WPI is -0.81.

22 The strong seasonal in the German expected inflation might make it harder to see the Fisher effect, because the seasonal does not appear in the euro rate. However, seasonally adjusted CPI data still do not provide evidence for a strong Fisher effect; the correlation of seasonally adjusted expected inflation and the nominal euro rate is only 0.17.

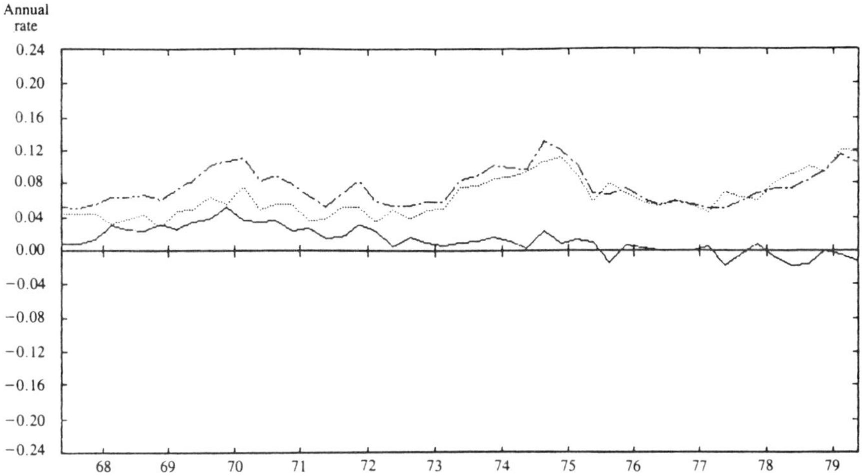

Key to figures 9–15

———————— estimated real rate, $\hat{rr}_t$

– — — — — — nominal interest rate (three-month euro rate)

.... estimated expected inflation rate, $\hat{\pi}_t^e$

FIGURE 9 U.S. dollar; nominal interest rates, estimated real rates and estimated expected inflation

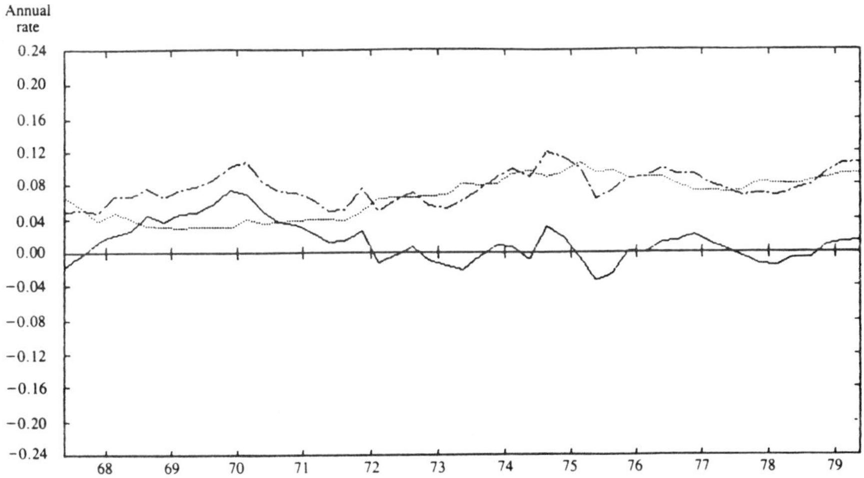

FIGURE 10 Canadian dollar; nominal interest rates, estimated real rates and estimated expected inflation

Canada, and the United Kingdom, and hence in these countries nominal interest rates have been a potentially misleading indictor of financial market conditions. Movements in nominal interest rates in France, Germany, the Netherlands, and Switzerland, by contrast, are closely associated with movements in the real rate. Thus nominal rates appear to be more informative about the tightness of financial markets

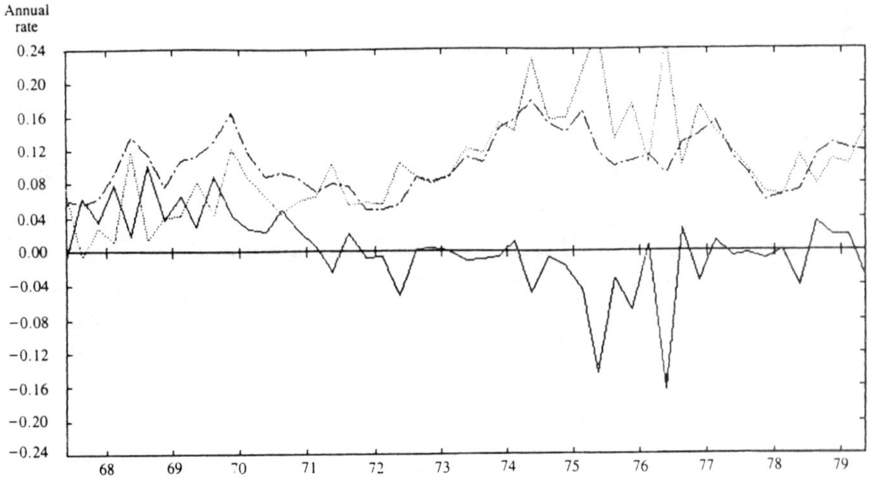

FIGURE 11 United Kingdom pound sterling; nominal interest rates, estimated real rates and estimated expected inflation

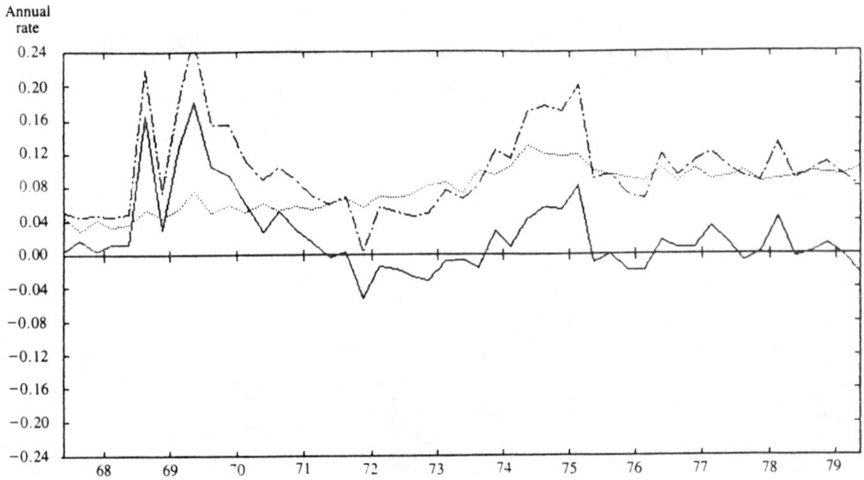

FIGURE 12 French franc; nominal interest rates, estimated real rates and estimated expected inflation

in these countries. This does not mean that targeting on nominal rates would be less harmful in these countries than it potentially has been in the United States. On the contrary, the results here suggest that a change to a monetary policy regime in which nominal interest rates are targeted might significantly alter their informational content.

More formal statistical tests

The real rates in these seven countries shown in the figures above do not appear to constant. The null hypothesis of the constancy of the euro real rates is studied here

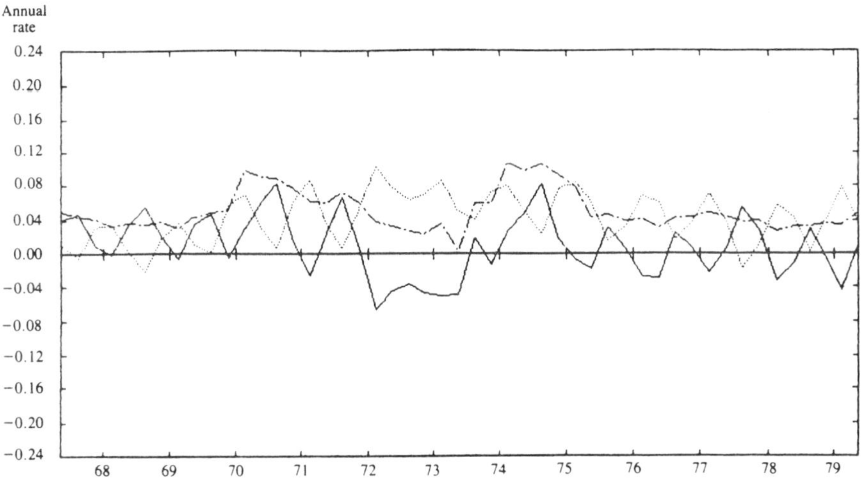

FIGURE 13 West Germany Deutschemark; nominal interest rates, estimated real rates and estimated expected inflation

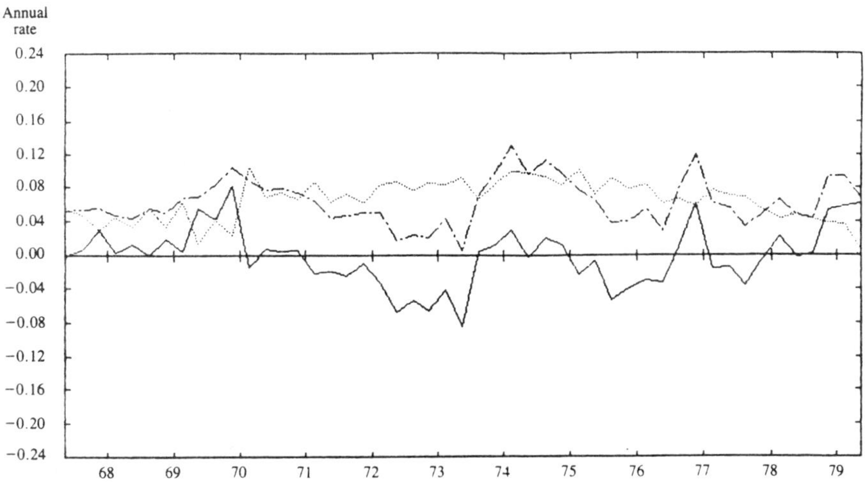

FIGURE 14 Dutch guilder; nominal interest rates, estimated real rates and estimated expected inflation

with two types of tests, which are similar to those carried out in Fama (1975) and Mishkin (1981). These tests correspond to the weak-form / semi-strong-form distinction discussed in the efficient markets literature by Fama (1970).

Table 2 contains the weak form tests that look at the first twelve autocorrelations of the ex post real rates. The constancy of the real rate implies that all the autocorrelations should equal zero. It is formally tested with the adjusted Q-statistic suggested by Ljung and Box (1978). The $Q(12)$ statistic is distributed approximately as $\chi^2(12)$, and its marginal significance level is the probability of getting that value of the test statistic or higher under the null hypothesis that all autocorrelations equal

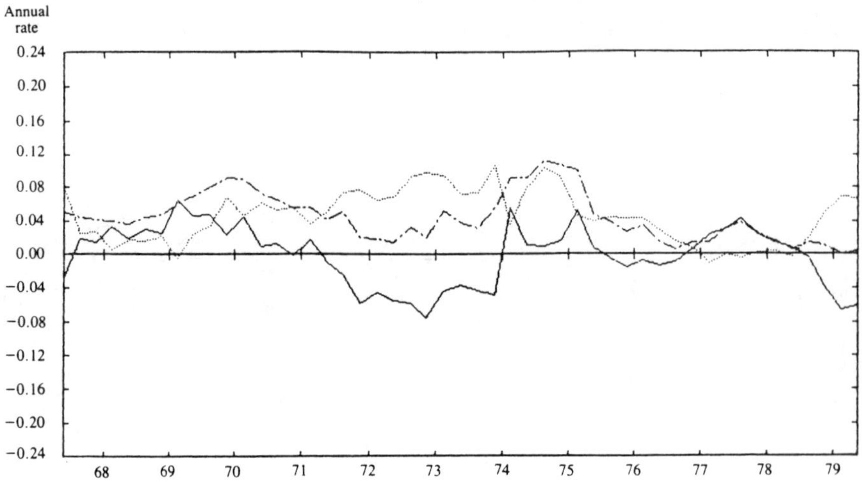

FIGURE 15 Swiss franc; nominal interest rates, estimated real rates and estimated expected inflation

zero; that is, a marginal significance level of less than 0.05 indicates a rejection of the null hypothesis at the 5 per cent level. The serial correlation pattern for the ex post real rate in table 1 is similar to that found for U.S. Treasury bill data in Mishkin (1981). The first four or five autocorrelations are usually positive, with a high percentage significantly different from zero. The $Q(12)$ statistic rejects the null hypothesis implied by the constancy of the real rate (at the 5 per cent level) in six out of seven cases, and only the ex post real rate for the Dutch guilder displays no evidence of serial correlation.

Table 3 contains the semi-strong-form tests for whether the ex post real rates in the seven OECD countries – and hence the real rates – are correlated with other variables whose values are known when the real rate is determined, that is, at time $t - 1$. The F-statistics in table 3 test the null hypothesis that all coefficients of the explanatory variables in the real rate model for each country, except the constant terms, are zero. Line 3.1 follows Mishkin (1981) in conducting a mechanical test of the constancy of the real rate by postulating that the real rate for each country moves with a fourth order polynomial in time. The rationale behind this test is explained in more detail in the appendix. The rejection of the constancy of the euro real rates is very strong, with the marginal significance level indicating that the probability of getting such a high value of the test statistic under the null hypothesis is less than one in ten million. Line 3.2 uses the economic variables discussed earlier to explain real rate movements, while line 3.3 uses both the economic and the non-economic time variables to explain real rates. Note that the ex post real rate regressions for each country use only that country's economic variables for explanatory variables. Clearly, other countries' economic variables might affect domestic real rates, but if each country's regressions included all other countries' economic variables, almost all degrees of freedom would be used up. Again, the rejection of the null hypothesis is strong, and in one case the

TABLE 1

Correlations of nominal euro rates, expected inflation, and real euro rates

Countries	US	CA	UK	FR	FD	ND	SW
1.1 Correlation of nominal euro rates and expected inflation	0.75	0.40	0.58	0.37	0.11	−0.00	0.30
1.2 Correlation of real euro rates and expected inflation	−0.48	−0.70	−0.82	−0.12	−0.76	−0.66	−0.65
1.3 Correlation of real and nominal euro rates	0.21	0.38	−0.02	0.87	0.56	0.75	0.53

NOTE FOR ALL TABLES:
US = United States
CA = Canada
UK = United Kingdom
FR = France
FD = West Germany
ND = Netherlands
SW = Switzerland

marginal significance level drops below 10^{-38}. The rejection in table 3 of the constancy of the real rates jointly in all seven countries is stronger than in any country alone.[23] This demonstrates the increased power of joint statistical tests for several countries.

Tables 4 through 6 explore in more detail the association of euro real rate movements in the seven countries with their own economic variables. Considering the negative correlation of expected inflation and real rates found in the figures, we would expect to find a negative correlation of real rates and lagged inflation when inflation is positively autocorrelated. Positive serial correlation of inflation appears in all the countries, but it is strongest in the United States, Canada, the United Kingdom, and France. System 4.2 in table 4 indicates that a negative association of each country's real rate and lagged inflation appears in all seven countries. However, only two of these seven negative coefficients are significantly different from zero, and the *F*-test for whether all the inflation coefficients are zero is not rejected at the 5 per cent level. Particularly surprising is the weak association of the U.S. euro dollar real rate and lagged U.S. inflation, considering the strong association found with Treasury bill data in Mishkin (1981).

A clue to why the results for the euro dollars differ from the results for U.S. Treasury bills is provided by the premium of the euro dollar rate over the *T*-bill rate, plotted in figure 8. The premium varies substantially over time. Two periods are particularly important: both 1969 and 1974 displayed a very large premium of the three-month euro dollar rate over the three-month U.S. Treasury bill rate. Both

23 For example, the smallest marginal significance level for the test in one country alone of the null hypothesis that the time variables do not have explanatory power is 3×10^{-5} versus 1×10^{-8} for the joint test.

TABLE 2

Autocorrelations of ex post real rates

Country	Autocorrelation at lag 1	2	3	4	5	6	7	8	9	10	11	12	$Q(12)$	Marginal significance level
	Panel A: ex post real rates using CPI													
US	0.34	0.16	0.21	0.47	0.23	0.08	0.21	0.16	0.11	−0.03	0.19	0.08	33.67	0.0008
CA	0.39	0.30	0.23	0.26	0.13	0.01	0.14	0.14	0.10	−0.19	−0.02	−0.14	26.92	0.0079
UK	0.23	0.33	−0.02	0.46	0.05	0.11	−0.07	0.29	−0.06	0.01	−0.15	0.23	31.85	0.0015
FR	0.37	0.29	0.37	0.07	0.13	−0.01	−0.01	0.02	−0.09	−0.14	−0.18	−0.13	25.35	0.0132
FD	0.22	−0.12	0.07	0.41	−0.03	−0.41	−0.12	0.22	−0.03	−0.38	−0.03	0.25	39.70	0.0001
ND	0.28	0.15	−0.01	0.23	−0.06	−0.09	−0.18	0.09	0.09	−0.11	−0.13	0.02	13.78	0.3150
SW	0.27	0.29	0.24	0.32	−0.05	0.15	−0.08	0.05	−0.24	−0.14	−0.25	−0.11	28.73	0.0043

NOTE: $Q(12)$ = adjusted Box-Pierce statistic (Ljung and Box (1978)]
$= n(n+2)\sum_{k=1}^{12}(n-k)^{-1}\rho_k^2$ where n = number of observations and ρ_k is the autocorrelation at lag k: $Q(12)$ is distributed approximately as $\chi^2(12)$ under the null hypothesis that $\rho_1 = \rho_2 = , \ldots , \rho_{12} = 0$ approximate standard error of the autocorrelations $= 1/n^{\frac{1}{2}}$, where n = number of observations = 49.

TABLE 3

Joint tests of the constancy of the real euro rate in the seven countries

	Explanatory variables in real rate model for each country	Panel A: using CPI F-statistic	Marginal significance level
3.1	TIME, TIME^2, TIME^3, TIME^4	$F(28,308) = 3.63$	1.12×10^{-8}
3.2	MG(-1), i, 4 lags of π	$F(42,294) = 9.56$	7.17×10^{-35}
3.3	MG(-1), i, 4 lags of π, TIME, TIME^2, TIME^3, TIME^4	$F(70,266) = 8.79$	1.19×10^{-39}

NOTE:
Variables:
TIME = time trend = 0.01 in 1967–II, … , 0.49 in 1979–II: superscript indicates TIME raised to that power
π = inflation rate for each country
MG(-1) = money growth for each country, lagged one period
i = nominal euro rate for each country, maturing at time t, but known at time $t-1$ and thus in the information set ϕ_{t-1}

periods were also a time of high inflation.[24] Hence, the positive correlation of the risk premium to inflation might be obscuring the negative relationship of real rates and inflation. This possibility is explored by adjusting the euro dollar rates for the risk premium by substracting the premium of the three-month euro dollar rate over the three-month U.S. Treasury bill from each country's euro rate. In the case of the United States this leaves us with the three-month Treasury bill rate that is adjusted for the pure euro market risk but not for any political risk borne by securities denominated in a particular currency. (See Aliber, 1974.) The resulting estimates can be found in system 4.2. All the inflation coefficients are negative. Now the inflation coefficient in the U.S. regression is statistically significant and has a value very similar to that found in Mishkin (1981), which used a somewhat different sample period. The joint test of the null hypothesis that the inflation variables have no explanatory power is now rejected at the 5 per cent level.

Systems 4.3 and 4.4 add three more lags of inflation to the models of Systems 4.1 and 4.2 because they have significant additional explanatory power,[25] and here the evidence is far stronger for the negative relationship of real rates and inflation. The

24 One factor behind the positive correlation of the premium and inflation could be Regulation Q. When inflation rises, nominal interest rates would rise in the United States via a standard Fisher effect. With Regulation Q binding so that banks cannot compete for deposits in the United States, they might go into the euro market and bid for funds, thus possibly raising euro rates relative to U.S. domestic rates. Another factor might be the greater uncertainty in the international financial system as a result of financial crises: the Penn Central bankruptcy and major bank failures such as Franklin National and the Herstadt bank. The determination of the premium on euro dollar rates over U.S. T-bill rates is an interesting question that deserves further research.

25 The null hypothesis that their coefficients are different from zero can be rejected at the one percent level. $F(21,308) = 3.61$ while the critical F at 1 per cent is 1.9. Note, however, that the three lags of inflation may solely be picking up the seasonality in the ex post real rates. With seasonally adjusted inflation data, these extra lags do not provide significant additional explanatory power.

TABLE 4

Relationship of real rates and inflation

	Dependent variables: ex post real euro rates			
	Coefficients of constant	$\pi(-1)$	Constant	4 lags[a] of π
Country	System 4.1		System 4.3	
	0.0060	−0.1950	0.0065	−0.2331
US	(2.97)	(−1.61)	(2.75)	(−1.56)
	0.0074	−0.2761	0.0091	−0.3909
CA	(2.94)	(−2.01)	(3.02)	(−2.23)
	0.0068	−0.2554	0.0156	−0.6124
UK	(1.81)	(−2.10)	(4.43)	(−4.92)
	0.0073	−0.0873	0.0070	−0.0821
FR	(1.51)	(−0.37)	(1.32)	(−0.31)
	0.0032	−0.0925	0.0061	−0.3754
FD	(1.42)	(−0.55)	(2.20)	(−1.51)
	0.0022	−0.1587	0.0076	−0.5000
ND	(0.65)	(−0.88)	(1.60)	(−1.79)
	−0.0001	−0.0084	0.0025	−0.2488
SW	(−0.06)	(−0.05)	(0.86)	(−1.10)
F-test[b]		$F(7,329) = 1.28$		$F(28,308) = 3.19$
Marginal significance level		0.2577		3.87×10^{-7}
	Dependent variables: ex post real euro rates adjusted for risk premium			
Country	System 4.2		System 4.4	
	0.0034	−0.3292	0.0046	−0.4120
US	(2.02)	(−3.26)	(2.28)	(−3.27)
	0.0035	−0.3257	0.0050	−0.4265
CA	(1.49)	(−2.53)	(1.81)	(−2.61)
	0.0017	−0.2365	0.0101	−0.5785
UK	(0.45)	(−1.97)	(2.79)	(−4.53)
	0.0036	−.1373	0.0038	−0.1575
FR	(0.77)	(−0.61)	(0.74)	(−0.61)
	−0.0016	−0.0784	0.0028	−0.5127
FD	(−0.74)	(−0.48)	(1.10)	(−2.24)
	−0.0023	−0.1706	0.0047	−0.6066
ND	(−0.68)	(−0.96)	(1.00)	(−2.23)
	−0.0036	−0.1171	0.0000	−0.4446
SW	(−1.52)	(−0.73)	(0.01)	(−1.99)
F-test[b]		$F(7,329) = 2.50$		$F(28,308) = 3.50$
Marginal significance level		0.0161		3.33×10^{-8}

NOTES

[a]Sum of coefficients and *t*-statistics on sum of coefficients.

[b]*F*-test for whether the coefficient of this variable (or variables) equals zero for all countries.

T-statistics are in parentheses.

π = inflation rate for each country.

TABLE 5

Relationship of real rates and money growth

	Panel A: using CPI			
	Ex post real euro rates		Ex post real euro rates adjusted for risk premium	
Dependent variables	Coefficients of constant	MG(−1)	Coefficients of constant	MG(−1)
Country	System 4.1		System 4.2	
US	0.0039	−0.0644	−0.0015	−0.0098
	(2.86)	(−0.83)	(−1.18)	(−0.14)
CA	0.0035	−0.0244	−0.0014	−0.0139
	(2.70)	(−1.22)	(−1.16)	(−0.72)
UK	0.0076	−0.2778	0.0020	−0.2388
	(2.27)	(−2.79)	(0.58)	(−2.40)
FR	0.0064	−0.0349	0.0009	0.0028
	(2.52)	(−0.45)	(0.36)	(0.04)
FD	0.0038	−0.0668	−0.0011	−0.0577
	(1.57)	(−0.79)	(−0.46)	(−0.70)
ND	0.0058	−0.2513	0.0010	−0.2460
	(2.83)	(−4.18)	(0.49)	(−4.17)
SW	0.0006	−0.0404	−0.0041	−0.0391
	(0.26)	(−0.57)	(−1.91)	(−0.54)
F-test[a]		$F(7,329) = 3.70$		$F(7,329) = 3.28$
Marginal significance level		0.0007		0.0022

NOTES

[a]F-test for whether the coefficient of this variable (or variables) equals zero for all countries.

T-statistics are in parentheses.

MG(−1) = money growth for each country, lagged one period.

sum of the inflation coefficients in each country is always negative, and the explanatory power of the inflation variables is highly significant: the null hypothesis that their coefficients equal zero is rejected at extremely small marginal significance levels. All these results are even stronger when the WPI rather than the CPI is used to construct the inflation data.

Mishkin (1981) found evidence that, as we might expect from standard monetary theory, money growth and real rates in the United States are negatively correlated. However, only weak evidence was found that money growth has explanatory power over and above its association with inflation. Table 5 yields evidence on this issue for the seven countries studied here. Note that only one lag of each country's money growth is used as an explanatory variable because additional lags did not contain significant additional explanatory power.[26] The results in table 5 show that real rates

26 The null hypothesis that coefficients on three more lags on money growth are zero cannot be rejected at the 5 per cent level. Using the CPI, $F(21,308) = 1.46$, while the critical value of F at 5 per cent is 1.6. Note that the $M1$ data used here, which are obtained from the IFS tape, are seasonally adjusted; it is not surprising that the extra lags do not provide significant explanatory power.

TABLE 6

Relation of real rates and nominal rates

	Panel A: using CPI			
	Ex post real euro rates		Ex post real euro rates adjusted for risk premium	
Dependent variables	Coefficients of Constant	i	Coefficients of Constant	i^a
Country	System 6.1		System 6.2	
US	−0.0001	0.1657	0.0073	−0.2917
	(−0.03)	(1.01)	(1.98)	(−1.18)
CA	−0.0065	0.4854	0.0005	0.1665
	(−1.30)	(1.94)	(0.11)	(0.58)
UK	0.0011	−0.0256	0.0043	−0.1816
	(0.14)	(−0.09)	(0.64)	(−0.62)
FR	−0.0149	0.8162	−0.0116	0.8423
	(−6.02)	(9.26)	(−4.98)	(8.54)
FD	−0.0087	0.8562	−0.0057	0.9780
	(−3.02)	(4.18)	(−2.32)	(3.74)
ND	−0.0162	1.0022	−0.0126	1.0975
	(−4.70)	(4.98)	(−4.27)	(4.66)
SW	−0.0075	0.6601	−0.0071	1.0800
	(−2.81)	(3.25)	(−3.34)	(4.32)
F-test[b]		$F(7,329) = 17.26$		$F(7,329) = 18.02$
Marginal significance level		4.55×10^{-11}		2.45×10^{-11}

NOTES
[a]The nominal euro rate here has also been adjusted for the risk premium in order to make the tests in system 6.2 comparable to those in 6.1.
[b]F-test for whether the coefficient of this variable (or variables) equals zero for all countries.
T-statistics are in parentheses.
i = nominal euro rate for each country, maturing at time t, but known at time $t-1$ and thus in the information set ϕ_{t-1}.

for each country except the United States are negatively associated with lagged money growth in that country. The money growth coefficients are negative in thirteen out of fourteen cases and the hypothesis that all the money growth coefficients equal zero is always rejected at the 1 per cent level.[27] In addition, when lagged inflation for each country is included in the regressions, the money growth coefficients continue to be negative and significantly different from zero. The finding here of an independent association of money growth and real rates, over and above the connection with

27 For example, when one lag of inflation for each country is added as an explanatory variable to the regressions in system 4.1, the null hypothesis that the coefficients on money growth are zero can be rejected at the 1 per cent level, $F(7,322) = 3.70$, while the critical value of F at 1 per cent is 2.04. Although we could interpret this result as indicating that monetary policy has an independent effect on real rates, it is also possible that money growth has significant explanatory power because it helps forecast inflation, and it is expected inflation that is negatively correlated with the real rate.

inflation, is stronger than was found for U.S. data alone, as in Mishkin (1981). Again this finding demonstrates the usefulness of analysing data from many countries. The WPI results (not reported here) display a much weaker tendency for real rates and money growth to be negatively associated. The money growth coefficients for each country are negative in nine out of fourteen cases in a table corresponding to table 5 in Mishkin (1982a), and the explanatory power of money growth is not strong; the null hypothesis of zero money growth coefficients cannot be rejected at the 5 per cent level.

Formal tests of whether movements in the nominal rate provide reliable information on movements in the real rate, and hence on the tightness of financial market conditions, are presented in table 6. As would be expected from figures 9 through 15, the real and nominal rates are not significantly correlated for the United States, Canada, and the United Kingdom. However, not only are the real and nominal rates significantly positively correlated for the other four countries, but the null hypothesis that the real euro rate moves one for one with the nominal euro rate cannot be rejected.[28]

CONCLUSION

This paper has studied real interest rate movements in seven OECD countries over the 1967–II to 1979–II sample period. One valuable feature of this study is that it indicates that certain empirical findings appear to be quite robust when the empirical analysis is extended to other countries besides the United States. The constancy of real rates is decisively rejected, and a negative correlation of the real rates and expected inflation appears for all seven countries. Not only have short-term bonds in the United States been a poor inflation hedge, even in an ex ante sense, but this has also been true for short-term bonds denominated in other currencies. The pattern of high real rates in the United States in the 1960s, followed by lower rates in the 1970s, is repeated in the other countries studied here.

Extending the analysis to other countries also reveals that Fama's (1975) propositions concerning the relationship of nominal interest rates with either expected inflation or real rates are not generally valid outside the United States. Whereas in the United States movements in nominal rates in the post-war period have mostly reflected changes in expected inflation rather than real interest rates, this is not true for France, Germany, the Netherlands, and Switzerland. In these countries the Fisher effect is quite weak and movements in nominal rates seem to reflect a one-for-one

28 The positive association between real and nominal rates is not as strong for the WPI results as for the CPI results. Only France and the Netherlands display a significant positive correlation of real and nominal rates, and when the real euro rate is adjusted for default risk, the correlation is no longer significant for the Netherlands. Nevertheless the pattern displayed in the CPI results is repeated in the WPI results: real rates in France, Germany, the Netherlands, and Switzerland are more positively associated with nominal rates than in the United States, Canada, and the United Kingdom.

movement in the real rate. This raises the tantalizing question of what has been different in those countries, particularly in their monetary policy regimes, that might explain why the behaviour of their financial market variables differs.

APPENDIX: SOME ECONOMETRIC ISSUES

What if relevant information is excluded from X_{t-1}?

Consider the example in which the true real rate has the following linear relationship to X_{t-1} and another relevant set of information Z_{t-1}, which has been ignored by the econometrician:

$$rr_t = X_{t-1}\beta^* + Z_{t-1}\delta, \tag{A1}$$

then

$$P(rr_t|X_{t-1}) = X_{t-1}(X'X)^{-1}X'(X\beta^* + Z\delta) = X_{t-1}[\beta^* + (X'X)^{-1}Z\delta]. \tag{A2}$$

Equation (A2) above tells us that the $\hat{\beta}_{OLS}$ estimate from the ex post real rate regression when Z_{t-1} is excluded will not be a consistent estimate of β^*. Indeed the larger δ is and the more correlated Z_{t-1} is with X_{t-1}, the more serious this bias becomes. Hence, even if X_{t-1} were exogenous, leaving out relevant information would lead to inconsistent estimates of the effects from changes in X_{t-1}.

The measurement error of the real rate is

$$rr_t - \hat{rr}_t = X_{t-1}(\beta - \hat{\beta}) + u_t = X_{t-1}(X'X)^{-1}X'(\epsilon - u) + u_t. \tag{A3}$$

whose probability limit is

$$\text{plim}\,(rr_t - \hat{rr}_t) = u_t, \tag{A4}$$

since rational expectations implies plim $(X'\epsilon/T) = 0$ and the definition of u indicates plim $(X'u/T) = 0$. In the example above where the relevant information Z_{t-1} has been left out of the regression equation,

$$u_t = rr_t - P(rr_t|X_{t-1}) = Z_{t-1}\delta - X_{t-1}(X'X)^{-1}Z\delta$$
$$= [Z_{t-1} - P(Z_{t-1}|X_{t-1})]\delta. \tag{A5}$$

The following points about the $\hat{rr}_t$ estimate of the real rate are now easily seen. It will be a consistent estimate of rr_t only if u_t equals zero. This will occur if no relevant information is left out of the explanatory variables in the ex post real rate regression, or if the information left out is perfectly correlated with the X_{t-1} information. Therefore, the consistency of the real rate estimate does not depend on the consistency of the $\hat{\beta}$ estimate. Indeed, paradoxically, the more highly correlated the information that is left out correlates with X_{t-1}, the more inconsistent is the $\hat{\beta}$ estimate but the more consistent is the $\hat{rr}_t$ estimate.

Calculation of the F-statistic for joint tests

The correct variance-covariance of the stacked OLS parameter estimates is

$$V(\hat{\beta} - \beta) = \begin{bmatrix} \sigma_1^2(X_1'X_1)^{-1} & . & . & . & \sigma_{1m}(X_1'X_1)^{-1}X_1'X_m(X_m'X_m)^{-1} \\ . & . & & & \\ . & & . & & \\ . & & & . & \\ . & & & & . \\ \sigma_{1m}(X_1'X_1)^{-1}X_1'X_m(X_m'X_m)^{-1} & . & . & . & \sigma_m^2(X_m'X_m)^{-1} \end{bmatrix}, \qquad \text{(A6)}$$

where

X_i = the nxk_i (n = number of observations) matrix of explanatory variables for country i,
σ_{ij} = cov $(u_{it} - \epsilon_{it'}u_{jt} - \epsilon_{jt})$,
σ_i^2 = cov $(u_{it} - \epsilon_{it'}u_{it} - \epsilon_{it})$,
m = the number of countries.

The $F(q, mn - \Sigma_{i=1}^{m} k_i)$ statistic used in this paper to conduct joint tests is then

$$\frac{(mn - \sum_{i=1}^{m} k_i)}{q} \frac{(R\hat{\beta} - b)' [R\hat{V}(\hat{\beta} - \beta)R']^{-1}(R\hat{\beta} - b)}{(\hat{u} - \hat{\epsilon})' (\hat{\Sigma}^{-1} \oplus I) (\hat{u} - \hat{\epsilon})}. \qquad \text{(A7)}$$

where there are q constraints, $R\hat{\beta} = b$, and $\hat{\Sigma}$ = the variance-covariance matrix of the stacked $\hat{u} - \hat{\epsilon}$.

Tests with time trend variables

The time variables should be seen as a proxy for the smoothly moving component of economic variables that are related to real rates. For example, if the real rate projection against all available information, ϕ_{t-1}, is

$$P(rr_t|\phi_{t-1}) = X_{t-1}{}^E\beta$$

and

$$P(X_{t-1}{}^E|T_{t-1}) = T_{t-1}\theta,$$

where T_{t-1} = vector of the four time variables at $t - 1$, and $X_{t-1}{}^E$ = vector of the economic variables at $t - 1$, then

$$eprr_t = T_{t-1}\theta\beta + u_t' - \epsilon_t,$$

where

$$u_t' = rr_t - p(rr_t|T_{t-1}).$$

The null hypothesis of the constancy of the real rate implies that $\beta = 0$, and thus the coefficients on T_{t-1} in the ex post real rate regression, $\theta\beta$, must also equal zero. The main advantage of this mechanical test is that it does not require knowledge of what the $X_{t-1}{}^E$ variables are; it may thus capture some effects from variables that belong in the relevant information set but have been ignored by econometricians.

REFERENCES

Aliber, R.Z. (1974) 'Attributes of national monies and the interdependence of national monetary policies.' In R.Z. Aliber, ed., *National Monetary Policies and the International Financial System* (Chicago: University of Chicago Press)

— (1980) 'The equivalence of real interest rates in a multi-currency world.' In P. Oppenheimer, ed., *Issues in International Economics* (Stocksfield: Oriel Press)

Barro, R.J. (1980) 'A capital market in an equilibrium business cycle model.' *Econometrica* 48

Boskin, M.J. (1978) 'Taxation, saving and the rate of interest.' *Journal of Political Economy* 86, S3–S27.

Box, G.E.P. and G.M. Jenkins (1970) *Time Series Analysis, Forecasting and Control* (San Francisco: Holden Day)

Cargill, J.A. (1976) 'Anticipated price changes and nominal interest rates in the 1950's.' *Review of Economics and Statistics* 58, 364–7

Carlson, J.A. (1977) 'Short-term interest rates as predictors of inflation: comment.' *American Economic Review* 67, 469–75

Cumby, R., J. Huizinga, and M. Obstfeld (1980) 'Two-step, two-stage least squares estimation in models with rational expectations.' Discussion Paper Series No. 71, Department of Economics, Columbia University, forthcoming, *Journal of Econometrics*

Cumby, R.E. and M. Obstfeld (1981) 'A note on exchange rate expectations and nominal interest differentials: a test of the Fisher Hypothesis.' *Journal of Finance* 36, 697–704

— (1982) 'International interest-rate and price-level linkages under flexible exchange rates: a review of recent evidence.' Paper, National Bureau of Economic Research

Dornbusch, R. (1976) 'Expectations and exchange rate dynamics.' *Journal of Political Economy* 84, 1161–76

Fama, E.F. (1970) 'Efficient capital markets: a review of theory and empirical work.' *Journal of Finance* 25, 383–417

— (1975) 'Short-term interest rates as predictors of inflation.' *American Economic Review* 65, 269–82

— (1976) 'Inflation, uncertainty and expected return on treasury bills.' *Journal of Political Economy* 84, 427–48.

Fama, E.F. and M.R. Gibbons (1982) 'Inflation, real returns and capital investment.' *Journal of Monetary Economics*

Fama, E.F. and G.W. Schwert (1977) 'Asset returns and inflation.' *Journal of Financial Economics* 5, 115–46

— (1979) 'Inflation, interest, and relative prices.' *Journal of Business* 52, 183–209

Feldstein, M. (1980a) 'Tax rules and the mismanagement of monetary policy.' *American Economic Review* 70, 182–209.

— (1980b) 'Comment on Shiller in *Rational Expectations and Economic Policy*, S. Fischer, ed. (Chicago: University of Chicago Press)

Fisher, I. (1930) *The Theory of Interest* (New York: Macmillan)

Frenkel, J.A. (1979) 'On the mark: a theory of floating exchange rates based on real interest differentials.' *American Economic Review* 69, 610–27

— (1981) 'The collapse of purchasing power parity during the 1970's.' *European Economic Review* 16, 146–65

Garbade, K. and P. Wachtel (1978) 'Time variation in the relationship between inflation and interest rates.' *Journal of Monetary Economics* 4, 755–65

Gibson, W.E. (1972) 'Interest rates and inflationary expectations: new evidence.' *American Economic Review* 62, 834–65

Goldfeld, S. and R.E. Quandt (1965) 'Some tests for homoscedasticity.' *Journal of the*

American Statistical Association 60, 539–47
Grossman, S.J. and L. Weiss (1982) 'Heterogeneous information and the theory of the business cycle.' *Journal of Political Economy* 90, 699–727
Hansen, L.P. and R.J. Hodrick (1980) 'Forward exchange rates as optimal predictors of future spot rates: an econometric analysis.' *Journal of Political Economy* 88, 829–53
Hess, P.J. and J.L. Bicksler (1975) 'Capital asset prices versus time series models as predictors of inflation: the expected real rate of interest and market efficiency.' *Journal of Financial Economics* 2, 341–60
Hester, D. (1981) 'Innovations and monetary control.' *Brookings Papers on Economic Activity* 1, 141–200
Hodrick, R.J. (1980) 'Some evidence on the equality of expected real interest rates across countries.' Working Paper No. 8-79-80, Graduate School of Industrial Administration, Carnegie-Mellon University
Howrey, R.P. and S.H. Hymans (1978) 'The measurement and determination of loanable-funds savings.' *Brookings Papers on Economic Activity*, 3: 655–85.
Huizinga, J. and F.S. Mishkin (1983) 'The measurement of short-term real interest rates on assets with different risk characteristics.' Working Paper No. 95, Center for Research in Security Prices, Graduate School of Business, University of Chicago
Joines, D. (1977) 'Short-term interest rates as predictors of inflation: comment.' *American Economic Review* 67, 476–7
Lahiri, K. (1976) 'Inflationary expectations: their formation and interest rate effects.' *American Economic Review* 66, 124–31
Ljung, C.M. and G.E.P. Box (1978) 'On a measure of lack of fit in time series models.' *Biometrica* 65, 297–303
Lucas, R.E., Jr (1975) 'An equilibrium model of the business cycle.' *Journal of Political Economy* 83, 1113–44
Lucas, R.E., Jr and L. Rapping (1969) 'Real wages, employment and inflation.' *Journal of Political Economy* 77, 721–54
Mishkin, F.S. (1981) 'The real interest rate: an empirical investigation.' *The Cost and Consequences of Inflation, Carnegie-Rochester Conference Series on Public Policy*, vol. 15, 151–200
— (1982a) 'The real interest rate: a multi country empirical study.' NBER Working Paper No. 1048, Cambridge, MA
— (1982b) 'Are real interest rates equal across countries? An empirical investigation of international parity conditions.' NBER Working Paper No. 1048, Cambridge, MA
— (1983) *A Rational Expectations Approach to Macroeconometrics: Testing Policy Ineffectiveness and Efficient Markets Models* (Chicago: University of Chicago Press)
Mussa, M. (1982) 'A model of exchange rate dynamics' *Journal of Political Economy* 90, 74–104.
Nelson, C.R. and G.W. Schwert (1977) 'Short-term interest rates as predictors of inflation: on testing the hypothesis that the real rate of interest is constant.' *American Economic Review* 67, 478–86
Pearce, D.K. (1979) 'Comparing survey and rational measures of expected inflation: forecast performance and interest rate effects.' *Journal of Money, Credit and Banking* 11, 447–56
Roll, R. (1979) 'Violations of purchasing power parity and their implications for efficient international commodity markets.' In Sauret and Szego, eds, *International Finance and Trade*, vol. 1 (New York: Ballinger)
Sargent, T.J. (1981) *Macroeconomics* (New York: Academic Press)
Shiller, R.J. (1980) 'Can the Fed control real interest rates?' In S. Fisher, ed., *Rational Expectations and Economic Policy* (Chicago: University of Chicago Press)
Summers, L.H. (1978) 'Tax policy in a life cycle model.' National Bureau of Economic Research Working Paper #302, Cambridge, Mass.
— (1982) 'The non-adjustment of nominal interest rates: a study of the Fisher effect.' NBER Working Paper No. 836, Cambridge, MA

THE JOURNAL OF FINANCE • VOL. XXXIX, NO. 5 • DECEMBER 1984

Are Real Interest Rates Equal Across Countries? An Empirical Investigation of International Parity Conditions

FREDERIC S. MISHKIN*

ABSTRACT

This paper conducts empirical tests of the equality of real interest rates across countries. The empirical evidence strongly rejects the hypothesis of real rate equality and the joint hypotheses of uncovered interest parity and ex ante relative PPP, or the unbiasedness of forward rate forecasts and ex ante relative PPP. The evidence suggests that it is worth studying open economy macroeconomic models which allow: 1) domestic real rates to differ from world rates, 2) time varying risk premiums in the forward market, or 3) deviations from ex ante relative PPP.

THE RELATIONSHIP OF REAL interest rates across countries is of central importance to our understanding of open economy macroeconomics. In some models where there is costless international arbitrage in goods and financial assets, real interest rates for comparable securities should be equal across countries. This has been a feature of much of the early research in the monetary approach to exchange rates, e.g., Frenkel [11] and Bilson [2]. On the other hand, finance theory indicates that risk premia may well differ for comparable securities denominated in different currencies (Solnick [27], Roll and Solnick [26], Stulz [28], Fama and Farber [7], Hansen and Hodrick [17], and Dornbusch [6]), and more recent theoretical models in the exchange rate literature, such as Dornbusch [5], Frankel [10], and Mussa [24], depend on real rates differing between countries in the short run.

The proposition that real rates are equal across countries is worth studying because it sheds light on these theoretical models and because it is also an important issue to policy makers. If it is true, then domestic monetary authorities have no control over their real rate relative to the world rate, limiting the impact of their stabilization policies. In addition, as Feldstein [8] has pointed out, unless real rates can differ across countries, policies directed at increasing domestic savings cannot increase the rate of capital formation and hence productivity. We shall also see that the equality of real rates is also worth investigating because it

* Graduate School of Business, Columbia University and NBER. I thank the following for their helpful comments: Robert Cumby, Thomas Doan, Robert Gordon, Fumio Hayashi, Craig Hakkio, Marjorie McElroy, Michael Mussa, Michael Parkin, and the participants in workshops at the University of Liverpool Seminar in Open Economy Macroeconomics, The Board of Governors of the Federal Reserve, the University of Illinois, Champaign-Urbana, Northwestern University, University of Western Ontario, Columbia University, Tulane University, and the University of Florida. This research is part of the National Bureau of Economic Research's Program in Economic Fluctuations. The National Science Foundation and the Sloan Foundation have provided research support. The usual disclaimer applies.

is intimately linked to and provides information on the basic parity conditions featured so prominently in open economy macro models.

This paper conducts empirical tests of the equality of real rates across countries, an ex ante version of purchasing power parity, uncovered interest parity, and the unbiasedness of forward rate forecasts of exchange rates over the 1967-II to 1979-II sample period. The next section develops the methodology of the tests. It is then followed by a discussion of the data and the empirical results. The final section summarizes the empirical evidence and provides some concluding remarks.

I. The Methodology of the Tests

Each country's real rate of interest for one-period bonds is defined from the Fisher [9] equation as

$$rr_t^j = i_t^j - \pi_t^{ej} \tag{1}$$

where

i_t^j = the nominal interest rate earned on a one-period bond denominated in country j's currency that matures at time t, i.e., it is the nominal return from holding the one-period bond from $t-1$ to t,
π_t^{ej} = the country's rate of inflation from $t-1$ to t expected at time $t-1$,
rr_t^j = the one-period real rate of interest.[1]

The real rate defined above, which is more precisely referred to as the ex ante real rate, is unobservable in contrast to the ex post real rate, which is defined as

$$eprr_t^j = i_t^j - \pi_t^j = rr_t^j - (\pi_t^j - \pi_t^{ej}) = rr_t^j - \epsilon_t^j \tag{2}$$

where

$eprr_t^j$ = the one-period ex post real rate for the bond maturing at time t,
π_t^j = the actual inflation rate from $t-1$ to t,
$\epsilon_t^j = \pi_t - \pi_t^{ej}$ = the forecast error of inflation.

The critical assumption behind the methodology developed here is the rationality of expectations in the bond market, which yields the condition that the forecast error of inflation, ϵ_t^j, is unforecastable and hence

$$rr_t^j = E(eprr_t^j \mid \phi_{t-1}) \tag{3}$$

[1] All returns, inflation, and interest rates in the empirical work here are continuously compounded so that the usual second-order term is not necessary in the Fisher equation (1). Note that if holding period returns are used in the empirical work here rather than continuously compounded returns, there is almost no change in the results. Note also that this definition of a country's real rate matches up the euro security denominated in its currency with its inflation rate. Clearly, a domestic resident might be interested in the real rate obtained by purchasing a euro security denominated in a foreign currency. However, given that uncovered interest parity holds, in this case he will earn the same real return. As will become obvious shortly, uncovered interest parity is intimately related to the equality of real rates across countries and thus it is only necessary to test the equality of real rates using the definition above.

The equality of the real rates across countries then implies

$$rr_t^j - rr_t^i = E(eprr_t^j - eprr_t^i \mid \phi_{t-1}) = 0 \tag{4}$$

for all countries i and j. This equation indicates that the ex post real rate differential between all countries is unforecastable given *any* information that is available at time $t - 1$.

With m countries, there are $m(m-1)/2$ equations of the type above, but only $m - 1$ of them are independent. Thus, the test of the null hypothesis of real rate equality for all countries is obtained by jointly testing $\alpha^j = 0$ in the $m - 1$ ordinary least squares (OLS) regressions

$$eprr_t^j - eprr_t^1 = X_{t-1}\alpha^j + u_t^j, \qquad j = 2, \cdots, m \tag{5}$$

where

X_{t-1} = any variables in the available information set ϕ_{t-1},
$u_t^j = \epsilon_t^i - \epsilon_t^j$ under the null hypothesis, so that $E(u_t^j \mid \phi_{t-1}) = 0$ under rational expectations, and hence u_t^j will be serially uncorrelated under the null.[2]

There are two important points to make about this test. As the condition in Equation (4) makes clear, the test procedure is valid for *any set of variables in* X_{t-1} *as long as they are contained in the information set* ϕ_{t-1}.[3] Even if information relevant to the determination of real rates in different countries is excluded from X_{t-1}, the test procedure described here is valid; that is, a rejection of the null hypothesis is indeed a rejection of the equality of real rates across countries. That the test procedure is valid even when relevant information is ignored is a common feature of rational expectations tests (see Abel and Mishkin [1]).

One pitfall to beware is that these joint tests cannot be conducted by estimating each country's OLS constrained and unconstrained regressions separately, adding up their sum of squares, and then carrying out the usual comparison to construct the F-test. This yields incorrect test statistics because the covariance of the OLS parameter estimates in different equations is assumed to be zero. Instead the covariance of the parameter estimates must be allowed for by using generalized least squares (GLS) when constructing the test statistics.[4]

As we have seen, the test procedure is valid regardless of the variables included in X_{t-1} as long as they are available information at time $t - 1$. However, as the condition in Equation (4) makes clear, the information set X_{t-1} must be chosen

[2] The parameters and their variance-covarance matrix will be estimated consistently with OLS under the null, so that test statistics will have the appropriate asymptotic distributions. However, if the null is false, the u_t^j could be serially correlated and then the power of the test might not be high. Therefore, if there is a failure to reject the null, we would want to be sure that this is not the result of serial correlation in the u_t^j. There are three countries that display significant first-order serial correlation in the Equation (5) regression using WPI data (Durbin-Watson statistics of 1.03 to 1.36), but first-order serial correlation is not present when CPI data are used. In any case, strong rejections of the null hypothesis arise for both CPI and WPI regressions. In the regression tests of uncovered interest parity, the unbiasedness of the forward rate, and ex ante purchasing power parity, no evidence of first-order serial correlation is found.

[3] This statement is proved more formally in a working paper version of this article, Mishkin [22].

[4] Note that the parameter estimates from the GLS procedure will be identical to the OLS parameter estimates because in the tests here the explanatory variables in each country's regression are identical.

so that it has significant explanatory power in the ex post real rate regressions for these countries if the statistical test is to have any power. The tests here specify the right-hand side of Equation (5) as a fourth-order polynomial in time; that is, the X_{t-1} variables are a constant term and the four variables TIME, TIME^2, TIME^3, and TIME^4. These time variables are used in the statistical tests here because in previous research (Mishkin [23]), they have been found to have significant explanatory power, while using up few degrees of freedom.[5]

Clearly, the time variables used in the tests here do not contain all the information relevant to predicting real rates in the countries we examine. However, it is important to remember that the validity of the test proposed here does not require that all relevant information be included in the regressions. Indeed, we can think of the time variables as a proxy for the smoothly moving (low frequency) component of economic variables that are related to real rates.[6] Using them in the tests here has the advantage that the tests will only pick up deviations in real rates across countries that move smoothly over time. Since these low frequency deviations from real rate equality are potentially most important to investment and consumption decisions, they are probably of greatest interest to economists.

The second set of tests conducted in this paper involve the basic parity conditions discussed in the international economics literature. Roll [25] has noted that 1) interest parity, 2) an ex ante version of purchasing power parity (PPP), and 3) the unbiasedness of the forward rates as a predictor of the spot exchange rate are linked to the proposition that real rates are equal across countries. We can see this as follows. Denoting the log of the spot exchange rate and one-period ahead forward rate for country j relative to country i given at time $t-1$ as s^j_{t-1} and ${}_{t-1}f^j_t$, respectively, the interest parity condition (IP) is

$$i^j_t - i^i_t = {}_{t-1}f^j_t - s^j_{t-1} \qquad (6)$$

The ex ante version of relative PPP is[7]

$$E(\pi^j_t - \pi^i_t - (s^j_t - s^j_{t-1}) \mid \phi_{t-1}) = 0 \qquad (7)$$

and the unbiasedness of forward rate forecasts is

$${}_{t-1}f^j_t = E(s^j_t \mid \phi_{t-1}) \qquad (8)$$

[5] In Mishkin [23], four lags of inflation, the lagged money growth rate, and the nominal euro rate for each country have been found to be significant explanatory variables in the ex post real rate regressions for each country. If we included them in the X_{t-1} information set when the number of countries, m, is 7, then there would be 42 variables in each regression. The total number of constraints to be tested would then be a very large number, 252, and we would expect this test to have very little statistical power. The test with the time trend variables, on the other hand, only involves 5 variables per regression, for a total of 30 constraints to be tested. Because these time variables have been found to have significant explanatory power in regressions for all these countries, we would expect this test to have much greater power because fewer restrictions are tested.

[6] This issue is discussed more extensively in Mishkin [22].

[7] This is a weaker condition than the usual relative PPP condition because it will be satisfied even if the log of the real exchange rate follows a random walk. Thus, findings such as Frenkel's [12] rejecting PPP but finding that the deviations follow a random walk would be consistent with Equation (7). However, evidence discussed later suggests that even ex ante relative PPP is violated.

Combining (6) and (8), we obtain the uncovered interest parity condition (UIP), which is also known as the Fisher-open hypothesis, i.e.,

$$E(i_t^j - i_t^i - (s_t^j - s_{t-1}^j) \mid \phi_{t-1}) = 0 \tag{9}$$

Subtracting (7) from (9) we have

$$E(eprr_t^j - eprr_t^i \mid \phi_{t-1}) = 0 = rr_t^j - rr_t^i \tag{10}$$

which is the condition for the equality of real rates.

As the above derivation shows, a breakdown in any of the conditions in (6)–(9) can lead to a rejection of the equality of real rates.[8] Frenkel and Levich [13, 14] and McCormick [20] have shown that deviations from the interest parity condition are quite small in the euro currency market. Indeed, since interest rate parity is a pure arbitrage condition for euro rates, there is some suspicion that many of the deviations may be the result of data problems.[9] Thus, the tests that follow focus on the other conditions.

The tests of the parity conditions are conducted in a similar fashion to the tests of the equality of real rates. For example, uncovered interest parity implies that $\delta^j = 0$ in the following regressions:

$$i_t^j - i_t^1 - (s_t^j - s_{t-1}^j) = X_{t-1}\delta^j + \eta_t^j, \qquad j = 2, \cdots, m \tag{11}$$

where

η_t^j = error term with the property $E(\eta_t^j \mid \phi_{t-1}) = 0$ under the null.[10]

Ex ante relative PPP implies that $\partial^j = 0$ in

$$\pi_t^j - \pi_t^1 - (s_t^j - s_{t-1}^j) = X_{t-1}\partial^j + \omega_t^j, \qquad j = 2, \cdots, m \tag{12}$$

where

ω_t^j = error term with the property $E(\omega_t^j \mid \phi_{t-1}) = 0$ under the null.

The tests involve estimating these regression equations and testing for $\delta^j = 0$ in the $m - 1$ regressions of (11) or $\partial^j = 0$ in the $m - 1$ regressions of (12).

II. The Empirical Results

A. The Data

Obviously, there is no unique real interest rate. The magnitude of a real rate depends not only on the risk characteristics of the security being studied, but also on the price index used to calculate real returns. What the appropriate price

[8] Note that if the deviation from one of these conditions is exactly offset by a deviation from one of the others, real rates could still be equal. But since this is extremely unlikely, it is reasonable to view a breakdown in one of these conditions as leading to a violation of real rate equality.

[9] For example, conversations with Harris Bank personnel indicate that the timing of the euro rate data on the Harris tape used in the tests here can differ by up to an hour from that of the forward premium. This would lead to spurious deviations from interest parity.

[10] Under the null, the η_t^j and ω_t^j error terms are as defined in Equations (13) and (14). Rationality of expectations then clearly implies that $E(\eta_t^j \mid \phi_{t-1}) = E(\omega_t^j \mid \phi_{t-1}) = 0$.

index is depends on what economic decision is being analyzed. For example, if we are interested in the savings-consumption decision, a price index based on a commodity bundle of consumption goods, such as the CPI, is appropriate. If, on the other hand, we are interested in decisions to trade among countries, then a price index with tradeable goods as a larger proportion of its commodity bundle, such as the WPI, is more appropriate.

This study analyzes real interest rates in the euro deposit market in the 1967-II to 1979-II period for the following countries: the United States, Canada, the United Kingdom, France, West Germany, the Netherlands, and Switzerland. Euro deposits denominated in different countries' currencies are offshore securities issued by the same bank and therefore have similar default risk. Hence, a comparison of real euro rates across countries will not have to be adjusted for differing default risk or non-comparability because of capital controls. Quarterly data has the advantage that the data are non-overlapping and timing problems that would arise with monthly data are avoided.[11] The dating convention is as follows. The ex post real rate for a quarter is the actual real return on a three-month euro deposit held from the beginning of the quarter to the end of that quarter, continuously compounded. Both the CPI and WPI are used in the empirical analysis to calculate inflation rates for the reasons discussed above. Quarterly data on three-month euro rates, spot exchange rates, and forward exchange rates are used in this study, and were obtained from the Harris Bank tape. Both the seasonally unadjusted CPI and WPI were obtained from the International Financial Statistics (IFS) tape maintained by the International Monetary Fund.[12]

B. The Results

Line 1.1 of Table I conducts a test for the equality of the mean real rates in the seven countries by only including the constant term in the information set X_{t-1}. The equality of the mean real rates is rejected at the 1 percent level when the CPI is used to calculate the ex post real rate, but not when the WPI is used. However, when the time variables are added to the information set in the tests of line 1.2, we now see very strong rejections of the equality of real rates in both the WPI and CPI results.

Even though real rates are not equalized across countries, it is possible that they have a different mean, but move similarly over time. This proposition is tested in line 1.3, where the information set has the same variables as in line 1.2. Here only the coefficients of the time variables are tested for equality, while the mean real rates across countries are allowed to differ by not constraining the

[11] See Mishkin [21].

[12] Only seven of the ten countries' data available in the tape are used here because three of the countries—Italy, Belgium, and Japan—either had a high proportion of the data missing or did not satisfy interest parity because of two-tiered exchange rates. In the few cases where euro rate data were missing for the seven countries, the euro rate was calculated from the interest parity condition. The data were checked by 1) verifying that there were no large deviations from interest parity, 2) checking that the forward premiums used in these calculations were consistent with the forward rate and spot rate data, and 3) plotting all the series to look for outliers. Several obvious errors in the tape were found in this manner and corrected.

equality of the constant terms. The rejections continue to be strong, indicating that real rates in different countries do have dissimilar movements.[13]

A basic finding of this paper is that the equality of real rates across countries can be significantly rejected statistically. But it is always important to ask not only whether a rejection is statistically significant, but whether it is economically significant as well. Evidence in Mishkin [23] which provides measures of ex ante real rates indicates that real rate differentials are economically significant; they are often very sizable, over ten percentage points or more.

Table II conducts tests corresponding to those in line 1.2 of Table I for uncovered interest parity and ex ante relative PPP, which together imply the equality of real rates. Line 2.1 of Table II tests $\delta^j = 0$ in the six independent regressions of Equation (11) where X_{t-1} includes the constant term and the four time variables. Line 2.2 conducts a similar test for ex ante relative PPP of $\partial^j = 0$ in the six independent regressions of Equation (12). Neither ex ante relative PPP nor uncovered interest parity (UIP) are rejected at the 5 percent level in these tests. However, when these hypotheses are tested jointly in line 2.3—that is, $\delta^j = 0$ and $\partial^j = 0$ are tested in the twelve regressions of (11) and (12)—they are rejected, and especially strongly in the CPI results.

At first glance the findings above are surprising. When the UIP and PPP conditions are implicitly tested together, as in tests of the equality of real rates in Table I, or when tested jointly as in Table II, they are rejected. Yet when these conditions are tested independently, they are not rejected. What explains this phenomenon?

The answer to this puzzle comes from investigating the error terms of the regressions in the tests above. Taking expectations conditional on the available information set ϕ_{t-1} of (11) and (12) and subtracting them from their respective equations, the error terms are seen to be:[14]

$$\eta_t^j = -[s_t^j - E(s_t^j \mid \phi_{t-1})] \tag{13}$$

$$\omega_t^j = [\pi_t^j - \pi_t^1 - E(\pi_t^j - \pi_t^1 \mid \phi_{t-1})] - [s_t^j - E(s_t^j \mid \phi_{t-1})] \tag{14}$$

[13] As is pointed out in Mishkin [23], the French data and real rate estimates are somewhat peculiar. We might suspect then that France alone is the source of the rejections of real rate equality. To check this suspicion, the equality of real rates was tested with France excluded and the rejections were still strong. The 1.2 test using CPI data was $F(25, 264) = 2.63$ with a marginal significance level of 7.4×10^{-5}, while for the WPI, $F(25, 264) = 2.11$ with a marginal significance level of 0.0021. Bilateral tests carried out in Mishkin [22] also indicate that the hypothesis that real rates are equal in the United States, Canada, and the United Kingdom cannot be rejected. When France, Germany, the Netherlands, and Switzerland are included in the bilateral comparisons, significant rejections of the equality of real rates now occur, both with each other and with the first group of countries. One interesting coincidence found in Mishkin [23] that might help us find an explanation for this phenomenon is that the countries which lead to rejections of the equality of real rates are also the countries that display a stronger positive correlation between nominal interest rates and real rates, as well as a weaker Fisher effect.

[14] The derivations of the error terms are done here under the null hypotheses. If the nulls are false, then an additional term of $P[i_t^j - i_t^1 - (s_t^j - s_{t-1}^j) - E(i_t^j - i_t^1 - (s_t^j - s_{t-1}^j) \mid \phi_{t-1}) \mid X_{t-1}]$ should be added to the right-hand side of the η_t^j-equation (13), where $P[\cdots \mid X_{t-1}]$ is the linear projection onto X_{t-1} and an additional error term $P[\pi_t^j - \pi_t - (s_t^j - s_{t-1}^j) - E(\pi_t^j - \pi_t^1 - (s_t^j - s_{t-1}^j) \mid \phi_{t-1}) \mid X_{t-1}]$ should be added to the right-hand side of the ω_t^j-equation (14). The basic point made here is not altered by these additional terms.

Table I

Tests of Equality of Real Rates Across Countries

	Using CPI		Using WPI	
	F-test	Marginal Significance Level	F-test	Marginal Significance Level
1.1 Equality of Constants (Mean Real Rate)	$F(6,288) = 3.28$	0.0039	$F(6,288) = 1.24$	0.2857
1.2 Equality of Constants, TIME, TIME^2, TIME^3, TIME^4 Coefficients	$F(30,264) = 2.68$	1.48×10^{-5}	$F(30,264) = 2.07$	0.0013
1.3 Equality of TIME, TIME^2, TIME^3, TIME^4 Coefficients, Allowing Mean Real Rate to Differ Across Countries	$F(24,264) = 2.44$	0.0003	$F(24,264) = 2.28$	0.0008

Table II

Tests of Uncovered Interest Parity (UIP) and Ex Ante Relative Purchasing Power Parity (PPP)

	Using CPI		Using WPI	
	F-test	Marginal Significance Level	F-test	Marginal Significance Level
2.1 Test of UIP	$F(30,264) = 0.84$	0.7046	$F(30,264) = 0.84$	0.7046
2.2 Test of Ex Ante Relative PPP	$F(30,264) = 1.10$	0.3363	$F(30,264) = 0.88$	0.6512
2.3 Joint Test of UIP and Ex Ante Relative PPP	$F(60,528) = 2.12$	6.88×10^{-6}	$F(60,528) = 1.45$	0.0198

That is, the error term in the UIP regression is minus the forecast error of the spot rate, while the error term in the PPP regression is the forecast error of the inflation differential minus the forecast error of the spot rate. Frenkel and Mussa [15] have documented that the spot exchange rate is highly volatile and is apparently quite hard to predict. On the other hand, inflation rates are substantially less volatile. The forecast error of the spot rate should then have a large variance which would be substantially greater than the variance of the forecast error of the inflation differential. This would imply that the variance of η and ω would be large and thus independent tests of (11) and (12) would have low power and would be unlikely to reject even if the null hypothesis were untrue. On the other hand, the contemporaneous correlation of η and ω for the same country should be highly positive[15] and thus when (11) and (12) are tested jointly, properly

[15] Denoting the variance of the unexpected inflation differential as σ_π^2, the variance of the unexpected spot rate as σ_s^2, their correlation coefficent as $\rho_{s\pi}$ and the ratio of their variances as k, then the correlation η and ω is

$$\frac{1 - \rho_{s\pi}k}{\sqrt{1 + k^2 - 2\rho_{s\pi}k}}$$

It is easy to show that the minimum correlation occurs when $\rho_{s\pi} = k$, equaling $\sqrt{1 - k^2}$. When k is small, this minimum correlation is necessarily highly positive.

allowing for the covariance of their error terms, the test should have greater power and be more likely to reject if the null hypothesis were untrue. The evidence is consistent with the above story; the correlation of the contemporaneous η and ω for the same country is always greater than 0.9 and the UIP and PPP conditions are jointly rejected although they are never rejected when tested independently.

The ability to reject the equality of real rates in Table I, but not uncovered interest parity and ex ante relative PPP individually, also is explained by the error terms in the regressions. Subtracting (12) from (11), we get the regressions that are used to test the equality of real rates across countries, and the error terms are $\eta_t^j - \omega_t^j$. Here the forecast error of the spot rate cancels out and we are left with only the forecast error of the inflation differential. By the reasoning above, this error term has much smaller variance than the error term in either the UIP or PPP regressions. Hence, the test of the equality of real rates will be more powerful than tests of uncovered interest parity and ex ante PPP when conducted independently.

If the interest parity condition holds closely, then replacing the UIP condition (9) by the unbiasedness of the forward rate forecast condition in (8) should have no appreciable effect on test results.[16] This is the finding in Table III which conducts tests where $s_t^j - {}_{t-1}f_t^j$ replaces $i_t^j - i_t^1 - (s_t^j - s_{t-1}^j)$ in (11). The test statistics in Table III are almost identical to those in Table II, never differing by more than 2 percent. This illustrates that results from uncovered interest parity tests can be used to make inferences about the unbiasedness of forward rate forecasts and the potential existence of risk premiums in the forward rate market. This is useful information because frequently data are available to test uncovered interest parity, as in Cumby and Obstfeld [3], but are not as readily available to test the unbiasedness of the forward rate forecasts.

Because of the potential non-normalities of error terms in the fixed exchange rate period—i.e., this is the Peso problem discussed by Krasker [19]—the tests on the equality of real rates, the unbiasedness of forward rate forecasts, and ex ante relative PPP for the flexible exchange rate period from 1973-III to 1979-II are reported in Table IV. The tests of uncovered interest parity for this sample period are not reported here because, as expected, the test statistics are very close to those for the unbiasedness of forward rate forecasts. Note that X_{t-1} again includes the constant term and the four time variables in these tests.

The general flavor of these results is similar to that found for the longer sample period. Joint tests yield much stronger rejections than independent tests of ex ante relative PPP and the unbiasedness of forward rate forecasts. However, now we do see rejections of the unbiasedness of the forward rate forecasts at the 5

[16] Note that when tests of interest parity are conducted the same way the tests of uncovered interest parity are conducted in the text, a strong rejection occurs: $F(30,264) = 5.12$ with a marginal significance level of 6.47×10^{-14}. However, the deviations from interest parity, although they produce a statistically significant rejection, are quite small. In the seven countries, the mean deviations from interest parity (using quarterly rates) range from 0.02 to 0.06 percent; and the standard deviations range from 0.05 to 0.18 percent. As the comparison of Tables II and III indicates, athough the rejection of interest parity is statistically significant, it is not economically significant. Of course, even the statistical rejections are probably spurious because of the data problems described in footnote 9, and the fact that Harris Bank personnel indicate that they quote euro rates as if interest parity held perfectly.

Table III

Tests of Unbiasedness of Forward Rate Forecasts and Ex Ante Relative Purchasing Power Parity

	Using CPI		Using WPI	
	F-test	Marginal Significance Level	*F*-test	Marginal Significance Level
3.1 Test of Unbiasedness of Forward Rate Forecasts	$F(30,264) = 0.85$	0.7016	$F(30,264) = 0.85$	0.7016
3.2 Test of Ex Ante Relative PPP	$F(30,264) = 1.10$	0.3363	$F(30,264) = 0.88$	0.6512
3.3 Joint Test of Unbiasedness of Forward Rate Forecasts and Ex Ante Relative PPP	$F(60,528) = 2.10$	8.73×10^{-6}	$F(60,528) = 1.47$	0.0152

Table IV

Flexible Exchange Rate Period: 1973-III to 1979-II Tests of Unbiasedness of Forward Rate Forecasts, Ex Ante Relative Purchasing Power Parity, and the Equality of Real Rates Across Countries

	Using CPI		Using WPI	
	F-test	Marginal Significance Level	*F*-test	Marginal Significance Level
4.1 Test of Unbiasedness of Forward Rate Forecasts	$F(30,114) = 1.71$	0.0229	$F(30,114) = 1.71$	0.0229
4.2 Test of Ex Ante Relative PPP	$F(30,114) = 1.61$	0.0395	$F(30,114) = 1.03$	0.4427
4.3 Joint Test of Unbiasedness of Forward Rate Forecasts and Ex Ante Relative PPP	$F(60,228) = 2.78$	2.52×10^{-8}	$F(60,228) = 5.64$	6.09×10^{-22}
4.4 Test of Equality of Real Rates Across Countries	$F(30,114) = 2.39$	0.0005	$F(30,114) = 5.32$	3.26×10^{-11}

percent level, although not at the 1 percent level, and a rejection of ex ante relative PPP for the CPI at the 5 percent level. The rejections of these hypotheses jointly is also stronger and is especially so using the WPI where the marginal significance level is below 10^{-20}. The equality of real rates, as expected from the above results, is also rejected quite strongly using both the CPI and WPI.

III. Conclusions

The empirical evidence in this paper strongly rejects the hypothesis of the equality of real euro rates across countries. The joint hypothesis of uncovered interest parity and ex ante relative PPP, or the unbiasedness of forward rate forecasts and ex ante relative PPP, are also strongly rejected. Yet independent tests of uncovered interest parity, the unbiasedness of forward rate forecasts, and ex ante relative PPP yield few rejections and high marginal significance levels.

These results can be characterized in the following way. When tests are set up so that their power will be high, as in the case of the tests of real rate equality or the joint tests of the parity conditions, we find that the null hypothesis is strongly rejected. When the tests are not set up to have high power, as in the case of the independent tests of the parity conditions, significant rejections of the null hypothesis occur far less frequently. The same pattern appears in the literature. Roll [25] conducts an independent test of ex ante relative PPP and he rarely rejects this hypothesis. As argued here, this is likely to be the result of the low power of his tests. When more powerful statistical procedures are used to test this hypothesis, as in Cumby and Obstfeld [4], we do see significant rejections. Similarly, independent tests of the unbiasedness of forward rate forecasts or of uncovered interest parity do not frequently reject the null hypothesis when tests of low statistical power are used as in Frenkel [12]. However, more powerful statistical tests, such as Hansen and Hodrick [16, 17] and Cumby and Obstfeld [3, 4], do reject these null hypotheses. Hodrick [18] conducts independent bilateral tests of the equality of real rates in the United States versus other countries, finds the evidence mixed, and concludes that the results are reasonably supportive of the null hypothesis.[17] More powerful joint tests here strongly reject the equality of real rates and this is consistent with Cumby and Obstfeld's [3, 4] tests which, using a different methodology, also strongly reject this proposition.

An important caveat about the evidence discussed here is that severe measurement error in inflation, due to mismeasurement of the price indices, could bias the results against the equality of real rates and purchasing power parity.[18] This mismeasurement of inflation could arise because of the use of inadequate statistical procedures in calculating the price indices, but it also could arise because of the imposition of wage and price controls or even direct manipulation of the price indices by the government.

Overall, the evidence presented in this paper is not supportive of the equality of real rates across countries. However, this result does not imply the existence of irrationality or unexploited profit opportunities in international financial markets. In a world of risk-averse economic agents, real rates can differ across countries because risk premiums in the forward exchange market and for securities denominated in different currencies should exist, differ across countries,

[17] Hodrick [18] actually uses the interest parity condition to test this hypothesis using forward and spot exchange rates rather than euro rates, but as shown above, this would have no appreciable effect on the results. One problem with just looking at one set of bilateral tests independently, as in Hodrick [18], is that which country you chose as the base country for the bilateral comparisons might lead you to very different conclusions. For example, in the 1.1 CPI and 1.2 WPI tests, when the U.S. is the base country, there are no rejections of the equality of real rates in the independent bilateral comparisons. On the other hand, with a different base country, such as France or Germany, bilateral rejections do occur. This problem does not arise with joint tests of real rate equality, and the results in Table I indicate that jointly we can reject the equality of the U.S. real rates with those from the other six countries.

[18] The nature of the tests conducted here indicates that if measurement errors of inflation tend to be offsetting, then the tests will not be biased against real rate equality. For example, the inflation rate over two subsequent quarters might be measured as 5% and 10% although the actual inflation rate was the same, 7.5%, in both quarters. Because the time variables will only pick up slow moving deviations from real rate equality, this mismeasurement will not have an appreciable effect on the test results.

and undergo variation over time. (See Solnick [27], Roll and Solnick [26], Stulz [28], Fama and Farber [7], Hansen and Hodrick [17], and Dornbusch [6].) Furthermore, transactions costs and non-substitutability of different countries' goods can imply the violation of purchasing power parity even when there are no unexploited profit opportunities.[19]

The evidence then suggests that it is worth studying open economy macro models which allow domestic real rates to differ from world real rates. The evidence also leaves open the possibility for policy makers to exert some control over their domestic real rate, relative to those in the rest of the world. However, the evidence does not rule out that there is a tendency for real rates across countries to equalize over time, and this is an important topic for further research.

[19] That marginal tax rates on euro interest payments might differ across countries might also be a factor in differing real rates.

REFERENCES

1. A. Abel and F. S. Mishkin. "An Integrated View of Tests of Rationality, Market Efficiency and the Short-Run Neutrality of Monetary Policy." *Journal of Monetary Economics* 11 (January 1983), 3–24.
2. J. F. O. Bilson. "Rational Expectations and the Exchange Rate." In J. A. Frenkel and H. G. Johnson (eds.), *The Economics of Exchange Rates: Selected Studies.* Reading, Mass.: Addison-Wesley, 1978.
3. R. E. Cumby and M. Obstfeld. "A Note on Exchange-Rate Expectations and Nominal Interest Differentials: A Test of the Fisher Hypothesis." *Journal of Finance* 36 (June 1981), 697–704.
4. ———. "International Interest-Rate and Price-Level Linkages Under Flexible Exchange Rates: A Review of Recent Evidence." In J. Bilson and R. Marston (eds.), *Exchange Rate Theory and Practice.* Chicago: University of Chicago Press, 1984.
5. R. Dornbusch. "Expectations and Exchange Rate Dynamics." *Journal of Political Economy* 84 (December 1976), 1161–76.
6. ———. "Exchange Rate Risk and the Macroeconomics of Exchange Rate Determination." *Research in International Business and Finance* 3 (1983), 3–27.
7. E. Fama and A. Farber. "Money, Bonds and Foreign Exchange." *American Economic Review* 69 (September 1979), 639–49.
8. M. Feldstein. "Domestic Savings and International Capital Movements in the Long-Run and the Short-Run." NBER Working Paper No. 947, July 1982.
9. I. Fisher. *The Theory of Interest.* New York: MacMillan, 1930.
10. J. A. Frankel. "On the Mark: The Theory of Floating Exchange Rates Based on Real Rate Differentials." *American Economic Review* 69 (September 1979), 610–22.
11. J. A. Frenkel. "A Monetary Approach to the Exchange Rate: Doctrinal Aspects and Empirical Evidence." *Scandinavian Journal of Economics* 78 (May 1976), 200–24.
12. ———. "Flexible Exchange Rates, Prices, and the Role of News: Lessons from the 1970's." *Journal of Political Economy* 89 (August 1981), 667–705.
13. ——— and R. M. Levich. "Covered Interest Arbitrage: Unexploited Profits?" *Journal of Political Economy* 83 (April 1975), 325–38.
14. ——— and ———. "Transactions Costs and Interest Arbitrage: Tranquil Versus Turbulent Periods." *Journal of Political Economy* 85 (December 1977), 1209–26.
15. ——— and M. Mussa. "The Efficiency of the Foreign Exchange Market and Measures of Turbulence." *American Economic Review* 70 (May 1980), 374–81.
16. L. P. Hansen and R. J. Hodrick. "Forward Exchange Rates as Optimal Predictors of Future Spot Rates: An Econometric Analysis." *Journal of Political Economy* 88 (October 1980), 829–53.
17. ——— and ———. "Risk Averse Speculation in the Foreign Exchange Market: An Econometric Analysis." In J. Frenkel (ed.), *Exchange Rates and International Macroeconomics.* Chicago: University of Chicago Press, 1983, pp. 113–42.

18. R. J. Hodrick. "Some Evidence on the Equality of Expected Real Rates Across Countries." Working Paper No. 8-79-80, GSIA, Carnegie-Mellon University, January 1980.
19. W. S. Krasker. "The Peso Problem in Testing Efficiency of Forward Exchange Markets." *Journal of Monetary Economics* 6 (April 1980), 269–76.
20. F. McCormick. "Covered Interest Arbitrage: Unexploited Profits? Comment." *Journal of Political Economy* 87 (April 1979), 411–17.
21. F. S. Mishkin. "The Real Interest Rate: An Empirical Investigation." *The Cost and Consequences of Inflation, Carnegie-Rochester Conference Series on Public Policy* 15, (Autumn 1981), 151–200.
22. ———. "Are Real Interest Rates Equal Across Countries? An Empirical Investigation of International Parity Conditions." NBER Working Paper No. 1048, December 1982.
23. ———. "The Real Interest Rate: A Multi-Country Empirical Study." *Canadian Journal of Economics* 17 (May 1984), 283–311.
24. M. Mussa. "A Model of Exchange Rate Dynamics." *Journal of Political Economy* 90 (1982), 74–104.
25. R. Roll. "Violation of Purchasing Power and Their Implications for Efficient International Commodity Markets." In M. Sarnat and G. P. Szego (eds.), *International Finance and Trade*, Vol. 1, Cambridge, Mass.: Ballinger, 1979, pp. 133–76.
26. ——— and B. Solnik. "A Pure Foreign Exchange Asset Pricing Model." *Journal of International Economics* 7 (May 1977), 161–79.
27. B. Solnik. *European Capital Markets: Toward a General Theory of International Investment.* Lexington, Mass.: Lexington Books, 1973.
28. R. Stulz. "A Model of International Asset Pricing." *Journal of Financial Economics* 9 (December 1981), 383–406.

Journal of International Money and Finance (1986), **5**, 5–23

The International Linkage of Real Interest Rates: The European–US Connection

ROBERT E. CUMBY

Graduate School of Business, New York University, 100 Trinity Place, New York NY 10006, USA

AND

FREDERIC S. MISHKIN*

Graduate School of Business, Columbia University, New York NY 10027, USA

In this paper we present evidence on several questions regarding the movement in short term real interest rates in eight countries: Have *ex ante* real rates in the United States and Europe been high during recent years? Has there been a link between US real rates and those in other countries? Can this link be quantified? The basic finding in this paper is that real rates have climbed dramatically from the 1970s to the 1980s in both the European countries and the United States. There is also strong evidence that there is a positive association between movements in US real rates and those in Europe. However, European real rates typically do not move one-for-one with US real rates, still leaving open the possibility that European monetary policy can influence domestic economic activity.

In recent years real interest rates in the United States have risen sharply and remained high relative to historical standards.[1] Many observers have claimed that these high real rates have been transmitted abroad and have led to high real rates in the rest of the industrialized countries. Concern over the level of real rates has been widespread in the analyses by economic policy makers both in Europe and in the United States. The current focus on the high worldwide level of real interest rates and their effect on the economies of the world calls for an econometric examination of the recent movements in real rates and the degree of linkage between real rates in different countries.

Several attempts have been made recently to test whether there is complete international linkage of real rates by testing for the equality of real rates across

* An earlier draft of this paper was presented at the conference, 'Europe and the Dollar,' sponsored by the Instituto Bancario di San Paolo, June 3–5, 1984, Turin, Italy. We thank the participants in that conference and seminars at Columbia University and New York University as well as the referees for helpful comments. This research has been supported by the National Science foundation, the Andre Meyer Fellowship, and the Sloan Foundation.

0261–5606/86/01/0005–19$03.00

countries (for example, Hodrick 1979, Mishkin 1984b, Cumby and Obstfeld 1984, and Mark 1985). These tests have generally provided evidence against the hypothesis that real short term interest rates in the industrialized countries have been equal during the past decade. However, they have not provided any evidence concerning the extent to which real rates in the major industrial countries move together over time.

In this paper we present evidence on several questions regarding the movement in short term real interest rates in eight countries: Have *ex ante* real rates outside of the United States been high during recent years? Has there been a link between US *ex ante* real rates and those in other countries? Can this link be quantified? Have real rates within Europe been more closely linked together than they are with real rates in the United States? We also examine the issue of the equality of real rates across these countries because our sample period contains data at least two years more recent than in previous studies. These two years are important since they are characterized by extreme movements in real rates and consequently including them should lead to conclusions that are stronger and possibly different from previous work.

Determining the extent to which real interest rates in different countries move independently of one another is important for issues involving stabilization policy in general as well as for shedding light on the recent policy-debate. If real interest rates in an economy move one-for-one with those abroad, an important avenue for monetary policy to influence the domestic economy emphasized in many open economy macro-economic models is removed. In many of these models, equality of real rates fails due to relative price changes. Deviations from purchasing power parity that are due to sticky prices give rise to independent real interest rate movements in the models of Dornbusch (1976), Frankel (1979), and Mussa (1982). Changes in the relative price of home goods account for real interest rate movements in the intertemporal optimizing model of Dornbusch (1983) and in the imperfect information model of Stockman and Koh (1982). Obstfeld (1983) presents an intertemporal maximizing model in which real interest rate differentials arise from terms of trade changes. Deviations from uncovered interest parity are behind real interest rate inequality in other models. For example, the portfolio balance models of Branson (1979) and Girton and Henderson (1977) exhibit independent real interest rate movements arising from changes in the supply of outside assets.[2]

In the next section we turn to the econometric methodology for estimating *ex ante* real rates and testing the linkage between real rates in different countries. The central problem that the methodology deals with is that expected inflation, and hence the *ex ante* real interest rate itself, is not observable. We must therefore obtain estimates based on observed data, and are careful to take account of the statistical properties of these estimates in making inferences about *ex ante* real rates. We then produce estimates of real interest rates in the United States, Canada, and six European countries and test to what extent real rate movements outside of the United States are associated with movements in the US real rate. We also test the association of European real rate movements with each other.

Our basic finding is that real rates have climbed dramatically from the 1970s to the 1980s in all countries studied and that there is a significant positive association between movements in US real rates and those abroad. However, European real rates typically do not move one-for-one with US real rates, still leaving open the possibility that monetary policy can influence domestic economic activity. The association of movements of European real rates with each other is not found to be any stronger than the association of European with US real rates.

I. Methodology

For each country, the *ex ante* real interest rate (which we will also refer to as the real rate) on a j period bond which is held for j periods is defined from the Fisher (1930) equation as,[3]

$$\langle 1 \rangle \qquad rr_{t,j} = i_{t,j} - \pi^{e}_{t,j}$$

where,

$rr_{t,j}$ = the expectation at time t of the real return earned by holding the j-period bond from time t to $t+j$,

$i_{t,j}$ = the nominal interest rate at time on the j-period bond, held to maturity at $t+j$.[4]

$\pi'_{t,j}$ = the expectation at time t of the inflation rate in that country from t to $t+j$.

This real rate is unobservable, so that we are forced to work with the observable, *ex post* real rate defined as,

$$\langle 2 \rangle \qquad eprr_{t,j} = i_{t,j} - \pi_{t,j}$$

where,

$eprr_{t,j}$ = the realized real return on the j-period bond held from t to $t+j$,

$\pi_{t,j}$ = the inflation rate from t to $t+j$ in that country.

Combining equations ⟨1⟩ and ⟨2⟩ the *ex post* real rate can be expressed as

$$\langle 3 \rangle \qquad eprr_{t,j} = (rr_{t,j} - \pi_{t,j} - \pi'_{t,j}) = rr_{t,j} - \varepsilon_{t,j}$$

where, $\varepsilon_{t,j} = \pi_{t,j} - \pi'_{t,j}$ = the forecast error of inflation.

The underlying assumption behind the econometric methodology used here is the rationality of expectations, which implies

$$\langle 4 \rangle \qquad E(\varepsilon_{t,j} | \phi_t) = 0$$

where, ϕ_t = all available information at time t.

This condition implies that the forecast error of inflation $\varepsilon_{t,j}$ is unforecastable, that is, it is uncorrelated with any information available at time t. The econometrician observes a set of variables X_t that are included in the available information set ϕ_t and are correlated with the real rate $rr_{t,j}$. A logical choice for an estimate of the real rate is the best linear predictor of $rr_{t,j}$ given X_t, that is, the linear projection of $rr_{t,j}$ onto X_t, which we represent as

$$\langle 5 \rangle \qquad P(rr_{t,j} | X_t) = X_t\beta$$

The projection equation for $rr_{t,j}$ can then be written as

$$rr_{t,j} = X_t\beta + u_{t,j} \tag{6}$$

where,

$u_{t,j}$ = the projection equation error, $rr_{t,j} - P(rr_{t,j}|X_t)$, which by construction has the property $P(u_{t,j}|X_t) = 0$,

and substituting ⟨6⟩ into ⟨2⟩ we obtain the regression equation,

$$eprr_{t,j} = X_t\beta + u_{t,j} - \varepsilon_{t,j} = X_t\beta + \eta_{t,j} \tag{7}$$

Because $eprr_{t,j}$ and X_t are observable, this equation can be estimated by ordinary least squares (OLS). We can then use as our estimates of *ex ante* real rates in each country, $\hat{rr}_{t,j}$, the fitted values from the OLS regression ⟨7⟩,

$$\hat{rr}_{t,j} = X_t\hat{\beta}_{\text{OLS}} \tag{8}$$

To understand the properties of the resulting estimates, there are two important features of the error term of this equation, $\eta_{t,j}$, that merit discussion. The assumption of rational expectations implies that the forecast error of inflation, $\varepsilon_{t,j}$, is uncorrelated with any information available at time t which includes X_t. Therefore, $\varepsilon_{t,j}$ is orthogonal to X_t and by construction, $u_{t,j}$ is also orthogonal to X_t. As is shown by Mishkin (1981), the resulting orthogonality of the error term, $\eta_{t,j}$, with X_t then implies that estimating equation ⟨7⟩ by OLS produces consistent estimates of the projection equation β's. This indicates that, although we cannot observe the *ex ante* real rate $rr_{t,j}$, we can infer information about its relationship with variables known at time t via *ex post* real rate regressions.

The usual case in the literature, that of non-overlapping data, has j equal to 1, so that the holding period and the observation period are the same. On the other hand, in the empirical analysis in this paper in which we examine real interest rates over three-month holding periods, we use monthly observations rather quaterly data in order to increase the efficiency of our estimates: thus, j equals 3 and the data will be overlapping.[5] For example, $rr_{t,3}$ will be a three period return which equals the sum of the one period returns in $t+1$, $t+2$ and $t+3$. $rr_{t+1,3}$ then overlaps $rr_{t,3}$ because both include the one period returns for $t+2$ and $t+3$.

In order to obtain confidence intervals around our estimates of real rates, we must have a consistent estimate of the variance–covariance matrix of $\hat{\beta}_{\text{OLS}}$. Unfortunately, the variance–covariance matrix from OLS regressions reported by standard regression packages can be very misleading when there is serial correlation in the $\eta_{t,j}$ error term. In the non-overlapping case where $j=1$, $\varepsilon_{t-1,1}$ is realized at time t and so is included in the available information set ϕ_t. The rational expectations condition then implies that $E(\varepsilon_{t,1}|\varepsilon_{t-1,1}) = 0$, implying that $\varepsilon_{t,1}$ will be serially uncorrelated. Even though the $u_{t,1}$ error term does not have to be serially uncorrelated, if X_t includes most of the relevant information used to predict the real rate, then the variance of $u_{t,1}$ will be small and $\eta_{t,1}$ will be dominated by the serially uncorrelated movement of $\varepsilon_{t,1}$. In this case, any serial correlation in $\eta_{t,1}$ will be sufficiently small that the bias to the standard errors reported by OLS regression packages will be negligible.

When the data are overlapping, as in our analysis here where $j=3$, then $\varepsilon_{t,3}$ is not realized until 3 periods in the future. Thus, $\varepsilon_{t-1,3}$ and $\varepsilon_{t-2,3}$ are not in the information set ϕ_t and can be correlated with $\varepsilon_{t,3}$. This means that $\varepsilon_{t,3}$ will follow a second order moving average process (MA(2)). Even if the $u_{t,3}$ error term has small variation relative to $\varepsilon_{t,3}$ then $\eta_{t,3}$ will be serially correlated, and the variance–covariance matrix of $\hat{\beta}_{\text{OLS}}$ will not be consistently estimated by OLS regression packages.

Consistent estimates of the $\hat{\beta}_{\text{OLS}}$ variance–covariance matrix are calculated with a method outlined by Hansen (1982) and Cumby, Huizinga and Obstfeld (1983), which allows for serial correlation in the error term of rational expectations regression equations. The estimates we use here are similar to those used by Hansen and Hodrick (1980), but they are more general because they allow for conditional heteroscedasticity in the regression residuals. This is a particularly attractive feature of this technique since the assumption of conditional homoscedasticity is usually rejected in financial markets.[6]

An accurate measure of the *ex ante* real rate using the methodology described here requires that most of the relevant information for predicting the real rate be included in X_t so that $u_{t,3}$ is small. When this is the case, $\eta_{t,3}$ will have the time series properties of the forecast error of inflation term, $\varepsilon_{t,3}$. Thus a diagnostic check of the adequacy of the X_t specification is to see whether the residuals from the *ex post* real rate regressions have the MA(2) time series process implied by rational expectations for $\varepsilon_{t,3}$.

After obtaining measures of *ex ante* real rates in both the European countries and the United States, we want to test whether there is a linkage between the European real rates and the US real rates and to test the international equality of real rates. We construct a test of this linkage as follows. Consider a regression of the *ex ante* real rate in country *m* on the US real rate,

$$\langle 9\rangle \qquad rr^m_{t,j} = \alpha^m + \gamma^m rr^{US}_{t,j} + \omega^m_{t,j}$$

The hypothesis that real rates in the United States and those abroad are fully linked implies $\gamma = 1$ while the hypothesis that there is no link between US real rates and European real rates implies that $\gamma = 0$. Equality of real rates between the United States and country *m* implies that $\gamma = 1$ and $\alpha = 0$.

Because these *ex ante* real rates are unobservable, this regression equation cannot be estimated. Using the expression for the *ex post* real rate in equation ⟨3⟩, we can rewrite equation ⟨9⟩ as:

$$\langle 10\rangle \qquad eprr^m_{t,j} = \alpha_m + \gamma_m eprr^{US}_{t,j} + \omega^m_{t,j} - \varepsilon^m_{t,j} + \gamma^m \varepsilon^{US}_{t,j}$$

Because the *ex post* real rates for country *m* and the United States are observable, this equation can be estimated. However, the error term of this equation is not orthogonal to the explanatory variable, $eprr^{US}_{t,j}$, because $eprr^{US}_{t,j}$ is realized only at time $t+j$ and thus will be correlated with the inflation forecast error terms. McCallum (1976) pointed out that consistent estimates of this equation could be obtained by estimating it with instrumental variables, provided the instruments are in the available information set ϕ_t so that the instruments will be uncorrelated with the expectation errors, $\varepsilon^m_{t,j}$ and $\varepsilon^{US}_{t,j}$. Consistency also requires that the instruments be uncorrelated with $\omega^m_{t,j}$, the disturbance in ⟨9⟩. This disturbance is, by construction, the part of movements in the real rate in country *m* that is not explained by movements in the US real rate. Therefore, the instruments should exert no additional influence on the real rate in country *m* apart from their influence on the real rate in the United States.[7]

However, if the data are overlapping so that the ε's and hence the error term of the equation are serially correlated, then the McCallum procedure will not lead to consistent estimates of the estimated parameters' standard errors and misleading inference can result. The solution to this problem is to use the two-step, two stage least squares (2S2SLS) procedure developed by Cumby, Huizinga and Obstfeld (1983). Not only does this procedure provide consistent estimates of the covariance matrix of the coefficient estimates when the error is serially correlated or conditionally heteroscedastic, but it produces more efficient parameter estimates as well.[8] There are two criteria for choosing the instruments to be used in this procedure. First, the instruments must be in the available information set ϕ_t in order to achieve consistent estimates. Second, the instruments should have good explanatory power for the *ex post* real rate on the right-hand-side of the equation so that the power of the test is as high as possible. A natural choice for instruments are then the variables in X_t that have been found to predict the US *ex post* real rate well.

In summary: measures of real interest rates when the data are overlapping, as in the empirical analysis of this paper, can be obtained by estimating *ex post* real rate regressions with ordinary least squares and using the fitted values as estimates of the *ex ante* real rates. Correct statistical inference requires that the standard errors of these estimates be corrected for the serial correlation due to overlapping data using the 2S2SLS procedure outlined by Cumby, Huizinga and Obstfeld (1983). Tests of the linkage between United States and European real rates can be conducted by estimating a regression of the European country's *ex post* real rate on the *ex post* real rate in the United States with the 2S2SLS technique using as instruments the same variables that were used to estimate the measures of the real rates.

II. The Data

In this paper we study short-term real interest rates in the Euro deposit and domestic money markets using monthly data from June 1973 until December 1983 for eight industrialized countries: the United States, Canada, the United Kingdom, Italy, the Netherlands, France, West Germany and Switzerland. Since capital controls, both actual and potential, may drive a wedge between onshore money market interest rates and the corresponding Euro deposit rate, we examine both of these interest rates in our tests here. We have chosen to examine real rates calculated using changes in the consumer price index (CPI) as the relevant measure of price inflation since this is the most reliable price index available for the countries in our sample. We study three-month real interest rates on Euro deposits and domestic money market instruments because the timing problem of the inexact dating of the monthly price indices is somewhat lessened by looking at real interest rates of maturities longer than one month.[9] The time period is chosen to begin shortly after the onset of generalized floating exchange rates and to include the most recently available data.

The dating convention is as follows. The *ex post* real rate at month *t* is the actual real rate of return on a three-month Euro deposit or domestic money market instrument held from the end of that month to three months in the future: for the observation in January, it is the real rate of return from January 31 until April 30. For each country, the *ex post* real rate is constructed by subtracting the continuously compounded inflation rate for that country from the continuously compounded nominal interest rate on the Euro deposit or money market instrument denominated in that country's currency.

The three-month Eurocurrency deposit rates come from a variety of sources. Prior to January 1976, the Euro rates are taken from Data Resources, Inc. for the United States, Germany, and Switzerland and from the *Weekly Review* of the Harris Bank of Chicago for the remaining countries. Following January 1976, all rates (except the Euro lira rate) are taken from Morgan Guaranty Trust's *World Financial Markets*. The money market rates are taken from Morgan Guaranty Trust's *World Financial Markets*. These are representative three-month rates measured at or near the end of the month. Interbank rates are used for France, Germany, Italy, the Netherlands,[10] Switzerland, and the United Kingdom. For Canada three-month prime finance company paper is used and for the United States three month prime industrial paper is used.

The consumer price indices for each country except the United States are obtained from the International Financial Statistics (IFS) tape (line 64). The US consumer price index is the CPI-UX1, which uses the new rental equivalence procedure for measuring housing costs.[11]

III. Measuring Real Rates in the Eight Countries

We employ a constant term, a time trend, the nominal interest rate, $i_{t,3}$, and three values of lagged inflation, $\pi_{t-3,3}$, $\pi_{t-6,3}$, and $\pi_{t-12,3}$ as our X_t variables in the regressions used to generate the *ex ante* real rate estimates.[12] (The regressions for each country contains only domestic variables.) There is quite strong evidence that the stochastic structure of real rate movements in the United States undergoes a major shift sometime around the change in the Federal Reserve's operating procedure in October 1979 (see Huizinga and Mishkin, 1984) and we find similar evidence of a shift in the stochastic structure for six of the other countries studied.[13] Only in the Swiss case are we unable to reject the null hypothesis of stability at standard significance levels. In the case of the United Kingdom, the sample is split at the beginning of the Thatcher government in June 1979. For the other European countries the beginning of the European Monetary System in April 1979 is chosen as the break point. The estimated real rates for each country are thus constructed from a separate regression for each of the two sub-periods.[14]

Before looking at the estimated real rates obtained from these regressions, we should first look at the autocorrelations of the residuals, reported in Table 1. Because there may be spurious seasonality of the *ex post* rates,[15] the small but significant autocorrelations at lag twelve are not of great concern. What is more important is the fact that, except for the autocorrelations at the seasonal lags, there are rarely significant autocorrelations at lags greater than 2. This provides some indication that enough relevant information is included in X_t so that the $u_{t,3}$ are small relative to $\varepsilon_{t,3}$ and that our estimates of the real rates will be reliable.

Figures 1 through 8 display the estimated real rates using the consumer price index for the eight countries studied here for domestic money market

TABLE 1. Autocorrelations of residuals[a].

A. Three month Eurocurrency deposits

	Lag											
Country	1	2	3	4	5	6	7	8	9	10	11	12
US	0.69	0.26	−0.04	−0.04	−0.02	−0.03	−0.16	−0.22	−0.12	0.05	0.12	0.05
CA	0.66	0.34	0.03	0.05	0.02	0.02	0.04	0.08	0.03	−0.06	−0.11	−0.10
UK	0.73	0.31	−0.05	−0.08	0.01	0.05	−0.05	−0.22	−0.33	−0.32	−0.21	−0.10
ND	0.57	0.38	−0.04	−0.10	−0.13	−0.05	0.03	0.07	−0.07	−0.15	−0.19	−0.11
IT	0.65	0.21	−0.22	−0.28	−0.16	0.03	0.01	−0.07	−0.19	−0.17	−0.09	−0.02
FR	0.73	0.32	−0.09	−0.23	−0.21	−0.10	−0.07	−0.08	−0.09	−0.01	0.04	0.08
WG	0.60	0.11	−0.22	−0.18	−0.04	−0.02	−0.13	−0.17	−0.17	−0.10	−0.06	−0.10
SW	0.74	0.41	0.04	−0.04	−0.04	−0.01	−0.04	−0.04	−0.01	0.06	0.03	−0.03

B. Domestic money market instruments

	Lag											
Country	1	2	3	4	5	6	7	8	9	10	11	12
US	0.68	0.23	−0.08	−0.08	−0.03	−0.03	−0.15	−0.20	−0.13	0.01	0.06	0.03
CA	0.66	0.34	0.04	0.06	0.02	0.02	0.04	0.08	0.03	−0.06	−0.11	−0.10
UK	0.72	0.32	−0.05	−0.08	−0.02	0.02	−0.07	−0.22	−0.31	−0.31	−0.19	−0.09
ND	0.56	0.38	−0.04	−0.09	−0.13	−0.05	0.02	0.06	−0.08	−0.15	−0.20	−0.11
IT	0.70	0.21	−0.20	−0.28	−0.16	−0.02	−0.02	−0.14	−0.24	−0.14	0.03	0.12
FR	0.74	0.34	−0.06	−0.19	−0.18	−0.08	−0.08	−0.12	−0.13	−0.06	0.03	0.08
WG	0.60	0.09	−0.25	−0.19	−0.05	−0.01	−0.13	−0.18	−0.17	−0.08	−0.03	−0.05
SW	0.71	0.33	−0.02	−0.06	−0.04	−0.08	−0.17	−0.22	−0.15	−0.01	0.03	0.04

[a] Under the null hypothesis that the errors are iid, the autocorrelations have asymptotic standard errors of $(1/T)^{0.5} = 0.09$.

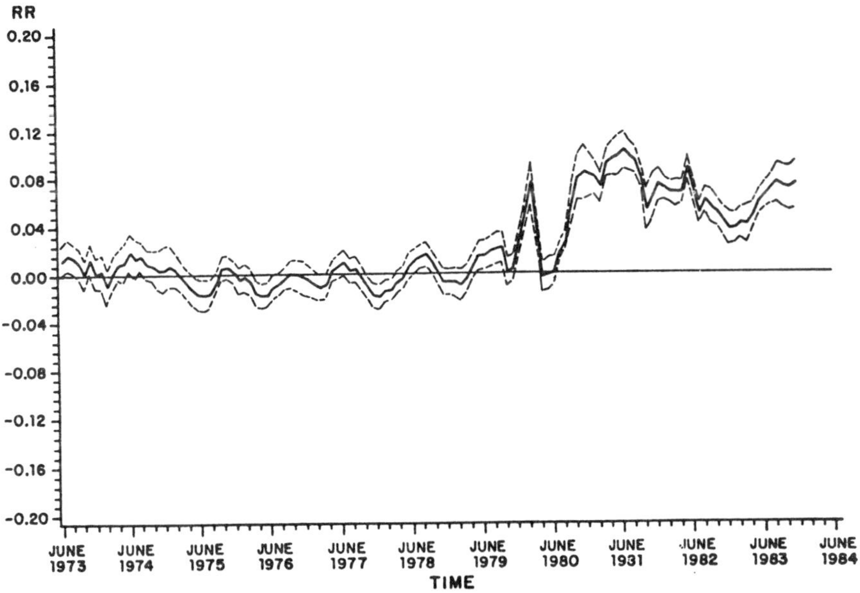

FIGURE 1. *Ex ante* real rates: United States (domestic money market rates).

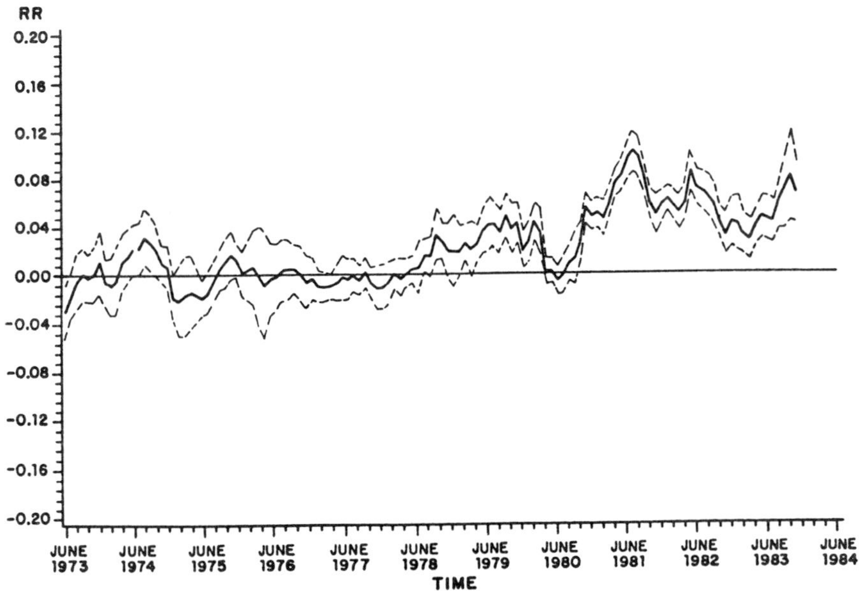

FIGURE 2. *Ex ante* real rates: Canada (domestic money market rates).

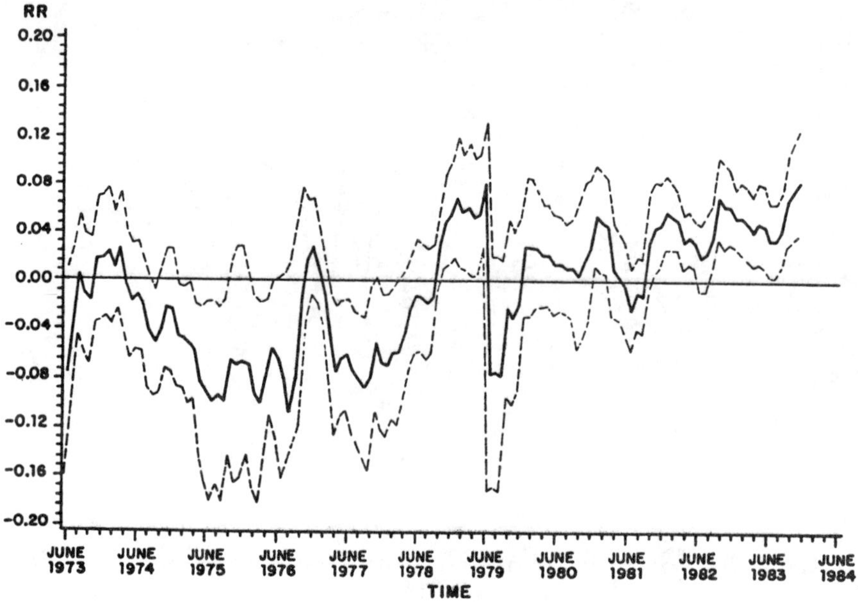

FIGURE 3. *Ex ante* real rates: United Kingdom (domestic money market rates).

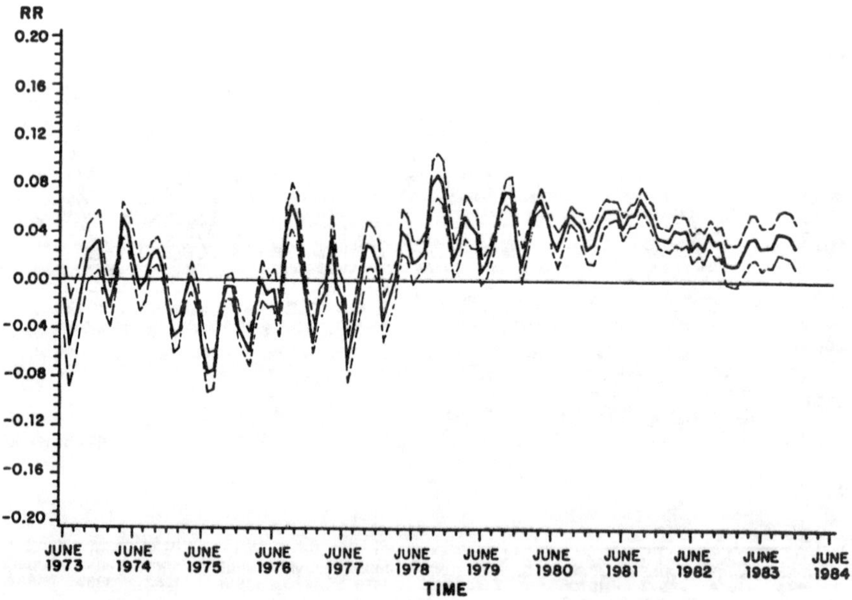

FIGURE 4. *Ex ante* real rates: Netherlands (domestic money market rates).

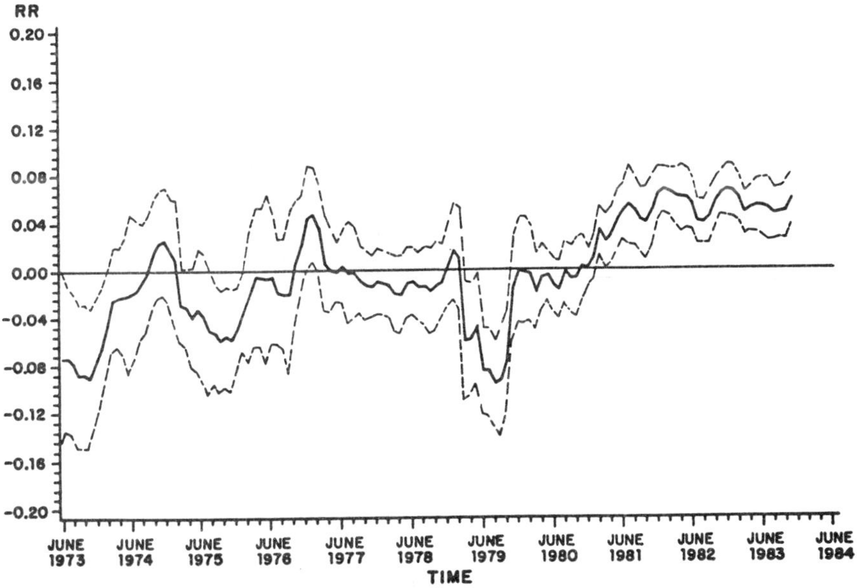

FIGURE 5. *Ex ante* real rates: Italy (domestic money market rates).

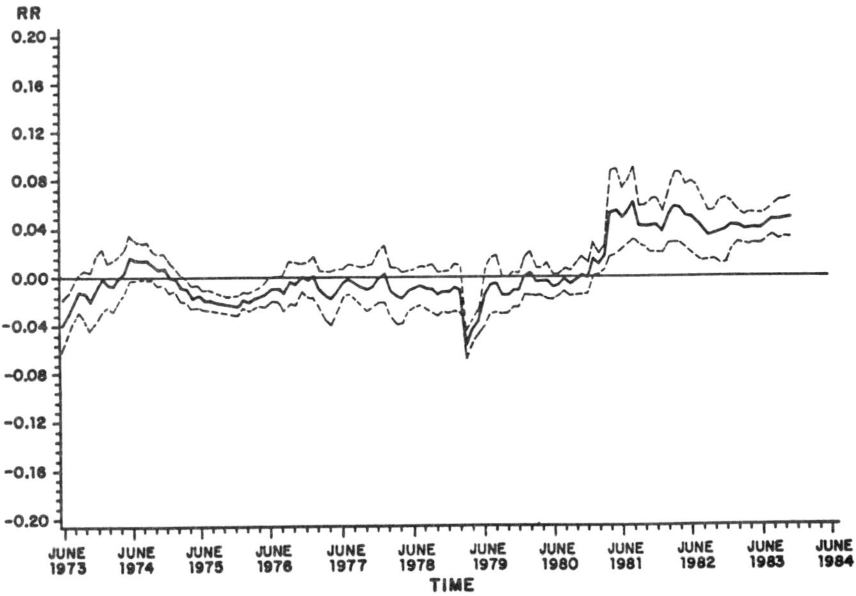

FIGURE 6. *Ex ante* real rates: France (domestic money market rates).

instruments.[16] The heavy solid lines show the estimated *ex ante* real rates, while the lighter lines surrounding the estimated real rates provide 95 per cent confidence intervals for these estimates under the sssumption that the variances of the forecast error term, $\varepsilon_{t,3}$, are large relative to the variance of $u_{t,3}$.[17]

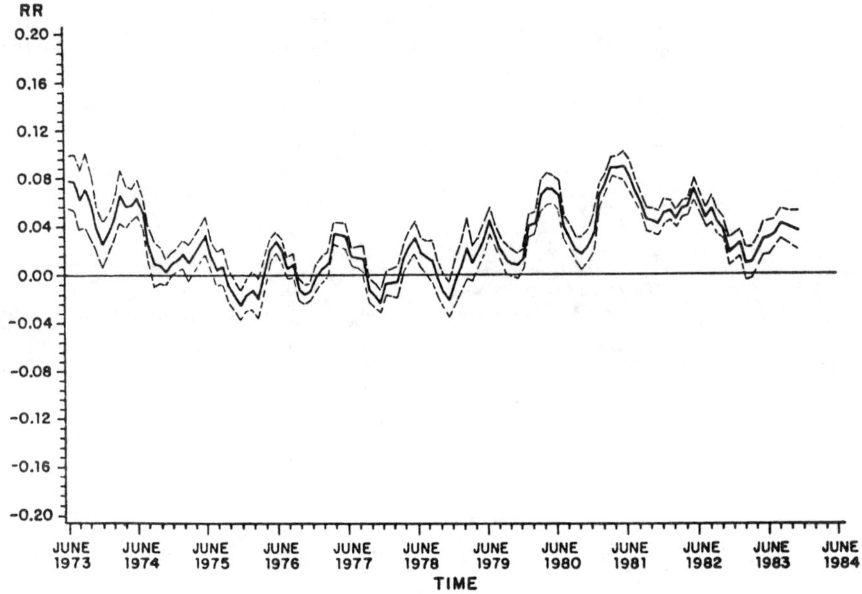

FIGURE 7. *Ex ante* real rates: West Germany (domestic money market rates).

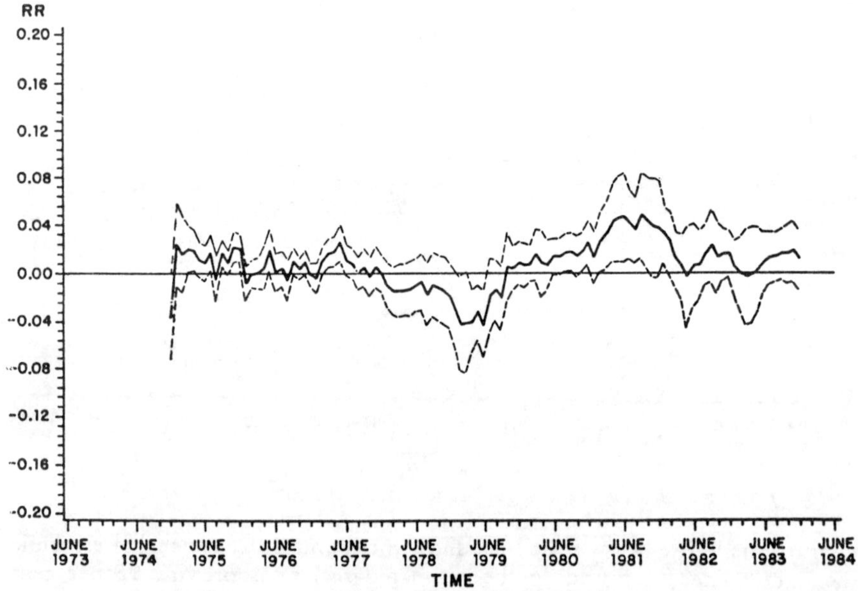

FIGURE 8. *Ex ante* real rates: Switzerland (domestic money market rates).

The estimated real rates for the United States in Figure 1 exhibit a sharp change in behavior after 1979, having a substantially higher level and increased volatility. The US real rates were low from the middle of 1973 until October 1979, have a substantial rise after the change in the Fed policy regime, a brief decline in the middle of 1980 when nominal interest rates decline temporarily, and a sustained period of high real rates thereafter. An important finding here is that in the 1980s real rates in the United States have approached 10 per cent at an annual rate, a level unprecedented in the post-war period, and they remain statistically significantly different from zero continuously from 1981 through 1983. The only period in US history where real interest rates appear to be as high was during the contraction phase of the Great Depression.[18] Complaints that real interest rates in the United States are exceedingly high seem to be well justified.

The estimated real rate for Canada seems to follow the US pattern reasonably closely, although Canadian real rates are actually declining from mid-1979 to mid-1980, when they begin their big rise. The UK real rates start their climb in late 1979 coincident with the rise in the US real rate, but are significantly positive only after August 1981.

The Italian and Dutch real rates do appear to be higher on average in the 1980s than in the 1970s, but they both have a brief period in late 1976 when they are particularly high. The timing of the real rate movements for these countries also does not appear to be as closely tied to real rate movements in the United States. The increase in real rates in the Netherlands occurs in 1978 with substantial upward and downward movements thereafter. The italian real rates have a very sharp decline and rise in late 1979 and in early 1981 the real rates are near zero.

The German and French real rate movements are particularly interesting. Although German real rates do rise in late 1979 as US real rates do, the rise is much smaller. The major climb in German real rates does not begin until late 1980, several months after the US increase. The increase in the French real rates is even more delayed. French real rates remain quite low until early 1981, hovering around zero. An increase then occurs, taking the real domestic money market rate rate to approximately 6 per cent.[19]

The Swiss real rates do appear to have a somewhat different pattern from the other real rates we have been looking at. Although there is a rise in Swiss real rates, which reach their highest levels in 1981, the extent of the rise is much less than in other countries, and they are only statistically significantly different from zero for a one year period in 1981. The amount of variation in Swiss real rates seems to be smaller than in other countries. In addition, the climb in real rates in Switzerland begins in early 1979, well before the increase in US real rates.

The general conclusions from these estimates from the eight countries is that they all show a tendency to have higher real interest rates in the 1980s than in the 1970s.[20] However, there are differences in the timing and extent of real rate movements in these countries. In light of the sometimes substantial confidence intervals around the real rate estimates, we need to examine more closely the degree to which real rates in different countries move together. We conduct statistical tests on this issue in the next section.

IV. Testing the Linkage Between Real Rates

Table 2 contains the first set of results on the degree of international association of real rates obtained from the regression of the real rates in the seven countries on the real rate in the United States. Of particular interest in these tables is the coefficient γ that describes the amount of movement in a country's real rate for a given movement in the US real rate. We test three hypotheses about real rate movements between the United States and these other countries. The first is that real rates are fully linked internationally ($\gamma=1$); the second is that there is no linkage between real rates in different countries ($\gamma=0$). The third is that real rates are equal across countries ($\alpha=0$ and $\gamma=1$).

Panel A contains the results on Euro deposits and Panel B the results on domestic money market instruments. In general the evidence is not favorable to either the hypothesis that real rates are fully linked or to the hypothesis that no international linkage exists. For both the Euro deposit rates and the domestic money market rates, the hypothesis of no linkage ($\gamma=0$) can be rejected at the five per cent level for all countries except Switzerland. The hypothesis of full linkage ($\gamma=1$) is rejected at the five per cent level for five countries for both instruments studied. In all cases the γ coefficients lie between 0 and 1. Canada has the highest coefficients, which are quite close to 1, especially for the domestic money market real rate. Germany has coefficients around 0.4; and Switzerland has the lowest coefficients, which are below 0.2. The remainder of the countries have coefficients between 0.5 and 0.8.[21] Table 2 also contains the χ^2 statistics for the hypothesis that real rates in each country are equal to real rates in the United States. The hypothesis of real rate equality is rejected in in all cases but France for the three-month Euro rates and in all cases but Canada for the domestic money market rates.[22]

In general then it appears that while real rates in all of the countries studied exhibit a statistically significant association with US real rate movements, this linkage is not complete. We then would want to ask whether there is a close association among real rates in the European countries? We explore this question by running regressions of the *ex post* real rate in European countries on the West Germany *ex post* real rate using the techniques outlined in Section I.

The results from these regressions can be found in Table 3, which gives roughly similar results to those we found in Table 2. The association between European real rates and West German real rates appears to be no closer than the association of European real rates with US real rates. The γ coefficients are not closer to one and the Swiss coefficients continue to be the lowest. It is also interesting to note that real rates in the EMS countries are no more closely related to German real rates than are real rates outside of the EMS. The standard errors of the γ coefficient are generally larger than those in Table 2, so that although we see significant rejections of both hypotheses that $\gamma=0$ or 1, these rejections are not as frequent.

V. Conclusions

In this paper we demonstrate that real interest rates have risen significantly in recent years and have been considerably higher since 1980 than during the 1970s. This increase in the general level of real rates has occurred in Canada and

TABLE 2. The link with US real interest rates. Consumer prices (June 1973–December 1983)[a].

A. Three-month Eurocurrency deposit rates

Country	α	γ	Test of equality of real rates[b] ($\alpha=0$, $\gamma=1$)
Canada	−0.0013 (0.0010)	0.8585 (0.0984)	13.50
United Kingdom	−0.0035 (0.0042)	0.5544 (0.2865)	22.28
Netherlands	0.0001 (0.0010)	0.5275 (0.0435)	375.53
Italy	0.0024 (0.0027)	0.5416 (0.1923)	8.72
France	0.0009 (0.0013)	0.7541 (0.1159)	4.53
West Germany	0.0020 (0.0010)	0.4281 (0.0773)	86.18
Switzerland	0.0026) (0.0012)	0.0703 (0.1024)	123.46

B. Domestic money market interest rates

Country	α	γ	Test of equality of real rates[b] ($\alpha=0$, $\gamma=1$)
Canada	0..0005 (0.0008)	0.9128 (0.0674)	1.67
United Kingdom	−0.0063 (0.0033)	0.7673 (0.2853)	22.01
Netherlands	0.0010 (0.0009)	0.5175 (0.0434)	241.36
Italy	−0.0032 (0.0022)	0.6370 (0.1477)	89.85
France	−0.0028 (0.0007)	0.5814 (0.0940)	55.41
West Germany	0.0037 (0.0010)	0.4373 (0.0915)	38.51
Switzerland	0.0023 (0.0009)	0.1635 (0.1043)	73.97

[a] The regressions begin in January 1976 for the Swiss money market interest rates. Standard errors are in parentheses. The instruments used in all cases were a constant, the nominal interest rate in the United States, three lagged values of inflation in the United States, and a time trend. These variables are also included multiplied by a dummy variable that is set equal to zero prior to October 1979 and one thereafter.

[b] Distributed as $\chi^2(2)$ under the null hypothesis. The critical value at the 5 per cent level is 5.99 and at the 1 per cent level is 9.21.

TABLE 3. The link among European real interest rates. Consumer prices (June 1973–December 1983)[a].

A. Three-month Eurocurrency deposit rates

Country	α	γ	Test of equality of real rates[b] ($\alpha=0$, $\gamma=1$)
France	0.0032 (0.0018)	0.5668 (0.3035)	56.09
Switzerland	0.0003 (0.0014)	0.1288 (0.1146)	213.34
Netherlands	0.0021 (0.0007)	0.4968 (0.1014)	26.88
Italy	0.0052 (0.0019)	0.3531 (0.1778)	13.30
United Kingdom	0.0021 (0.0035)	0.1538 (0.2762)	15.44

B. Domestic money market interest rates

Country	α	γ	Test of equality of real rates[b] ($\alpha=0$, $\gamma=1$)
France	−0.0013 (0.0014)	0.2395 (0.1460)	56.09
Switzerland	0.0004 (0.0005)	0.1254 (0.0419)	758.12
Netherlands	0.0025 (0.0011)	0.3776 (0.1408)	32.73
Italy	−0.0063 (0.0016)	0.7913 (0.1594)	39.94
United Kingdom	−0.0011 (0.0033)	0.1210 (0.2431)	29.41

[a] The regressions begin in January 1976 for the Swiss money market interest rates. Standard errors are in parentheses. The instruments used in all cases were a constant, three lagged values of inflation in West Germany, the nominal interest rate in West Germany, and a time trend. These variables are also included multiplied by a dummy variable that is set equal to zero prior to April 1979 and one thereafter.

[b] Distributed as $\chi^2(2)$ under the null hypothesis. The critical value at the 5 per cent level is 5.99 and at the 1 per cent level is 9.21.

several European countries as well as in the United States.[23] We also find that there is a significant positive correlation between real rate movements in the United States and those in seven other industrialized countries, and that the degree of international linkage in real rates, while significantly positive, is also significantly less than complete. In addition, the evidence suggests that real rates within Europe are not more closely linked with one another than they are with US real rates.

Recent claims that real interest rates are currently at levels unprecedented in recent history receive strong support from our findings that real rates have increased significantly. In addition, our evidence that there is a significant positive association between real rates in the United States and those in other countries is consistent with the frequently advanced argument that high US real rates have been transmitted abroad. However, it should be emphasized that, while consistent with these arguments, our estimates provide no evidence on the direction of causation of real rate movements: they do not necessarily imply that high US real rates have caused high real rates elsewhere.

The evidence we present also points to significant independence in real rate movements in the countries in our sample, a point that has received little attention in recent discussions by policy makers.[24] This finding of a less than complete linkage in real rates has important implications for questions concerning the ability of domestic stabilization policies to influence the economy by affecting real interest rates. Our evidence is consistent with models that, for example, allow monetary policy to have real effects. However, since we do not provide evidence on the source of these significant differences in real rates, our results cannot rule out models in which money is neutral and real rate differences arise due to relative price movements resulting from real shocks to the economy.

Notes

1. This widely-noted change in the level of real rates in the United States has been carefully documented by Huizinga and Mishkin (1984).
2. For further references see the surveys of Frenkel and Mussa (1984) and Obstfeld and Stockman (1984).
3. The methodology outlined here has been discussed more extensively in Mishkin (1981, 1984a) and Huizinga and Mishkin (1984). All returns, inflation and interest rates in the analysis here are continuously compounded so that the additional second order term is not needed in equation ⟨1⟩. Note that there has been a change in the timing of the notation here from Mishkin (1981, 1984a, 1984b) necessitated by the use of overlapping data. What was called rr_t in Mishkin (1981, 1984a, 1984b) corresponds to $rr_{t-1,1}$ in the notation adopted here.
4. Since we are considering assets held to maturity, there is no uncertainty about nominal interest rates.
5. Hansen and Hodrick (1980) show that using overlapping data to sample observations more frequently increases the efficiency of estimates.
6. Huizinga and Mishkin (1984) reject the hypothesis of conditional homoscedasticity of inflation forecast errors for the United States as do Cumby and Obstfeld (1984) for five countries, including the United States. Models of the changing conditional variance of inflation are presented in Engle (1983) and Hasbrouck (1984) for the United States and by Engle (1982) for the United Kingdom.
7. The instruments in our empirical analysis are US nominal interest rates, past US inflation rates, a constant term and a time trend. These instruments should satisfy the criteria described above.
8. In the special case where the number of parameters to be estimated is equal to the number of instrumental variables, two-step two stage least squares reduces to McCallum's instrumental variables estimator with the correct standard errors and hence provides no gain in efficiency.
9. See Mishkin (1981).
10. Prior to January 1977, three-month municipal loans are used.

11. This series is described more extensively in Huizinga and Mishkin (1984).
12. The addition of other variables such as money growth and industrial production provided no significant explanatory power. These variables were therefore omitted in order to conserve on degrees of freedom. The programs used to perform all of the calculations in this paper are available from the authors upon request.
13. As Huizinga and Mishkin (1984) point out, the breakpoint of October 1979 is somewhat arbitrary. It is entirely possible that the breakpoint occurred somewhat before or after this date.
14 We have also split the sample period for all the countries at October 1979 and the results did not change appreciably.
15. See Mishkin (1981).
16 We have not presented the estimated real Euro deposit rates in the interest of saving space. The estimates of the real Euro rates were similar to the estimates of the real domestic money market rates except in the case of the French franc, as is noted below.
17. The formulae for the standard error bounds are given in Mishkin (1981). This assumption on the relative importance of the two components of the composite error term in equation ⟨7⟩ is supported by the correlogram of the residuals in Table 1.
18. See Mishkin (1981).
19. The real rate on Euro French franc deposits shows a very similar pattern, although we do see the effect of capital controls. The real Euro rates rise much more than the real domestic money market rates, reaching a level of over 15 per cent.
20. Mishkin (1984) presents estimates of *ex ante* real rates for the countries studied here but his sample ends in the second quarter of 1979. His estimates therefore do not include the widespread dramatic increase in real rates we find here.
21. It would also have been interesting to test the joint hypothesis that all γ's equal 0 and the joint hypothesis that all γ's equal 1. However, this did not prove to be computationally feasible.
22. The critical value for a χ^2 with 2 degrees freedom is 5.99 at the 95 per cent level and 9.21 at the 99 per cent level. It is interesting to note that the rejections of real rate equality we obtain are stronger than those obtained in the bilateral tests in Cumby and Obstfeld (1984) except in the case of Canada.
23. Two caveats should be mentioned. The first is the 'peso problem' (Krasker 1980), which is essentially a problem in finite-sample inference. Suppose, for example, that for a substantial portion of the period of declining *ex post* inflation in the 1980s, agents rationally expected inflation to increase again. While these agents' expectations would be correct on average in an infinite sample, we have only ten years of data at our disposal. Since no increase in inflation was realized in the sample, the 'peso problem' may lead us to underestimate expected inflation during part of the sample and, therefore, to overestimate real rates during the same period. The second caveat is that we estimate *pre-tax* real rates. As pointed out by Darby (1975), after tax real rates will rise by more than pre-tax rates when inflation declines. Our estimates may then underestimate the increase in after-tax real rates in the 1980s. In addition, if marginal tax rates differ internationally, after tax real rates may be equal even if pre-tax real rates differ. However, to the extent that marginal tax rates move little over time, differential taxes may explain significant constant terms in the regressions in Tables 2 and 3, but not slope coefficients that differ insignificantly from one. See Mark (1985).
24. This point has received attention in the academic literature, however. Darby, Lothian, *et al.* (1983) provide considerable empirical evidence regarding the degree of independence of interest rates and inflation rates.

References

Branson, W.H., 'Exchange Rate Dynamics and Monetary Policy,' in A. Lindbeck, ed., *Inflation and Unemployment in Open Economies,* Amsterdam: North-Holland, 1979.

Cumby, R. E., J. Huizinga, and M. Obstfeld, 'Two-Step Two-Stage Least Squares Estimation in Models with Rational Expectations,' *Journal of Econometrics,* April 1983, **21**: 333–355.

Cumby, R.E. and M. Obstfeld, 'International Interest-Rate and Price-Level Linkages under Flexible Exchange Rates: A Review of Recent Evidence,' in J.F.O. Bilson and R. Marston, eds, *Exchange Rates: Theory and Practice,* Chicago: University of Chicago Press for the NBER, 1984.

DARBY, M.R., 'The Financial and Tax Effects of Monetary Policy on Interest Rates,' *Economic Inquiry*, June 1975, **8**: 266–276.

DARBY, M.R., J.R. LOTHIAN, A.E. GANDOLFI, A.J. SCHWARTZ, AND A.C. STOCKMAN, *The International Transmission of Inflation*, Chicago: University of Chicago Press for the NBER, 1983.

DORNBUSCH, R., 'Expectations and Exchange Rate Dynamics,' *Journal of Political Economy*, December 1976, **84**: 1161–1176.

DORNBUSCH, R., 'Real Interest Rates, Home Goods, and Optimal External Borrowing,' *Journal of Political Economy*, February 1983, **91**: 141–153.

ENGLE, R., 'Autoregressive Conditional Heteroscedasticity with Estimates of United Kingdom Inflation,' *Econometrica*, July 1982, **50**: 987–1007.

ENGLE, R., 'Estimates of the Variance of U.S. Inflation Based upon the ARCH Model,' *Journal of Money, Credit, and Banking*, March 1983, **15**: 286–301.

FISHER, I., *The Theory of Interest*, New York: Macmillan, 1930.

FRANKEL, J.A., 'On the Mark: A Theory of Flating Exchange Rates Based on Real Interest Differentials,' *American Economic Review*, September 1979, **69**: 610–622.

FRENKEL, J.A. AND M.L. MUSSA, 'Asset Markets, Exchange Rates and the Balance of Payments,' in P. Kenen and R. Jones, eds, *Handbook of International Economics*, Amsterdam: North Holland, 1984.

GIRTON, L. AND D. HENDERSON, 'Central Bank Operations in Foreign and Domestic Assets under Fixed and Flexible Exchange Rates,' in P.B. Clark, D. Logue, and R. Sweeny, eds, *The Effects of Exchange Rate Adjustments*, Washington: US Government Printing Office, 1977.

HANSEN, L.P., 'Large Sample Properties of Generalized Method of Moments Estimators,' *Econometrica*, July 1982, **50**: 1029–1054.

HANSEN, L.P. AND R.J. HODRICK, 'Forward Exchange Rates as Optimal Predictors of Future Spot Exchange Rates,' *Journal of Political Economy*, October 1980, **88**: 829–853.

HASBROUCK, J., 'Forecaster Discord and Consensus Prediction Error: An Econometric Investigation,' Working Paper, New York University, 1984.

HODRICK, R.J., 'Some Evidence on the Equality of Expected Real Interest Rates Across Countries,' Working Paper, Carnegie-Mellon University, 1979.

HUIZINGA, J. AND F.S. MISHKIN, 'Inflation and Real Interest Rates on Assets with Different Risk Characteristics,' *Journal of Finanace*, July 1984, **39**: 699–712.

KRASKER, W.S., 'The "Peso Problem" in Testing the Efficiency of Forward Exchange Markets,' *Journal of Monetary Economics*, April 1980, **6**: 269–276.

MCCALLUM, B.T., 'Rational Expectations and the Natural Rate Hypothesis: Some Consistent Estimates,' *Econometrica*, January 1976, **44**: 43–52.

Mark, N.C., 'Some Evidence on the International Inequality of Real Interest Rates,' *Journal of International Money and Finanace*, June 1985, **4**: 189–208.

MISHKIN, F.S., 'The Real Interest Rate: An Empirical Investigation,' *Carnegie-Rochester Conference Series on Public Policy*, Autumn 1981, **15**: 151–200.

MISHKIN, F.S., 'The Real Interest Rate: A Multicountry Empirical Study,' *Canadian Journal of Economics*, May 1984, **17**: 283–311 (1984a).

MISHKIN, F.S., 'Are Real Interest Rates Equal Across Countries: An Empirical Investigation of International Parity Conditions,' *Journal of Finanace*, December 1984, **39**: 1345–1357 (1984b).

MUSSA, M.L., 'A Model of Exchange Rate Dynamics,' *Journal of Political Economy*, February 1982, **90**: 74–104.

OBSTFELD, M., 'Intertemporal Price Speculation and the Optimal Current Account Deficit,' *Journal f International Money and Finanace*, August 1983, **2**: 135–145.

OBSTFELD, M. AND A.C. STOCKMAN, 'Exchange Rate Dynamics,' in P. Kenen and R. Jones, eds, *Handbook of International Economics*, Amsterdam: North-Holland, 1984.

STOCKMAN, A.C. AND A.T.KOH, 'Models of Business Cycles in Open Economics,' Working Paper, University of Rochester, 1982.

Carnegie-Rochester Conference Series on Public Policy 24 (1986) 231-274
North-Holland

MONETARY POLICY REGIME SHIFTS AND THE UNUSUAL BEHAVIOR OF REAL INTEREST RATES*

JOHN HUIZINGA
University of Chicago
and
National Bureau of Economic Research
and
FREDERIC S. MISHKIN
Columbia University
and
National Bureau of Economic Research

I. INTRODUCTION

A striking phenomenon of the early 1980s is the climb in real interest rates to levels unprecedented in the post-World War II period. In order to understand this phenomenon, it is not enough to focus on the recent high level of real rates, as in several recent papers;[1] research has also revealed a significant shift in the stochastic process of real interest rates.[2] Modern monetary theory suggests that regime changes have an important impact on the stochastic process of many economic variables. Thus, a change in a policy regime (by which we mean a change in the direction of policy or the way in which policy is conducted) may explain the unusual real rate experience in recent years.

In this paper, we investigate the nature and timing of shifts in the

*We thank Depaio Tang and Wilbur Coleman for research assistance and the Alfred P. Sloan Foundation, the General Motors Corporation Faculty Research Fellowship, and the NSF for financial support. We also thank Andrew Abel, Robert Cumby, Eugene Fama, Albert Hart, Allan Meltzer, Maurice Obstfeld, Adrian Pagan, William Schwert, and participants at the Carnegie-Rochester Conference and seminars at Columbia University, the Federal Reserve Bank of Kansas City, the Hoover Institution, Northwestern University, and the University of Virginia. This research is part of the National Bureau of Economic Research's program in Economic Fluctuations. The usual disclaimer applies.

[1]See for example. Blanchard and Summers (1984) and Holland (1984).

[2]See Huizinga and Mishkin (1984).

real rate process to determine if the unusual behavior of real rates is associated with monetary policy regime changes. We find that when the Federal Reserve alters its behavior as in October 1979 and October 1982, there are statistically significant shifts in the stochastic process of real rates. Statistical analysis designed to determine the timing of the shifts in the real rate process indicates that these dates are also the most likely choices for breakpoints.

The above evidence suggests that the Fed's changes in the monetary policy regime are likely candidates for explaining the recent unusual behavior of real interest rates. Our search for an understanding of how these changes might have altered real rate behavior proceeds along two dimensions. First, since the Fed's 1979 changes in operating procedures were associated with increased variability of interest rates, money supply growth, and inflation, we explore whether increased uncertainty about these variables plays a significant role in real rate movements.[3] We find little evidence supporting the importance of uncertainty in the recent unusual behavior of real rates.

Second, we look for other periods in which there is a clearly defined change in the monetary policy regime that bears similarities to the recent regime changes.[4] In a sense, we are looking for other "controlled experiments" that provide information on how monetary policy regime changes affect real interest rates. One such "experiment" is in 1920, when the Federal Reserve sharply raised its discount rate twice. This episode is a natural one to study because the economy was suffering from a high and persistent inflation before the regime shift, while afterwards a sharp disinflation occurred. This is similar to what we have seen in recent years and thus we might expect to find parallels between the two periods.

Our analysis of the period surrounding 1920 reveals a significant shift in the stochastic process of real interest rates which has many similarities to the recent experience. For example, the 1920 monetary regime change and the subsequent disinflation is associated with a weakening of

---

[3]Mascaro and Meltzer (1983) have argued that increased monetary uncertainty is an important factor in the recent rise in real rates. Fama (1976) has found a link among real interest rates, inflation uncertainty, and nominal interest-rate uncertainty. Hartman and Makin (1982) also find a link between inflation uncertainty and interest rates.

[4]Shiller (1980) has also examined historical episodes to see if a change in the monetary policy regime affects real interest rates. For the end of Fed-Treasury accord he finds a noticeable change in the behavior of real interest rates.

the Fisher effect and a shift to a sustained higher level of real interest rates, which are also characteristic of the recent period. Although our analysis does not reveal the precise mechanism through which changes in monetary policy regimes affect real interest rates, it does suggest that disinflation is a more important factor in the recent policy regime shift than is the increased variability of money growth, inflation, and interest rates.

Other studies have examined competing explanations for the recent unusual behavior of real interest rates -- e.g., budget deficits, investment booms, favorable changes in business taxation, and the declining relative price of energy. Although these competing explanations have met with mixed success, our evidence lends substantial support to the view that monetary policy regime changes have been and continue to be an important source of shifts in the behavior of real interest rates. Future research should focus on how changes in monetary policy regimes produce shifts in real interest rate movements.

II. THE METHODOLOGY

The real interest rate of concern to economists is more precisely referred to as the ex ante real interest rate. At time t, this ex ante rate is defined as the expectation at time t of the ex post real return on an asset when it is held from time t to t+1. In the case of a one-period, default-free, nominal bond, whose expected nominal return is equal to its nominal interest rate at time t, the ex ante real interest rate is:

$$rr_t \equiv i_t - \pi_t^e \qquad (1)$$

where

rr_t = the ex ante real interest rate on the one-period bond at time t: i.e., the ex ante real return from time t to t+1.

i_t = the nominal interest rate on the one-period bond at time t: i.e., the nominal return from time t to t+1.

π_t^e = the inflation rate from time t to t+1 expected at time t.

The ex post real rate is defined as,

$$eprr_t = i_t - \pi_t = rr_t - \varepsilon_t \tag{2}$$

where

$eprr_t$ = the ex post real interest rate on the one-period bond at time t: i.e., the realized real return from time t to t+1.

π_t = the actual inflation rate from time t to t+1.

ε_t = the inflation forecast error, $\pi_t - \pi_t^e$.

Although the ex post real rate is observable, the ex ante rate is not. Thus, in order to measure and make inferences about the ex ante real rate, some identifying assumptions are needed. In this paper we use the identifying assumptions that expectations of inflation are rational and that the ex ante real rate can be reasonably approximated by linear projection onto an observable information set. The assumption of rational expectations implies that inflation forecast errors are unforecastable given any information available at time t: i.e.,

$$E(\varepsilon_t \mid \phi_t) = 0 \tag{3}$$

where

ϕ_t = represents all the information available at time t.

$E(\ldots \mid \phi_t)$ = the mathematical expectations operator conditional on the information set ϕ_t.

Describing the ex ante real interest rate as a linear projection onto an observable information set X_t gives,

$$rr_t = X_t\beta + u_t \tag{4}$$

where

X_t = a subset of ϕ_t.

u_t = the error from projecting rr_t on X_t, which by construction is uncorrelated with X_t.

Combining equations (1) through (4) generates the following ex post real rate regression equation,

$$eprr_t = X_t\beta + u_t - \varepsilon_t \tag{5}$$

As shown in Mishkin (1981), ordinary least squares (OLS) estimation of this regression equation yields consistent estimates of the parameters in β. This conclusion stems from the orthogonality of the composite error term $u_t - \varepsilon_t$ with X_t.[5]

Within the above framework, a logical way to test for a shift in the stochastic process of the ex ante real rate is to test for the constancy of β when equation (5) is estimated over different samples. We do this with a conventional F-test (Chow test). We date when the real rate process shifts using a procedure proposed by Quandt (1958, 1960). This procedure involves finding the breakpoints that maximize the likelihood of the ex post real rate regression. Specifically, for each set of potential breakpoints, we calculate minus twice the log of the Quandt likelihood ratio -- the maximized likelihood assuming there are no breaks, divided by the maximized likelihood conditional on that set of breakpoints. When this statistic reaches its maximum, we have found the set of breakpoints that maximizes the likelihood function.

Are the procedures for testing and dating of breakpoints meaningful? How are they to be interpreted if there is information Z_t in ϕ_t that is relevant for predicting the ex ante real rate but is unknown to the econometrician and has thus been excluded from X_t? To examine these questions, consider the hypothetical case in which the ex ante real rate can be expressed as

$$rr_t = X_t\beta^* + Z_t\delta \tag{6}$$

This implies that the coefficient β in equation (4) and (5) can be expressed as,

$$\beta = \beta^* + \lambda\delta \tag{7}$$

where

[5]Note that there has been a change in the timing of the notation here from Mishkin (1981, 1984a,b): $eprr_t$, rr_t, u_t and ε_t in the notation here correspond to $eprr_{t+1}$, rr_{t+1}, u_{t+1} and ε_{t+1} in the earlier Mishkin papers.

λ = the regression coefficient of X_t in a regression of Z_t on X_t.

A change in β represents either (1) a change in the way information is used to predict ex ante real rates (a change in β^* or δ), or (2) a change in the relation between the variables in the information set (a change in λ). Either of these changes can cause a change in the stochastic process of real rates.

We are interested not only in verifying a break in the stochastic process of real interest rates but also in examining measures of the ex ante real rate to see how the stochastic process changes. Given the consistency of $\hat{\beta}$, it is logical to estimate the ex ante real rate as the fitted values obtained from OLS estimation of equation (5): i.e.,

$$\hat{rr}_t = X_t\hat{\beta} \tag{8}$$

where

$\hat{\beta}$ = the OLS estimate of β.

How good is this estimate? In a large sample the estimated ex ante real rate defined in equation (8) will differ from the true ex ante real rate by u_t, so that when u_t has small variance, $\hat{rr}_t$ is an accurate measure.

While it would be desirable to know that the variance of u_t is small, unfortunately its variance is not identifiable. However, there may be information in the data concerning the variance of u_t. Our information is limited to the variances and autocovariances of the regression residual from the ex post real rate regression, $u_t - \varepsilon_t$. Under rational expectations, ε_t is serially uncorrelated, yet u_t may be autocorrelated or correlated with past values of ε_t. If this is the case and the variance of u_t is large, then the regression residual, $u_t - \varepsilon_t$, is serially correlated. However, if the variance of u_t is small, then the regression residual, $u_t - \varepsilon_t$, is dominated by ε_t and is necessarily serially uncorrelated. Thus a diagnostic check of the X_t specification involves examining the residuals from the ex post real rate regressions to see if they are white noise.[6]

The last remaining issue is how we choose the information set X_t. As described above, the choice of the variables in X_t comprises part of the identifying of assumptions for measuring real interest rates. A variety of previous research uses the identifying assumption that ex ante real rates follow a random walk:[7] i.e., $X_t = rr_{t-1}$ and the coefficient $\beta = 1$. Evidence in Litterman and Weiss (1985) is inconsistent with this assumption: they find the ex ante real rate follows an AR(1) process with the AR coefficient significantly less than one.[8]

In light of this finding and the lack of a compelling theoretical justification for the random walk specification, we feel it appropriate to use a less restrictive set of identifying assumptions about the time series process for the ex ante real rate. This can be accomplished by including a distributed lag of ex post real rates and inflation rates in X_t.[9] This methodology also allows us to relax another assumption used by proponents of the random walk specification -- that unexpected inflation between time t-1 and t has no explanatory power for the ex ante real rate at t. Again, there is no compelling theoretical justification for this assumption and it is inconsistent with evidence in Litterman and Weiss (1985).[10]

By including other economic variables known at time t in X_t, we allow additional factors to help predict ex ante real interest rate movements, making our approach even more general. Specifically, we can include a measure of supply shocks which may affect ex ante real interest rates by

---

[6]Although the diagnostic check described here is valuable, it is not powerful against certain alternatives. If u_t is not serially correlated or correlated with past ε_t, then the regression residual $u_t - \varepsilon_t$ will not be serially correlated even if the variance of u_t is large. For example, if the X_t specification includes many lags of $eprr_t$, then u_t will not display any serial correlation and the diagnostic check will have little power.

[7]See, for example, Garbade and Wachtel (1978), Fama and Gibbons (1982), and Antoncic (1983).

[8]Evidence in Huizinga and Mishkin (1985) also suggests that the random walk assumption for the ex ante real rate is inappropriate.

[9]See Huizinga and Mishkin (1985).

[10]This assumption is not an assumption about monetary neutrality. Real factors can lead to unexpected inflation and have a lasting effect on the ex ante real interest rate. Litterman and Weiss (1985) estimate the correlation coefficient between unexpected inflation and the innovation in the ex ante real rate to be -.64.

affecting current and/or expected future investment opportunities.[11] We can also include the nominal interest rate at time t which may be able to capture other, hard to measure, influences on the ex ante real rate. The nominal rate is likely to reflect these other influences because it is composed of the ex ante real rate itself, as well as expected inflation, which a variety of evidence has shown to be negatively related to ex ante real rates.[12]

III. THE DATA

Two monthly data sets are used in this paper: one for the time-period from January 1953 to December 1984 and the other for the time-period from January 1916 to December 1927. We begin the postwar period in January 1953 because the quality of the CPI was substantially upgraded at this time. We stop in December 1984 because of data availability. We begin the earlier period in January 1916 because this is the beginning of the sustained inflation that lasted until the middle of 1920. We end in December 1927 because data availability requires us to use assets with risk premiums which begin to undergo substantial fluctuations after this date.

For the 1953-84 period, the nominal interest rates are computed from one-month United States Treasury Bill prices (end of the month) obtained from the bond file of the Center for Research in Security Prices (CRSP) at the University of Chicago. The rates are continuously compounded rates, expressed at a monthly rate.

The inflation rate is computed as the one-month change in the log of the consumer price index (CPI). To obtain a price index that appropriately treats housing costs on a rental-equivalence basis, we use four series to

[11]It is not clear a priori what effect a supply shock that raises the relative price of energy would have on ex ante real rates. The most common story, outlined by Wilcox (1983), has a rise in the relative price of energy decreasing investment opportunities, which lowers the demand for loanable funds and hence ex ante real rates. However, it is also possible that a rise in the relative price of energy might increase the returns to new capital even though it reduces the value of old capital. Then we might expect ex ante real rates to rise rather than fall, with an increase in the relative price of energy. Both Wilcox (1983) and Huizinga and Mishkin (1985) find that a rise in the relative price of energy is associated with a fall in ex ante real interest rates.

[12]Fama and Gibbons (1982), Huizinga and Mishkin (1985), Litterman and Weiss (1985), Nelson and Schwert (1977), Mishkin (1981), and Summers (1983).

construct our CPI measure. From January 1983 to December 1984, we use the Bureau of Labor Statistics (BLS) widely reported CPI-U series, which is on a rental-equivalence basis. Before January 1983, however, the CPI-U series is not on a rental-equivalence basis which leads to serious biases in measures of real rates in the 1970s.[13] Thus, from January 1954 to December 1982, we use the series CPI-UX, a series which is consistent with the currently produced CPI-U series. This is actually two series because the data from January 1967 to December 1982 are obtained from the BLS, while the data from January 1954 to December 1966 are obtained from the Congressional Budget Office. Prior to January 1954, we use the CPI-U series.

Our measure of supply shocks is calculated as the log of the relative price of fuel and related products in the producer price index. The data were obtained from the BLS. Money supply growth is calculated as the one-month change in the log of monthly averages of seasonally adjusted M1. The money supply data were obtained from the Board of Governors of the Federal Reserve System. They include the February 1984 benchmark revisions, but not those of February 1985.

For the 1916-27 period, we use three nominal interest rate series because a series for a one-month government bond is unavailable. The three series are monthly averages of the rate on 4/6-month prime commercial paper, the rate on 90-day stock exchange time loans, and the average rate on stock exchange call loans (renewal rate). These data are obtained from the Board of Governors of the Federal Reserve System, Banking and Monetary Statistics 1914-1941.[14] Monthly averaged data are used because last-week-of-the-month data are available only after 1919. We have used the last-week-of-the-month data in the 1919-1927 period and have obtained similar results to those found for monthly averaged data. All rates are treated as though they were one-month rates and have been converted to continuously compounded rates, expressed at a monthly rate.

Inflation in the 1916-27 period is measured as the one-month change in the log of the CPI-U series provided by the BLS.

[13] See Huizinga and Mishkin (1984). Note that the BLS does not revise earlier CPI-U data when it changes the procedures for its calculations. This requires us to construct a consistent CPI series using the procedures outlined above.

[14] Macaulay (1938), Appendix E, describes background information on these rates including a description of why they are the most representative of market-clearing interest rates in this period.

The timing of variables is as follows. The real interest rates we examine are for a one-month holding period.[15] The ex post real interest rate ($eprr_t$) for 1953:1 is the realized real return for a one-month United States Treasury Bill over the month of January 1953. It equals the nominal interest rate on the one-month bill (i_t) on December 31, 1952 minus the inflation rate (π_t) calculated using the December 1952 and January 1953 CPI. The supply variable for 1953:1 ($SUPPLY_t$) is calculated using the January 1953 fuel and related products component of the PPI and the January 1953 overall PPI. For 1916:1, the ex post real interest rate for each of the three assets ($eprr_t$) equals its average nominal interest rate (i_t) for December 1915 minus the inflation rate (π_t) calculated using the December 1915 and January 1916 CPI.

IV. THE NATURE AND TIMING OF SHIFTS IN THE REAL RATE PROCESS: 1953-84

Our discussion of methodology in Section II suggests that X_t, the explanatory variables in the ex post real rate regression, should include lags of ex post real rates and inflation as well as other economic variables known at time t, such as the nominal interest rate and a supply shock variable. In practice, the variables that should be included in X_t must be limited in order to avoid overfitting the data. This is especially necessary in the present analysis because we are examining time periods as short as 26 months.

This need for parsimony has led us to terminate lag lengths and omit variables when doing so does not significantly diminish the explanatory power of the ex post real rate regression. To arrive at our specification, we examined separate regressions for the 1953:1 to 1979:10, 1979:11 to 1982:10, and 1982:11 to 1984:12 sample periods. We chose this division of sample periods to correspond with our prior belief that the changes in the

[15] In previous work [Mishkin (1981) and Huizinga and Mishkin (1984, 1985)] we have argued that one-month holding periods have timing problems that arise because the appropriate dating for the CPI is unclear. Although three-month holding periods have the advantage of reducing the relative magnitude of this timing problem, they have the disadvantage of reducing the number of nonoverlapping observations. In our empirical analysis here, which centers on dating breakpoints and thus requires estimation over short sample periods, we feel that the loss of degrees of freedom resulting from the use of three-month holding periods outweighs the benefits from reducing the timing problem.

Federal Reserve operating procedures in October 1979 and October 1982 constitute regime shifts. Variables which entered significantly at the 5% level in any of the three periods were included in our final specification for X_t. The resulting specification of X_t includes a constant term, the one-month nominal interest rate (i_t), the one-month inflation rate lagged one and two months (π_{t-1} and π_{t-2}), and the supply shock variable lagged one month ($SUPPLY_{t-1}$).[16]

Recall that a diagnostic check of the X_t specification involves examining the residuals from the ex post real rate regression to see if they are white noise. Table 1 reports the autocorrelations of the regression residuals for the three sample periods mentioned above. In all three sample periods there is little evidence of serial correlation of the residuals.[17] The first twelve autocorrelations are small and the Ljung-Box (1978) Q(12) statistic, which is distributed asymptotically as $\chi^2(12)$ under the null hypothesis that the residuals are serially uncorrelated, is not significant at the 5% level for any of the three periods. Given that we have found no evidence which contradicts our specification, we proceed to an examination of the nature and timing of shifts in the real rate process.

The October 1979 change in operating procedures away from interest-rate smoothing is a natural candidate for a monetary policy regime shift. The deemphasis of monetary aggregates by the Fed in October 1982 is another natural candidate. Our next set of results examines whether there were shifts in the real rate process at these dates. The stability test reported in the first column of Table 2 indicates that there was a highly

[16]Variables which we have examined but have dropped from our final specification include lags of the ex post real rate, additional lags of inflation and supply shocks, and lags of industrial production and detrended industrial production. Note that adding lags of nominal rates is equivalent to adding lags of the ex post real rate, given that we have included lags of inflation. Other potentially relevant variables -- for example, the unemployment rate, investment, budget deficits, and, most notably, money supply growth -- were not included in our specification search either because monthly data were unavailable or because previous research fails to find that these variables have significant explanatory power for ex ante real rates. For example, Litterman and Weiss (1985) and Mishkin (1981) find that money supply growth does not help to predict ex ante real rates. However, it is important to realize that this finding does not imply that monetary policy is unimportant for the determination of ex ante real interest rates.

[17]There is some evidence of seasonality in the residuals because the autocorrelation at lag 12 in the 1953:1 to 1979:10 sample period is significantly different from zero at the 5% level, although not at the 1% level. However, as pointed out in Mishkin (1981), we do not devote much attention to this seasonality because it may well be spurious due to the fixed-weight nature of the CPI.

Table 1

Autocorrelations of Ex Post Real Rate Regression Residuals

1953-1984

	Autocorrelation at Lag														
Sample Period	1	2	3	4	5	6	7	8	9	10	11	12	SE	Q(12)	MSL
1953:1 - 1979:10	.01	-.01	-.03	-.02	-.04	-.01	-.04	-.02	.07	.11	.03	.14	.06	14.72	.26
1979:11 - 1982:10	-.06	-.04	-.07	.08	.15	.07	-.15	.05	-.15	-.12	.10	.10	.17	6.07	.91
1982:11 - 1984:12	.14	.06	.03	-.14	.07	-.14	.04	-.10	.17	-.03	-.06	.18	.20	5.61	.93

SE = Asymptotic standard error of the estimated autocorrelations under the assumption that the true residuals are serially uncorrelated.

Q(12) = Adjusted Q-statistic suggested by Ljung and Box (1978) which is distributed asymptotically as $X^2(12)$ under the null hypothesis that the residuals are serially uncorrelated.

MSL = Marginal significance level of Q-statistic, i.e., the probability of obtaining that value of the X^2 statistic or higher under the null hypothesis that the residuals are serially uncorrelated.

Residuals from a regression of the ex post real rate, $eprr_t$, on a constant, $\pi_{t-1}, \pi_{t-2}, i_t$ and $SUPPLY_{t-1}$.

Table 2

Stability Tests for Ex Post Real Rate Regressions

1953-1984

F-Test for Equality of Coefficients in			
1953:1 - 1979:10 and 1979:11 - 1982:10	1979:11 - 1982:10 and 1982:11 - 1984:12	1953:1 - 1979:10 and 1982:11 - 1984:12	1953:1 - 1966:5 and 1966:6 - 1979:10
$F(5,348) = 12.14$**	$F(5,52) = 3.99$**	$F(5,338) = 8.90$**	$F(5,312) = 1.12$
(1.7×10^{-10})	(.0039)	(5.9×10^{-8})	(.34)

Regressions of the ex post real rate, $eprr_t$, on $\pi_{t-1}, \pi_{t-2}, i_t$ and $SUPPLY_{t-1}$.

Marginal significance levels in parentheses; i.e., the probability of obtaining that value of the F-statistic or higher under the null hypothesis the coefficients in the ex post real rate regression are equal in the two periods.

* = significant at the 5% level

** = significant at the 1% level

significant change in the real rate process in October 1979. The F(5,348) = 12.14 statistic indicates that the null hypothesis that the coefficients of the ex post real rate regression remain unchanged from the 1953:1-1979:10 period to the 1979:11-1982:10 period is rejected at a marginal significance level of 1.7×10^{-10}.[18]

The F-test presented in the second column of Table 2 shows that there is a second significant shift in the real rate process in October 1982. The finding of a second significant shift is surprising. Although the finding that there is a shift in the real rate process in October 1979 could have been guessed by a casual examination of the dramatic rise in ex post real rates in 1980, such an examination would not have revealed a further shift in October 1982 because ex post real rates remained high through the end of 1984.

An additional interesting finding, reported in the third column of Table 1, is that the stochastic process of real rates after October 1982 does not represent a return to the pre-October 1979 process. The F-statistic which tests for coefficient equality in the pre-October 1979 and post-October 1982 periods is highly significant.

Since we have found significant shifts in the stochastic process of real rates after October 1979, it is interesting to ask whether similar shifts occurred in our sample prior to this date. The final column addresses this question by testing for coefficient stability in the two halves of the pre-October 1979 period. The F-statistic does not reveal a shift in the real rate process. We have also examined coefficient stability over various three-year samples in the 1953:1-1979:10 period. Although we find one three-year sample whose coefficients are significantly different from those in the remainder of the period, the change is not nearly as

---

[18]We did not find any evidence of significant heteroscedasticity across the sample periods examined in Table 2 and thus did not correct for it when computing the F-tests. (The test for heteroscedasticity involved an F-test of the ratio of the estimated variances over the differing sample periods.) We also tested for equality of coefficients in the 1953:1-1979:10 and 1979:11-1984:12 sample periods, obtaining F(5,374) = 11.44, with a marginal significance level of 3.7×10^{-10}. Our results are consistent with the finding of Clarida and Friedman (1984) that the relationship of nominal interest rates with other economic variables shifted after October 1979.

significant as the change in October 1979.[19] Further, dropping this three-year sample from the 1953:1-1979:10 period does not alter the significant rejection of coefficient stability pre- and post-October 1979.

While we have found significant shifts in the coefficients of the ex post real rate regressions, we have not yet determined the dates at which the real rate process shifts: i.e., determined the breakpoints. Table 3 reports minus twice the log of the Quandt likelihood ratio for pairs of breakpoints surrounding the October 1979 and October 1982 dates. Remarkably, the Quandt procedure indicates that October 1979 and October 1982 are the breakpoints that maximize the likelihood of the ex post real rate regressions.[20] The evidence in Table 3 reinforces that of Table 2 by suggesting that the shifts in the monetary policy regime may account for the unusual behavior of real interest rates in recent years.

One reason why we have reported minus twice the log of the Quandt likelihood ratio for so many pairs of breakpoints is to indicate that the likelihood function around these breakpoints is quite flat.[21] For example, the pair of breakpoints at (1979:4, 1982:10) has a value of 76.74, which is very close to the maximum of 77.48 found at (1979:10, 1982:10). Similarly, the pair breakpoints at (1979:10, 1983:4) has a value of 75.40, again close to the maximum of 77.48. Therefore, although we have found that the most likely breakpoints in the real rate process coincide with the recent changes in the Fed operating procedures, the evidence does not appear to be sufficiently strong to convince someone with prior beliefs that the breakpoints occur at 1979:10 and 1983:4, for example, that they are incorrect.

Given that the evidence is consistent with breakpoints at October 1979 and October 1982, we construct estimates of the ex ante real rate using

---

[19] Of the nine 3-year periods from 1953:1-1979:10, we find significantly different coefficients only in 1973:11-1976:10 [$F(5,312) = 2.99$, marginal significance level = .012.] We also tested for coefficient equality in each 3-year sample and the subsequent 26-month sample. Of the eight tests we conducted, none is significant at the 5% level. This latter finding gives us confidence that our rejection of equal coefficients in 1979:11-1982:10 and 1982:11-1984:12 is not due to small sample problems.

[20] We have also examined minus twice the log of the Quandt likelihood ratio for breakpoint dates outside the range reported in Table 3. The pair of breakpoints at October 1979 and October 1982 is the global maximum.

[21] Although we report minus twice the log of the Quandt likelihood ratio, Quandt (1960) has pointed out that the maximum value across all possible breakpoints of this statistic is not distributed as χ^2. His Monte Carlo simulations indicate that the distribution of the statistic has fatter tails than the χ^2 distribution.

Table 3

Dating of Breakpoints in 1953-84 Period

Minus Twice the Log of the Quandt Likelihood Ratio

Second Breakpoint	First Breakpoint												
	1979:4	1979:5	1979:6	1979:7	1979:8	1979:9	1979:10	1979:11	1979:12	1980:1	1980:2	1980:3	1980:4
1982: 4	72.16	71.04	71.52	71.76	71.72	71.68	71.68	69.90	69.58	67.60	66.96	67.52	59.52
5	70.08	68.98	69.46	69.70	69.68	69.66	69.94	68.48	68.30	66.08	65.36	65.96	57.54
6	75.64	74.54	75.00	74.98	75.22	74.92	75.46	73.82	73.58	71.26	70.44	71.00	62.34
7	74.98	73.88	74.36	74.60	74.58	74.56	75.10	73.56	73.42	71.26	70.36	71.08	62.20
8	71.94	70.62	71.38	71.64	71.90	71.64	72.40	71.22	71.40	69.00	68.14	68.60	60.00
9	76.86	75.80	76.32	76.56	76.82	76.58	77.08	75.82	75.72	73.34	72.78	73.52	64.08
10	76.74	75.68	76.46	76.70	76.96	76.98	77.48	76.52	76.72	74.30	73.46	74.20	65.06
11	73.12	71.86	72.88	73.16	73.42	73.48	74.20	73.26	73.74	71.38	70.58	71.06	62.40
12	71.64	70.40	71.42	71.68	72.20	72.24	72.74	72.06	72.28	69.92	69.10	69.60	61.48
1983: 1	71.02	69.76	70.78	71.04	71.56	71.60	72.34	71.52	71.72	69.34	68.78	69.00	60.92
2	72.06	70.84	71.88	72.16	72.68	72.76	73.22	72.28	72.26	70.22	69.46	69.76	62.52
3	74.00	72.78	73.82	74.10	74.62	74.46	74.92	73.46	73.44	71.42	70.92	71.22	63.96
4	73.96	72.78	73.82	74.34	74.84	74.96	75.40	74.52	74.54	72.52	71.82	72.12	64.76

fitted values from three separate ex post real rate regressions, estimated over the periods 1953:1-1979:10, 1979:11-1982:10, and 1982:11-1984:12.[22] The heavy solid line in Figure 1 displays the estimated ex ante real rates, while the dotted lines surrounding the estimated real rates provide the 95% confidence interval for these estimates under the assumption that the variance of inflation forecast errors are large relative to the variance of u_t.[23]

The estimated ex ante real rates from 1953:1 to 1979:10 are consistent with earlier findings that real rates were generally positive prior to late

---

[22]The regressions for the three sample periods are as follows:

1953:1 to 1979:10

$$eprr_t = .000697 + .2467\ i_t - .1204\ \pi_{t-1} - .2000\ \pi_{t-2}$$
$$(.00025)\quad(.1035)\quad(.0544)\quad(.0542)$$
$$-\ .002390\ SUPPLY_{t-1}$$
$$(.00083)$$

Standard Error = .001982 R^2 = .1598 Durbin-Watson = 1.98

1979:11 to 1982:10

$$eprr_t = -.017305 + .9368\ i_t - .6088\ \pi_{t-1} + .2920\ \pi_{t-2}$$
$$(.00520)\quad(.1750)\quad(.1709)\quad(.1563)$$
$$+\ .01652\ SUPPLY_{t-1}$$
$$(.00623)$$

Standard Error = .002133 R^2 = .6809 Durbin-Watson = 1.98

1982:10 to 1984:12

$$eprr_t = -.00093 - .0528\ i_t - .1940\ \pi_{t-1} + .3195\ \pi_{t-2}$$
$$(.01246)\quad(.6864)\quad(.2047)\quad(.2005)$$
$$+\ .006256\ SUPPLY_{t-1}$$
$$(.012032)$$

Standard Error = .001679 R^2 = .1521 Durbin-Watson = 1.70

Note that the coefficients of the constant term and $SUPPLY_{t-1}$ above have not been multiplied by 100 as in Table 4.

[23]The formula for the confidence interval is given in Mishkin (1981).

1973 when the first oil shock occurs, ranging at an annual rate from -1% to 2.5%. After 1973, they are generally negative, falling to as low as -2.5%. Following the break in October 1979, estimated real rates remain low until late 1980 when they begin to rise to over 7%. They fluctuate around this level until June 1982 when they fall sharply with the decline in nominal interest rates. Following the break in October 1982, estimated real rates fluctuate around the 5% level.[24]

One striking feature of Figure 1 is that the Fed's switch to its new operating procedures in October 1979 is associated with a notable rise in the variability of ex ante real interest rates. Following the Fed's abandonment of these operating procedures in October 1982, the variability of ex ante real rates falls sharply to a level comparable to that before October 1979. The standard deviation of estimated ex ante real rates (annual rate) is 1.0% from 1953:1 to 1979:10, 3.5% from 1979:11 to 1982:10, and .8% from 1982:11 to 1984:12.[25]

Another interesting feature of Figure 1 is that our dating of the first break in the real rate process at October 1979 does not coincide with the substantial rise in the estimated real rates which occurs in late 1980. This finding indicates why focusing solely on the level of real interest rate does not provide an accurate characterization of the unusual behavior of real interest rates.

Figure 1 provides one way of characterizing the nature of the shifts in the real rate process. The regression results presented in Table 4 provide another way. Table 4 describes the relationship of ex ante real rates with expected inflation, nominal interest rates, and the supply shock

---

[24]The sharp rise in the estimated real rates from 1982:10 to 1982:11 is probably an artifact of splitting the sample for the ex post real rate regressions at 1982:10.

[25]The standard deviation of the estimated ex ante real rate for the 1953:1 to 1979:10 period may give a somewhat misleading impression of the variability of ex ante real interest rates because there is an apparent shift in the mean at the end of 1973 (see Figure 1). The standard deviation of the estimated ex ante real rate (annual rate) for the 1953:1 to 1973:12 period is .6%, while for the 1974:1 to 1979:10 period it is .7%. These standard deviations suggest that the variability of ex ante real interest rates before October 1979 may be slightly lower than the standard deviation for the 1953:1 to 1979:10 period suggests.

Figure 1

Estimated Ex Ante Real Interest Rate, 1953-84

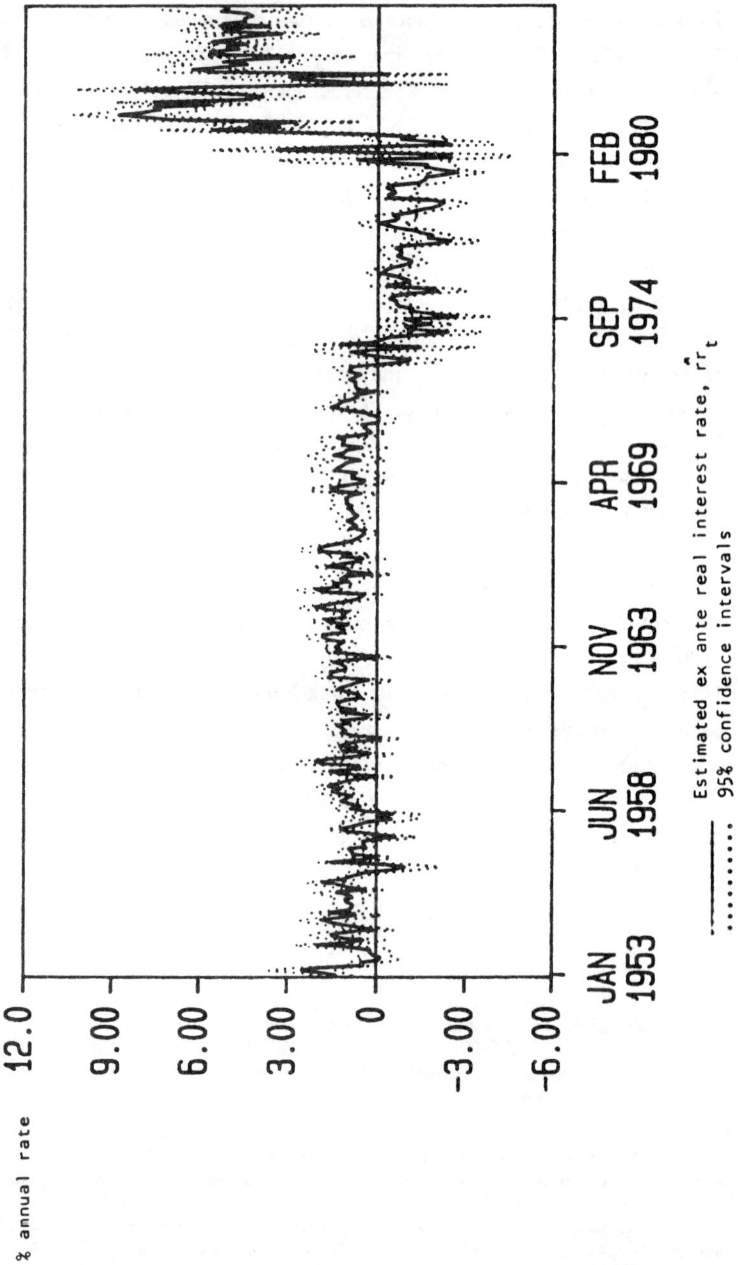

Table 4

The Relationship of Ex Ante Real Interest Rates
with Nominal Interest Rates,
Expected Inflation and Supply Shocks, 1953-84

Dependent Variable: Ex Post
Real Interest Rate on a 1-month U.S.
Treasury Bill, $eprr_t$
Estimation Method: Ordinary Least Squares

Sample Period	Constant term[a]	Coefficient of π_t^e	i_t	$SUPPLY^a_{t-1}$	SER	DW
1953:1 - 1979:10	.12**	-.29**			.0021	1.71
	(.01)	(.04)				
	.12**		-.26**		.0021	1.59
	(.03)		(.07)			
	.07**			-.41**	.0020	1.68
	(.01)			(.07)		
1979:11 - 1982:10	.89**	-.91**			.0031	1.55
	(.13)	(.19)				
	-.61**		.93**		.0029	.81
	(.21)		(.22)			
	-2.21**			3.08**	.0029	1.22
	(.60)			(.74)		
1982:11 - 1984:12	.56**	-.53**			.0016	1.42
	(.05)	(.16)				
	.69		-.40		.0017	1.29
	(.40)		(.57)			
	-.28			.88	.0017	1.35
	(.79)			(1.01)		

standard errors in parentheses
* = significant at the 5% level
** = significant at the 1% level
SER = standard error of the regression
DW = Durbin-Watson Statistic

[a]Coefficients and their standard errors have been multiplied by 100.

variable in the three sample periods defined by the breakpoints.[26] The regression results of Table 4 indicate that in all three sample periods, there is a significant negative correlation between ex ante real rates and expected inflation.[27] This finding is a surprisingly robust one, having been found in previous research for many different sample periods in the United States and other countries.[28]

In contrast to the robustness of the relationship between expected inflation and ex ante real rates, the relationship between nominal interest rates and ex ante real rates changes dramatically with the policy regime shifts in October 1979 and October 1982. In the pre-October 1979 period, nominal rates are a misleading indicator of ex ante real interest rates because the two rates are significantly negatively correlated. With the Fed's deemphasis of interest-rate smoothing following October 1979, the correlation of nominal and ex ante real interest rates becomes significantly positive. Following the Fed's abandonment of the new operating procedures, the correlation of nominal and estimated ex ante real rates returns to being negative.

The shifts in the real rate process are also reflected in the changing strength of the Fisher effect (i.e., the positive correlation between expected inflation and the nominal interest rate). The Fisher effect is strong in the pre-October 1979 period, is nonexistent from November 1979 to October 1982, and is strong again after October 1982: the correlation coefficient between the nominal interest rate and our measure of expected in-

---

[26]The regressions of Table 4 use the ex post real rate as the dependent variable. The coefficient estimates would be numerically the same if the dependent variable were the estimated ex ante real rate because, by construction, the regressors are orthogonal to the difference between the ex post and the estimated ex ante real rates. Further, the coefficient estimates would be asymptotically the same as those obtained in regressions with the true ex ante real rate as the dependent variable. See Mishkin (1981).

[27]The expected inflation variable, π^e_t, which is an explanatory variable in the regressions, is calculated as the nominal interest rate minus our estimated values of the ex ante real rate. Since this involves the two-step procedure of first estimating expected inflation and then regressing the ex post real rate on this measure, the standard errors of the coefficients typically reported will be incorrect. We have obtained consistent estimates of the standard errors by using the instrumental variables procedure outlined by McCallum (1976) and Pagan (1984). Since some of the Durbin-Watson statistics are low, we have also estimated the standard errors correcting for possible serial correlation of the error terms using the procedure outlined in Cumby, Huizinga, and Obstfeld (1983). Although the standard errors rose slightly, there was no appreciable difference in the significance of the coefficients.

[28]Mishkin (1981, 1984) and Summers (1983).

flation is .95 for 1953:1-1979:10, .08 for 1979:11-1982:10, and .81 for 1982:11-1984:12. The lack of a Fisher effect from 1979:11 to 1982:10 is not surprising considering the dramatic increase in the variability of the estimated ex ante real rate during this period. Only if there were a similar rise in the variability of expected inflation or a change in the correlation of expected inflation with ex ante real rates could this fail to be the case.

The relationship of ex ante real rates and the supply shock variable also shifts following October 1979. Whereas before October 1979 a rise in the relative price of energy is associated with a significant decrease in ex ante real rates, after this date it is associated with a rise in ex ante real rates. Given the theoretical ambiguity associated with the effects of supply shocks on ex ante real rates and this change in sign of its regression coefficient, we have some concern that the supply-shock variable may be proxying for other economic factors.[29]

Our characterization of the real rate process suggests that there are strong similarities between the 1953:1-1979:10 and 1982:11-1984:12 periods. Both periods display a negative correlation between nominal interest rates and ex ante real rates, a strong Fisher effect, and similar

---

[29]Because of our concern about the interpretation of the supply shock variable, we have conducted the stability tests described in Table 2 excluding the supply shock variable from the list of regressors. We continue to find significant shifts in the real rate process in October 1979 and October 1982. The test for equality of coefficients in 1953:1-1979:10 and 1979:11-1982:10 yields $F(4,350) = 10.73$ (marginal significance level = 3.3×10^{-8}). The test for equality of coefficients in 1979:11-1982:10 and 1982:11-1984:12 yields $F(4,54) = 3.71$ (marginal significance level = .0096).

variability in ex ante real rates.[30] In contrast, the 1979:11-1982:10 period, when the Fed deemphasized interest rate smoothing, displays a positive correlation between nominal and ex ante real rates, a weak Fisher effect, and variability in ex ante real rates that is substantially higher than in the periods before or after.

The characterization of the ex ante real rate process from 1979:11-1982:10 is not totally without precedent, however. As found in Mishkin (1984a), West Germany, the Netherlands and Switzerland also have a positive correlation between nominal and ex ante real rates, a weak Fisher effect, and greater variability of ex ante real rates than the United States in the period 1967-79. Could it be that the change in the Fed operating procedures in October 1979 produced a monetary policy regime similar to that found in these countries before 1979?

---

[30]Blanchard and Summers (1984) suggest that an upward shift in investment profitability may have been an important source of high ex ante real interest rates after 1982. Following Blanchard and Summers, we have also examined forecast errors from time series models of real gross private fixed investment to see if investment has been strong since October 1979.

Because residuals from a regression of investment on current and past values of real GNP appear to be nonstationary, our forecasting models regress the change in investment on the current and lagged changes in real GNP over the 1953:I-1979:III period. We then conducted dynamic simulations for the period beginning with 1979:IV to obtain forecasts of investment to compare with actual investment. As long as four lags of real GNP changes are included as regressors, further lags of real GNP and alternative ARIMA specifications for the error term produce similar findings.

For real gross business fixed investment (gross private fixed investment excluding residential investment), the dynamic forecast errors are positive after 1980 and grow in size in 1983 and 1984, averaging $20 billion (1972 dollars) for all of 1984. This evidence provides support for the Blanchard and Summers contention that investment spending has been strong recently. However, for real gross private fixed investment (including residential investment), there is much less evidence for buoyant investment spending before 1983. Dynamic forecast errors are negative until 1983:IV, and they average only $5 billion (1972 dollars) in 1984.

An upward shift in profitability may help to explain why the stochastic process of real rates after October 1982, although similar in many ways to that before October 1979, is significantly different. In particular, the overall level of ex ante real rates is substantially higher after October 1982 than it was before October 1979, and this may be related to the strong investment performance in this period. A test for whether coefficients remain stable across these two periods if the constant terms are allowed to differ [$F(4,338) = 1.41$ (marginal significance level = .23)] indicates that the source of the significant difference between the two periods is an upward shift in the level of ex ante real rates. (Note, however, that this test may not have much power because we also found that, when comparing the 1982:11-1984:12 and 1979:11-1982:10 periods, we could not reject stability of the other coefficients besides the constant term.)

V. UNCERTAINTY AND EX ANTE REAL RATES

Casual inspection of the data for the October 1979 to October 1982 period reveals that the adoption of the Fed's new operating procedures led to increased uncertainty about interest rate movements, money supply growth, and possibly inflation. This, combined with the results of the previous section which suggest that the Fed's change in operating procedures may account for the shifts in the real rate process, makes it worth examining whether this increased uncertainty is the critical feature of the monetary policy regime shift that has altered real rate movements in recent years. Such a view has been espoused by Mascaro and Meltzer (1983) who argue that increased money growth uncertainty caused the rise in ex ante real interest rates after October 1979. Research by Fama (1976) and Hartman and Makin (1982) has also pointed to uncertainty about inflation and interest rates as possible factors affecting ex ante real interest rates.

Because the Mascaro and Meltzer (1983) results concerning the effects of money growth uncertainty on interest rates are so striking, we extend our analysis to include a measure of money growth uncertainty which was constructed using their procedure. Specifically, we have fit univariate time series models to the M1 money growth series in order to extract a series of forecast errors.[31] The money growth uncertainty measure (σ^{mm}_{t-1}) equals the square root of the average sum of squared forecast errors over the previous twelve months.

Table 5 presents estimates of ex post real rate regressions that include σ^{mm}_{t-1} in the information set X_t. We look at the 1953:1 to 1979:10 period to see whether money growth uncertainty had any explanatory power before the Fed adopted its new operating procedure. We look at the 1953:1 to 1984:12 period to see whether uncertainty can help to explain the recent

---

[31]After performing Box-Jenkins (1970) identification procedures, the following ARIMA models were fit to data for the three periods: for 1952:1-1979:10, an autoregressive model with AR parameters at lags 2, 3, 4, and 6; for 1979:11-1982:10 and 1982:10-1984:12, autoregressive models with AR parameters at lag 1 The σ^{mm} measure constructed from the one-step-ahead forecast errors from these models is the one used in Table 5. In order to check for robustness, we also constructed another σ^{mm} measure from the forecast errors of an autoregressive model with AR parameters at lags 1, 3, and 6, fit to the entire 1952:1-1984:12 sample period. Results of using this measure were roughly similar; the signs of the estimated coefficients on σ^{mm}_{t-1} were identical to those reported in Table 5 and were insignificant in all but the last regression where it entered with a coefficient of .12 and a t-statistic of 2.28.

Table 5

Correlation of the Ex Ante Real Interest Rate with Mascaro-Meltzer Measure of Money Growth Uncertainty

Dependent Variable: Ex Post Real Interest Rate, $eprr_t$

Estimation Method: Ordinary Least Squares

	Coefficients of							
	Constant[a] term	i_t	π_{t-1}	π_{t-2}	$SUPPLY^a_{t-1}$	σ^{mm}_{t-1}	SER	DW
1953:1 - 1979:10	.11**	.23*	-.11*	-.20**	-.24**	-.09	.0020	1.97
	(.03)	(.10)	(.05)	(.05)	(.08)	(.05)		
	.07**					-.10	.0021	1.52
	(.02)					(.06)		
1953:1 - 1984:12	.01	.61**	-.31**	-.26**	.09	-.02	.0022	2.02
	(.03)	(.08)	(.05)	(.05)	(.06)	(.05)		
	.05					.10	.0025	1.13
	(.03)					(.06)		

standard errors in parentheses

* = significant at the 5% level

** = significant at the 1% level

SER = Standard Error of the Regression

DW = Durbin-Watson Statistic

[a]Coefficients and their standard errors have been multiplied by 100.

unusual behavior of ex ante real interest rates. The results do not support the proposition that money growth uncertainty is an important determinant of ex ante real interest rates. In contrast to Mascaro and Meltzer (1983), we find that the σ^{mm}_{t-1} coefficients enter with a negative sign in three out of four cases so that they cannot explain the rise in ex ante real rates after October 1979. In addition they are never significantly different (at the 5% level) from zero.[32]

We have also tested whether the inclusion of this measure of money growth uncertainty affects the conclusion that significant shifts in the real rate process occured in October 1979 and October 1982. Not surprisingly, the rejections of stability continue to be strong. For example, the test for equality of coefficients in the 1953:1-1979:10 and 1979:11-1982:10 periods yields an $F(6,346) = 10.80$ (marginal significance level = 5.1×10^{-11}). The test for equality of coefficients in the 1979:11-1982:10 and 1982:11-1984:12 periods yields an $F(6,50) = 2.69$ (marginal significance level = 2.4×10^{-4}).

The failure of the results in Table 5 to provide evidence that money growth uncertainty is an important determinant of ex ante real interest rates may be attributable to econometric difficulties. Measuring uncertainty with a weighted average of past squared forecast errors and then including it in an OLS regression can be thought of as a classic errors-in-variables problem.[33] A way around this problem has been suggested by Pagan (1984). His procedure involves including the contemporaneous measure of uncertainty as a regressor and estimating the equation by instrumental variables using lagged measures of uncertainty as instruments.

Table 6 reports results obtained when Pagan's procedure is used to examine the association of ex ante real rates with uncertainty not only about money growth but also about inflation and nominal interest rates. The uncertainty variable for money growth (σ^{m}_{t}), inflation (σ^{π}_{t}), and

[32]While negative coefficients on σ^{mm}_{t-1} are the "wrong" sign from the point of view of explaining the rise in ex ante real rates after October 1979, they are not inconsistent with some theoretical models of how uncertainty affects ex ante real interest rates. For example, see Bohn (1985).

[33]The uncertainty variable that presumably belongs in the regression is the true standard deviation of the forecast error, which is measured imperfectly as the square root of an equally weighted average of past squared forecast errors. This mismeasurement never disappears, even if the sample size grows to infinity, because the number of forecast errors used in the estimation is independent of sample size.

Table 6

Correlation of the Ex Ante Real Interest Rate with Money Growth, Inflation, and Nominal Interest Rate Uncertainty

Dependent Variable: Ex Post Real Interest Rate, $eprr_t$
Estimation Method: Instrumental Variables

Sample Period	Constant[a]	i_t	π_{t-1}	π_{t-2}	$SUPPLY^{a}_{t-1}$	σ^m_t	σ^π_t	σ^i_t	SER	DW
		Coefficients of								
1953:1 - 1979:10	.13**	.25*	-.12*	-.22**	-.22*	-.19			.0021	1.97
	(.04)	(.11)	(.06)	(.06)	(.09)	(.10)				
	.09**					-.18			.0022	1.55
	(.03)					(.11)				
	-.01	.26*	-.16*	-.21**	-.19		.57		.0023	1.98
	(.08)	(.12)	(.07)	(.06)	(.10)		(.52)			
	.01						.21		.0022	1.52
	(.07)						(.45)			
	.10**	.32**	-.11*	-.16	-.27**			-2.65	.0021	1.95
	(.04)	(.12)	(.06)	(.06)	(.09)			(2.04)		
	.15**							-4.33**	.0023	1.64
	(.04)							(1.61)		
1953:1 - 1984:12	.02	.61**	-.31**	-.27**	.09	-.06			.0022	2.02
	(.03)	(.08)	(.05)	(.05)	(.06)	(.10)				
	.07*					.03			.0025	1.12
	(.04)					(.11)				
	-.14	.57**	-.36**	-.26**	.14		1.10		.0028	2.02
	(.09)	(.11)	(.07)	(.06)	(.08)		(.61)			
	.02						.40		.0027	1.17
	(.08)						(.54)			
	.00	.62**	-.31**	-.26**	.09			-.11	.0022	2.02
	(.02)	(.09)	(.05)	(.05)	(.06)			(.71)		
	.04							1.20**	.0025	1.18
	(.02)							(.45)		

standard errors in parentheses
* = significant at the 5% level
** = significant at the 1% level
SER = Standard Error of the Regression
DW = Durbin-Watson Statistic

Instruments are a constant, i_t, π_{t-1}, π_{t-2}, $SUPPLY_{t-1}$, and four lags of the σ variable in the equation.

[a]Indicates that the coefficient, and its standard error, have been multiplied by 100.

interest rates (σ_t^i) are contemporaneous absolute values of forecast errors obtained from time series models.[34] The results for the money growth uncertainty variable are similar to those reported in Table 5. The signs of the σ_t^m coefficients are identical to those found for σ_{t-1}^{mm}, and none of these coefficients is significant at the 5% level.

In all the regressions, the results on inflation uncertainty are consistent with the premise that increases in inflation uncertainty raise ex ante real interest rates. However, none of the σ_t^π coefficients is significantly different from zero. Results on interest rate uncertainty are somewhat more mixed. The σ_t^i coefficients are significant when no other information is included in the regressions.[35] However, when other information is added to the regressions, nominal interest rate uncertainty has no significant additional explanatory power for ex ante real interest rates. Furthermore, in the specification in which the coefficients of σ_t^i are significantly different from zero, the coefficients change signs when the 1953:1-1979:10 sample is extended through 1984:12.[36]

In summary, uncertainty variables do not have much explanatory power

[34]For money growth, we use the same forecast errors that were used in constructing the Mascaro-Meltzer uncertainty measure. Forecast errors for nominal interest rates were constructed from univariate time series models developed, using Box-Jenkins identification procedures. The following ARIMA models for the change in the nominal interest rate were fit to data for the three periods: for 1952:1-1979:10, an autoregressive model with AR parameters at lags 1, 4, and 6; for 1979:11-1982:10 and 1982:10-1984:12, a white noise specification. Forecast errors for inflation were generated from the ex post real rate regressions estimated separately over the three periods. The results in Table 6 use four lags of the absolute values of the forecast errors as instruments. In order to check for robustness, we also estimated these regressions with only one lag and also twelve lags of the absolute of the forecast errors as instruments. We also obtained forecast errors from time series models estimated over the entire 1952:1-1984:12 sample period. The ARIMA model for money growth and the ex post real rate regression used to generate inflation forecast errors have already been described for this period, while the ARIMA model for the change in the nominal interest rate is an autoregressive model with AR parameters at lag 7 and 8. Results with all of these alternative specifications are similar to those found in Table 6. The signs of the σ coefficients are typically the same, and they are only significant in the same cases that they are significant in Table 6. These results are available from the authors by request.

[35]The finding of a significant negative coefficient in the 1953:1-1979:10 period is in agreement with the findings of Fama (1976).

[36]Bodie, Kane, and McDonald (1983) also fail to find evidence that the riskiness of nominal bonds can explain the recent rise of ex ante real rates on short maturity assets.

for ex ante real rates.[37] Thus to understand how the recent changes in monetary policy regime might have affected ex ante real rates, it is necessary to look elsewhere.

VI. EX ANTE REAL RATES AND THE 1920 MONETARY REGIME SHIFT

We have presented evidence suggesting that recent shifts in a monetary policy regime have been important determinants of the behavior of real interest rates. If this is true, there should be breaks in the stochastic process of real rates in other periods which contain similar changes in the direction of monetary policy. One such period is 1916-27. In January and June of 1920, the Federal Reserve carried out the steepest rises in the discount rate in the first 50 years of its history -- raising the discount rate by 1-1/4% in January and 1% in June. Two aspects of this period make it especially attractive to study. First, since discount rate changes were the primary tool of monetary policy in this period, the sharp rises in the discount rate represented a definite change in the direction of monetary policy. Changes in the discount rate were particularly potent at this time because the total amount of member-bank borrowing from the Fed exceeded the amount of nonborrowed reserves. Second, this regime shift has several similarities to the more recent regime shift. In both periods, the United States had been experiencing a sustained high level of inflation, and the dollar was facing foreign-exchange pressure prior to the shift. After the regime change there was a rapid disinflation in both periods.

Our analysis of ex ante real interest rate behavior surrounding the time of the regime shift uses the same techniques we applied previously.

---

[37]Although a variable may not be statistically significant, it is always worth asking whether the size of its coefficient might make it economically significant. Given that uncertainty for money growth, inflation, and interest rates rose in the 1979:11-1982:10 period, we examine what would be the largest positive effect on ex ante real interest rates arising from increased uncertainty by applying the most positive coefficients in Table 6 to the change in the standard deviations of these variables from 1953:1-1979:10 to 1979:11-1982:10. The result of this exercise is that the largest positive effect on ex ante real rates from uncertainty is 10 basis points for monetary growth, 20 basis points from inflation, and 189 basis points from nominal interest rates. The first two are clearly economically insignificant. Although the third can be considered economically important, recall that we must assume that no information other than nominal interest rate uncertainty is helpful for predicting ex ante real rates (something we can statistically reject) in order to arrive at this figure.

The major difficulty we encounter when examining this period is that reliable monthly data on one-month, default-free, government bonds are not available. The only reliable interest-rate data are for 4/6-month commercial paper, 90-day stock exchange time loans, and stock exchange call loans. Since maturities of these assets span the one-month maturity we desire, and also because they have different risk characteristics, our strategy is to examine results based on interest rates from all three assets. Findings that are consistent for all three assets, would presumably extend to the ex ante real rate on a one-month United States Treasury Bill, had such an asset existed. Another difficulty is that inflation data for this period are of lower quality than current inflation data. Nonetheless, the results for this period are so striking that we doubt they would be substantially altered if higher quality data were available.

Our specification of the X_t variables in the ex post real rate regressions for the 1916-1927 period is the same as for the 1953-84 period, with the exception that data were not readily available to construct the supply shock variable, so they were not included. This means that for each asset, the information set X_t contains a constant term, the nominal interest rate on that asset (i_t), and two lags of inflation (π_{t-1} and π_{t-2}). The results from the diagnostic check of the X_t-specification for the 1916-27 period appear in Table 7. There is no evidence of any serial correlation of the residuals from the ex post real rate regressions for any asset in either time period. Thus, we have found no evidence that we have omitted information relevant for predicting ex ante real rates from our regressions.

Table 8 contains the tests of coefficient stability in the ex post real rate regressions in the 1916-27 period. Given the two sharp rises in the discount rate in January and June of 1920, choosing a date for the monetary policy regime shift is somewhat ambiguous. In practice it does not make a difference: choosing either date, we find a highly significant shift of the real rate process. Since timing evidence presented in Table 9 indicates that the breakpoint occurs in June of 1920, the results of Table 8 use this dating.

The test for equality of the coefficients in the 1916:1-1920:6 and

Table 7

Autocorrelations of Ex Post Real Rate Regression Residuals, 1916-1927

Sample Period and Asset	Autocorrelation at Lag 1	2	3	4	5	6	7	8	9	10	11	12	SE	Q(12)	MSL
1916:1 - 1920:6															
4/6-Month Commercial Paper	-.00	.02	-.10	-.11	-.10	-.12	-.14	.05	-.15	-.11	-.06	.00	.14	6.81	.87
Stock Exchange Time Loans, 90 days	-.01	.02	-.11	-.10	-.11	-.12	-.14	.05	-.15	-.10	-.06	.01	.14	6.76	.87
Stock Exchange Call Loans	-.02	.02	-.11	-.09	-.10	-.09	-.12	.05	-.15	-.07	-.05	.01	.14	5.62	.93
1920:7 - 1927:12															
4/6-Month Commercial Paper	-.04	.06	-.12	.06	.06	.02	-.02	-.04	-.02	-.06	.07	-.01	.11	3.59	.99
Stock Exchange Time Loans, 90 days	-.02	.02	-.11	.05	.06	.03	-.01	-.03	-.01	-.05	.04	-.04	.11	2.71	.99
Stock Exchange Call Loans	-.02	.04	-.08	.09	.10	.02	-.02	-.02	-.02	-.08	-.01	-.07	.11	3.94	.99

SE = Asymptotic standard error of the estimated autocorrelations under the assumption that the true residuals are serially uncorrelated.

Q(12) = Adjusted Q-statistic suggested by Ljung and Box (1978) which is distributed asymptotically as $X^2(12)$ under the null hypothesis that the residuals are serially uncorrelated.

MSL = Marginal significance level of Q-statistic, i.e., the probability of obtaining that value of the X^2 statistic or higher under the null hypothesis that the residuals are serially uncorrelated.

Table 8

Stability Tests for Ex Post Real Rate Regressions

1916-1927

Ex Post Real Rate Regression For	F-Tests for Equality of Coefficients in 1916:1 - 1920:6 and 1920:7 - 1927:12	1916:1 - 1918:3 and 1918:4 - 1920:6	1920:7 - 1924:3 and 1924:4 - 1927:12
4/6-Month Commercial Paper	F(4,136) = 13.60** (2.4 x 10^{-9})	F(4,46) = .50 (.74)	F(4,82) = .96 (.43)
Stock Exchange Time Loans, 90 Days	F(4,136) = 12.77** (7.5 x 10^{-9})	F(4,46) = .47 (.76)	F(4,82) = 1.16 (.33)
Stock Exchange Call Loans	F(4,136) = 12.89** (6.3 x 10^{-9})	F(4,46) = 1.02 (.41)	F(4,82) = 1.79 (.14)

Marginal significance levels in parentheses: i.e., the probability of obtaining that value of the F-statistic or higher under the null hypothesis that the coefficients in the ex post real rate regressions are equal in the two periods.

* = significant at the 5% level

** = significant at the 1% level.

1920:7-1927:12 periods is very similar for all three assets.[38] All the F(4,136) statistics are larger than 12 and are significant at the 10^{-8} level.[39] The additional tests presented in Table 8 indicate that there is only one significant shift in the real rate process during the 1916-27 period.[40]

Table 9 presents the results of using the Quandt procedure for dating the timing of the shift in the real rate process. In contrast to the likelihood surface examined for the 1953-84 period, the likelihood function is well-defined for all three assets in the 1916-27 period. Evidence for all three assets is in agreement that the most likely date for the break in the real rate process is June 1920, the date of the second large increase in the discount rate.

The timing evidence for the 1916-27 period indicates that, just as in October 1979, a monetary regime change is associated with a significant shift in the stochastic process of real interest rates. This evidence adds further support to the view that the recent changes in the monetary regime have been an important source of the unusual behavior of real rates.

We now proceed to examine the way in which the stochastic process of real rates changes at the time of the 1920 regime shift. Is the nature of the changes in the real rate process at the time of the regime shift similar to that found recently? We first examine this question by generating estimates of ex ante real interest rates using fitted values from the separate ex post real rate regressions for the 1916:1-1920:6 and 1920:7-1927:12

---

[38]The reason the results are so similar for all three assets is that there is little variation in the nominal interest rates for each asset, with the result that most of the variation in the ex post real interest rates is attributable to changes in inflation.

[39]An F-test using the ratio of the estimated variances of the two sample periods reveals that the variance of the residuals is significantly higher in 1916:1-1920:6 than in 1920:7-1927:12. Thus, we also conducted the stability tests correcting for heteroscedasticity. For 4/6-month commercial paper, F(4,136) = 12.54; for 90-day stock exchange time loans, F(4,136) = 11.58; for stock exchange call loans, F(4,136) = 11.73. These results lead to the same conclusion as those presented in Table 8.

[40]To check for the possibility of a second breakpoint, we used the Quandt procedure to locate the most likely pair of breakpoints in the 1916-27 sample period. The result was June 1920 and March 1922. When conducting the standard F-test for coefficient equality before and after the second breakpoint, we failed to find a significant shift despite using this search technique which maximizes the probability of finding a significant shift in the real rate process.

Table 9

Dating of Breakpoint in 1916-27 Period

Real Rate Regression for	Minus Twice the Log of Quandt Likelihood Ratio												
	1919:12	1920:1	1920:2	1920:3	1920:4	1920:5	1920:6	1920:7	1920:8	1920:9	1920:10	1920:11	1920:12
4/6-Month Commercial Paper	32.20	33.24	33.18	33.56	47.04	50.02	58.46	52.86	44.88	43.54	43.52	42.82	40.26
90-day Stock Exchange Time Loans	29.90	30.82	30.64	30.90	43.90	46.76	54.44	48.84	40.40	39.02	39.12	37.84	34.92
Stock Exchange Call Loans	29.70	30.90	30.76	31.58	45.78	48.58	54.80	49.50	40.84	38.48	37.30	35.64	32.94

264

periods.[41] Because the estimates are so familiar for all the assets, we report only those for stock exchange call loans in Figure 2.

We see that estimated ex ante real rates during the inflationary period prior to June 1920 are persistently negative, just as they were prior to October 1979. After the June 1920 monetary regime shift, they climb to extremely high levels, sometimes exceeding 25%, and then settle down to around the 4-1/2% level after mid-1922 when deflation is over and price stability is maintained.[42] The variability of the ex ante real rates also appears to be higher after June 1920 than before: the standard deviation of the estimated ex ante real rate is 2.1% in 1916:1-1920:6 and is 6.8% in 1920:7-1927:12. Even after price stability has been achieved, the variability of ex ante real rates continues to be higher than before June 1920: the standard deviation of the estimated ex ante real rate is 4.0%.

Although the rise in ex ante real rates is far greater after the 1920 regime shift than after October 1979, the general pattern we saw in the post-October 1979 period seems to be repeated.[43] After the regime shift in both periods, ex ante real rates climb to a temporarily high level and then settle down to a level that is permanently higher than in the pre-regime

[41]The stock exchange call loan regressions for the two sample periods are as follows:

1916:01 to 1920:06

$$eprr_t = -.00876 - .1507\ i_t - .1190\ \pi_{t-1} + .1388\ \pi_{t-2}$$
$$(.00365)\quad (.8401)\quad (.1400)\quad (.1412)$$

Standard Error = .0101 R^2 = .0301 Durbin-Watson = 2.04

1920:07 to 1927:12

$$eprr_t = -.01151 + 4.4196\ i_t - .2524\ \pi_{t-1} + .0597\ \pi_{t-2}$$
$$(.00300)\quad (.7718)\quad (.1014)\quad (.0950)$$

Standard Error = .007019 R^2 = .4020 Durbin-Watson = 2.04

Note that the coefficient of the constant term has not been multiplied by 100 as in Table 10.

[42]As was the case in Figure 1, the sharp rise in the estimated real rate at a breakpoint is likely to be an artifact of splitting the sample for the ex post real rate regressions at 1920:6.

[43]One possible reason why real rates climbed to much higher levels after June 1920 than after October 1979 is that the disinflation after June 1920 was far more rapid than the recent disinflation.

Figure 2

Estimated Ex Ante Real Interest Rates
for Stock Exchange Call Loans, 1916-27

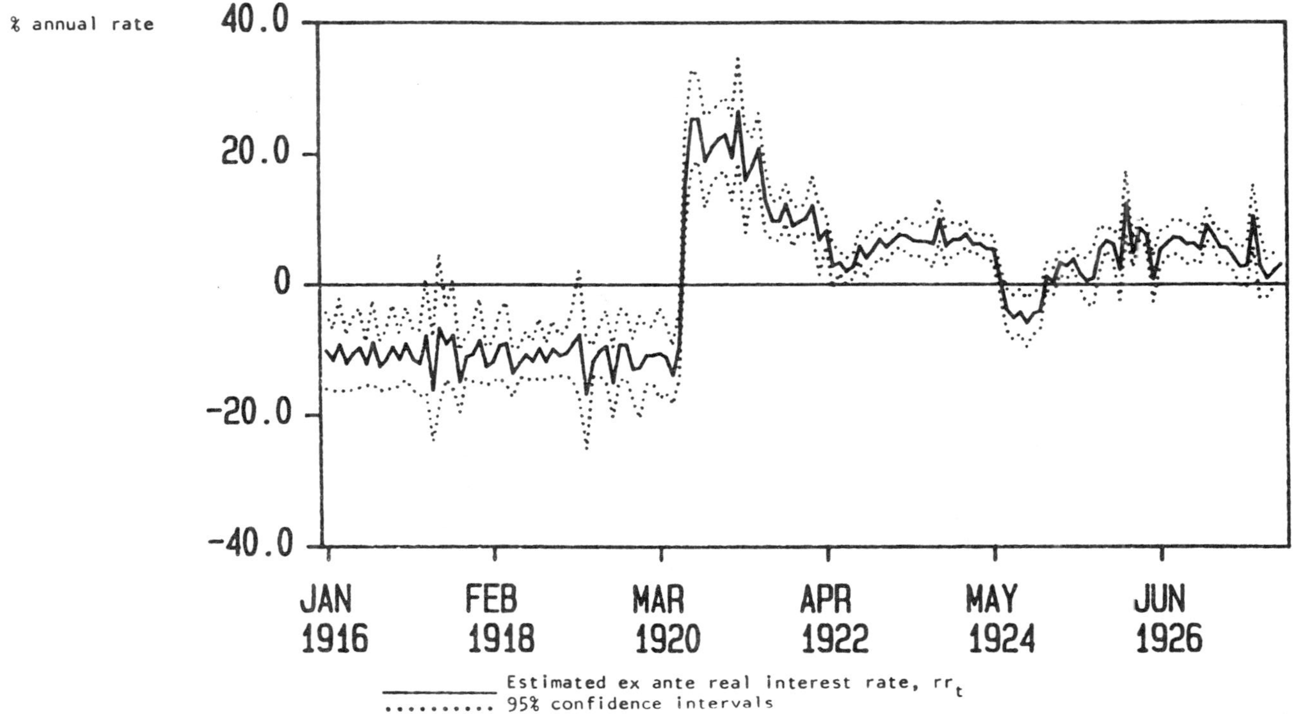

shift period. Although the securities used in Figures 1 and 2 are not strictly comparable, adjusting for these differences would probably not change the conclusion that the ex ante real interest rates we see currently are at a similar level to those found after 1922.

Further similarities between the behavior of real rates after the monetary regime shifts of June 1920 and October 1979 are evident in the regression results of Table 10. As we found for the entire post-World War II period, ex ante real rates are negatively correlated with expected inflation, usually significantly so. We also again find that during the inflationary period before the regime shift, the correlation between nominal interest rates and ex ante real rates is negative, while afterwards the correlation becomes positive. Furthermore, during the inflationary period we find a strong Fisher effect -- a positive correlation between nominal interest rates and our measure of expected inflation equal to .74; while after June 1920, the correlation between nominal interest rates and estimated expected inflation even becomes strongly negative, equaling -.92.

Our examination of the 1916-27 period reveals that the surprising behavior of ex ante real rates that we have been experiencing in the last ten years has historical precedent. In both periods, a central feature of the changes in monetary policy regime is that they are followed by a substantial disinflation. Our evidence that both regime shifts are closely associated with changes in the stochastic process of real interest rates suggests that disinflation may well be an important characteristic of the regime changes affecting ex ante real interest rates.

VII. CONCLUSIONS

This paper has examined evidence that changes in monetary policy regimes are important factors in explaining the recent unusual behavior of

Table 10

The Relationship of Ex Ante Real Interest Rates with Nominal Interest Rates and Expected Inflation: 1916-1927

Ex Post Real Rate Regression for	1916:1 to 1920:6					1920:7 to 1927:12				
	Coefficients of					Coefficients of				
	Constant term[a]	π_t^e	i_t	SER	DW	Constant term[a]	π_t^e	i_t	SER	DW
4/6-Month Commercial Paper	.12	-.76**		.0099	1.94	.37**	-1.21**		.0068	2.17
	(.17)	(.13)				(.02)	(.03)			
	-.34		-1.24	.0101	1.78	-1.54**		5.27**	.0069	1.68
	(.75)		(1.69)			(.28)		(.67)		
Stock Exchange Time Loans	-.03	-.65**		.099	1.93	.37**	-1.21**		.0070	2.14
	(.25)	(.19)				(.02)	(.03)			
	-.66		-.50	.0101	1.79	-1.48**		5.11**	.0072	1.58
	(.50)		(1.12)			(.31)		(.72)		
Stock Exchange Call Loans	-.27	-.49		.0100	1.92	.34**	-1.21**		.0070	2.14
	(.36)	(.27)				(.02)	(.03)			
	-.88		-.09	.0101	1.81	-1.36**		5.07**	.0072	1.55
	(.34)		(.79)			(.29)		(.72)		

standard errors in parentheses
* = significant at the 5% level
** = significant at the 1% level
SER = standard error of the regression
DW = Durbin-Watson Statistic

[a]Coefficients and their standard errors have been multiplied by 100.

ex ante real interest rates.[44] We find that not only are there significant shifts in the stochastic process of real interest rates in October 1979 and october 1982 when the Federal Reserve altered its behavior, but these dates are also found to be the most likely breakpoints in the real rate process.

Although these results point the finger at monetary regime changes as partly explaining the unusual behavior of ex ante real rates, we run the danger of fitting one historical episode into a tailor-made theory. Truly convincing evidence that monetary policy is important must rely on examining similar "controlled experiments" in other time periods. If we examine other time periods with similar monetary policy regime changes and we fail to find a correspondence between shifts in the stochastic process of ex ante real rates and the regime changes, then the results from the recent experience become less convincing. In contrast, if we do find such a correspondence, we have more confidence that monetary policy regime shifts have played an important role in the recent real rate experience.

Our examination of another time period, that surrounding the 1920 monetary regime shift when the discount rate was raised sharply, produces a striking correspondence between the regime change and the shift in the real rate process. As in October 1979, the shift away from an inflationary monetary policy regime in 1920 is associated with a change from a negative correlation between nominal and real interest rates to a positive correlation. In addition, the Fisher effect significantly diminishes with the change in monetary regime. Finally, the shift away from the inflationary monetary regime is associated with a sharp rise in ex ante real rates, while after the disinflation is complete, ex ante real rates remain at a high level.

In this paper, we have examined several pieces of evidence to provide an explanation of recent real rate behavior. Although each piece of evi-

---

[44] Another possible factor often cited as a source of the current high real interest rates is the current and prospective large budget deficit. Although evidence analyzing the link between budget deficits and real interest rates does not support a strong connection [Blanchard and Summers (1984), and Evans (1985)], the perspective in this paper suggests that the possible link between deficits and real rates might be better understood by concentrating on a regime shift in the budgetary process. Evidence in Eisner and Pieper (1984) indicates that when the high-employment budget surplus as a percentage of GNP is appropriately corrected for price and interest effects, it is rarely negative in the postwar period. Beginning in 1982, it swings sharply into the negative range and can be expected to remain there for some time. This may indicate that there has been a shift in the budgetary regime which might be linked to recent behavior of real interest rates. However, Barro (1984) presents evidence that no regime shift for fiscal policy has occurred.

dence by itself may not be compelling, we find that taken together, there is strong support for the view that the recent shift in real rate behavior is a monetary phenomenon. Although our evidence does not rule out affects from such factors as the high budget deficits or financial deregulation in the 1980s, it does suggest that monetary factors are more important, since high budget deficits or financial deregulation were not a feature of the 1920s, a period which displays real rate behavior similar to that in recent years.[45]

Our findings also provide a different perspective on the recent behavior of real interest rates. When many economists discuss the recent behavior of real interest rates, they describe it as unusual. An important conclusion that comes out of our analysis is that what appears to be unusual behavior of real interest rates is only unusual from the perspective of the post-World War II United States experience. In a wider historical context the recent behavior of real interest rates is not unusual at all.

---

[45] Although the federal government ran substantial budget deficits in the years 1917-1919 as a result of World War I, there were budget surpluses in every year from 1920 to 1927. (See the federal budget series in the Historical Statistics of the United States, page 1104.)

References

Antoncic, M.
(1983) High and Volatile Real Interest Rates: Where Does the Fed Fit In? Federal Reserve Bank of New York. Unpublished paper.

Barro, R.J.
(1984) The Behavior of U.S. Deficits. *National Bureau of Economic Research*, Working Paper No. 1309.

Blanchard, O.J. and Summers, L.H.
(1984) Perspectives on High World Real Interest Rates. *Brookings Papers on Economic Activity*, 2: 273-324.

Bodie, A., Kane, A., and McDonald, R.
(1983) Why Are Real Interest Rates So High? School of Management, Boston University. Unpublished paper.

Bohn, H.
(1985) Indexed Bonds, Nominal Bonds and the Stochastic Structure of the Economy. Graduate School of Business, Stanford University, mimeo.

Box, G.E.P. and Jenkins, G.M.
(1970) *Time Series Analysis, Forecasting and Control*. San Francisco: Holden Day.

Clarida, R.H. and Friedman, B.M.
(1984) The Behavior of U.S. Short-Term Interest Rates Since October 1979. *Journal of Finance*, 39: 671-682.

Cumby, R.J., Huizinga, J., and Obstfeld, M.
(1983) Two-Step, Two-Stage Least Squares Estimation in Models with Rational Expectations. *Journal of Econometrics*, 21: 333-55.

Eisner, R. and Pieper, P.J.
(1984) A New View of the Federal Debt and Budget Deficits. *American Economic Review*, 74: 11-29.

Evans, P.

(1985) Do Large Deficits Produce High Interest Rates? *American Economic Review*, 75: 68-87.

Fama, E.F.

(1976) Inflation Uncertainty and Expected Returns on Treasury

_________ and Gibbons, M.G.

(1982) Inflation, Real Returns and Capital Investment. *Journal of Monetary Economics*, 9: 297-323.

Garbade, K. and Wachtel, P.

(1978) Time Variation in the Relationship Between Inflation and Interest Rates. *Journal of Financial Economics*, 4: 755-765.

Hartman, R. and Makin, J.H.

(1982) Inflation Uncertainty and Interest Rates: Theory and Empirical Tests. *National Bureau of Economic Research*, Working Paper No. 906.

Hasbrouck, J.

(1984) Forecaster Discord and Consensus Prediction Error: An Econometric Investigation. New York University. Unpublished paper.

Holland, A.S.

(1984) Real Interest Rates: What Accounts for their Recent Rise? *Review*, Federal Reserve Bank of St. Louis, 66: 18-29.

Huizinga, J. and Mishkin, F.S.

(1984) Inflation and Real Interest Rates on Assets with Different Risk Characteristics. *Journal of Finance*, 39: 699-712.

_________ and _________

(1985) The Measurement of Ex Ante Real Interest Rates on Assets with Different Risk Characteristics. *National Bureau of Economic Research*, Working Paper Series, forthcoming.

Litterman, R.B. and Weiss, L.

(1985) Money, Real Interest Rates, and Output: A Reinterpretation of Postwar U.S. Data. *Econometrica*, 53: 129-156.

Ljung, C.M. and Box G.E.P.

(1978) On a Measure of Lack of Fit in Time Series Models.

Lucas, R.E. Jr.

(1976) Econometric Policy Evaluation: A Critique. K. Brunner and A. Meltzer (eds.). *The Phillips Curve and Labor Markets*, Carnegie-Rochester Conference Series on Public Policy, 1: 19-46.

Macaulay, F.R.

(1938) *Some Theoretical Problems Suggested by the Movements of Interest Rates, Bond Yields, and Stock Prices in the United States Since 1856*. New York: National Bureau of Economic Research.

Mascaro, A. and Meltzer, A.H.

(1983) Long- and Short-Term Interest Rates in a Risky World. *Journal of Monetary Economics*, 12: 485-518.

McCallum, B.T.

(1976) Rational Expectations and the Natural Rate Hypothesis: Some Consistent Estimates. *Econometrica*, 44: 43-52.

Mishkin, F.S.

(1981) The Real Interest Rate: An Empirical Investigation. K. Brunner and A. Meltzer (eds.). *Consequences of Inflation*, Carnegie-Rochester Conference Series on Public Policy, 15: 151-200.

____

(1984a) The Real Interest Rate: A Multi-Country Empirical Study. *The Canadian Journal of Economics*, 17: 283-311.

Mishkin, F.S.

(1984b) Are Real Interest Rates Equal Across Countries? An Empirical Investigation of International Parity Conditions. *Journal of Finance*, 39: 1345-57.

Nelson, C.R. and Schwert, G.W.

(1977) Short-Term Interest Rates as Predictors of Inflation: On Testing the Hypothesis That the Real Rate of Interest is Constant. *American Economic Review*, 67: 478-86.

Pagan, A.

(1984) Econometric Issues in the Analysis of Regressions with Generated Regressors. *International Economic Review*, 25: 221-247.

Quandt, R.E.

(1958) The Estimation of the Parameters of a Linear Regression System Obeying Two Separate Regimes. *Journal of the American Statistical Association*, 53: 873-80.

____

(1960) Tests of the Hypothesis That a Linear Regression System Obeys Two Separate Regimes. *Journal of the American Statistical Association*, 55: 324-30.

Shiller, R.J.

(1980) Can the Fed Control Real Interest Rates? S. Fischer (ed.), *Rational Expectations and Economic Policy*. Chicago: University of Chicago Press.

Summers, L.H.

(1983) The Nonadjustment of Nominal Interest Rates: A Study of the Fisher Effect. J. Tobin (ed.), *A Symposium in Honor of Arthur Okun*. Washington: The Brookings Institution.

Wilcox, J.A.

(1983) Why Real Interest Rates Were So Low in the 1970s. *American Economic Review*, 73: 44-53.

Understanding Real Interest Rates

Frederic S. Mishkin

Real interest rates are among the most important economic variables and have been studied extensively. They figure prominently in discussions of the transmission mechanisms of monetary policy and also play a prominent role in explanations of business cycles and particular business cycle episodes. Real interest rates are a central element in savings-consumption decisions and in debates about how to encourage savings, a topic which has been prominent in recent years because of the rise of supply-side economics. Real interest rates are also a critical explanatory variable for investment decisions since they represent the real cost of borrowing. They are especially important in the agricultural sector because farmers must make extensive use of debt markets in order to finance their production.

This paper outlines an approach to measuring real interest rates and testing hypotheses on their behavior. It then describes what is known about real interest rates in the aggregate economy and provides estimates of real interest rates for the agricultural sector. Examining the behavior of real interest rates in the agriculture sector provides a better understanding of some of the woes of the farming industry in recent years.

Methodology

The real interest rate of concern to economists is more precisely referred to as the *ex ante* real interest rate. The *ex ante* real interest rate for a one-period bond, that is, its expected real return, is

$$rr_t = i_t - \pi_t^e, \quad (1)$$

where rr_t is the *ex ante* real interest rate on the one-period bond at time t: i.e., the *ex ante* real return from time t to $t + 1$; i_t is the nominal interest rate on the one-period bond at time t: i.e., the nominal return from time t to $t + 1$; and π_t^e is the inflation rate from time t to $t + 1$ expected at time t.

The problem with measuring the *ex ante* real interest rates is that expected inflation, π_t^e, is not directly observable and so neither is the *ex ante* real interest rate. Several approaches have been used to measure *ex ante* real interest rates. In one approach, real interest rates have been calculated by subtracting survey data on inflation expectations, such as the Livingston data, from nominal interest rates. However, survey-based measures of real interest rates are only as good as the survey measure of inflation expectations, and the survey respondents may have little incentive to answer accurately. An even more telling criticism of survey-based measures, often ignored in the literature, is that the behavior of market expectations is driven by economic agents at the margin who are eliminating unexploited profit opportunities. Market expectations, therefore, are unlikely to be well measured by the average expectations of survey respondents (Mishkin 1981a).

Another approach is to use futures market data to examine real interest rate behavior. Futures market data can be used to directly construct own-commodity real interest rates, i.e., the *ex ante* real return on a bond in terms of specific commodities. Then the own-commodity real rates can be used to make inferences about the real interest rate for the aggregate economy. As pointed out by Mishkin (1987), however, this approach also runs into problems because own-commodity real rates constructed using futures market data contain information not only about the real interest rate for the aggregate economy or for a particular sector but also about *ex ante* relative price movements for the particular commodity. Since, as demonstrated in Mishkin (1987), these *ex ante* relative price movements (which can be thought of as noise) are far greater in

---

Frederic S. Mishkin is with the Graduate School of Business, Columbia University, and the National Bureau of Economic Research.

This research is part of the NBER's research program in "Economic Fluctuations and Financial Markets and Monetary Economics." The usual disclaimer applies.

The data in the figures in this paper as well as the other data used in the analysis will be made available free of charge to any researcher who will send the author a standard formatted 360 KB diskette with a self-addressed mailer.

magnitude than movements in the aggregate real interest rate (the signal), then the noise-to-signal ratio in own-commodity real rates will be very high. Own-commodity real rates constructed using futures market data will thus contain little information about the aggregate real interest rate of primary concern to economists.[1]

Although the *ex ante* real interest rate is not directly observable, the *ex post* real interest rate, which is the actual real return from holding the one-period bond from t to $t + 1$, is observable. It is defined as

$$eprr_t = i_t - \pi_t = rr_t - \epsilon_t, \tag{2}$$

where $eprr_t$ is the *ex post* real interest rate on the one-period bond at time t: i.e., the realized real return from time t to $t + 1$; π_t is the actual inflation rate from time t to $t + 1$; and ϵ_t is the inflation forecast error, $\pi_t - \pi_t^e$. The approach for measuring *ex ante* real interest rates outlined here makes use of *ex post* real interest rate data with the assumption of rational expectations. Specifically, the assumption of rational expectations implies that inflation forecast errors are unforecastable given any information at time t: i.e., $E(\epsilon_t|\phi_t) = 0$, where $E(\ldots|\phi_t)$ is the mathematical expectations operator conditional on all information available at time t, ϕ_t.

If the *ex ante* real rate is correlated with observable variables, X_t, we can describe the *ex ante* real interest rate as a linear projection onto X_t:

$$rr_t = X_t\beta + u_t, \tag{3}$$

where X_t is a set of variables in the available information set ϕ_t and u_t is the error from projecting rr_t onto X_t, which by definition is uncorrelated with X_t. Finally, combining equations (1) through (3) we obtain the following regression equation:

$$eprr_t = X_t\beta + u_t - \epsilon_t. \tag{4}$$

Since data on $eprr_t$ and X_t are observable, equation (4) can be estimated by ordinary least squares (OLS) and hypothesis tests can be conducted on β. Measures of the *ex ante* real rate can be constructed from the fitted values obtained from the OLS estimate of this regression equation: i.e.,

$$\widehat{rr}_t = X_t\hat{\beta}_{OLS}. \tag{5}$$

In a similar fashion, estimates of expected inflation are generated by

$$\hat{\pi}_t^e = i_t - \widehat{rr}_t = i_t - X_t\hat{\beta}_{OLS}. \tag{6}$$

The question arises: what are the properties of the estimated β's and of the measures of the *ex ante* real interest rate and expected inflation described above? The answers to this question are outlined briefly in the following set of econometric points. More formal demonstrations of these points can be found in Mishkin (1981b, 1984b).

(*a*) The $\hat{\beta}_{OLS}$ estimate is a consistent estimate of the projection equation β in (4). This follows directly from the fact that u_t is orthogonal to X_t by definition, while ϵ_t is also orthogonal to X_t because X_t is in the information set ϕ_t and rational expectations implies that ϵ_t is orthogonal to any information included in ϕ_t. Another way of thinking about the result is that a regression using *ex post* real rates will asymptotically yield the same estimates of β as a regression using *ex ante* real rates. Thus we can make inferences about the relationship of the *ex ante* real interest rate with variables known at time t via *ex post* real rate regressions, even though the *ex ante* real rate is unobservable.

(*b*) However, we do lose information by using *ex post* real rates in a regression rather than *ex ante* real rates. The appearance of the error term ϵ_t in the *ex post* real rate regression equation (4) means that $\hat{\beta}_{OLS}$ will have higher standard errors and will be measured less precisely. Furthermore, as a result, the statistical power of tests on the β-coefficients may be quite low.

(*c*) The β and its consistent estimate $\hat{\beta}_{OLS}$ do not imply causation from X_t to the *ex ante* real rate for two reasons: (*i*) the X_t variables are not necessarily exogenous, and (*ii*) information relevant to real rates that is correlated with X_t may have been excluded from the explanatory variables of the regression equation. Without further identifying information, the $\hat{\beta}_{OLS}$ can be interpreted only as reflecting the correlation of *ex ante* real rates with the X_t variables.

(*d*) The rr_t and $\hat{\pi}_t^e$ estimates will be good estimates of real interest rates and expected inflation only if the variance of the u_t error term is small. This will be the case if no relevant information is excluded from the *ex post*

[1] On the other hand, an own-commodity real interest rate measured with futures market data may provide valuable information on the real cost of borrowing to a producer of that commodity. For a hog farmer, a high own-commodity real rate in terms of hogs indicates a high cost of financing hog storage or production.

real rate regression or if the relevant information left out is highly correlated with X_t.

(*e*) An important diagnostic check for a good specification of X_t that produces a small u_t involves examining the residuals from the *ex post* real rate regression to see if they are white noise. Under rational expectations, ϵ_t is serially uncorrelated because with the holding period matching the observation interval (nonoverlapping data), all past ϵ's are in the information set ϕ_t and are thus uncorrelated with ϵ_t.[2] On the other hand, u_t may be autocorrelated or correlated with past values of ϵ_t. If this is the case and the variance of u_t is large, then the regression residual, $u_t - \epsilon_t$, will be serially correlated. However, if the variance of u_t is small, then the regression residual, $u_t - \epsilon_t$, is dominated by ϵ_t and is necessarily serially uncorrelated. Thus the absence of serial correlation in the residuals of the *ex post* real rate regression is a necessary condition for a small variance of u_t, and hence for good $\widehat{rr}_t$ and $\hat{\pi}_t^e$ estimates.[3]

(*f*) In order for OLS to yield correct standard errors for the β-estimates, the regression residuals must satisfy the Gauss-Markov conditions that they not be heteroskedastic or serially correlated. Satisfying the diagnostic check described above is therefore also important because it helps insure that the OLS standard errors of the coefficients are correct.[4]

Real Interest Rates for the Aggregate Economy: What Do We Know?

Using the methodology above, a number of basic facts about the behavior of the real interest rates have been uncovered. The interested reader is directed to papers by Fama, Nelson and Schwert, Mishkin (1981b, 1984a,b) Fama and Gibbons, Summers, Huizinga and Mishkin (1984, 1986), and Cumby and Mishkin. All of these results involve the measurement of an *ex ante* real interest rate for the aggregate economy in which inflation is measured with a broad-based price index such as the CPI.

(*a*) The hypothesis that the real interest rate is constant (i.e., that β-coefficients on all variables except the constant term equal zero in equation (4) is strongly rejected for most sample periods. Only in the unusual sample period from 1953 to 1971 studied by Fama, in which there was very little variation in the data, is the constancy of the real rate not rejected. Even in this sample period, the failure to reject constancy of the real rate should not be taken as strong evidence that the real interest rate was constant in that period: rather it appears to be a reflection of the lack of statistical power of tests on the beta-coefficients.

(*b*) The real interest rate is negatively correlated with expected inflation. This finding is an extremely robust one, having been found for sample periods going back over a hundred years and for other countries besides the United States. Another way of characterizing this result is that bonds have been a poor inflation hedge even in an *ex ante* sense.

(*c*) Increased money supply growth is associated with a decline in real interest rates. However, little evidence has been found that money growth affects real interest rates other than through its effect on inflation, although this result could be due to the low power of the statistical tests.

(*d*) In the postwar period in the United States, fluctuations in nominal interest rates have typically reflected changes in expected inflation rather than in real interest rates. This so-called Fisher effect, in which there is a high correlation between nominal interest rates and expected inflation, is not a general phenomenon. There is little evidence of a Fisher effect in the United States in the period between the two world wars and during the change in Federal Reserve operating procedures from October 1979 to November 1982.

(*e*) Movements in nominal interest rates are often not a reliable indicator of movements in real rates. The correlation of nominal interest rates with real rates in the United States has been found to be negative in most of the postwar period, with the exception of the October 1979 to October 1982 period. However, in that period, nominal interest rates became highly

[2] If the data are overlapping, say the observation interval is one period and the holding period and time to maturity of the bond is j periods, then ϵ_t will be serially correlated and will have an MA $(j-1)$ time-series process. This occurs because ϵ_{t-1} to ϵ_{t-j+1} can be correlated with ϵ_t, since they will not be realized at time t and thus will not be in the information set ϕ_t. In the overlapping data case, the diagnostic check examines whether ϵ_t is uncorrelated with ϵ's lagged j periods or more.

[3] Although the diagnostic check described here is valuable, it is not powerful against certain alternatives. If u_t is not serially correlated or correlated with past ϵ_t, then the regression residual, $u_t - \epsilon_t$, will not be serially correlated even if the variance of u_t is large.

[4] Although OLS produces consistent estimates of β in the overlapping data case of footnote 2, in which ϵ_t is serially correlated, the OLS standard errors of the coefficients will be incorrect. The standard errors can be corrected, however, using the techniques outlined by Hansen and Hodrick and Cumby, Huizinga and Obstfeld (see references in Huizinga and Mishkin 1986).

positively correlated with real interest rates, moving one-for-one with them.

(*f*) Other countries often display a different relation between nominal interest rates with either expected inflation or real interest rates than is found in the United States. Even before 1979, several other countries had only a very weak Fisher effect, with low correlation between nominal interest rates and expected inflation, yet have had a strong positive correlation between nominal and real rates.

(*g*) Real interest rates were extremely high during the contraction phase of the Great Depression. From the perspective of real interest rates, money was extremely tight in this period.

(*h*) Real interest rates were positive in the 1950s and 1960s, turned negative in the mid- to late 1970s, jumped up dramatically in the early 1980s to levels comparable to those during the contraction phase of the Great Depression, and although having declined somewhat have continued to remain at levels above those in the 1950s and 1960s.

(*i*) Real interest rates in other developed countries tend to move in tandem with those in the United States. Just as in the United States, real interest rates in these countries declined from the 1960s to the 1970s and then rose to levels unprecedented in the postwar period. Although there is a statistically significant link between real interest rates in these countries and those in the United States, real rates in these countries do not move one-for-one with those in the United States. As a result, the equality of real interest rates across countries can be strongly rejected.

An important puzzle in the list of facts above is why real interest rates became so high in the 1980s. Politicians and many economists blame the high real rates on the dramatic jump in the U.S. budget deficit after 1981, but closer scrutiny of the data does not give strong support to this view (e.g., see Blanchard and Summers, Evans). Instead, recent research by Huizinga and Mishkin (1986) points to monetary policy as the source of high real interest rates. Because the issue of why real interest rates have been so high in recent years is such an important one, particularly to the agricultural sector, it is worthwhile describing the evidence for the conclusion that the high real interest rates in the 1980s are a monetary phenomenon.

Modern monetary theory (Lucas) suggests that regime changes have an important impact on the stochastic process of many economic variables. With the change in monetary regime in October 1979, the Federal Reserve Board changed the method of conducting monetary policy in order to reverse the inflationary monetary policy of the 1970s. The basic question is whether this disinflationary, monetary regime change is associated with a shift in the stochastic process of real interest rates which resulted in the high real rates in the 1980s.

The answer appears to be yes. When the Federal Reserve Board altered its behavior in October 1979, there was a statistically significant shift in the stochastic process of real interest rates. In addition, if one asks when the shift in the stochastic process of real rates actually occurred, statistical evidence indicates that it corresponded exactly to the October 1979 change in the monetary policy regime. These results point the finger at Paul Volcker's change to a disinflationary monetary policy regime as a major factor causing the high level of real rates.

The research strategy described above is one in which we look for a clearly definable historical event such as the October 1979 change in Federal Reserve operating procedures and then see if there is a significant change in the behavior of a particular economic variable immediately afterward. Suppose that for historical reasons we know the first event is exogenous, so that it occurs as a result of an independent action that could not possibly be caused by the other economic variable. Then when a significant change in the economic variable follows the exogenous event, we have strong evidence that the first event is causing the change in the behavior of the economic variable. In a sense then, we are treating the October 1979 change in the Federal Reserve operating procedures as an exogenous event—in other words, a controlled experiment; and when we see the shift in the behavior of the real interest rate, we are ascribing causation from the monetary regime shift to the change in real rate behavior.

The approach described above actually provides identification using historical knowledge to rule out such problems as reverse causation. It is one method for getting around the identification problem posed by the rational expectations revolution (see Sims). However, one danger of such a historical-econometric approach is that it runs the danger of fitting one historical episode with one tailor-made theory. Truly convincing evidence that the

Federal Reserve's monetary policy regime change led to high real interest rates must involve examination of similar "controlled experiments" in other time periods. Examination of another episode of a monetary regime shift in 1920 that has many similarities to the October 1979 shift provides exactly this kind of evidence.

At the beginning of 1920, the pursuit of the real bills doctrine by the Federal Reserve led to rapid money supply growth, a sustained high level of inflation with double-digit levels similar to that of the late 1970s, and a weak dollar. In January and June of 1920, the Federal Reserve decided to reverse its inflationary monetary policy by raising the discount rate sharply—by 1¼% in January and 1% in June. In the early years of the Federal Reserve System, changing the discount rate was the main tool of monetary policy, and it was particularly potent at this time because the total amount of member bank borrowing from the Federal Reserve exceeded the amount of nonborrowed reserves. The result of this policy was a rapid disinflation (in fact, a deflation). This disinflation was similar to the one we saw in the early 1980s, and thus we might expect to find parallels between the two periods.

The empirical analysis of the period surrounding 1920 reveals a significant shift in the stochastic process of real interest rates which has many similarities to the experience of the 1980s. Not only is the shift significant, but the dating of the shift is coincident with the Federal Reserve Board's taking action to raise the discount rate in June 1920. Furthermore, the 1920 monetary regime change and the subsequent disinflation is associated with a strengthening of the correlation of nominal interest rates and real interest rates and a shift to a sustained higher level of real interest rates.[5] The striking correspondence between the impact of the monetary regime shifts on real interest rates in 1920 and 1979 provides strong support for the view that the recent shift in real rate behavior is a monetary phenomenon. Particularly important in this regard is that high budget deficits were not a feature of the 1920s,[6] thus suggesting that monetary factors are more important than budget deficits to the recent behavior of real interest rates.[7]

Now that we have discussed what we know about real interest rate behavior for the aggregate economy, we might ask whether the real interest rate that is more applicable to the agricultural sector has behaved in a similar way. This is what we turn to now.

Real Interest Rate Behavior for the Agricultural Sector

Clearly, there is no unique real interest rate. The real rate depends not only on the risk characteristics of the particular security being studied, but more importantly also on the price index used to calculate real returns. The real interest rate relevant to production decisions in the agricultural sector is not the real interest rate calculated with a broad-based price index such as the CPI, the one discussed above. Instead, a real interest rate relevant to the agricultural sector should be measured with a price index that reflects the prices of agricultural output.

Using the farm products component of the producer price index and one-month Treasury bills, *ex post* real interest rates for the agricultural sector have been constructed for the January 1953–December 1986 sample period. *Ex post* real rate regressions for the pre-October 1979 and post-October 1979 sample periods have been run using the same explanatory variables as in Huizinga and Mishkin (1986), but the only explanatory variable with a statistically significant coefficient in either period is the one-month bill rate (i_t).[8] Even with just this one explanatory variable in the regressions, the diagnostic check for serial correlation of the residuals does not reveal any evidence of serial correlation.[9] Not only are

[5] The 1920 regime shift is also associated with a weakening of the Fisher effect, just as occurred after October 1979.

[6] Although the federal government ran substantial budget deficits in the years 1917–19 as a result of World War I, there were budget surpluses in every year from 1920 to 1929.

[7] Financial deregulation, investment tax credits, and oil price shocks were also not present in the 1920s. Thus, the correspondence between the 1920s and the 1980s of real interest rate behavior also weakens the case that these were important factors affecting recent real rate behavior.

[8] The list of explanatory variables examined included the one-month bill rate, two lags of the inflation rate (calculated using the farm products price index) and one lag of a supply shock variable measured as the relative price of energy in the PPI.

[9] Goldfeld-Quandt tests also reveal no evidence of heteroscedasticity in the post-October 1979 sample period but do reject homoscedasticity in the pre-October 1979 period. However, when the pre-October 1979 regression is rerun with a weighted least-squares correction for heteroscedasticity along the lines of Glesjer, the results are very similar to those reported in the text; the coefficient of the bill rate is still negative and insignificantly different from zero.

the Durbin-Watson statistics near two, but Q-statistics cannot reject that the first twelve autocorrelations of the residuals are zero. Thus there is no evidence that the specification of the X_t information set is inadequate. The regression results with standard errors of coefficients in parentheses are as follows:[10]

Sample period January 1953–October 1979:

$$eprr_t = \underset{(3.69)}{3.27} - \underset{(.81)}{.53}i_t + \epsilon_t,$$

$R^2 = .001$, standard error = 30.49, Durbin-Watson = 2.05.

Sample period November 1979–December 1986:

$$eprr_t = \underset{(9.74)}{-15.22} + \underset{(1.01)}{2.73}i_t + \epsilon_t,$$

$R^2 = .080$, standard error = 26.48, Durbin-Watson = 1.73.

The first striking feature of these results is the very large standard error of the regression, which is on the order of 30 percentage points. Because the absence of serial correlation in the residuals suggests that most of the variation of the regression residuals can be attributed to the forecast error of inflation, these regressions indicate that one-month forecast errors for farm products inflation have a standard deviation of thirty percentage points at an annual rate. On the other hand, for the same time periods, standard errors of the regression for *ex post* real rate regressions using the CPI price index are on the order of 2 to 2.5 percentage points, which is less than one-tenth as large.[11] The exceedingly large forecast errors for farm products inflation is not surprising considering how volatile farm prices are, but it does mean, as the earlier discussion of methodology suggests, that *ex post* real rate regressions for the agricultural sector will have low statistical power. This helps explain why only the T-bill rate is found to be a significant explanatory variable in the regressions.

Despite the low statistical power, the *ex post* real rate regressions above for farm products yield similar conclusions to ones estimated using the CPI price index. They suggest that in the pre-October 1979 period *ex ante* real rates for the agricultural sector are negatively correlated with nominal interest rates, while after the monetary regime shift in 1979 they become positively correlated. In addition, an F-test for the stability of the coefficients in the two sample periods indicates that the stochastic process of real rates for the farm sector also undergoes a significant shift in October 1979: $F(2,404) = 3.57$, while the critical value at the 5% level is 3.00.

Using the fitted values of the above regressions to construct measures of expected farm products inflation, we can run regressions of *ex post* real rates on expected inflation. The results are that the coefficient on expected inflation is −.35 in the pre-October 1979 period with a standard error of .34, and the coefficient is −1.58 in the post-October 1979 period, also with a standard error of .34.[12] Thus, similar to results using broader-based price indices such as the CPI, real rates for farm products are found to be negatively correlated with expected inflation.

Figure 1 displays the estimates of the real interest rate for farm products derived from the above regressions, along with 95% confidence intervals for these estimates.[13] Over the January 1953 to October 1979 period, the estimated real rate is relatively constant but has a slight downward trend. The real rate has an average of 1% over the period but has small negative values in the late 1970s. After October 1979, the behavior of the real rate changes dramatically. It jumps to near the 30% level in the 1980–81 period, with even the lower bound of the 95% confidence interval above 10%, and it remains high afterwards. The real rate estimates for the agricultural sector in figure 1 suggest one factor that has led to

[10] The one-month bill rate data was obtained from the Center for Security Prices (CRSP) at the University of Chicago. The bill rate and *ex post* real rate are continuously compounded percentages at an annual rate. The timing of the data is as follows: a January bill rate observation uses the end of December bill rate, while the January observation for the one-month inflation rate is calculated as the logarithmic change from the December to January values of the farm products ppi index (multiplied by 1200 to put it as percent as an annual rate). The January *ex post* real rate observation equals the January bill rate observation minus the January farm products inflation observation.

[11] Huizinga and Mishkin (1986) report the standard errors of these regressions on page 247. Note, however, that the Huizinga-Mishkin standard errors have to be multiplied by 1200 to be in percent at an annual rate.

[12] The standard errors of the expected inflation coefficient are estimated with an instrumental variables procedure described by McCallum and Pagan (see references in Huizinga and Mishkin 1986). This is necessary because OLS estimates of the standard errors will be incorrect since OLS estimation involves a two-step procedure in which expected inflation is estimated first and then *ex post* real rates are regressed on this measure.

[13] The formula for the confidence interval is derived under the reasonable assumption that the variance of inflation forecast errors are large relative to the variance of u_t. The formula is given in Mishkin (1981b).

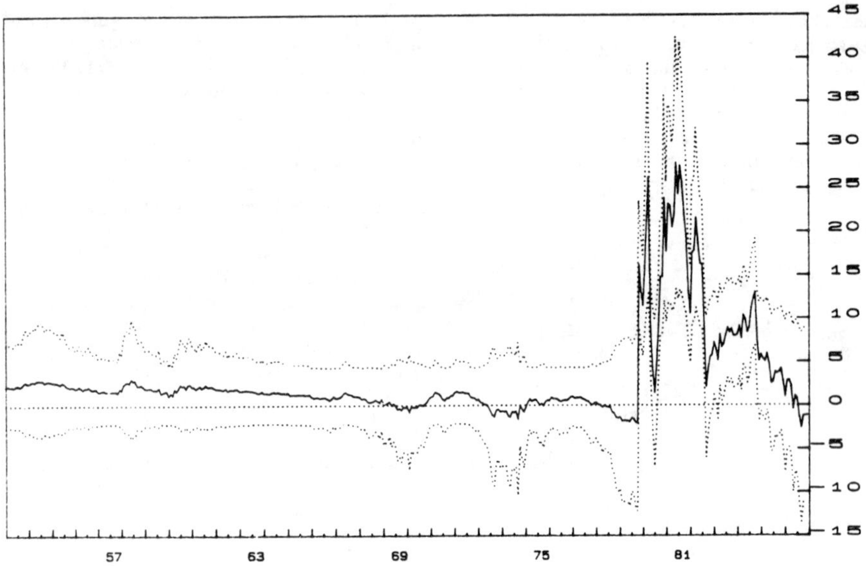

Legend: ____________ farm products real rate:
.... 95% confidence interval.

Figure 1. Estimated real interest rate for farm products

the difficulties of the agricultural sector in the 1980s is that farmers faced a real cost of borrowing in terms of their production of almost 30% in 1980–81 and an average of 10% for the entire November 1979 to December 1986 period. Real rates of this magnitude certainly have made life difficult for the American farmer in recent years.

A natural question to ask is: has the striking behavior of real interest rates for the agricultural sector been similar to that of real interest rates for the aggregate economy? This question is answered in figure 2, which compares estimated *ex ante* real rates for farm products with estimated *ex ante* real rates using the CPI price index.[14] As we can see in figure 2, the general pattern of real rate movements is the same for the aggregate economy and for the agricultural sector. The aggregate real rate also has small positive values in the 1950s and 1960s, has small negative values in the late 1970s, then also jumps dramatically to levels above 8% in the 1980–81 period and remains high thereafter. Indeed, the real rate for the agricultural sector looks like an amplified movement of the real rate for the aggregate economy. This is confirmed by regressing the estimated real rate for farm products on the CPI estimated real rate. The estimated coefficient on the CPI real rate is 1.52 with a standard error of .70,[15] so that there is a statistically significant comovement of these two series (t = 2.16) in which the farm products real rate moves more than one-for-one with the CPI real rate.

Conclusion

The evidence presented in this paper indicates that real interest rates for the agricultural economy have been extremely high in the 1980s and that their behavior seems to be linked to that found for real rates in the aggre-

[14] The estimated rates using the CPI price index are estimated using the regression specification of Huizinga and Mishkin (1986).

[15] For reasons similar to those described in footnote 12, correct standard errors of this coefficient are obtained with an instrumental variables technique. This procedure is described in Cumby and Mishkin.

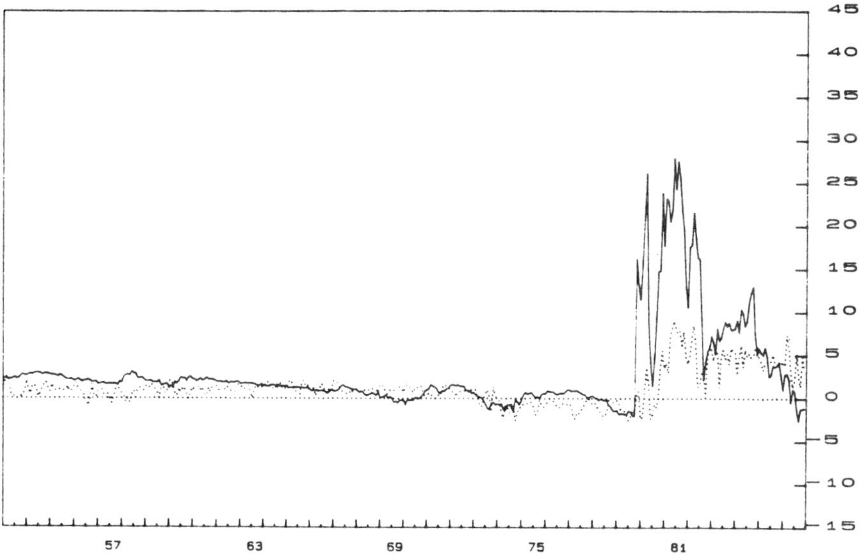

Legend: ____________ farm products real rate;
.... CPI real rate.

Figure 2. Comparison of farm products real rate and CPI real rate

gate economy. What has been the source of these high real rates? Apparently, it was the result of a concerted effort by the monetary authorities to disinflate the economy. However, the brunt of the Federal Reserve Board's disinflationary policy has fallen more heavily on the farm sector, which has had to face far higher real rates than the rest of the economy. Although breaking the back of inflation was certainly a worthy goal for the Federal Reserve, farmers have had to pay a heavy price. They have had to suffer for the sins of an economy that was excessively inflationary, which then had to be brought back into line with disinflationary policy.

References

Blanchard, O. J., and L. H. Summers. "Perspectives on High World Real Interest Rates." *Brookings Pap. on Econ. Activ.* 2(1984):273–324.

Cumby, Robert E., and Frederic S. Mishkin. "The International Linkage of Real Interest Rates: The European-US Connection." *J. Int. Money and Finan.* 5(1986):5–23.

Evans, P. "Do Large Deficits Produce High Interest Rates?" *Amer. Econ. Rev.* 75(1985):68–87.

Fama, Eugene F. "Short Term Interest Rates as Predictors of Inflation." *Amer. Econ. Rev.* 65(1975):269–82.

Fama, Eugene F., and Michael R. Gibbons. "Inflation, Real Returns and Capital Investment." *J. Monetary Econ.* 14(1982):297–323.

Glesjer, H. "A New Test for Heteroscedasticity." *J. Amer. Statist. Assoc.* 64(1969):316–23.

Goldfeld, S., and R. E. Quandt. "Some Tests for Heteroscedasticity." *J. Amer. Statist. Assoc.* 60(1965):539–47.

Huizinga, John, and Frederic S. Mishkin. "Inflation and Real Interest Rates on Assets with Different Risk Characteristics." *J. Finan.* 39(1984):699–712.

———. "Monetary Policy Regime Shifts and the Unusual Behavior of Real Interest Rates." *Carnegie-Rochester Conference Series on Public Policy* 20(Spring 1986):231–74.

Lucas, R. E., Jr. "Econometric Policy Evaluation: A Critique." *The Phillips Curve and Labor Markets*, ed. K. Brunner and A. Meltzer. *Carnegie-Rochester Conference Series on Public Policy* 1(1976):19–46.

Mishkin, Frederic S. "Are Market Forecasts Rational?" *Amer. Econ. Rev.* 71(1981a):295–306.

———. "Are Real Interest Rates Equal Across Countries? An Empirical Investigation of International Parity Conditions." *J. Finan.* 39(1984a):1345–57.

———. "Can Futures Market Data Be Used to Understand the Behavior of Real Interest Rates?" National Bureau of Economic Research Work. Pap. No. 2400, Columbia University, Oct. 1987.

———. "The Real Interest Rate: A Multi-Country Empirical Study." *Can. J. Econ.* 17(May 1984b):283–311.

———. "The Real Interest Rate: An Empirical Investigation." *Carnegie-Rochester Conference Series on Public Policy* 15(Fall 1981b):151–200.

Nelson, Charles R., and G. William Schwert. "Short-Term Interest Rates as Predictors of Inflation: On Testing the Hypothesis That the Real Rate of Interest Is Constant." *Amer. Econ. Rev.* 67(1977):478–86.

Sims, C. "Macroeconomics and Reality." *Econometrica* (1980).

Summers, L. H. "The Nonadjustment of Nominal Interest Rates: A Study of the Fisher Effect." *A Symposium in Honor of Arthur Okun*, ed. J. Tobin. Washington DC: The Brookings Institution, 1983.

THE JOURNAL OF FINANCE • VOL. XLV, NO. 1 • MARCH 1990

Can Futures Market Data Be Used to Understand the Behavior of Real Interest Rates?

FREDERIC S. MISHKIN*

ABSTRACT

This paper examines whether futures market data can be used to understand the behavior of real interest rates. Several ways of examining the data indicate that futures market data are not particularly informative about real interest rates. Not only does this evidence cast some doubt on results in previous research that make use of futures market data to draw inferences about real interest rates, but it also indicates that future research on real interest rates may need to turn to a different line of attack.

UNDERSTANDING THE BEHAVIOR OF real interest rates is a central issue in financial economics. In previous research on this topic, several approaches have been used to measure real interest rates. In one approach, real interest rates have been calculated by subtracting survey data on inflation expectations, such as the Livingston data, from nominal interest rates.[1] The problem with survey-based measures of real interest rates is that they are only as good as the survey measure of inflation expectations and there may be little incentive for the survey respondents to answer accurately. An even more telling criticism of survey-based measures, often ignored in the literature, is that the behavior of market expectations is driven by economic agents at the margin who are eliminating unexploited profit opportunities. Market expectations are unlikely, therefore, to be well measured by the average expectations of survey respondents.[2]

Because of doubts about survey-based measures of real interest rates, other researchers have used the assumption of rational expectations and ex-post real interest rate data calculated with aggregate price level data to make inferences about real interest rate behavior.[3] There are several difficulties with this approach

* Graduate School of Business, Columbia University, and National Bureau of Economic Research. This research has been supported by the Center for the Study of Futures Markets and the Faculty Research Fund at the Graduate School of Business, Columbia University. I thank Depaio Tang and Jae-Won Park for research assistance. I also thank for their helpful comments, Robert Cumby, Franklin Edwards, Alberto Giovannini, Bruce Hamilton, David Modest, Krishna Ramaswamy, Arthur Warga, the Editor of his journal and participants at seminars at Columbia University, Johns Hopkins University, Queens University, University of British Columbia, University of Texas at Austin, University of Washington, Wharton and Yale University. The research reported here is part of the NBER's programs in Economic Fluctuations and Financial Markets and Monetary Economics. The usual disclaimer applies. The data used in this paper will be made available free of charge to any researcher who will send me a standard formatted 360KB diskette with a self addressed, stamped mailer.

[1] For example, see Gibson (1972), Cargill (1976), Lahiri (1976), Carlson (1977), Levi and Makin (1979), Tanzi (1980) and Wilcox (1983).

[2] See Mishkin (1981a).

[3] For example, see Mishkin (1981b), Fama and Gibbons (1982), Hamilton (1985) and Huizinga and Mishkin (1986).

as well. First is the need for the rational expectations assumption. Although rational expectations is a maintained hypothesis in much current research in monetary and financial economics, there are questions about its validity particularly when there is a shift from one policy regime to another. An additional problem with this approach is that unanticipated inflation appears as a component of the error term in the statistical analysis. As a result, statistical tests may have low power.[4] Another consequence of the presence of unanticipated inflation in the error term is that the variability of real interest rates cannot be examined directly.

Because of the difficulties with the analysis of ex-post real interest rates derived with aggregate price level data, recent research has begun to use futures market data for contracts on individual commodities to examine real interest rate behavior. This paper examines whether futures market data for contracts on individual commodities can be used to understand the behavior of real interest rates. All the evidence consistently casts doubt on the usefulness of futures market data for understanding real interest rate behavior. Not only does this cast some doubt on results in previous research that make use of futures market data to draw inferences about real interest rates,[5] but it also indicates that future research on real interest rates may need to turn to a different line of attack.

The paper begins with a comparison of approaches for measuring real interest rates, Section II examines the usefulness of futures market data in evaluating real interest rate behavior, and Section III concludes.

I. A Comparison of Approaches

The own-commodity real rate for a particular commodity equals the ex-ante return on a one-period bond in terms of that specific commodity. With the existence of a futures market, an investor can lock in this ex-ante real return at time t by selling the commodity j at a price of S_t^j, use the proceeds to purchase a one-period bond with a nominal return (interest rate) of i_t, and then transform the proceeds received at time $t+1$ back into the commodity at the futures price set at time t, F_t^j. The own-commodity real rate for commodity j is thus defined as

$$rr_t^j = i_t - \ln(F_t^j/S_t^j), \tag{1}$$

where

rr_t^j = the own-commodity real rate at time t for commodity j,
$\ln(F_t^j/S_t^j)$ = the logarithmic basis,
F_t^j = the futures price at time t for delivery of commodity j at time $t+1$,[6]
S_t^j = the spot price at time t for commodity j.

[4] See Nelson and Schwert (1977) and Mishkin (1981a) for a discussion of this point.

[5] See Cornell and French (1986) and Hamilton (1987), for example.

[6] Strictly speaking, F_t^j in equation (1) should be the price of a forward contract rather than a futures contract. As Black (1976) has pointed out, futures contracts are priced differently from forward contracts. However, this difference should be minor relative to movements of real interest rates. To the extent that prices of forward contracts and futures contracts differ, this is just one more

An attractive feature of the own-commodity real rate rr_t^j defined above is that it is directly observable at time t and does not require any assumption about expectations formation, such as rational expectations, in order to be measured.

To see how own-commodity real rates are linked to the real interest rate, we can note, as in Cornell and French (1986), that if futures markets existed for all commodities in the commodity bundle of the aggregate price index, then the riskless real interest rate for the aggregate economy, rr_t, can be written as a weighted average of all the own-commodity real rates.

$$rr_t = \sum_{j=1}^{n} \omega_j rr_t^j = i_t - \sum_{j=1}^{n} \omega_j \ln(F_t^j/S_t^j), \tag{2}$$

where

rr_t = the (aggregate) real interest rate,
n = the number of commodities in the economy,
ω_j = the expenditure weight for commodity j—i.e., the relative expenditure on commodity j in the futures commodity bundle—where $\sum_{j=1}^{n} \omega_j = 1$.

Using (1) and (2), we can describe the own-commodity real rate for commodity j as follows:

$$\begin{aligned} r_t^j &= rr_t - [\ln(F_t^j/S_t^j) - \sum_{j=1}^{n} \omega_j \ln(F_t^j/S_t^j)] \\ &= rr_t - \varphi_t^j, \end{aligned} \tag{3}$$

where

φ_t^j = the ex-ante relative price movement for commodity j at time t (assuming there is no risk premium embedded in futures prices due to uncertainty about relative price movements).[7]

We can thus think of each own-commodity real rate as a measure of the aggregate real interest rate which is subject to a measurement error of φ_t^j, the ex-ante relative price movement.

The real interest rate usually studied in the literature is the ex-ante real return on a nominally riskless bond, which is defined as

$$rr_t^* = i_t - \pi_t^e, \tag{4}$$

where

rr_t^* = the expected real return at time t of a one-period bond maturing at time $t+1$,
π_t^e = the expected rate of change (at time t) in the aggregate price level from time t to $t+1$.

---

reason why futures market data may not provide reliable information about the behavior of real interest rates.

[7] Even if a risk premium reflecting uncertainty about relative price movements were present, the basic thrust of the analysis would remain unchanged. However, the φ_t^j term would have a different interpretation because it would include this risk premium.

Note that this real interest rate is not riskless in real terms because there is uncertainty about the inflation rate. It will thus differ from the riskless real interest rate, rr_t, by a risk premium. It is straightforward to calculate estimates of this risk premium using a capital asset pricing (CAPM) framework, and the estimated risk premium is found to be quite small—11 basis points (0.11 percentage points)[8]—while upper and lower bounds for the possible values of this risk premium are ±40 basis points. These CAPM calculations suggest that even if this risk premium is time varying, it and its possible variation is extremely small relative to measured movements in real interest rates which have undergone large swings in recent years (by as much as 1000 basis points from the late 1970s to the early 1980s).[9] Thus it seems plausible that for all practical purposes we can assume that $rr_t = rr_t^*$, and to simplify the discussion, we will treat rr_t and rr_t^*, as identical in the remainder of the paper.

The intuition for why this risk premium may be so small is that the amount of inflation uncertainty is very small relative to uncertainty for the market return. In the 1967–85 sample period examined in this paper, the standard deviation of inflation uncertainty is less than five percent of the standard deviation of the real market return. Thus the beta for a nominally riskless bond must necessarily also be very small, resulting in a small risk premium.

The real interest rate in (4) is not observable because π_t^e is unobservable, but, as discussed in Mishkin (1981a), we can examine the ex-post real rate which is defined as,

$$eprr_t = i_t - \pi_t^e, \tag{5}$$

where

$eprr_t$ = the realized real return on the one-period bond held from time t to $t + 1$,

π_t^e = the change in the aggregate price level from time t to $t + 1$.

The ex-post real rate can be written in terms of the real interest rate as

$$eprr_t = i_t - \pi_t^e - (\pi_t - \pi_t^e) = rr_t - \epsilon_t, \tag{6}$$

where

$$\epsilon_t = \pi_t - \pi_t^e = \text{the forecast error of inflation.}$$

The equation above thus tells us that the ex-post real rate is just equal to the real interest rate plus an error term which is the forecast error of inflation.

Two disadvantages of using ex-post real interest rate data to examine the behavior of real interest rates are readily understandable from the equation above. The presence of the ϵ_t forecast error of inflation term in ex-post real rates means that the researcher cannot directly examine how the variability of the real

[8] This calculation is found in a longer version of this paper, Mishkin (1989). Bodie, Kane and McDonald (1985) reach a very similar conclusion even though they use a model with different assumptions. Their estimate of 15 basis points for this risk premium is very close to my estimate of 11 basis points.

[9] See Huizinga and Mishkin (1986).

interest rate changes over time. Specifically, without knowledge about the variability of inflation forecast errors, information about the variability of the real interest rate cannot be directly extracted from information about the variability of the ex-post real interest rate. The second disadvantage stems from the fact noted in Mishkin (1981a) that the presence of the ϵ_t inflation forecast error term implies that statistical tests using ex-post real rates will have low statistical power. Equation (3) and our discussion of own-commodity real rates indicates, however, that they are also subject to a similar disadvantage. Specifically, for both ex-post real rates and own-commodity real rates there is a signal to noise problem. For own-commodity real rates, the noise is the ex-ante relative price movement, φ_t^j, while for ex-post real rates, the noise is the inflation forecast error, ϵ_t. If the ex-ante relative price movements, φ_t^j, are far greater in magnitude than movements in the real interest rate, then examining own-commodity real rates is unlikely to help us understand the behavior of real interest rates. Furthermore, if the variance of φ_t^j greatly exceeds the variance of ϵ_t, then we are likely to obtain better information about the behavior of real interest rates from using ex-post real rate data than from own-commodity real rate data constructed using futures market data.

Now that we understand the issues relating to the advantages and disadvantages of using futures market data, we can go on to examine what the data on own-commodity actually looks like.

II. An Examination of the Own-Commodity Real Rate Data

The futures market data were obtained from the Center for the Study of Futures Markets, Columbia Business School. The empirical analysis requires a choice of non-financial commodities with equal spacing between contracts that also were traded for a substantial period both before and after October 1979. Precious metals are not included in the study because they are most likely to be subject to cash-and-carry arbitrage which implies that they will contain little information about real interest rates. These criterion lead to the selection of five commodities: live cattle (id #2), live hogs (id #4), soybeans (id #17), frozen orange juice (id #12), and lumber (id #27). The sample period for cattle, hogs and soybeans extends from January or February, 1967 until November or December 1985. Because earlier data was not available, the sample period for orange juice extends from January 1968 until November 1985, while that for lumber is from January 1971 until November 1985.

These commodities have contracts maturing every two months, so that the observation interval and holding period for the own-commodity real rates is two months long. In calculating the logarithmic basis, it is important to make sure that the future and spot prices pertain to the exact same commodity. Thus the futures price for the maturing contract is used as the spot price for the commodity. For example, the logarithmic basis for cattle (at an annual percentage rate) in February, 1967 is calculated as 600 times the log of the April futures price at the closing on January 31, 1967 minus the log of the February futures price at the closing on January 31, 1967. The nominal interest rate is computed as a continuously compounded percent an annual rate from beginning of month prices of U.S. Treasury bills with two months to maturity (obtained from the Center for Research in Security Prices at the University of Chicago). For the February, 1967 own-commodity real rate, the nominal interest rate is 600 times the log of 100 minus the two-month bill price at the closing on January 31, 1967.

Figure 1 contains plots of the own-commodity real rates for the five commodities. The most prominent feature of the own-commodity real rates is their tremendous variability.[10] The own-commodity rates often are outside the range ±50% (annual rate) and the standard deviations for the five commodities are

Cattle	Hogs	Soybeans	Orange Juice	Lumber
25.9%	41.7%	16.1%	28.5%	39.2%.

As a comparison, each plot in Figure 1 also contains a measure of the ex-ante aggregate real rate calculated using the CPI with the procedure found in Huizinga and Mishkin (1986). (The ex-post aggregate real rate is not shown in addition because it would be indistinguishable in the plots from the ex-ante aggregate real rate.) Not only is the variability of the ex-ante aggregate real rate an order of magnitude smaller than those of the own-commodity rates, but this is also the case for the ex-post aggregate real rate: the standard deviation of the ex-ante aggregate real rate is 2.6%, while it is 3.2% for the ex-post aggregate real rate.

As discussed in the previous section, the ex-post aggregate real interest rate differs from the ex-ante aggregate real interest rate by the forecast error of inflation. On the other hand, the own-commodity real rate differs from the ex-ante aggregate real rate by the amount of the ex-ante relative price movements for the specific commodity. Thus which approach gives more accurate inference about the behavior of real interest rates depends on whether the noise represented by the ex-ante relative price movements is greater than the noise attributable to the forecast error of inflation. The standard deviations of the own-commodity real rates and the ex-post aggregate real rate does provide us with information about the relative size of the noises. The upper bound on the standard deviation of the forecast error of inflation is easily shown to equal the standard deviation of the ex-post real interest rate, 3.2%.[11] The lower bounds on the standard deviations of the ex-ante relative price movements can be computed using the fact that the minimum possible variance of the ex-ante relative price movements

[10] Because the high variability of own commodity real rates is so striking, I did check outliers in the data for accuracy by comparing the Center for Futures Markets data with published quotes in the *Wall Street Journal.* In no case did I find a discrepancy between the two data sources. Furthermore, although at first glance it might appear as though the tremendous variability of an own-commodity real rate implies an unexploited profit opportunity, closer inspection of the market suggests that this is unlikely. For example, Bruce Hamilton has pointed out to me that the variability of the own-commodity real rate for hogs (which is the highest of the five commodities) is exactly what might be expected because hogs must be slaughtered at a specific point in their lives in order to get a good price for their meat.

[11] Because the forecast error of inflation is uncorrelated with the ex-ante aggregate real rate under rational expectations, the variance of the ex-post real rate is the sum of the variances of the ex-ante real rate and the forecast error of inflation. Hence the upper bound on the variance of the forecast error of inflation is reached when the variance of inflation is zero: i.e., when the upper bound equals the variance of the ex-post real interest rate.

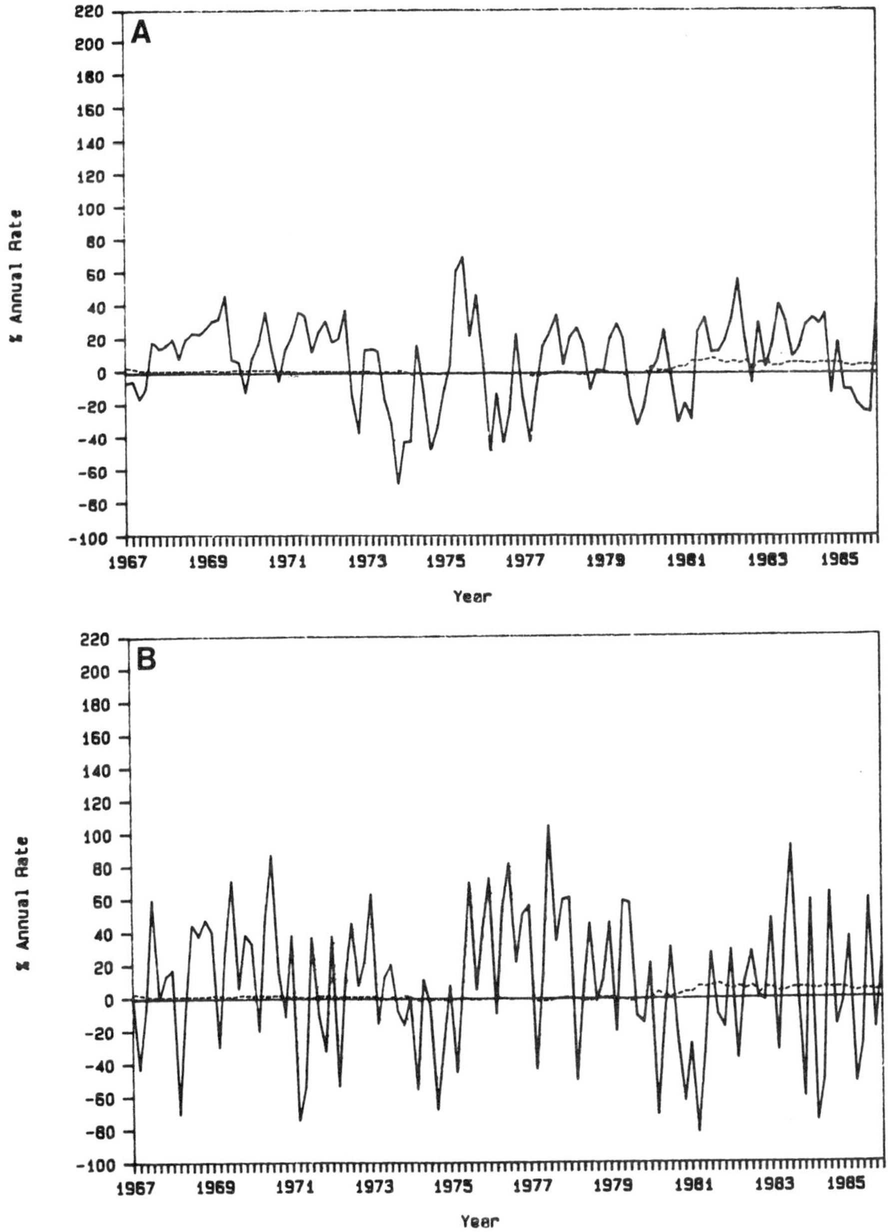

Figure 1. Own-commodity real rates and the aggregate real interest rate. The solid line in each panel is the own-commodity real rate for the commodity named in the panel, while the dashed line is the ex-ante aggregate real interest rate calculated using the CPI with the procedure described in Huizinga and Mishkin (1986). The own-commodity real rate for commodity j is defined as

$$rr_t^j = i_t - \ln(F_t^j/S_t^j),$$

where rr_t^j = the own-commodity real rate at time t for commodity j, $\ln(F_t^j/S_t^j)$ = the logarithmic basis, F_t^j = the futures price at time t for delivery of commodity j at time $t + 1$, and S_t^j = the spot price at time t for commodity j. Panel A: Cattle. Panel B: Hogs.

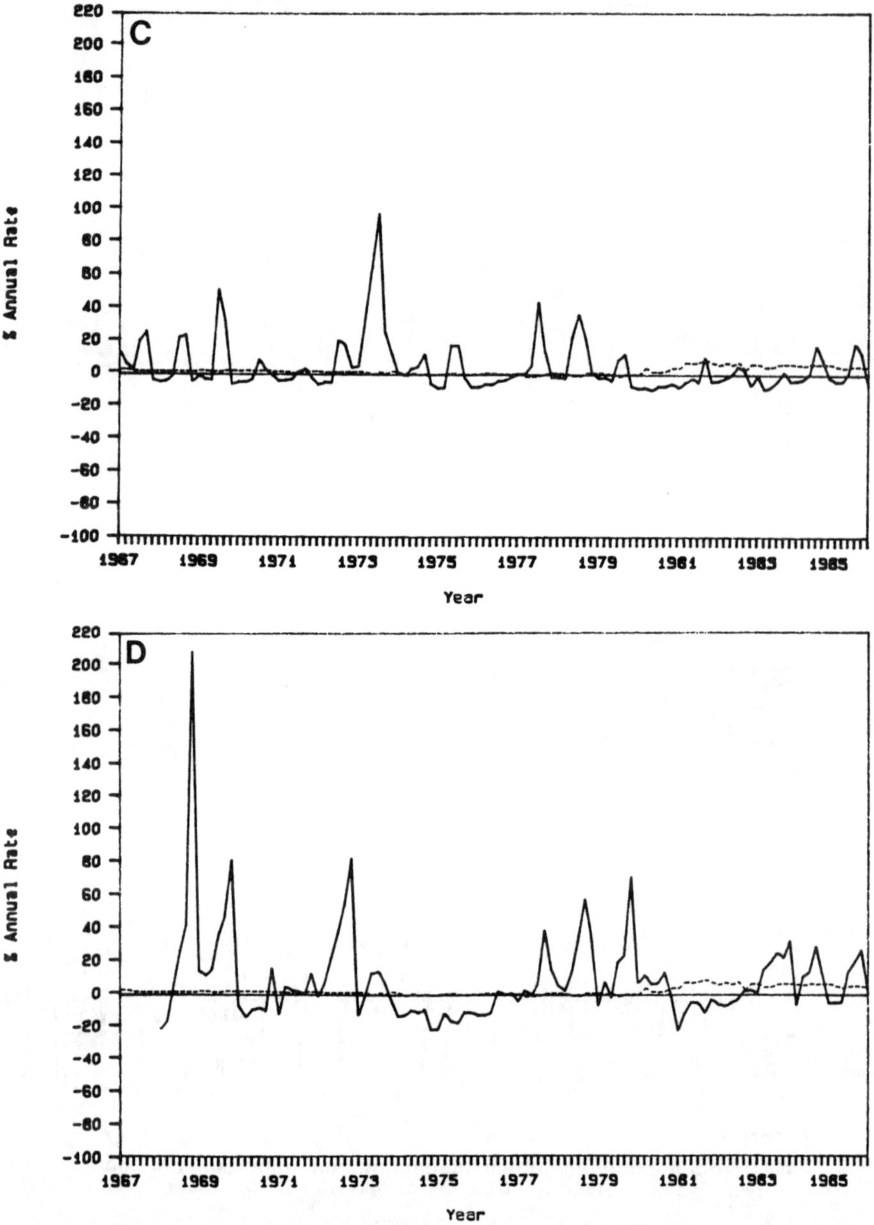

Figure 1. Own-commodity real rates and the aggregate real interest rate. The solid line in each panel is the own-commodity real rate for the commodity named in the panel, while the dashed line is the ex-ante aggregate real interest rate calculated using the CPI with the procedure described in Huizinga and Mishkin (1986). The own-commodity real rate for commodity j is defined as

$$rr_t^j = i_t - \ln(F_t^j/S_t^j),$$

where rr_t^j = the own-commodity real rate at time t for commodity j, $\ln(F_t^j/S_t^j)$ = the logarithmic basis, F_t^j = the futures price at time t for delivery of commodity j at time $t + 1$, and S_t^j = the spot price at time t for commodity j. Panel C: Soybeans. Panel D: Orange juice.

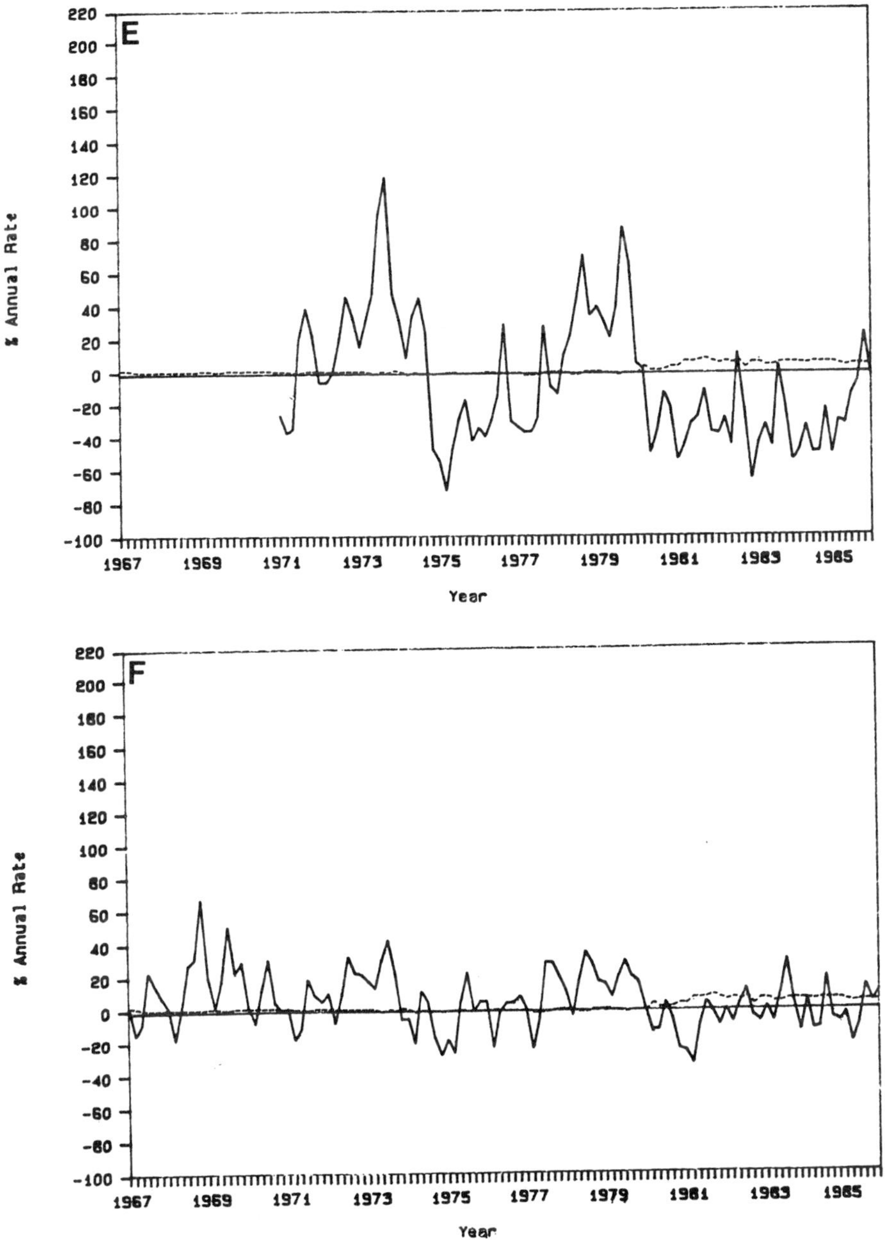

Figure 1. Own-commodity real rates and the aggregate real interest rate. The solid line in each panel is the own-commodity real rate for the commodity named in the panel, while the dashed line is the ex-ante aggregate real interest rate calculated using the CPI with the procedure described in Huizinga and Mishkin (1986). The own-commodity real rate for commodity j is defined as

$$rr_t^j = i_t - \ln(F_t^j/S_t^j),$$

where rr_t^j = the own-commodity real rate at time t for commodity j, $\ln(F_t^j/S_t^j)$ = the logarithmic basis, F_t^j = the futures price at time t for delivery of commodity j at time $t + 1$, and S_t^j = the spot price at time t for commodity j. Panel E: Lumber. Panel F: Average of own-commodity real rates.

occurs when the variance of the ex-ante aggregate real rate is at its upper bound and there is perfect negative correlation between the ex-ante relative price movements and the ex-ante aggregate real rate.[12] The lower bounds for the standard deviations of the ex-ante relative price movements for the five commodities are calculated to be the following:

Cattle	Hogs	Soybeans	Orange Juice	Lumber
22.7%	38.6%	13.0%	25.4%	36.0%.

All of these standard deviation are many times greater than the upper bound for the standard deviation of the forecast error of inflation of 3.2%. Hence, the data indicates that the noise in the own-commodity real rates is many times greater than the noise in the ex-post aggregate real rate. Indeed, on average, the variance of the ex-ante relative price movements seems to be on the order of at least 100 times greater than the variance of the forecast errors of inflation. Therefore, futures market data is unlikely to provide as reliable information about the behavior of the ex-ante aggregate real interest rate as ex-post aggregate real interest rate data does.

Since the upper bound for the standard deviation of the ex-ante aggregate real rate equals the standard deviation of the ex-post aggregate real interest rate,[13] 3.2%, the calculations above can be interpreted in a slightly different way. Ex-ante relative price movements (the noise) have a variance that is on the order of over 100 times greater than the variance for the aggregate real interest rate (the signal). Since the signal to noise ratio is apparently less than 1%, own-commodity real rates constructed with futures market data are unlikely to be useful in examining the behavior of aggregate real interest rates.

Another way of examining the value of own-commodity real rate data is to see whether this data confirms two widely accepted facts about the behavior of aggregate real interest rates since October 1979. The first fact is that aggregate real interest rose after October 1979 to levels well above those in the mid to late 1970s. We see evidence of this in Figure 1 where the measure of the ex-ante aggregate real rate averaged −0.8% from the beginning of 1975 until October 1979, while after October 1979 it averaged 4.5%. The conclusion that ex-ante aggregate real interest rates rose sharply after October 1979 is also supported by

[12] The lower bound for the standard deviation of the ex-ante relative price movements equals,

$$\sigma[\varphi^j]_{\min} = \sigma[rr^j] - \sigma[rr]_{\max} = \sigma[rr^j] - 3.2\%,$$

where $\sigma[\varphi^j]_{\min}$ is the lower bound for the standard deviation of the ex-ante relative price movement for commodity j, $\sigma[rr^j]$ is the standard deviation of the own-commodity rate, and $\sigma[rr]_{\max}$ is the upper bound for the standard deviation of the ex-ante aggregate real rate, which, as is shown in the subsequent footnote, equals the standard deviation of the ex-post aggregate real rate, 3.2%. The lower bound, $\sigma[\varphi_j]_{\min}$, is derived using equation (3) to write the variance of the own-commodity rate as

$$\sigma^2[rr^j] = \sigma^2[rr] - 2\rho\sigma[\varphi_j]\sigma[rr] + \sigma^2[\varphi_j],$$

where ρ is the correlation between φ^j and rr. Then recognizing that $\sigma^2[\varphi^j]$ reaches its minimum when $\rho = -1$ and $\sigma[rr]$ is at a maximum, we can solve for $\sigma[\varphi^j]_{\min}$.

[13] Using reasoning similar to that of footnote 11, the upper bound on the variance of the ex-ante real rate is reached when the variance of the forecast error of inflation is assumed to be zero; i.e., when the upper bound equals the variance of the ex-post real rate.

other approaches for measuring the ex-ante aggregate real interest rate, such as those using survey measures of expected inflation. The second fact is the increase in variability of ex-ante aggregate real rates after October 1979: From the beginning of 1975 to October 1979, the standard deviation of the ex-ante real rate measure in Figure 6 is 0.8%, and after October 1979 it is 2.2%. These two facts about the behavior of ex-ante real interest rates seem to be accepted by almost all economists, and yet they are not at all evident in the own-commodity real rate data.

In the first five panels of Figure 1 and the last panel which displays the average of the own-commodity real rates, we see that, rather than rising after October 1979, there was some tendency for the own-commodity real rates to fall: three of the own-commodity real rates (hogs, soybeans and lumber) tend to decline after October 1979, as does the average of all five own-commodity real rates. The average values of the own-commodity real rates for the five commodities in the 1975 to October 1979 period and the post-October 1979 period are shown in Table I. In addition, the variability of the own-commodity real rates usually fall after October 1979 rather than rise, as can also be seen in Table I.[14] Since the behavior of the own-commodity real rates before and after October 1979 seems to be at odds with what most analysis suggests occurred for ex-ante aggregate real rates, we have further evidence that using futures markets to examine real interest rate behavior may not be particularly illuminating.

Table I

Average Levels and Standard Deviations of Own-Commodity Real Rates

The own-commodity real rate for commodity j is thus defined as $rr^j_t = i_t - \ln(F^j_t/S^j_t)$, where rr^j_t = the own-commodity real rate at time t for commodity j, $\ln(F^j_t/S^j_t)$ = the logarithmic basis, F^j_t = the futures price at time t for delivery of commodity j at time $t + 1$, and S^j_t = the spot price at time t for commodity j.

Panel A. Average Levels of Own-Commodity Real Rates

	Cattle	Hogs	Soybeans	Orange Juice	Lumber	Average of Own-Rates
1975 to October 1979	7.7%	27.4%	4.1%	3.8%	−3.4%	7.9%
post-October 1979	9.0%	−4.2%	−2.1%	6.7%	−25.3%	−3.2%

Panel B. Standard Deviations of the Own-Commodity Real Rates

	Cattle	Hogs	Soybeans	Orange Juice	Lumber	Average of Own-Rates
1975 to October 1979	28.8%	39.8%	13.8%	18.9%	40.1%	16.6%
post-October 1979	24.1%	42.7%	7.2%	16.9%	25.8%	13.1%

[14] The finding here is however consistent with the evidence in Parks (1978) who suggests that there is a positive correlation between the level of inflation and relative price variability. Since the inflation level fell after October 1979, relative price variability would be expected to fall and this would be reflected in lower standard deviations of own-commodity real rates.

III. Conclusions

Rarely in monetary/macro economics does empirical work pay sufficient attention to the quality of the data it is analyzing. This paper is an attempt to be an exception since it asks whether a particular data set is appropriate for answering an important set of questions. The analysis here explores several pieces of evidence which provide information on the usefulness of own-commodity real rates constructed from futures market data for understanding the behavior of real interest rates. The evidence can be summarized as follows:

1. The noise in own-commodity real rates (the ex-ante relative price movements) is so large relative to the signal (the aggregate real interest rate) that own-commodity real rates are unlikely to contain much information about aggregate real interest rates.
2. Data on own-commodity real rates is not consistent with several widely accepted facts about the behavior of aggregate real interest rates, indicating that own-commodity real rates can provide misleading information about aggregate real interest rates.[15]

This paper would have a happier ending if it concluded that futures market data is useful for understanding real interest rate behavior. Instead, it indicates that a promising research line exploiting futures market data for analyzing real interest rates is not so promising. In order to learn more about real interest rates, we must pursue a different research route.

[15] In a longer version of this paper, Mishkin (1989), econometric analysis of own-commodity real rate behavior fails to find a shift in the stochastic process which has been documented for aggregate real interest rates. The failure of own-commodity real rate data to reveal a shift in the real rate process provides further evidence that any advantages of own-commodity real rate data for econometric analysis is overcome by the disadvantages stemming from the fact that the noise in the data is orders of magnitude larger than the signal.

REFERENCES

Black, Fischer, 1976, The pricing of commodity contracts, *Journal of Financial Economics* 3, 167–179.

Bodie, Zvi, Alex Kane, and Robert McDonald, 1985, Inflation and the role of bonds in investor portfolios, in Benjamin Friedman, ed.: *Corporate Capital Structures in the United States* (University of Chicago Press, Chicago, IL).

Cargill, Thomas F., 1976, Anticipated price changes and nominal interest rates in the 1950s, *Review of Economics and Statistics* 58, 364–367.

Carlson, John A., 1977, Short-term interest rates as predictors of inflation: Comment, *American Economic Review* 67, 469–475.

Cornell, Bradford and Kenneth French, 1986, Commodity own rates, real interest rates, and money supply announcements, *Journal of Monetary Economics* 18, 3–20.

Fama, Eugene and Michael R. Gibbons, 1982, Inflation, real returns and capital investment, *Journal of Monetary Economics* 14, 297–323.

Gibson, William E., 1972, Interest rates and inflationary expectations: New evidence, *American Economic Review* 62, 854–865.

Hamilton, James, 1985, Uncovering financial markets expectations of inflation, *Journal of Political Economy* 93, 1224–1241.

———, 1987, Monetary factors in the Great Depression, *Journal of Monetary Economics* 19, 145–169.

Huizinga, John and Frederic S. Mishkin, 1986, Monetary policy regime shifts and the unusual behavior of real interest rates, *Carnegie-Rochester Conference Series on Public Policy* 20, 231–274.

Lahiri, Kajal, 1976, Inflationary expectations: Their formation and interest rate effects, *American Economic Review* 66, 124–131.

Levi, Michael D. and John H. Makin, 1979, Fisher, Phillips, Friedman and the measured impact of inflation on interest, *Journal of Finance* 34, 35–52.

Mishkin, Frederic S., 1981a, The real interest rate: An empirical investigation, *Carnegie-Rochester Conference Series on Public Policy* 15, 151–200.

———, 1981b, Are market forecasts rational, *American Economic Review* 71, 295–306.

———, 1989, Can futures market data be used to understand the behavior of real interest rates, First Boston Working Paper Series #FB-87-18R, Graduate School of Business, Columbia University.

Nelson, Charles R. and G. William Schwert, 1977, Short-term interest rates as predictors of inflation: On testing the hypothesis that the real rate is constant, *American Economic Review* 67, 478–486.

Parks, Richard W., 1978, Inflation and relative price variability, *Journal of Political Economy* 86, 79–96.

Tanzi, Vito, 1980, Inflationary expectations, economic activity, taxes and interest rates, *American Economic Review* 70, 12–21.

Wilcox, James A., 1983, Why real interest rates were so low in the 1970s, *American Economic Review* 73, 44–53.

PART III

THE INFORMATION IN THE TERM STRUCTURE ABOUT FUTURE INFLATION AND INTEREST RATES

[11]

JOURNAL OF APPLIED ECONOMETRICS, VOL. 3, 307–314 (1988)

THE INFORMATION IN THE TERM STRUCTURE: SOME FURTHER RESULTS

FREDERIC S. MISHKIN
Graduate School of Business, Columbia University, New York N.Y. 10027, U.S.A. and National Bureau of Economic Research

SUMMARY

This paper provides some refinements and updating of Fama's (1984) evidence on the information in the term structure about future spot interest rate movements. First, it uses econometric techniques that properly correct standard errors for overlapping data and for conditional heteroscedasticity. Second, it makes use of a new data set that has some potential advantages over Fama's, and which has more recent data. Overall, the results are in broad agreement with those of Fama. The term structure does help predict spot interest rate movements several months into the future. Indeed, updating Fama's results indicates that the forecast power of forward rates is generally higher during the October 1982 to June 1986 period than it was during the sample periods Fama examined.

1. INTRODUCTION

In a recent important paper, Fama (1984) resurrects the view that the term structure of interest rates contains information about the future movements of spot interest rates. Using ordinary least-squares estimation, Fama finds evidence that the forward rate–spot rate differential helps predict changes in the spot rate, while the difference between adjacent maturity forward rates helps predict the future 1-month changes in the spot rate.

This paper provides some refinements of Fama's regression evidence. First, it uses econometric techniques that properly correct standard errors for overlapping data and for conditional heteroscedasticity. Second, it makes use of a new data set that has some potential advantages over Fama's and which has more recent data.*

2. THE METHODOLOGY AND DATA

In examining the information in the term structure about future movements in spot interest rates. Fama runs the following ordinary least-squares (OLS) regressions:

$$R_{t+\tau} - R_{t+1} = \alpha_1 + \beta_1(F\tau_t - R_{t+1}) + \eta^{\tau}_{t+\tau-1}, \tag{1}$$

$$R_{t+\tau} - R_{t+\tau-1} = \alpha_2 + \beta_2(F\tau_t - F(\tau-1)_t) + \eta^{\tau}_{t+\tau-1}, \tag{2}$$

*All the results in this paper have been produced using an IBM PC with the GAUSS programming language. The data and all the computer programs used to produce this paper will be made available free of charge to any researcher who will send me a standard formatted 360 KB diskette with a self-addressed mailer.

0883–7252/88/040307–08$05.00

Received October 1987
Revised April 1988

where:

$R_{t+\tau}$ = the 1-month spot rate observed at time $t+\tau-1$;
$F\tau_t$ = the forward rate for month $t+\tau$ observed at time t.

The error term in these regressions will be serially correlated when $\tau > 2$ because the error term, which can be thought of as a forecast error, is realized only after $\tau - 1$ periods. Thus $\eta^{\tau}_{t+\tau-1}$ is likely to be correlated with $\eta^{\tau}_{t+1}, \eta^{\tau}_{t+2}, \ldots, \eta^{\tau}_{t+\tau-2}$, and therefore $\eta^{\tau}_{t+\tau-1}$ will follow a MA($\tau - 2$) process. Because of the resulting serial correlation, the OLS standard errors of the coefficients—which is what Fama (1984) reports—will not be correct.

A solution to this problem is provided by Hansen and Hodrick (1980), who develop the following consistent estimate of the variance–covariance matrix of the parameter estimates,

$$V_\tau = (X_\tau' X_\tau)^{-1} X_\tau' \Omega_\tau X_\tau (X_\tau' X_\tau)^{-1}, \tag{3}$$

where:

V_τ = the variance–covariance matrix for the parameter estimates of the equation τ;
X_τ = the matrix of explanatory variables for equation τ, which is $T \times k$ (T = the number of observations, k = the number of explanatory variables);
Ω_τ = the variance–covariance matrix of the residuals $E(\eta_\tau \eta_\tau')$,

and the (i, j)th element of the estimated Ω_τ is defined as

$$\omega_\tau(i,j) = \sum_{s=p+1}^{T} \hat{\eta}^{\tau}_s \hat{\eta}^{\tau}_{s-p}, \quad \text{for } p \leqslant q \tag{4}$$
$$= 0, \qquad \text{otherwise}$$

where $p = |i-j|$ and q = the order of the MA process, $\tau - 2$.

Because researchers have found that interest rate volatility has changed markedly in the postward sample period that Fama examined, the error terms in equations (1) and (2) are likely to be conditionally heteroscedastic.* To obtain the correct standard errors when there is conditional heteroscedasticity, the Hansen–Hodrick variance–covariance matrix needs to be modified using the method described by White (1980). This involves redefining $\omega_\tau(i, j)$ to be

$$\omega_\tau(i,j) = \hat{\eta}^{\tau}_i \hat{\eta}^{\tau}_j, \quad \text{for } p \leqslant q \tag{5}$$
$$= 0. \qquad \text{otherwise}$$

A problem with the Hansen–Hodrick estimate of the variance–covariance matrix and the variant allowing for conditional heteroscedasticity is that it need not be positive-definite in finite samples. In practice this means that standard errors of coefficients and test statistics may turn out to be negative. Newey and West (1985) have proposed a solution to this problem which

*There is some evidence for conditional heteroscedasticity in the regression equations here, but it is not always very strong. In Fama's February 1959 to July 1982 sample period when $\tau = 2$, for example, White's (1980) test for conditional heteroscedasticity yields a test statistic (distributed as $\chi^2(1)$) of 3·65. This statistic indicates a rejection of conditional homoscedasticity at the 10% level but not at the 5% level. On the other hand, Engle's (1982) test for autoregressive conditional heteroscedasticity, in which squared residuals are regressed on one lag of the squared residuals, provides strong evidence for conditional heteroscedasticity: in the February 1959 to July 1982 sample period when $\tau = 2$, the lagrange multiplier statistic (distributed as $\chi^2(1)$) equals 21·95 which is highly significant. To check on the robustness of the results, I also have calculated the standard errors for the coefficients of regressions (1) and (2) under the assumption of conditional homoscedasticity. Although the calculated standard errors do sometimes differ appreciably from those found in the text (sometimes larger and sometimes smaller), the conclusions from these results are the same as the conclusions discussed in the text.

involves down-weighting the off-diagonal elements of the Ω_τ matrix to produce a consistent estimate of the variance–covariance matrix which is guaranteed to be positive–definite. The Newey–West estimate of the variance–covariance matrix allowing for conditional heteroscedasticity calculates the $\omega_\tau(i, j)$ elements of Ω_t as follows:

$$\omega_\tau(i,j) = [1 - p/(q+1)]\,\hat{\eta}_i^T\hat{\eta}_j^T, \quad \text{for } p \leqslant q \qquad (6)$$
$$= 0. \qquad \text{otherwise}$$

As in Fama (1984), the end-of-month Treasury bill rate data were obtained from the Center for Research on Security Prices (CRSP) at the University of Chicago, and the 1-month bill was defined to have a maturity of 30·4 days, the 2-month bill 60·8 days, on up to the 6-month bill with a maturity of 182·5 days. For each defined maturity the interest rate was interpolated from the two bills that were closest to the defined maturity. In effect this means that the slope of the term structure is assumed to be constant between these two bills. Fama (1984) instead chooses a bill that has a maturity closest to 6 months and then keeps on taking the interest rate from this same bill every month as its maturity shortens in order to get interest rates on one to 6-month bills. In effect, Fama is assuming that the slope of the term structure is zero around the desired maturity of the bill. The procedure used here, which assumes the slope around the desired maturity is constant rather than zero, is less restrictive. This is an advantage when you are examining the ability to predict future spot rate movements, as in this paper. However, Fama's procedure makes use of actual transaction price data, which is an advantage when you are focusing on predicting future premiums as in his paper.

3. THE RESULTS

Table I, which corresponds to Fama's (1984) Table 4, shows the estimated β's, their standard errors and the R^2's for regression equation (1), which regresses the change in the spot rate on the forward-spot differential. The first six rows contain the results for the sample periods in Fama (1984), and the coefficient estimates are typically quite close to those found there. The standard errors of the coefficients, however, are sometimes quite different from those found in Fama (1984).* For example, in Fama's full sample period, February 1959 to July 1982, the standard errors of the coefficients for $\tau = 2$ to 6 were 0·07, 0·10, 0·12, 0·10, and 0·10; the corresponding standard errors in the first row of Table I are 0·11, 0·18, 0·24, 0·15, and 0·11, which are larger and in one case is twice as large.† In general, however, the conclusion from the results is similar to Fama's. In all cases the forward rate-spot differential for 1 month ahead, $F2_t - R_{t+1}$, has significant predictive power for the change in the spot rate one month ahead, $R_{t+2} - R_{t+1}$. The forward-spot differential also has significant explanatory power for changes in spot rates further out in the future, although the number of significant β-coefficients (five) is less than in Fama's Table 4 (nine).

The last four rows of Table I contain results for a longer sample period than Fama's, January 1959 to June 1986, and for three subperiods January 1959 to September 1979, October 1979 to September 1982, and October 1982 to June 1986. These subperiods are examined because

*This stems from the estimation technique and not from the modification of Fama's data set. Ordinary least-squares estimates with the modified data set used here produced standard error estimates that were very close to those reported in Fama (1984).

†However, it is not always the case that the estimated standard errors here are larger than those found in Fama (1984). For example, the standard errors in the February 1979 to July 1982 sample are smaller in Table I than in Fama's Table 4.

Table I. Regressions of the change in the spot rate, $R_{t+\tau} - R_{t+1}$, on the forward rate minus the current spot rate, $F\tau_t - R_{t+1}$: $R_{t+\tau} - R_{t+1} = \hat{\alpha} + \hat{\beta}(F\tau_t - R_{t+1}) + \hat{\eta}_{t+\tau-1}$

	Dependent variable									
	$R_{t+2} - R_{t+1}$		$R_{t+3} - R_{t+1}$		$R_{t+4} - R_{t+1}$		$R_{t+5} - R_{t+1}$		$R_{t+6} - R_{t+1}$	
Sample period	$\hat{\beta}$	R^2	$\hat{\beta}$	R^2	$\hat{\beta}$	R^2	$\hat{\beta}$	R^2	$\hat{\beta}$	R^2
2/59–7/82	0·41**	0·11	0·27	0·03	0·25	0·01	0·21	0·01	0·16	0·01
	(0·11)		(0·18)		(0·24)		(0·15)		(0·11)	
2/59–1/64	0·44**	0·22	0·34**	0·16	0·28	0·06	0·05	0·00	0·06	0·01
	(0·12)		(0·10)		(0·16)		(0·11)		(0·14)	
2/64–1/69	0·52**	0·39	0·40**	0·19	0·22	0·04	0·32**	0·18	0·26**	0·14
	(0·13)		(0·14)		(0·12)		(0·09)		(0·08)	
2/69–1/74	0·32**	0·12	0·17	0·01	0·61**	0·13	0·07	0·00	0·15	0·02
	(0·07)		(0·16)		(0·18)		(0·17)		(0·11)	
2/74–1/79	0·69**	0·10	0·10	0·00	0·31	0·02	0·20	0·02	−0·12	0·01
	(0·17)		(0·25)		(0·29)		(0·22)		(0·18)	
2/79–7/82	0·61**	0·15	0·43	0·04	0·29	0·01	0·43	0·03	0·50	0·03
	(0·21)		(0·32)		(0·37)		(0·33)		(0·37)	
1/59–6/86	0·40**	0·11	0·30*	0·04	0·29	0·02	0·20	0·02	0·16	0·01
	(0·09)		(0·15)		(0·19)		(0·11)		(0·10)	
1/59–9/79	0·44**	0·14	0·25**	0·04	0·34**	0·05	0·12	0·01	0·05	0·00
	(0·06)		(0·08)		(0·10)		(0·09)		(0·09)	
10/79–9/82	0·71**	0·20	0·59	0·08	0·47	0·03	0·58	0·06	0·64*	0·07
	(0·23)		(0·33)		(0·35)		(0·31)		(0·30)	
10/82–6/86	0·51**	0·26	0·64**	0·23	0·61**	0·17	0·13	0·02	−0·03	0·00
	(0·12)		(0·15)		(0·21)		(0·17)		(0·17)	

Notes for all tables
Standard errors of coefficients in parentheses.
* = significant at the 5 per cent level.
** = significant at the 1 per cent level.

the Federal Reserve altered its techniques of monetary control in October 1979 and October 1982, and because previous research (Huizinga and Mishkin, 1986 and Roley, 1986) have documented shifts in the stochastic process of interest rates in October 1979 and October 1982. The results in these sample periods indicate that forward rates do have predictive power for spot rates several months in the future. The β-coefficient estimates for 1, 2 and 3 months in the future ($\tau = 2$ to 4) are statistically significant at the 1 per cent level in both the pre-October 1979 and post-October 1982 sample periods. However, since the β-coefficient estimates for $\tau = 2$ to 4 are higher in the October 1979 to September 1982 period than in the pre-October 1979 period, the failure to find statistical significance when $\tau = 3$ and 4 in the October 1979 to September 1982 period is probably due to the shortness of the sample period, which is only 3 years long. Indeed, the β-coefficient estimates are generally higher in both the post-October 1979 periods than in the pre-October 1979 period, as are the R^2's of the regressions. These results provide some support to the conclusion in Hardouvelis (1986) that the term structure has more predictive power for spot rates after October 1979 than before.*

*Mishkin (1987) has outlined a seemingly unrelated regression (SUR) procedure that can take advantage of additional information in the term structure by exploiting the correlation of error terms of equations for different maturity T-bills. In the context of examining the information in the term structure about future inflation, Mishkin (1987) finds that the SUR procedure resulted in the estimated standard error of coefficients falling by over 50 per cent. In a longer, working paper version of this paper (Mishkin, 1988), the SUR procedure is applied to the equations estimated here. In contrast to the results in Mishkin (1987), the estimated standard errors do not decline substantially when the SUR procedure is used, and the results are very similar to those found in Tables I and III of this paper.

Table II. Tests for shifts in parameters of Table I regressions

	Dependent variable				
	$R_{t+2} - R_{t+1}$	$R_{t+3} - R_{t+1}$	R_{t+4} R_{t+1}	$R_{t+5} - R_{t+1}$	$R_{t+6} - R_{t+1}$
Test of equality of $\hat{\beta}$ coefficients in 2/59–1/64, 2/64–1/69, 2/69–1/74, 2/74–1/79, 2/79–7/82 sample periods					
$\chi^2(4) =$	6·15	2·19	3·25	4·58	5·06
Marginal significance level	0·1876	0·7001	0·5162	0·3330	0·2815
Test of equality of $\hat{\alpha}$ and $\hat{\beta}$ coefficients in 2/59–1/64, 2/64–1/69, 2/69–1/74, 2/74–1/79, 2/79–7/82 sample periods					
$\chi^2(8) =$	10·67	3·45	4·67	5·82	6·30
Marginal significance level	0·2209	0·9033	0·7923	0·6774	0·6134
Test of equality of $\hat{\beta}$ coefficients in 1/59–9/79, 10/79–9/82, 10/82–6/86 sample periods					
$\chi^2(2) =$	1·51	5·92	1·35	2·12	3·94
Marginal significance level	0·4696	0·0518	0·5085	0·3466	0·1395
Test of equality of $\hat{\alpha}$ and $\hat{\beta}$ coefficients in 1/59–9/79, 10/79–9/82, 10/82–6/86 sample periods					
$\chi^2(4) =$	16·47**	9·51*	6·23	6·70	7·63
Marginal significance level	0·0024	0·0496	0·1826	0·1523	0·1061

Table II provides Wald tests for whether the coefficients remain unchanged in Fama's five subperiods and the three subperiods with breaks in October 1979 and October 1982. The tests do not indicate that the coefficients change over Fama's five subperiods; the marginal significance levels of the test statistics are quite high, indicating that the probability of obtaining the value of the test statistic or higher under the null hypothesis that the coefficient estimates are equal in the five periods is high. The tests for whether the coefficients change in October 1979 and October 1982 do provide some evidence that the α and β coefficients shift when $\tau = 2$ or 3. However, tests for changes in the β-coefficients alone do not provide significant rejections of the equality of the β-coefficients in the three subperiods. Overall, there is little support for instability of the information in the term structure about future spot rate movements. However, it should be recalled that the Wald tests reported here may not have very great statistical power, and in addition, there is some evidence that, for 1 and 2 months in the future, the information in the term structure did change with the shift in the Federal Reserve's operating procedures in October 1979 and October 1982.

The results on the marginal predictive power of forward rates on the 1-month changes in future spot rates is obtained from the equation (2) regression of the future 1-month changes in the spot rate, $R_{t+\tau} - R_{t+\tau-1}$, on the forward rate spread, $F\tau_t - F(\tau - 1)_t$. Table III (which corresponds to Fama's (1984) table 5) provides the β-coefficients, their standard errors and the R^2's for these regressions. Although the results are similar to those of Fama (1984), they are slightly less favourable to the view that the term structure has marginal predictive power for

Table III. Regressions of the change in the spot rate, $R_{t+\tau}-R_{t+\tau-1}$, on the forward rate spread, $F\tau_t - F(\tau-1)_t$: $R_{t+\tau}-R_{t+\tau-1} = \hat{\alpha} + \hat{\beta}(F\tau_t - (F\tau-1)_t) + \hat{\eta}_{t+\tau-1}$

	Dependent variable									
	$R_{t+2}-R_{t+1}$		$R_{t+3}-R_{t+2}$		$R_{t+4}-R_{t+3}$		$R_{t+5}-R_{t+4}$		$R_{t+6}-R_{t+5}$	
Sample period	$\hat{\beta}$	R^2	$\hat{\beta}$	R^2	$\hat{\beta}$	R^2	$\hat{\beta}$	R^2	$\hat{\beta}$	R^2
2/59–7/82	0·41**	0·11	−0·03	0·00	−0·02	0·00	0·04	0·00	0·00	0·00
	(0·11)		(0·12)		(0·11)		(0·08)		(0·06)	
2/59–1/64	0·44**	0·22	0·45**	0·21	0·25*	0·07	0·11	0·03	0·19**	0·09
	(0·12)		(0·10)		(0·11)		(0·09)		(0·06)	
2/64–1/69	0·52**	0·39	0·34**	0·21	0·18	0·04	0·21	0·14	0·12	0·07
	(0·13)		(0·12)		(0·14)		(0·11)		(0·07)	
2/69–1/74	0·32**	0·12	0·21	0·06	0·16	0·04	−0·08	0·01	−0·08	0·04
	(0·07)		(0·12)		(0·09)		(0·06)		(0·06)	
2/74–1/79	0·69**	0·10	−0·00	0·00	−0·55	0·10	−0·02	0·00	−0·09	0·02
	(0·17)		(0·23)		(0·49)		(0·16)		(0·08)	
2/79–7/82	0·61**	0·15	−0·59*	0·07	−0·36	0·02	0·03	0·00	0·26	0·01
	(0·21)		(0·28)		(0·29)		(0·23)		(0·37)	
1/59–6/86	0·40**	0·11	0·03	0·00	0·07	0·00	0·05	0·00	0·02	0·00
	(0·09)		(0·11)		(0·10)		(0·07)		(0·06)	
1/59–9/79	0·44**	0·14	0·25**	0·06	0·06	0·00	0·02	0·00	−0·03	0·00
	(0·06)		(0·08)		(0·11)		(0·06)		(0·05)	
10/79–9/82	0·71**	0·29	−0·56*	0·07	−0·24	0·01	0·09	0·00	0·25	0·01
	(0·23)		(0·27)		(0·27)		(0·22)		(0·34)	
10/82–6/86	0·51**	0·26	0·42*	0·13	0·60**	0·28	0·14	0·03	0·06	0·00
	(0·12)		(0·17)		(0·16)		(0·12)		(0·13)	

changes in the spot rate that are more than 1 month in the future. For 2 months ahead or more ($\tau \geqslant 3$), only four β-coefficients are significant and positive in the Fama sample periods, and one coefficient is even significantly negative; in contrast. Fama found six significant positive coefficients and no significant negative coefficients. The results for the post-October 1982 sample period, however, provide additional evidence that the term structure has marginal predictive power for changes in the spot rate more than 1 month in the future. The results in the last row of Table III indicate that forward rate spreads provide significant predictive power for the change in the spot rate up to 3 months in the future ($\tau \leqslant 4$), a result also found in Hardouvelis (1986).

Table IV, which provides tests for shifts in the coefficients of the Table III regressions, suggests that there is more coefficient instability for the marginal prediction equations of Table III than there were for the regressions in Table I. In the first row of the table there are two significant rejections of the equality of the β-coefficients in the Fama subperiods; while the last two rows of the table indicate that for $\tau = 2$, 3 and 4 there are significant shifts in the coefficients in October 1979 and October 1982.

4. CONCLUSION

This paper provides some refinements and updating of Fama's (1984) evidence on the information in the term structure about future spot interest rate movements. Overall, the results are in broad agreement with those of Fama. The term structure does help predict spot interest rate movements several months into the future. Indeed, updating Fama's results indicates that

Table IV. Tests for shifts in parameters of Table III regressions

	Dependent variable				
	$R_{t+2} - R_{t+1}$	$R_{t+3} - R_{t+2}$	$R_{t+4} - R_{t+3}$	$R_{t+5} - R_{t+4}$	$R_{t+6} - R_{t+5}$
Test of equality of $\hat{\beta}$ coefficients in 2/59–1/64, 2/64–1/69, 2/69–1/74, 2/74–1/79, 2/79–7/82 sample periods					
$\chi^2(4) =$	6·16	14·74**	6·02	6·68	14·11**
Marginal significance level	0·1876	0·0053	0·1973	0·1538	0·0069
Test of equality of $\hat{\alpha}$ and $\hat{\beta}$ coefficients in 2/59–1/64, 2/64–1/69, 2/69–1/74, 2/74–1/79, 2/79–7/82 sample periods					
$\chi^2(8) =$	10·67	15·00	7·97	8·96	15·03
Marginal significance level	0·2209	0·0591	0·4367	0·3458	0·0585
Test of equality of $\hat{\beta}$ coefficients in 1/59–9/79, 10/79–9/82, 10/82–6/86 sample periods					
$\chi^2(2) =$	1·51	9·99**	10·02**	0·80	1·03
Marginal significance level	0·4696	0·0068	0·0067	0·6706	0·5966
Test of equality of $\hat{\alpha}$ and $\hat{\beta}$ coefficients in 1/59–9/79, 10/79–9/82, 10/82–6/86 sample periods					
$\chi^2(4) =$	16·47**	10·23*	10·68*	4·02	2·89
Marginal significance level	0·0024	0·0368	0·0304	0·40	0·5762

the forecast power of forward rates is generally higher during tne October 1982 to June 1986 period than it was during the sample periods Fama examined.

ACKNOWLEDGEMENTS

I thank the General Motors Corporation Faculty Research Fellowship for financial support. I also thank John Campbell for supplying me with a computer program, and the anonymous referees and editor of this journal for helpful comments. This research is part of the National Bureau of Economic Research's programs in Economic Fluctuations and Financial Markets and Monetary Economics. The usual disclaimer applies.

REFERENCES

Engle, R. F. (1982), 'Autoregressive conditional heteroscedasticity with estimates of the variance of United Kingdom inflation', *Econometrica*, **50**, 987–1007.

Fama, E. F. (1984), 'The information in the term structure', *Journal of Financial Economics*, **13**, 509–528.

Hansen, L. and R. Hodrick (1980), 'Forward exchange rates as optimal predictors of future spot rates', *Journal of Political Economy*, **88**, 829–853.

Hardouvelis, G. A. (1986), 'The predictive power of the term structure during recent monetary regimes', Barnard College, mimeo. *Journal of Finance* (forthcoming).

Huizinga, J. and F. S. Mishkin (1986), 'Monetary policy regime shifts and the unusual behavior of real interest rates', *Carnegie–Rochester Conference Series on Public Policy*, **24**, 231–274.

Mishkin, F. S. (1987), 'What does the term structure tell us about future inflation?' Graduate School of Business, Columbia University (unpublished manuscript).

Mishkin, F. S. (1988), 'The information in the term structure: some further results', NBER Working Paper no. 2575.

Newey, W. and K. West (1985), 'A simple, positive definite, heteroskedasticity and autocorrelation consistent covariance matrix'. Discussion Paper 92 (Princeton University, Woodrow Wilson School: Princeton, N.J.).

Roley, V. V. (1986), 'The response of interest rates to money announcements under alternative operating procedures and reserve retirement systems'. NBER Working Paper 1812.

White, H. (1980), 'A heteroskedasticity-consistent covariance matrix estimator and direct tests for heteroskedasticity', *Econometrica*, **48**, 817–838.

[12]

Journal of Monetary Economics 25 (1990) 77–95. North-Holland

WHAT DOES THE TERM STRUCTURE TELL US ABOUT FUTURE INFLATION?

Frederic S. MISHKIN*

Columbia University, New York, NY 10027, USA
National Bureau of Economic Research, Cambridge, MA 02138, USA

Received November 1988, final version received June 1989

This empirical analysis indicates that for maturities of six months or less, the term structure of nominal interest rates provides almost no information about the future path of inflation but does provide information about the term structure of real interest rates. However, as maturities lengthen to nine and twelve months, the nominal term structure begins to contain information about future inflation, but ceases to provide information about the real term structure. These results are explained by differences in the relative variability of expected future inflation changes and real term structure slopes at different points in the term structure.

1. Introduction

Much recent research has focused on the information in the term structure of interest rates. Specifically, this research explores to what extent the relationship between interest rates for different maturities helps to predict the future movement of short-term interest rates. Although Shiller, Campbell, and Schoenholtz (1982) and Mankiw and Summers (1984) have questioned the value of the term structure in predicting future short-term interest rates, recent evidence in Fama (1984), Fama and Bliss (1987), Campbell and Shiller (1987), Hardouvelis (1988), and Mishkin (1988a) indicates that the term structure is capable of forecasting future interest rates.

*I thank Jae-Won Park for research assistance, John Campbell for supplying me with a computer program, and John Huizinga for helpful advice and supplying me with data. I also thank for their helpful comments an anonymous referee, Louis K.C. Chan, Ken Froot, and participants in the NBER Universities Conference on Risk and Financial Markets and seminars at Columbia University, Northwestern University, the NBER Summer Institute, and the Federal Reserve Banks of New York and Philadelphia. Research support has been provided by the Faculty Research Fund of the Graduate School of Business, Columbia University. The research reported here is part of the NBER's research programs in Financial Markets and Monetary Economics and Economic Fluctuations. Any opinions expressed are those of the author and not those of the National Bureau of Economic Research. The data in this paper will be made available free of charge to any researcher who sends me a standard formatted $5\frac{1}{4}$ 360KB diskette with a stamped, self-addressed mailer.

0304-3932/90/$3.50

The information in the term structure can also be examined from a somewhat different perspective. Fama's (1975) classic study on interest rates as predictors of inflation suggests that movements in interest rates primarily reflect fluctuations in expected inflation (the so-called Fisher effect) rather than changes in real interest rates. Subsequent work [Nelson and Schwert (1977), Mishkin (1981), Fama and Gibbons (1982), and Huizinga and Mishkin (1986)] supports this conclusion for the postwar United States except for the period of the change in Federal Reserve operating procedures from October 1979 until October 1982. This evidence along with the evidence that the term structure contains information about future interest-rate movements suggests that the term structure might also contain information about the future path of inflation.

This paper examines empirically what the term structure of interest rates tells us about future inflation. This is an important topic because inflation is a major concern of policymakers. This paper will also provide evidence on the prevalent view that a downward sloping yield curve reflects expectations of a falling rate of inflation, while a steeply upward sloping yield curve indicates expectations of a rising rate of inflation. The behavior of the term structure has thus been a central element in research about whether anti-inflation policy has been credible or not, as in Blanchard (1984) and Dornbusch (1988), for example.

In addition, this paper provides evidence on whether movements in the term structure of real interest rates (which is not directly observable) are revealed by movements in the term structure of nominal interest rates (which is observable). This is also an important topic because it will tell researchers whether using stylized facts about the observable nominal term structure provides them with information about the behavior of the *real* term structure, which has an important role in understanding asset pricing and in theories of the business cycle.

2. The methodology

The main focus of the paper is on estimates of a forecasting equation that tell us whether the term structure helps to predict the future path of inflation. This equation, which will be referred to as the 'inflation-change equation', is a regression of the change in the future m-period inflation rate from the n-period inflation rate ($\pi_t^m - \pi_t^n$) on the 'slope' of the term structure ($i_t^m - i_t^n$),

$$\pi_t^m - \pi_t^n = \alpha_{m,n} + \beta_{m,n}[i_t^m - i_t^n] + \eta_t^{m,n}. \tag{1}$$

Tests of the statistical significance of the $\beta_{m,n}$ coefficient and whether it differs from one reveal how much information there is in the slope of the term structure about future changes in inflation.

It is important to recognize that using the regression equation above to test for whether there is information in the term structure about the future path of inflation implies that the word 'information' is being used quite narrowly. Because 'information' in the term structure about the path of future inflation refers only to the ability of the slope, $i_t^m - i_t^n$, to predict the change in the inflation rate, $\pi_t^m - \pi_t^n$, we are restricting ourselves to extracting information about the future path of inflation using only our knowledge of the slope of the term structure. None of the evidence in this paper focuses on predictive power for forecasting equations that make use of more complicated interactions of interest rates or that use additional economic variables in combination with the slope of the term structure.

The regression framework outlined above is quite simple, but we need to carefully examine the link between nominal interest rates, real interest rates, and expected inflation in order to understand how to clearly interpret the results. According to the Fisher (1930) equation, expected inflation over m periods is equal to the m-period nominal interest rate minus the m-period real interest rate:[1]

$$E_t\pi_t^m = i_t^m - rr_t^m, \tag{2}$$

where

E_t = expectations at time t,
π_t^m = inflation rate from time t to $t+m$,
i_t^m = m-period nominal interest rate at time t,
rr_t^m = m-period (*ex ante*) real interest rate at time t – i.e., the *ex ante* real return on an m-period bond from t to $t+m$.

The realized inflation rate over the next m periods can be written as the expected inflation rate plus the forecast error of inflation:

$$\pi_t^m = E_t\pi_t^m + \varepsilon_t^m, \tag{3}$$

where $\varepsilon_t^m = \pi_t^m - E_t\pi_t^m$ is the forecast error of inflation. Substituting in for $E_t\pi_t^m$ from eq. (2), we obtain

$$\pi_t^m = i_t^m - rr_t^m + \varepsilon_t^m. \tag{4}$$

In order to examine the information in the term structure about future changes in the inflation rate, we can subtract eq. (4) above for the n-period

[1] The real interest rate described above is the expected real return on a nominally riskless bond. As is pointed out in Benninga and Protopapadakis (1983), this will not be equal to the riskless real interest rate. It is not clear, however, that the difference between the riskless real interest rate and the real interest rate described in the text is very large for the short-term interest rates analyzed in this paper. For example, see Bodie, Kane, and McDonald (1985) and Mishkin (1990).

inflation rate from eq. (4) for the m-year inflation rate to obtain

$$\pi_t^m - \pi_t^n = i_t^m - i_t^n - rr_t^m + rr_t^n + \varepsilon_t^m - \varepsilon_t^n. \tag{5}$$

This equation can be rewritten in the form of the inflation-change forecasting equation (1) as follows:

$$\pi_t^m - \pi_t^n = \alpha_{m,n} + \beta_{m,n}[i_t^m - i_t^n] + \eta_t^{m,n},$$

where

$$\alpha_{m,n} = \overline{rr}^n - \overline{rr}^m, \qquad \beta_{m,n} = 1,$$

$$\eta_t^{m,n} = \varepsilon_t^m - \varepsilon_t^n - (u_t^m - u_t^n),$$

$$u_t^m = rr_t^m - \overline{rr}^m, \qquad u_t^n = rr_t^n - \overline{rr}^n.$$

If we assume that expectations are rational and the slope of the real term structure, $rr_t^m - rr_t^n$, remains constant over time, then ordinary least-squares (OLS) estimates of the forecasting equation above produce a consistent estimate of $\beta_{m,n}$. We see this by first recognizing that rational expectations implies that the forecast errors of inflation, ε_t^m and ε_t^n, are orthogonal to the right-hand regressors because under rational expectations $E_t\varepsilon_t^m = E_t\varepsilon_t^n = 0$ – i.e., forecast errors of inflation must be unforecastable conditional on all available information at time t which includes i_t^m and i_t^n. Constancy of the slope of the real term structure then makes OLS estimates consistent because the $(u_t^m - u_t^n)$ term disappears, leaving an error term for the forecasting equation of $\varepsilon_t^m - \varepsilon_t^n$ which is orthogonal to the right-hand-side regressors under rational expectations.

If the slope of the real term structure is not constant, then the nominal term structure rate can still contain information about future changes in the inflation rate, but it is no longer an optimal predictor because $(u_t^m - u_t^n)$ is no longer equal to zero. Furthermore, if the slope of the nominal term structure is correlated with the slope of the real term structure, then $u_t^m - u_t^n$ and hence $\eta_t^{m,n}$ is correlated with $i_t^m - i_t^n$, and the OLS estimate of $\beta_{m,n}$ will have a probability limit different from one. In addition, correlation of $\eta_t^{m,n}$ and $i_t^m - i_t^n$ implies that the OLS estimate of $\alpha_{m,n}$ will also not be a consistent estimate of the mean slope of the real term structure $(\overline{rr}^n - \overline{rr}^m)$.

The discussion above leads to the following conclusions about tests on the $\beta_{m,n}$ coefficient. If the null hypothesis $\beta_{m,n} = 0$ is rejected statistically, then the slope of the term structure, $i_t^m - i_t^n$, contains significant information about the change in the future m-period inflation rate from the n-period inflation rate. If the null hypothesis $\beta_{m,n} = 1$ is rejected, then the empirical evidence indicates that the slope of the real term structure is not constant over time (assuming rational expectations)[2].

We can look at tests of the $\beta_{m,m}$ coefficient in a slightly different way by subtracting $i_t^m - i_t^n$ from both sides of the forecasting equation (5) and then multiplying both sides by -1 to obtain the following regression equation which involves the difference between m-period and n-period *ex post* real interest rates:

$$eprr_t^m - eprr_t^n = -\alpha_{m,n} + [1 - \beta_{m,n}](i_t^m - i_t^n) - \eta_t^{m,n}, \tag{6}$$

where $eprr_t^m = i_t^m - \pi_t^m$ is the *ex post* real interest rate on a m-period bond at time t (i.e., the realized real return from t to $t + m$).

Now we see that $\beta_{m,n} = 1$ implies that the coefficient $[1 - \beta_{m,n}]$ on the slope of the nominal term structure, $i_t^m - i_t^n$, equals zero in the *ex post* real rate regression. Since the *ex ante* real interest rate is just the conditional expectation at time t of the *ex post* real interest rate, a rejection of $\beta_{m,n} = 1$ (or equivalently, $1 - \beta_{m,n} = 0$) in the inflation-change forecasting equation indicates that the slope of the term structure of nominal interest rates $(i_t^m - i_t^n)$ contains significant information about the slope of the term structure of *ex ante* real interest rates $(rr_t^m - rr_t^n)$. Using similar reasoning, a rejection of $\beta_{m,n} = 0$ (or equivalently, $1 - \beta_{m,n} = 1$) means that the null hypothesis that the slope of the term structure of real interest rates $(rr_t^m - rr_t^n)$ moves one-for-one with the slope of the nominal term structure $(i_t^m - i_t^n)$ is rejected.

To summarize: a statistical rejection of $\beta_{m,n} = 0$ provides evidence that (a) the term structure contains significant information about the future path of inflation and (b) the slopes of the term structures of real and nominal interest rates do not move one-for-one with each other. On the other hand, a statistical rejection of $\beta_{m,n} = 1$ provides evidence that (a) the slope of the real term structure is not constant over time and (b) the term structure of nominal interest rates provides information about the term structure of real interest rates.

3. The data

The empirical analysis makes use of monthly data on inflation rates and one-to twelve-month U.S. Treasury bills for the period February 1964 to December 1986. The sample starts with February 1964 because this is the first date that data on all the Treasury bills became available (twelve-month Treasury bills were not issued until late 1963). Because six-month Treasury

[2] Note that $\beta_{m,n} = 1$ might not be rejected asymptotically even if the slope of the real term structure is not constant. This could occur when the term $(u_t^m - u_t^n)$ is not zero if it is orthogonal to $i_t^m - i_t^n$.

bills were first issued in late 1958, tests using one to six-month Treasury bills can be conducted with sample periods starting in January 1959. The results are very similar to those for sample periods starting with February 1964 and are reported in an appendix to a longer version of this paper [Mishkin (1988b)]. End-of-month T-bill data were obtained from the Center for Research in Security Prices (CRSP) at the University of Chicago. The one-month bill was defined to have a maturity of 30.4 days, the three-month bill 91.25 days, on up to the twelve-month bill with a maturity of 365 days. For each defined maturity the interest rate was interpolated from the two bills that were closest to the defined maturity. In effect, this means that the slope of the term structure is assumed to be constant between these two bills.[3] The interest rates are expressed on a continuously compounded basis at an *annual rate in percent* as are the inflation rates. The inflation data is calculated from a CPI series which appropriately treats housing costs on a rental-equivalence basis throughout the sample period. For more details on this series see Huizinga and Mishkin (1984, 1986).

The timing of the variables is as follows. A January interest-rate observation uses the end-of-December bill-rate data. A January observation for a one-month inflation rate is calculated from the December and January CPI data, a three-month inflation rate from the December and March CPI data, and so on.[4]

4. The empirical results

Because of serial correlation induced by the use of overlapping data, in which the horizon of the interest rate and the inflation rate is longer than the observation interval, standard errors of the OLS parameter estimates in eq. (1) will be incorrect. Asymptotically valid standard errors are generated for the regression results in this paper using the method outlined by Hansen and Hodrick (1980), with a modification due to White (1980) that allows for

[3] Fama (1984) instead chooses a bill that has a maturity closest to six months and then keeps on taking the interest rate from this same bill every month as its maturity shortens in order to get interest rates on one to six-month bills. In effect, Fama is assuming that the slope of the term structure is flat around the chosen bill. The procedure for data construction in this paper, which assumes that the slope around the desired maturity is constant rather than zero, makes a less restrictive assumption than Fama's procedure. The differences between these two procedures, however, is very slight and makes no appreciable difference to the results.

[4] The appropriate dating for the CPI in a particular month is not clear since price quotations on the component items of the index are collected at different times during the month. As a result, there is some misalignment of the inflation data and the interest-rate data which is collected at the end of the month. In order to see if this misalignment could have an appreciable effect on the results, I also estimated the regressions in this paper lagging the interest-rate data one period (i.e., for the January observation I used the end-of-November bill rate). The results with the lagged interest-rate data are very similar to those found in the text and none of the conclusions of the paper changes.

conditional heteroscedasticity and a modification by Newey and West (1987) that insures the variance–covariance matrix is positive definite by downweighting the off-diagonal elements.[5] Although the corrected standard errors using the method described above will lead to correct inference asymptotically, there could be a large difference between the finite-sample distribution of the test statistics and the asymptotic distribution when there is overlapping data, as has been found in Huizinga and Mishkin (1984). Monte Carlo results reported later in the paper indicate that for short sample periods of 50 or fewer observations conducting inference using asymptotic distributions can be quite misleading when there is a fair amount of overlap in regressions of the type analyzed here. Thus to avoid the bias from using asymptotic distributions, all critical values and marginal significance levels of every test statistic reported in the following empirical analysis have been obtained from Monte Carlo simulation results.

Table 1 contains the estimates of the inflation-change forecasting equation which regress the change in the future m-period inflation rate from the n-period inflation rate ($\pi_t^m - \pi_t^n$) on the 'slope' of the term structure ($i_t^m - i_t^n$).[6] Panel A contains the results for the full sample period, February 1964 to December 1986, while panels B, C, and D contain the results for three subperiods, February 1964 to October 1979, November 1979 to October 1982, and November 1982 to December 1986. The sample has been split into these three subperiods because results in Clarida and Friedman (1984), Huizinga and Mishkin (1986), and Roley (1986) indicate that the relationship of nominal interest rates and inflation shifted with the monetary regime changes of October 1979 and October 1982.

[5]A White correction for heteroscedasticity is used here because Lagrange-multiplier tests outlined by Engle (1982) reject conditional homoscedasticity for the error term of the forecasting equation. Note also that u_t^m and u_t^n are assumed to have MA processes of order less than $m-1$. If u_t^m or u_t^n follow a higher-order MA process, then the composite error term $\eta_t^{m,n}$ will also follow a higher-order MA process. In order to allow for more gradual down-weighting of the off-diagonal elements of the variance–covariance matrix and the possibility that u_t^m or u_t^n has a MA process of order greater than $m-1$, I also constructed Newey–West estimates of the variance–covariance matrix where the number of lags for which the covariances are allowed to be nonzero is doubled to $2(m-1)$. The estimated standard errors of the coefficients typically were quite close to those reported in the tables and none of the conclusions were affected. The results thus do not appear to be sensitive to allowance for a higher-order MA process for the error terms or the use of a more gradual down-weighting scheme in the Newey–West procedure.

[6]Note that n is not kept constant at say one or three months in the reported regressions because this would not reveal the full amount of information in the slope of the term structure about the future path of inflation. As the results in table 1 indicate, for maturities of six months or less the term structure provides no information about future inflation changes. Thus even though table 1 reveals that there is information in the term-structure slope when maturities are greater than six months, regressions which look at the predictive ability of the interest-rate slope from $n = 1$ or 3 months to $m = 12$ months do not yield significant $\beta_{m,n}$ coefficients because the lack of information in the slope for maturities up to six months obscures the fact that there is information in the slope for maturities greater than six months.

Table 1

Estimates of inflation-change equations.[a]

$$\pi_t^m - \pi_t^n = \alpha_{m,n} + \beta_{m,n}[i_t^m - i_t^n] + \eta_t^{m,n}$$

m, n (months)	$\alpha_{m,n}$	$\beta_{m,n}$	R^2	SE	t-test of $\beta_{m,n}=0$	t-test of $\beta_{m,n}=1$
Panel A: February 1964 to December 1986 sample						
3, 1	0.1686 (0.1420)	−0.3182 (0.2595)	0.005	1.883	−1.23	5.08[c]
6, 3	−0.0433 (0.1236)	0.2330 (0.4150)	0.003	1.197	0.56	1.85
9, 6	−0.0411 (0.0712)	0.4902 (0.2901)	0.020	0.726	1.69	1.76
12, 6	−0.1351 (0.1108)	0.9493 (0.3327)	0.073	0.920	2.85[b]	0.15
12, 9	−0.0498 (0.0411)	1.1799 (0.3150)	0.087	0.501	3.75[c]	−0.57
Panel B: February 1964 to October 1979 sample						
3, 1	0.1421 (0.1851)	−0.3127 (0.4498)	0.002	1.754	−0.70	2.92[c]
6, 3	0.0379 (0.1427)	0.1813 (0.5499)	0.001	1.088	0.33	1.49
9, 6	0.0826 (0.0647)	0.0014 (0.2695)	0.000	0.692	0.01	3.71[c]
12, 6	0.0249 (0.1251)	0.7108 (0.4873)	0.033	0.895	1.46	0.59
12, 9	−0.0199 (0.0397)	1.5336 (0.3527)	0.145	0.461	4.35[c]	−1.51
Panel C: November 1979 to October 1982 sample						
3, 1	0.0086 (0.5638)	−0.1774 (0.3727)	0.003	2.397	−0.48	3.16[b]
6, 3	−0.6397 (0.1767)	0.5696 (0.6269)	0.036	1.442	0.91	0.69
9, 6	−0.3646 (0.1304)	1.3277 (0.3373)	0.239	0.765	3.94	−0.97
12, 6	−0.5736 (0.1452)	1.4179 (0.1978)	0.335	0.875	7.17[b]	−2.11
12, 9	−0.2292 (0.0691)	0.6740 (0.5152)	0.037	0.599	1.31	0.63
Panel D: November 1982 to December 1986 sample						
3, 1	0.6458 (0.5678)	−0.9540 (0.9125)	0.027	2.009	−1.05	2.14
6, 3	0.2666 (0.3702)	−0.5976 (0.9741)	0.007	1.346	−0.61	1.64
9, 6	0.0086 (0.2315)	0.1060 (0.6492)	0.000	0.739	0.16	1.38
12, 6	0.2676 (0.4582)	−0.7101 (1.0017)	0.021	0.894	−0.71	1.71
12, 9	0.1379 (0.2003)	−1.1027 (1.4242)	0.033	0.509	−0.77	1.48

[a] $\pi_t^m - \pi_t^n$ is the difference between the m-period inflation rate from time t to $t+m$ and the n-period inflation rate from t to $t+n$. $i_t^m - i_t^n$ is the difference between the m-period nominal interest rate and the n-period nominal interest rate at time t. Standard errors of coefficients in parentheses. SE = standard error of the regression.

[b] Significant at the 5% level using Monte Carlo results.

[c] Significant at the 1% level using Monte Carlo results.

As we can see in table 1, at the shortest end of the term structure (maturities six months or less) the results for the inflation-change equations is strikingly different than that found for inflation level regressions of the type popularized by Fama (1975). In contrast to Fama-type regressions, which find that the level of short-term interest rates, at least before October 1979, contain a great deal of information about the future level of inflation, there is little ability of the slope of the term structure to forecast future changes in inflation. For all sample periods and time horizons of six months or less in table 1, the R^2s of the inflation change equations are near zero and none of the $\beta_{m,n}$ coefficients is statistically significant. Further tests reported in the appendix of Mishkin (1988b), which look at all combinations of m and n, for m and n less than or equal to six months, also strongly confirm these findings. Apparently, *the term structure for maturities of six months or less contains almost no information about the path of future inflation*.

The results for the longer maturities, nine and twelve months, tell a different story, however. For the full sample period in panel A, the difference between the twelve-month and six-month rate and between the twelve-month and nine-month rate do have substantial information about the path of future inflation. The $\beta_{12,6}$ and $\beta_{12,9}$ coefficients are quite close to 1.0 and have t-statistics of 2.85 and 3.75, making them significantly different from zero at the 1% level. In looking at the subperiods, we see the $\beta_{12,9}$ coefficient is significantly different from zero in the February 1964 to October 1979 sample period, as is the $\beta_{12,6}$ coefficient in the November 1979 to October 1982 sample period. Indeed, the R^2s are particularly high for the regressions with $m, n = 9, 6$ and 12, 6 in the November 1979 to October 1982 period, indicating a large amount of forecast power for changes in inflation.

The t-tests of $1 - \beta_{m,n} = 0$ in table 1 indicate that the term structure of nominal interest rates contains information about the term structure of real interest rates for the shortest maturities. For $m = 3$, in all the sample periods the $[1 - \beta_{m,n}]$ terms are always positive, are never statistically significant from one, and are statistically significant from zero in all but the last sample period. Indeed, the $[1 - \beta_{3,1}]$ term is highly significant in the full sample period, with a t-statistic exceeding five. The evidence thus suggests that most fluctuations in the slope of the term structure at the very short end reflect changes in the slope of the term structure of real interest rates on a one-for-one basis and do not reflect changes in expectations about future changes in inflation.

The t-tests of $1 - \beta_{m,n}$ for the intermediate maturities, six and nine months, provide some evidence for the nominal term structure containing information about the real term structure, but the evidence is not always strong. For $m = 6$ and 9, $[1 - \beta_{m,n}]$ is positive in seven out of eight cases in table 1, but is statistically significant only once (when $m = 9$ in panel B, the February 1964 to October 1979 sample period). However, additional results in the appendix of Mishkin (1988b) lend stronger support to the view that the term structure of

Table 2

Tests of parameter shifts in the inflation-change regressions.[a]

m, n (months)	Test of shifts in $\beta_{m,n}$ $\chi^2(2)$	Marginal significance level	Test of shifts in $\alpha_{m,n}$ and $\beta_{m,n}$ $\chi^2(4)$	Marginal significance level
3, 1	0.62	0.74	0.89	0.77
6, 3	0.96	0.74	10.94	0.08
9, 6	10.70	0.08	20.54[b]	0.04
12, 6	6.17	0.27	17.58	0.12
12, 9	4.46	0.33	11.23	0.24

[a] Tests of null hypothesis that the parameters are equal in the three periods February 1964 to October 1979, November 1979 to October 1982, and November 1982 to December 1986. Note: Marginal significance levels are generated from Monte Carlo results.

[b] Significant at the 5% level using Monte Carlo results.

nominal interest rates provides information about the term structure of real interest rates for maturities up to six months.

At the longest end of the term structure studied here, however, the story is quite different. For m equal to twelve months, $[1-\beta_{m,n}]$ is never significantly different from zero. The evidence for maturities around twelve months thus suggests that the term structure of nominal interest rates does not provide information about the term structure of real interest rates, but is rather more likely to reflect changes in expectations about future changes in inflation.[7]

The pattern of changes in the $\beta_{m,n}$ coefficients over the three subperiods is quite different from what might have been expected from earlier research on the information in the level of interest rates about future inflation. Evidence in Huizinga and Mishkin (1986) shows that before October 1979 the level of nominal interest rates primarily reflect changes in expected inflation, but with the change in monetary regime from October 1979 to October 1982, the information in the term structure about future inflation completely disappears. The results in table 1 show an entirely different pattern. There is no evidence that the information in the term structure about the path of future inflation declines; indeed, in going from the pre-October 1979 sample to the November 1979 to October 1982 sample, four of five $\hat{\beta}_{m,n}$ coefficients rise rather than fall. Furthermore, formal statistical (Wald) tests for whether the coefficients in the inflation-change equations shift over the three subperiods in table 2 do not indicate there are changes in the information in the term structure about the

[7] A longer version of this paper, Mishkin (1988b) shows that more efficient, seemingly unrelated regression (SUR) estimates of inflation-change forecasting equations can be obtained by exploiting the fact that equation residuals across different time horizons are highly correlated. The SUR estimates do sometimes produce large efficiency gains, and they continue to support the conclusions reached with OLS and tend to strengthen them.

path of future inflation. The marginal significance levels of the tests for shifts in $\beta_{m,n}$ are all above 0.05, indicating that none of the test statistics reject the equality of the $\beta_{m,n}$ coefficients in the three periods.[8] Also, tests for shifts in both the $\alpha_{m,n}$ and $\beta_{m,n}$ coefficients only reject their equality across the three periods in one case, $m, n = 9, 6$, and the rejection is just barely at the 5% level. An important caveat about these Wald tests for parameter shifts must be mentioned, however: they are likely to have very low power because of the small number of observations in the last two subperiods.

4.1. *Interpretation*

Under the assumption of rational expectations, the interpretation of the inflation-change forecasting equation $\beta_{m,n}$ is quite straightforward. Following Fama (1984) and Hardouvelis (1988), $\beta_{m,n}$ can be derived to be

$$\beta_{m,n} = (\tilde{\sigma}^2 + \rho\tilde{\sigma})/(1 + \tilde{\sigma}^2 + 2\rho\tilde{\sigma}), \tag{7}$$

where

$\tilde{\sigma} = \sigma[E_t(\pi_t^m - \pi_t^n)]/\sigma[rr_t^m - rr_t^n]$ is the ratio of the standard deviation of the expected inflation change to the standard deviation of the slope of the real term structure, and

$\rho =$ correlation between the expected inflation change, $E_t(\pi_t^m - \pi_t^n)$, and the slope of the real term structure, $rr_t^m - rr_t^n$.

This expression is derived by writing down the standard formula for the projection-equation coefficient $\beta_{m,n}$ and recognizing that the covariance of the inflation forecast error with $rr_t^m - rr_t^n$ equals zero given rational expectations.

The equation above indicates that $\beta_{m,n}$ is determined by how variable the expected inflation change is relative to the variability of the slope of the real term structure [represented by $\tilde{\sigma}$, the ratio of the standard deviations of $E_t(\pi_t^m - \pi_t^n)$ and $(rr_t^m - rr_t^n)$] as well as by the correlation of the expected inflation change with the real term structure slope (ρ). Fig. 1 shows how $\beta_{m,n}$ varies with $\tilde{\sigma}$ and ρ.

In order to understand why we find different information in the term structure at different maturities, we calculate estimated values of $\tilde{\sigma}$ and ρ using the procedure outlined in Mishkin (1981), in which estimates of $rr_t^m - rr_t^n$ are obtained from fitted values of regressions of the *ex post* real rate differen-

[8] Note that the marginal significance levels are derived from Monte Carlo simulations, and this explains why none of the test statistics are significant even though some would be significant under the asymptotic distribution.

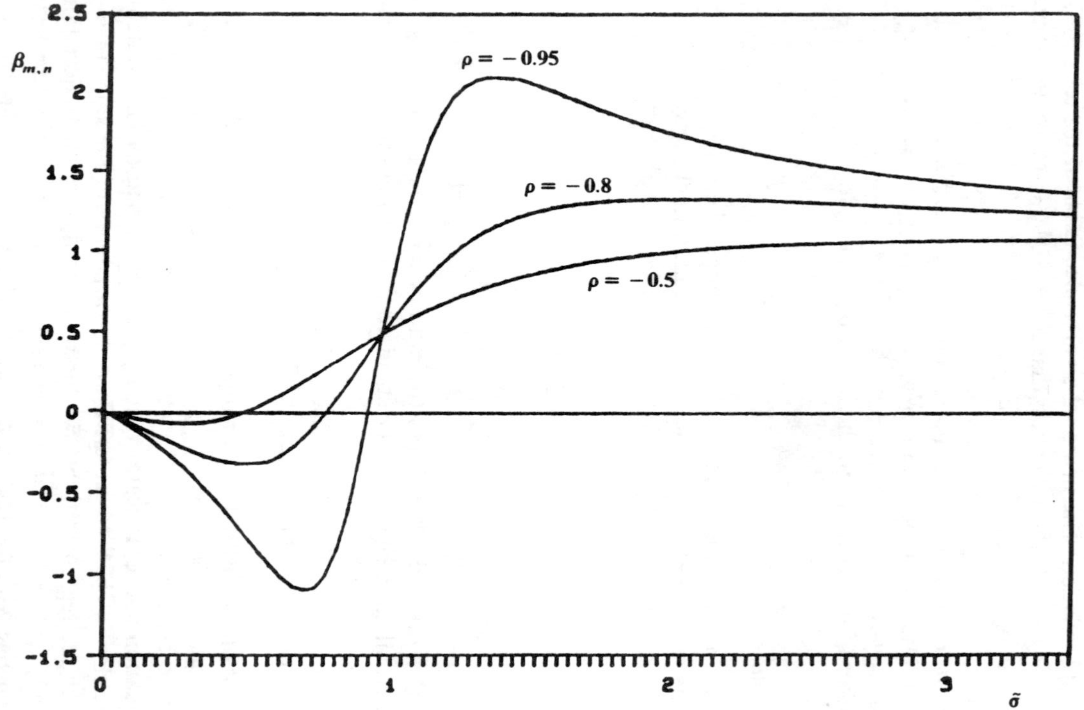

Fig. 1. How $\beta_{m,n}$ varies with $\tilde{\sigma}$ and ρ; $\beta_{m,n} = (\tilde{\sigma}^2 + \rho\tilde{\sigma})/(1 + \tilde{\sigma}^2 + 2\rho\tilde{\sigma})$, where $\tilde{\sigma} = \sigma[E_t(\pi_t^m - \pi_t^n)]/\sigma[rr_t^n - rr_t^m]$ is the ratio of the standard deviation of the expected inflation change to the standard deviation of the slope of the real term structure and ρ is the correlation between the expected inflation change, $E_t(\pi_t^m - \pi_t^n)$, and the slope of the real term structure, $rr_t^m - rr_t^n$.

tials on past inflation changes and past interest-rate spreads.[9] Then the estimated expected inflation change is calculated from the following definitional relationship:

$$\mathrm{E}_t(\pi_t^m - \pi_t^n) = i_t^m - i_t^m - (rr_t^m - rr_t^n). \tag{8}$$

Finally estimates of $\tilde{\sigma}$ and ρ are calculated from the estimated $\mathrm{E}_t(\pi_t^m - \pi_t^n)$ and $(rr_t^m - rr_t^n)$.

The estimated values of ρ for all the horizons and sample periods are quite negative, averaging around -0.8 and ranging between -0.5 and -0.97. These values of ρ follow from the fact that the variability of slope of the nominal term structure, $i_t^m - i_t^n$, is small relative to the variability of the slope of the real term structure, $rr_t^m - rr_t^n$, and thus, as is evident in eq. (8) above, the correlation between $\mathrm{E}_t(\pi_t^m - \pi_t^n)$ and $rr_t^m - rr_t^n$ must necessarily be quite negative. As can be seen in fig. 1, if the variability of expected inflation changes is less than the variability of the real term structure slope so that $\tilde{\sigma}$ is less than 1.0, then $\beta_{m,n}$ will be less than 0.5. This is exactly what we find for maturities six months or less in all the sample periods except for November 1979 to October 1982, where $\tilde{\sigma}$ is slightly above 1.0 for $m, n = 6, 3$. The failure to find information in the term structure at the shortest end of the term structure then just follows from the fact that the variability of expected inflation changes is dominated by the variability of the slope of the real term structure.

Research that suggests that term premiums should undergo substantial fluctuations over time provide a rationale for the low values of $\tilde{\sigma}$ at the shortest end of the term structure and the resulting inability of the term structure to provide information about the future path of inflation. [See, for example, Startz (1982), Jones and Roley (1983), Shiller, Campbell, and Schoenholtz (1983), Fama (1984), and Mankiw and Summers (1984).] Variation in the slope of the real term structure can be attributed to the variation of term premiums over time as well as changes in the average of expected one-period real interest rates over the next m-periods versus the next n-periods. High variation in these term premiums will then produce high variation in the slope of the real term structure and make it more likely that the variation of the real term structure slope will dominate the variation of expected future inflation changes. The outcome of substantial time variation of term premiums will then be a low $\tilde{\sigma}$ and a low $\hat{\beta}_{m,n}$ estimate, so that the term structure will provide little information about future inflation changes. The flip side of this

[9]The estimates described in the text were generated from OLS regressions in which the *ex post* real-rate differential, $eprr_t^m - eprr_t^n$, was regressed on $rr_t^m - rr_t^n$ and on the inflation change, $\pi^m - \pi^n$, lagged twelve months, eighteen months, and twenty-four months. I also experimented with other choices of lags and the estimated values of $\tilde{\sigma}$ and ρ were robust to different specifications of the regression equations.

argument is that substantial variation in term premiums, which produces low $\hat{\beta}_{m,n}$ estimates, lead to the finding that the term structure of nominal interest rates contains a great deal of information about the term structure of real interest rates.

The fact that, for all but the post-October 1982 sample period, the term structure at longer maturities now contains significant information about future inflation changes, but contains little information about the term structure of real interest rates, stems from the fact that as the maturity lengthens the variability of the real term structure slope declines relative to the variability of the expected inflation changes so that $\tilde{\sigma}$ rises well above 1.0. The result is that the $\hat{\beta}_{m,n}$ coefficients get larger at longer maturities and, for $m = 12$, are close to one.

In going from the pre-October 1979 sample period to the November 1979 to October 1982 period, there is a substantial increase in both the variability of real term structure slopes as well as expected inflation changes. However, except for $m, n = 12, 9$, the variability of expected inflation changes grows more than the variability of real term structure slopes. Thus, $\tilde{\sigma}$ is higher in the 1979–1982 period for all the horizons except $m, n = 12, 9$ and so the $\hat{\beta}_{m,n}$ coefficients rise. In the post-October 1982 sample period, both the variability of real term structure slopes and expected inflation changes decline somewhat, but the variability of expected inflation changes falls by more than the variability of real term structure slopes. Thus the $\tilde{\sigma}$s all decline and fall below 1.0, and hence the $\hat{\beta}_{m,n}$ decline and even sometimes become quite negative. Theoretical analysis in Evans (1989) suggests that the higher $\tilde{\sigma}$s and hence higher $\hat{\beta}_{m,n}$ coefficients in the 1979–1982 period might result from increased fluctuations in the uncertainty about nominal rather than real shocks during this period.

5. Monte Carlo results

To evaluate the degree of any small sample bias, table 3 reports the results from Monte Carlo simulations of one-thousand t-tests of the null hypothesis $\beta_{m,n} = 0$ in the inflation-change forecasting equation (1). The table reports the Monte Carlo results using the sample periods and m and n horizons for the regressions reported in the paper. Panel A has results for the full sample of 275 observations, panel B for the pre-October 1979 sample of 189 observations, panel C for the November 1979 to October 1982 sample with only 36 observations, and panel D for the post-October 1982 sample of 50 observations.

The Monte Carlo simulation experiments were conducted as follows. The inflation rates and $i_t^m - i_t^n$ slope variables were generated using ARIMA models whose parameters were estimated from the relevant sample periods. Because Lagrange-multiplier tests described by Engle (1982) revealed the

Table 3

Monte Carlo simulation results for t-test of $\beta_{m,n} = 0$.[a]

m, n (months)	Critical values of t from Monte Carlos — Significance levels 50%	25%	10%	5%	1%	% rejections using asymptotic 5% critical value	% rejections using asymptotic 1% critical value
	Panel A: February 1964 to December 1986 sample (275 observations)						
3, 1	0.64	1.06	1.53	1.81	2.43	3.2%	0.5%
6, 3	0.68	1.13	1.68	2.03	2.76	5.7%	1.2%
9, 6	0.70	1.25	1.76	2.07	3.07	6.8%	1.7%
12, 6	0.77	1.34	1.92	2.34	3.44	9.3%	3.2%
12, 9	0.75	1.26	1.76	2.06	2.97	6.2%	2.0%
	Panel B: February 1964 to October 1979 sample (189 observations)						
3, 1	0.67	1.14	1.70	1.98	2.62	5.4%	1.3%
6, 3	0.76	1.29	1.85	2.27	3.11	8.2%	2.5%
9, 6	0.79	1.31	1.89	2.25	3.08	9.1%	2.3%
12, 6	0.79	1.36	1.97	2.40	3.20	10.0%	3.6%
12, 9	0.78	1.34	1.97	2.33	3.46	10.2%	3.0%
	Panel C: November 1979 to October 1982 sample (36 observations)						
3, 1	0.82	1.40	2.05	2.58	3.43	11.3%	4.8%
6, 3	1.14	2.02	3.24	3.98	6.14	26.3%	16.4%
9, 6	1.27	2.35	3.54	4.49	7.47	31.7%	21.1%
12, 6	1.54	2.71	4.30	6.15	9.08	38.6%	26.4%
12, 9	1.29	2.22	3.11	4.03	5.91	31.7%	16.8%
	Panel D: November 1982 to December 1986 sample (50 observations)						
3, 1	0.80	1.30	1.86	2.27	3.03	8.4%	2.8%
6, 3	0.81	1.39	2.13	2.68	3.63	12.2%	5.8%
9, 6	0.87	1.48	2.22	2.79	4.30	13.6%	6.4%
12, 6	1.03	1.77	2.73	3.25	4.73	21.1%	11.4%
12, 9	0.97	1.70	2.59	3.30	5.36	20.5%	10.1%

[a] Results from Monte Carlo simulations of one-thousand t-tests of the null hypothesis $\beta_{m,n} = 0$ in the inflation-change forecasting equation (1) using the Hansen–Hodrick–White–Newey–West estimation procedure described earlier in the text. The details of how the simulation experiments were conducted are described in the text.

presence of ARCH (autoregressive conditional heteroscedasticity) in the error terms, the error terms were drawn from a normal distribution in which the variance follows an ARCH process whose parameters were also estimated from the relevant sample periods. Start-up values for AR terms in the times-series models were obtained from the actual realized data from six and seven years before the sample period (or at the start of the sample period if earlier data were unavailable) and then five years of draws from the random number generator produced start-up values for the error terms. Then a sample size corresponding to the relevant regression was produced using errors drawn from the distribution described above and the test statistics using the Hansen–Hodrick–White–Newey–West method described earlier were calculated. To check out the robustness of the Monte Carlo results, I also conducted experiments where the error terms were assumed to be i.i.d. rather than ARCH and also where the parameters of the ARIMA and ARCH processes were estimated only from the full sample period; the conclusions were the same as those reported in the text.

Panel A of table 3 indicates that, for the full sample, the difference between inference using the asymptotic distribution rather than the finite-sample distribution is fairly small. The last two columns show that the percentage of rejections in the Monte Carlo experiments under the null hypothesis is quite close to that predicted by the asymptotic distribution, except to some extent for the $m, n = 12, 6$ case where the percentage of rejections is somewhat higher than predicted by the asymptotic distribution. Indeed, as the columns showing the critical t-values from the Monte Carlo experiments indicate, a critical t-value of 2.0 is a reasonable critical value for rejection at the 5% level. The panel B results also indicate that the difference between the asymptotic distribution and the finite-sample distributions are not terribly large, although a t-value of around 2.3 is a more accurate critical value for rejection at the 5% level than is a value of 2.0.

When the sample size drops to 50 or lower, as in panel D and particularly in panel C, the amount of bias in the asymptotic distribution becomes quite severe. For example, with m over three months in the panel C results, the percentage of rejections using the 5% critical value from the asymptotic distribution is above 25%, over five times greater than is predicted by the asymptotic distribution. Critical 5% t-values with m greater than three months in panel C are 4.0 and higher, which are more than double the conventional 5% critical t-value of 1.96.

Additional Monte Carlo experiments have been conducted for t-tests of $1 - \beta_{m,n} = 0$, and they produce results which are quite close to those found in table 1. These additional results are not reported here in order to conserve space.

6. Conclusions

The empirical evidence in this paper indicates that the information in the term structure about the future path of inflation is quite different at the shortest end of the term structure (maturities six months or less) than it is for maturities nine months or greater. For maturities of six months or less, in all the sample periods examined – February 1964 to December 1986, February 1964 to October 1979, November 1979 to October 1982, November 1982 to December 1986 – the term structure provides almost no information about the future path of inflation. On the other hand at this end of the term structure, the results do indicate that the term structure of nominal interest rates contains a great deal of information about the term structure of *real* interest rates. This finding is quite important because it suggests that researchers can examine observable data on the shortest end of the nominal term structure to provide them with information about the behavior of the *real* term structure.

For maturities of nine and twelve months, the term structure does appear to contain information about the future path of inflation. The $\beta_{m,n}$ coefficients for these maturities are often highly significant in the full sample period and in the subperiods before October 1982.[10] At these longer maturities, however, there does not appear to be much information in the nominal term structure about the term structure of real interest rates.

The results in this paper on the information in the term structure strongly contrast with previous research which finds that, for much of the postwar period, nominal interest-rate movements reflect changes in expected inflation rather than real interest rates. The results also differ dramatically from previous research which finds that the degree to which the overall level of nominal interest rates reflects expectations of future inflation significantly decreases with the change in the monetary regime in October 1979. In contrast, this paper finds no evidence that the amount of information in the term structure about the future path of inflation decreases with the monetary regime shift in October 1979. The nature of the relationship between the term structure and future inflation is thus strikingly different from that found between the overall level of interest rates and future inflation.

The evidence in this paper suggests that some caution should be exercised in using the term structure of interest rates as a guide for assessing inflationary pressures in the economy. Although there is apparently significant information in the term structure about the future path of inflation for maturities greater than six months, there is no information about the future path of inflation that can be obtained from the shorter end of the term structure. Furthermore, as the interpretation of the results indicates, the $\beta_{m,n}$ regression coefficients are sensitive to the relative variability of expected future inflation changes and real term structure slopes, as well as to the correlation of these two variables. Any change in the method of conducting monetary policy, such as focusing on the term structure as a guide to monetary policy, is likely to change the correlation and relative variability of expected future inflation changes and real term structure slopes, thus causing the regression coefficients to change in the

[10] Using a somewhat different regression framework than that used here, Fama (1990) finds that the term structure is able to forecast changes in inflation more than one year out in the future, a result that is consistent with the evidence in this paper. His findings are supported by additional evidence in Mishkin (1989), which uses the same regression framework as in this paper, and finds that the longer-maturity term structure contains substantial information about the future path of inflation.

inflation-change forecasting equation. Thus the forecasting ability of the term structure for the path of future inflation could change dramatically, making the term structure a poor guide for monetary policy. This is, of course, just another example of the Lucas (1976) critique.

References

Benninga, S. and A. Protopapadakis, 1985, Real and nominal interest rates under uncertainty: The Fisher theorem and the term structure, Journal of Political Economy 91, 856–867.

Blanchard, O., 1984, The Lucas critique and the Volcker deflation, American Economic Review 74, 211–215.

Bodie, Z., A. Kane, and R. McDonald, 1985, Inflation and the role of bonds in investor portfolios, in: B. Friedman, ed., Corporate capital structures in the United States (University of Chicago Press, Chicago, IL) 167–194.

Campbell, J.Y. and R.J. Shiller, 1987, Cointegration and tests of present value models, Journal of Political Economy 95, 1062–1088.

Clarida, R.H. and B.M. Friedman, 1984, The behavior of U.S. short-term interest rates since October 1979, Journal of Finance 39, 671–682.

Dornbusch, R., 1988, Credibility, debt and unemployment: Ireland's failed stabilization, NBER working paper no. 2785.

Engle, R.F., 1982, Autoregressive conditional heteroscedasticity with estimates of the variance of the United Kingdom inflation, Econometrica 50, 987–1007.

Evans, M.D., 1989, What can the term structure tell us about expected inflation? A theoretical analysis, Mimeo. (Stern School of Business Administration, N.Y.U., New York, NY).

Fama, E.F., 1975, Short term interest rates as predictors of inflation, American Economic Review 65, 269–282.

Fama, E.F., 1984, The information in the term structure, Journal of Financial Economics 13, 509–528.

Fama, E.F., 1990, Term structure forecasts of interest rates, Inflation and Real Returns, Journal of Monetary Economics, this issue.

Fama, E.F. and R.R. Bliss, 1987, The information in long-maturity forward rates, American Economic Review 77, 680–692.

Fama, E.F. and M.R. Gibbons., 1982, Inflation, real returns and capital investment, Journal of Monetary Economics 9, 297–324.

Fisher, I., 1930, The theory of interest (Macmillan, New York, NY).

Hansen, L. and R. Hodrick, 1980, Forward exchange rates as optimal predictors of future spot rates, Journal of Political Economy 88, 829–853.

Hardouvelis, G.A., 1988, The predictive power of the term structure during recent monetary regimes, Journal of Finance 43, 339–356.

Huizinga, J. and F.S. Mishkin, 1984, Inflation and real interest rates on assets with different risk characteristics, Journal of Finance 39, 699–712.

Huizinga, J. and F.S. Mishkin, 1986, Monetary policy regime shifts and the unusual behavior of real interest rates, Carnegie–Rochester Conference Series on Public Policy 24, 231–274.

Jones, D.S. and V.V. Roley, 1983, Rational expectations and the expectations model of the term structure: A test using weekly data, Journal of Monetary Economics 12, 453–465.

Lucas, R.E. Jr., 1976, Econometric policy evaluation: A critique, Carnegie–Rochester Conference Series on Public Policy 1, 19–46.

Mankiw, N.G. and L.H. Summers, 1984, Do long-term interest rates overreact to short-term interest rates?, Brookings Papers on Economic Activity, 223–242.

Mishkin, F.S., 1981, The real rate of interest: An empirical investigation, Carnegie–Rochester Conference Series on Public Policy 15, 151–200.

Mishkin, F.S., 1988a, The information in the term structure: Some further results, Journal of Applied Econometrics 3, 307–314.

Mishkin, F.S., 1988b, What does the term structure tell us about future inflation, NBER working paper no. 2626.

Mishkin, F.S., 1989, The information in the longer-maturity term structure about future inflation. NBER working paper no. 3126.

Mishkin, F.S., 1990, Can futures market data be used to understand the behavior of real interest rates?, Journal of Finance 45.

Nelson, C.R. and G.W. Schwert, 1977, Short-term interest rates as predictors of inflation: On testing the hypothesis that the real rate of interest is constant, American Economic Review 67, 478–486.

Newey, W. and K. West, 1987, A simple, positive definite, heteroskedasicity and autocorrelation consistent covariance matrix, Econometrica 53, 703–708.

Roley, V.V., 1986, The response of interest rates to money announcements under alternative operating procedures and reserve retirement systems, NBER working paper no. 1812.

Shiller, R.J., J.Y. Campbell, and K.L. Schoenholtz, 1983, Forward rates and future policy: Interpreting the term structure of interest rates, Brookings Papers on Economic Activity, 173–217.

Startz, R., 1982, Do forecast errors or term premia really make the difference between long and short rates?, Journal of Financial Economics 10, 323–329.

White, H., 1980, A heteroskedasticity-consistent covariance matrix estimator and direct tests for heteroskedasticity, Econometrica 48, 817–838.

[13]

THE INFORMATION IN THE LONGER MATURITY TERM STRUCTURE ABOUT FUTURE INFLATION*

FREDERIC S. MISHKIN

I. INTRODUCTION

Recent research has begun to examine what information the term structure of interest rates contains about future inflation. Mishkin [1990] examines the term structure for U. S. Treasury bills and finds that, for maturities of six months or less, the term structure of nominal interest rates provides almost no information about the future path of inflation. On the other hand, at this shorter end of the term structure, the term structure of *nominal* interest rates does contain a great deal of information about the term structure of *real* interest rates. However, for longer maturities of nine and twelve months, the term structure of nominal interest rates provides information about the future path of inflation, although it contains little information about the term structure of real interest rates. Using a somewhat different regression framework, Fama [1990] finds that at even longer maturities the term structure helps forecast the future path of inflation.

This paper conducts a further examination of the information in the term structure of nominal interest rates about future inflation and the term structure of real interest rates. It looks at the information in the longer maturity term structure by examining data from U. S. Treasury bonds with maturities of one to five years. This is an important area of study because forecasting longer term inflation is a major concern of policymakers. This paper will also provide evidence on the prevalent view that a downward sloping yield curve at longer maturities reflects expectations of a declining rate of inflation, while a steeply upward sloping yield curve indicates expectations of a rising rate of inflation. In addition, this

*Research support has been provided by the Faculty Research Fund of the Graduate School of Business, Columbia University. I thank Jae-Won Park for research assistance and John Campbell, Ken Froot, Gene Fama, Gikas Hardouvelis, and participants in a seminar at the NBER Summer Institute for helpful comments. The research reported here is part of the NBER's research programs in Financial Markets and Monetary Economics and Economic Fluctuations. Any opinions expressed are those of the author and not those of the National Bureau of Economic Research. The data in this paper will be made available free of charge to any researcher who sends me a standard formatted 5¼" 360KB diskette with a stamped, self-addressed mailer.

The Quarterly Journal of Economics, August 1990

paper provides evidence on whether changes in the slope of the yield curve of real interest rates (which is not directly observable) are revealed by changes in the slope of the yield curve of nominal interest rates (which is observable).

II. The Methodology

In examining the information in the term structure about future inflation, the empirical analysis in this paper primarily focuses on estimation of the following inflation-change forecasting equation:

$$\pi_t^m - \pi_t^1 = \alpha_m + \beta_m[i_t^m - i_t^1] + \eta_t^m. \tag{1}$$

In this equation the change in the future m-year inflation rate from the one-year future inflation rate $(\pi_t^m - \pi_t^1)$ is regressed on the "slope" of the term structure, the spread between the m-year interest rate and one-year interest rate $(i_t^m - i_t^1)$.

Tests of the statistical significance of the β_m coefficient and whether it differs from 1.0 reveal how much information there is in the slope of the term structure about future changes in inflation. More specifically, as is described in Mishkin [1990], a statistical rejection of $\beta_m = 0$ provides evidence that (1) the term structure contains significant information about the future path of inflation, and (2) the slopes of the term structures of real and nominal interest rates do not move one-for-one with each other. On the other hand, a statistical rejection of $\beta_m = 1$ provides evidence that (1) the slope of the real term structure is not constant over time, and (2) the term structure of nominal interest rates provides information about the term structure of real interest rates.

Note that the phrase "information in the term structure" is being used in this paper quite narrowly. Information in the term structure about the path of future inflation refers only to the ability of the slope, $i_t^m - i_t^1$, to predict the change in the inflation rate, $\pi_t^m - \pi_t^1$. This paper focuses on the predictive power of the slope term, $i_t^m - i_t^1$, because it is the most natural piece of information in the term structure to examine.

Before going on to a discussion of the data and the empirical results, several econometric issues that have important consequences for hypothesis testing need to be mentioned. As is now well-known, the error term η_t^m will be serially correlated when the number of periods spanned by the interest rate and inflation is greater than the observation interval, as occurs in the following empirical analysis. In this overlapping data case, the forecast error is not realized until m-years in the future, with the result that it will follow a MA($12m - 1$) time series process. Asymptotically valid standard errors are generated here using the method outlined by Hansen and Hodrick [1980], with a modification due to White [1980] and Hansen [1982] that corrects for heteroskedasticity, and a modification suggested by Newey and West [1987] that insures the variance-covariance matrix is positive definite. Although the corrected standard errors using the method described above will lead to correct inference asymptotically, previous research (Huizinga and Mishkin [1984], for example) indicates that there could be large differences between finite sample distributions and asymptotic distributions when there is a large amount of data overlap as in the empirical analysis in this paper. To check out whether inference using asymptotic distributions might be misleading, a series of Monte Carlo simulations have been conducted and are contained in the Appendix. They indicate that inference using asymptotic distributions can be highly misleading when the data have a large amount of overlap (which ranges from 23 periods for monthly observations with $m = 2$ years, to 59 periods for monthly observations for $m = 5$ years). For this reason, all critical values and marginal significance levels of every test statistic reported in the following empirical analysis have been obtained from Monte Carlo simulation results.

III. The Data

The empirical analysis makes use of monthly data from 1953 to 1987 for inflation rates and interest rates on one- through five-year Treasury bonds. The inflation and interest rate data are all in *percent at an annual rate*. The inflation data are calculated from a CPI series that appropriately treats housing costs on a rental-equivalence basis throughout the sample period. For more details on this series see Huizinga and Mishkin [1984, 1986]. The interest rate data are McCulloch's [1987, Table A-1] zero coupon yield curve series that are continuously compounded, end-of-month data. Because interest rate data for longer term bonds must be obtained by fitting a yield curve through interest rates on the maturities available and then using the fitted values for the desired maturity dates, it is worthwhile checking whether results are robust to a different procedure for constructing the data set. To this end, all the regressions in this paper have also been run with an alternative data set constructed by Fama and Bliss [1987], which has been obtained from the Center for Research and Security Prices (CRSP) data tape. There are no major differences between the results from the Fama and Bliss data set versus the McCulloch data set. However, standard errors of coefficients tended to be somewhat smaller with the McCulloch data set, so the results with this data set are the ones reported in the text.

The timing of the variables is as follows. A January 1980 interest rate observation, for example, uses the end of December 1979 bond rate data. A January 1980 observation for the one-year inflation rate is calculated from the December 1979 and December 1980 CPI; a two-year inflation rate from the December 1979 and December 1981 CPI; and so on. Since the last CPI observation is December 1987, the last observation for the full sample in a regression when $m = 2$ years is December 1985; for $m = 3$ years it is December 1984; for $m = 4$ years it is December 1983; and for $m = 5$ years it is December 1982.[1]

IV. The Empirical Results

Table I contains the estimates of the inflation-change forecasting equations for horizons of one through five years. Panel A contains the results for the full sample period; while Panel B reports the results for the pre-October 1979 period; and Panel C the results for the post-October 1979 period. The sample has been split into these two subperiods because results in Clarida and Friedman [1984], Huizinga and Mishkin [1986], and Roley [1986] indicate that the relationship of nominal interest rates and inflation shifted dramatically with the monetary regime change of October 1979.[2]

The results in Table I indicate that there is a great deal of information in the longer maturity term structure about the future

1. Note that the appropriate dating for the CPI in a particular month is not clear since price quotations on the component items of the index are collected at different times during the month. As a result, there is some misalignment of the inflation data and the interest rate data that are calculated for the end of the month. To see whether this misalignment could have an appreciable effect on the results, the regressions in this paper have also been estimated lagging the interest rate one month (i.e., for the January 1980 observation, I used the November 1979 bond rate). Not surprisingly, the results with the lagged interest rate data are very close to those found in the text.

2. The sample is not split again in October 1982, as in Mishkin [1990], because with the long horizons used in this paper, there are often few data points after October 1982. For example, with $m = 5$ years, the last data point is December 1982.

TABLE I
ESTIMATES OF INFLATION-CHANGE FORECASTING EQUATIONS
$\pi_t^m - \pi_t^1 = \alpha_m + \beta_m[i_t^m - i_t^1] + \eta_t^m$

m (years)	α_m	β_m	R^2	SE	t-test of $\beta_m = 0$	t-test of $1 - \beta_m = 1$
		Panel A: Full sample				
2	−0.1439	1.0641	0.199	0.750	3.08*	−0.19
	(0.1152)	(0.3452)				
3	−0.2804	1.4096	0.306	1.097	3.38*	−0.98
	(0.1738)	(0.4167)				
4	−0.3568	1.6795	0.422	1.214	4.82**	−1.95
	(0.2359)	(0.3487)				
5	−0.3508	1.7700	0.480	1.265	8.08**	−3.52*
	(0.3367)	(0.2190)				
		Panel B: Pre-October 1979 sample				
2	−0.0546	1.5426	0.309	0.654	4.40**	−1.55
	(0.1047)	(0.3503)				
3	−0.1634	1.9506	0.451	0.916	5.90**	−2.88
	(0.1575)	(0.3305)				
4	−0.2322	2.0569	0.546	0.983	7.27**	−3.74*
	(0.2195)	(0.2829)				
5	−0.1905	1.8280	0.498	1.093	5.62*	−2.55
	(0.3393)	(0.3250)				
		Panel C: Post-October 1979 sample				
2	−0.7793	0.8749	0.320	0.694	4.77	0.68
	(0.1152)	(0.1835)				
3	−1.3962	0.7514	0.445	0.719	11.30**	3.74
	(0.1763)	(0.0665)				
4	−1.8124	0.7412	0.445	0.858	13.75*	4.80
	(0.2239)	(0.0539)				
5	−2.1476	0.7468	0.340	1.124	3.79	1.29
	(0.4347)	(0.1969)				

Notes to Table I:
Asymptotic standard errors of coefficients are in parentheses.
SE = standard error of the regression.
* = significant at the 5 percent level using Monte Carlo results.
** = significant at the 1 percent level using Monte Carlo results.

path of inflation. For the full sample in Panel A, the β_m coefficients at all horizons are positive and significantly different from zero (as indicated by the t-tests of $\beta_m = 0$), and for $m = 4$ and $m = 5$ the β_m coefficients are even significant at the 1 percent level. (Recall that statistical significance is determined using critical values derived from the finite sample distribution obtained from Monte Carlo simulations.) Furthermore, the R^2s of the forecasting regressions are quite high, particularly for the longer horizons: indeed for $m > 3$, over 40 percent of the variation in the change in inflation is explained by forecasts using the slope of the term structure.

The results for the two subperiods also reach the same conclusion that the term structure for maturities greater than a year contains a great deal of predictive power for changes in future inflation. The results are stronger for the pre-October 1979 period in Panel B, with all the β_m significant at the 5 percent level and three out of four significant at the 1 percent level. In addition, the R^2s of the forecasting regressions are higher than in the full sample. The post-October 1979 results in Panel C are somewhat weaker than the pre-October 1979 results: the R^2s of the regressions are lower; and only two of the β_m coefficients are significant. However, the β_m coefficients always remain positive, and the R^2s are still quite high.

The results found in Table I are quite different from those found in Mishkin [1990] for term structure maturities of one to twelve months. For maturities under nine months, the term structure contains no information about future changes in inflation: R^2s of regressions similar to those in Table I are never larger than 0.05. For maturities of nine and twelve months, there is significant information about the path of future inflation, but the R^2s of the forecasting regressions are still quite low, typically below 0.10. Taking these results and those in Table I together suggests that the term structure provides better forecasts of future changes in inflation at longer maturities.[3]

The t-tests of $1 - \beta_m = 0$ in the last column of Table I indicate that the nominal term structure for maturities greater than one year contains very little information about the term structure of real interest rates. Only in two cases can the null hypotheses that the slope of the real term structure is constant or that the slope of the nominal term structure reveals no information about the slope of the real term structure be rejected. However, even in these two cases

3. Another way to look at the information in the term structure follows along the lines of Fama [1984] who looks at whether forward rates help predict future changes in one-month interest rates. Table A1 in an appendix to a longer version of this paper [Mishkin, 1989], looks at whether forward rates help predict future changes in the one-year inflation rate; it reports regressions of the change in the one-year inflation rate, $\pi^1_{t+m} - \pi^1_t$, on the forward-spot rate differential at time t, $f_{t+m} - i^1_t$. (f_{t+m} = the forward rate at time t for the one-year interest rate m-years in the future.) For both the full sample period and the pre-October 1979 sample period, forward rates do have significant explanatory power for changes in one-year inflation rates up to three years out into the future. However, by the time one goes four years out, the forward-spot differential no longer has a significant β_m coefficient. This suggests that the information in the term structure about future inflation may begin to decrease when maturities begin to exceed five years.

of statistically significant $[1 - \beta_m]$ terms, the $[1 - \beta_m]$ are negative, indicating a negative correlation of the slope of the real term structure with the slope of the nominal term structure.

Again, the results on tests of $1 - \beta_m = 0$ in Table I are quite different from those found for shorter maturities in Mishkin [1990]. In contrast to the results in Table I, Mishkin [1990] finds that for maturities of six months or less the nominal term structure contains a great deal of information about the term structure of real interest rates. Indeed, the hypothesis that the slopes of the real and nominal term structure move one-for-one with each other cannot be rejected for these shorter maturities. This is exactly the opposite of what is found for the longer maturities reported on in Table I, where there is typically a negative relationship between the slopes of the nominal and real term structure.

An interesting set of results in Table I is that there is a major change in the β_m coefficients after October 1979. In the pre-October 1979 sample period the β_m coefficients are greater than one (and significantly so for $m = 4$), while they fall below one in the post-October 1979 sample period. This suggests that associated with the change in the procedures for conducting monetary policy, there was a change in the correlation of the slopes of the nominal and real term structure. Specifically, only after October 1979 does a steeper nominal term structure indicate that the real term structure slope has also steepened. This finding is similar to one found in Huizinga and Mishkin [1986], who document that only after October 1979 does a rise in nominal interest rates indicate that real interest rates have also risen.

Before making too much of the differences in the β_m coefficients before and after October 1979, we need to examine whether these differences are statistically significant. Table II reports on the results of tests for parameter shifts in the inflation change equations. As can be seen from the marginal significance levels of these tests, in no case can the null hypothesis that the coefficients are equal in the two periods be rejected at the 5 percent level, although there are rejections at the 10 percent level. However, because the change in the coefficients across the periods is substantial in magnitude, the failure to reject equality of the coefficients may be a reflection of the low power of the tests.

A. Interpretation

The most striking feature of the Table I results is how different they are from those found at shorter maturities of the term

TABLE II
TESTS FOR PARAMETER SHIFTS IN THE INFLATION-CHANGE FORECASTING EQUATIONS

m (years)	Test of shift in β_m $\chi^2(2) =$	Marginal significant level	Test of shift in α_m and β_m $\chi^2(4) =$	Marginal significance level
2	2.94	0.35	23.11	0.09
3	12.42	0.13	47.90	0.06
4	21.09	0.07	52.94	0.08
5	7.37	0.24	29.22	0.26

Tests of the null hypothesis that the parameters are equal in the pre-October 1979 and post-October 1979 sample periods.
Note that the marginal significance levels are derived from Monte Carlo simulations.

structure in Mishkin [1990]. What explains why there is so much more information in the term structure about future inflation at longer maturities than there is at shorter maturities?

As is described in Mishkin [1990], under the assumption of rational expectations β_m is determined by how variable the expected inflation change is relative to the variability of the slope of the real term structure (represented by $\tilde{\sigma}$, the ratio of the standard deviations of $E_t(\pi_t^m - \pi_t^1)$ and $(rr_t^m - rr_t^1)$), as well as by the correlation of the expected inflation change with the real term structure slope (ρ). Figure I shows how β_m varies with $\tilde{\sigma}$ and ρ. The key fact visible in Figure I is that β_m will be substantially above zero if the variability of expected inflation changes is greater than the variability of real term structure slopes so that $\tilde{\sigma}$ is greater than one.

We can calculate estimated values of $\tilde{\sigma}$ and ρ as described in Mishkin [1990] by using the procedure outlined in Mishkin [1981], in which estimates of real term structure slopes and expected inflation changes are obtained from fitted values of regressions of the ex post real rate differentials on past inflation changes and past interest rate spreads.[4] The above calculations readily explain why the β_m estimated at the longer maturities in this paper are so much higher than those found in Mishkin [1990] at shorter maturities,

4. The estimates described in the text were generated from OLS regressions in which the ex post real rate differential, $eprr_t^m - eprr_t^1$, was regressed on $i_t^m - i_t^1$, this differential lagged one through five years, and on the inflation change $(\pi_t^m - \pi_t^1)$ lagged two to five years, not including lagged values if they are not realized at time t. I also experimented with other choices of lags, and the estimated values of $\tilde{\sigma}$ and ρ were robust to different specifications of the regression equations.

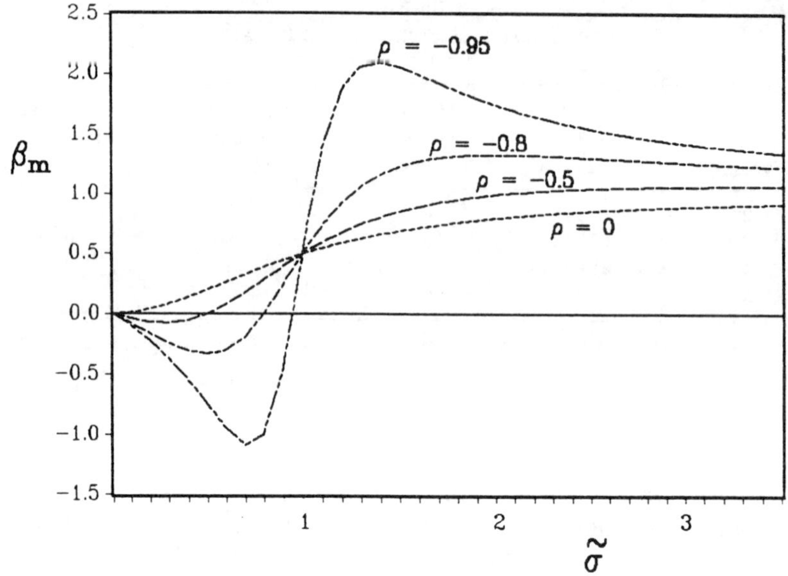

FIGURE I
How β_m Varies with $\tilde{\sigma}$ and ρ

particularly under nine months. For the longer maturities studied in this paper, the variation in expected inflation changes are substantially greater than the variation in real term structure slopes. For all horizons and sample periods, the $\tilde{\sigma}$s exceed 1.2 and range as high as 2.0. As we can see in Figure I, these high $\tilde{\sigma}$s lead to high β_ms. On the other hand, at shorter maturities under nine months the variability of expected inflation changes is dominated by the variability of the real term structure slopes, so that the resulting small $\tilde{\sigma}$s generate low estimated β_ms.

Empirical research that has investigated the time-variation of term premiums provides a rationale why the $\tilde{\sigma}$s are so much lower at the shortest end of the term structure and hence why only at longer maturities can the term structure provide information about the future path of inflation. (See, for example, Startz [1982]; Jones and Roley [1983]; Shiller, Campbell, and Schoenholtz [1983]; Fama [1984]; Mankiw and Summers [1984]; and Fama and Bliss [1987].) Variation in the slope of the real term structure can be attributed to the variation of term premiums over time as well as changes in the average of expected one-period real interest rates over the next m-periods versus the next n-periods. High variation in these term premiums will then produce high variation in the slope of the real term structure and make it more likely that the variation of the real term structure slope will dominate the variation of expected future inflation changes. However, research such as Fama and Bliss [1987] has found that variation in these term premiums is less important at longer maturities, and so at longer maturities it is more likely that the variation of expected inflation changes will now dominate the variation of real term structure slopes. The corollary of this argument is that at longer maturities in which the variation in term premiums no longer dominates, the term structure of nominal interest rates should contain very little information about the term structure of real interest rates.

The estimates of ρ, along with those for $\tilde{\sigma}$ discussed above, explain the pattern of the $\hat{\beta}_m$ coefficients in Table I. For the Panel A full sample, as the maturity increases, the estimated ρs decline from -0.7 to -0.95, while the $\tilde{\sigma}$s rise from 1.6 to 2.0. As Figure I indicates, the increasingly negative ρs as the maturity lengthens lead to larger β_m coefficients that will be substantially greater than one at the longest maturities. The Panel B pre-October 1979 sample displays estimated $\tilde{\sigma}$s which hover around 1.5 and ρs which decline from -0.89 to -0.95 as m reaches four years and then rise to -0.93 for $m = 5$ years, which explains why all the $\hat{\beta}_m$ coefficients are well above 1.0 and why the $\hat{\beta}_m$ coefficients fall as we move from $m = 4$ years to $m = 5$ years. The Panel C post-October 1979 sample has estimated $\tilde{\sigma}$s that are below those in the other samples (ranging from 1.2 to 1.4) and estimated ρs that are less negative than in the other samples (ranging from -0.4 to -0.6): the result is lower β_ms that are less than 1.0.

V. Conclusions

This paper provides empirical evidence on the information in the term structure for longer maturities about both future inflation and the term structure of real interest rates. The evidence indicates that there is substantial information in the longer maturity term structure about future inflation: the slope of the term structure does have a great deal of predictive power for future changes in inflation. These results are consistent with those in Fama [1990] who also finds that at longer maturities the term structure helps forecast future inflation. On the other hand, at the longer maturities, the term structure of nominal interest rates contains very little information about the term structure of real interest rates. These results are strikingly different from those found for very short-term maturities (six months or less) in previous work. For maturities of six months or less, the term structure contains no information about the future path of inflation, but it does contain a great deal of information about the term structure of real interest rates.

The evidence in this paper does indicate that, at longer maturities, the term structure of interest rates can be used to help assess future inflationary pressures: when the slope of the term structure steepens, it is an indication that the inflation rate will rise in the future and when the slope falls, it is an indication that the inflation rate will fall. However, some caution is warranted because, as the interpretation of the results indicates, changes in the correlation or relative variability of expected future inflation changes and real term structure slopes are likely to change the coefficients in the inflation-change forecasting equation. The results here also lend support to research that has used the term structure spread between long- (over two years) and short-term interest rates to assess the credibility of anti-inflation policies (as in Blanchard [1984] and Dornbusch [1988]).

Appendix: Monte Carlo Experiments

Table III reports the results from Monte Carlo simulations of 1,000 t-tests of the null hypothesis $\beta_m = 0$ in the inflation-change forecasting equation using the Hansen-Hodrick-White-Newey-West estimation method described above. The table contains results for the regressions with $m =$ two to five years, and for three sample periods: Panel A for the full sample, which has over 350, Panel B for the pre-October 1979 sample, which has 322 observations, and Panel C for the post-October 1979 sample with fewer than 75 observations.

The Monte Carlo simulations are conducted as follows. The inflation rates and the $i_t^m - i_t^1$ spread variables were constructed from ARMA models whose parameters were estimated from the relevant sample periods. Because Lagrange-multiplier tests described by Engle [1982] reveal the presence of ARCH (autoregressive conditional heteroskedasticity) in the error terms, the error terms are drawn from a normal distribution in which the variance follows an ARCH process whose parameters were also estimated from the relevant sample periods. Start-up values for AR terms in the time series models are obtained from the actual realized data from five and six years before the sample period, and then four years

TABLE III
MONTE CARLO SIMULATION RESULTS FOR t-TEST OF $\beta_m = 0$

m (years)	Critical values of t from Monte Carlos Significance levels 50%	25%	10%	5%	1%	% Rejections using asymptotic 5% critical value	% Rejections using asymptotic 1% critical value
			Panel A: Full sample				
2	0.93	1.71	2.38	2.80	4.38	18.3%	7.7%
3	0.96	1.72	2.43	3.10	4.56	18.2%	8.5%
4	0.99	1.73	2.53	3.06	4.80	18.4%	9.4%
5	0.98	1.76	2.68	3.22	4.71	20.4%	11.3%
			Panel B: Pre-October 1979 sample				
2	0.92	1.64	2.42	2.95	4.20	16.7%	7.5%
3	1.05	1.78	2.62	3.10	4.31	21.6%	10.6%
4	1.07	1.83	2.63	3.28	4.73	22.0%	10.4%
5	1.09	1.78	2.98	3.54	5.69	21.2%	14.7%
			Panel C: Post-October 1979 sample				
2	1.33	2.49	4.04	5.26	8.76	33.6%	23.3%
3	1.82	3.33	5.54	7.15	11.30	47.0%	35.5%
4	2.29	4.25	7.30	9.62	16.96	55.7%	45.2%
5	2.31	4.05	6.43	9.65	15.72	56.0%	43.4%

of draws from the random number generator produce start-up values for the error terms. Then a sample size corresponding to the relevant regression is produced using errors drawn from the distribution described above. To check out the robustness of the Monte Carlo results, I also conducted experiments where the error terms were assumed to be i.i.d. rather than ARCH and also where the test statistics were not corrected for heteroskedasticity; the results were very similar to those reported in the text. The Monte Carlo results reported in the text assume that the error terms for the inflation and yield slope equations are independent. Mankiw and Shapiro [1986] and Stambaugh [1986], however, point out that if the data-generating-mechanism has yield spreads correlated with past inflation rates because of contemporaneous correlation between their error terms, the small sample distribution of test statistics can be substantially affected. This problem is not an important one in the data here because the correlations between error terms from yield spread and inflation equations are not statistically significant. Monte Carlo simulations which allowed for this correlation as in Mankiw and Shapiro [1986] and Stambaugh [1986], as well as simulations allowing for additional effects of past inflation on yield spreads, were not appreciably different from those reported in the text. Note that the dating convention for interest rates in this paper is off by one period from the conventional dating used in Mankiw and Shapiro [1986] and Stambaugh [1986]. Hence allowing for contemporaneous correlation of the error terms from the π_t^m and i_t^m ARIMA models in the Monte Carlo simulations involves allowing for the correlation between the i_t^m error term and one lag of the π_t^m error term in the notation of this paper.

As the last two columns of Table III indicate, inference from using the asymptotic distribution can be highly misleading, even when the number of observations is in excess of 350. Using the 5 percent critical value from the asymptotic distribution, over 18 percent of the t-statistics from the Monte Carlo simulations using the full sample (Panel A) indicate rejection of the null hypothesis when it is true. Not surprisingly, the bias of the asymptotic distribution gets worse as the degree of overlap increases with increasing m. When we get to the Panel C results which have under 100 observations, the degree of bias becomes especially severe. For example, even using the 1 percent critical value from the asymptotic distribution, over 50 percent of the t-statistics for $m = 5$ indicate a rejection of the null when it is true.

The second through sixth columns of Table III provide more information about the characteristics of the finite sample distribution by providing the critical values for different marginal significance levels. In Panel A and Panel B the 5 percent critical values of the finite distributions are around 3.0 rather than 2.0 as with the asymptotic distribution, while the 1 percent critical values of the finite distribution are over 4.0. For samples with less than 100 observations in Panel C, the 5 percent critical values of the finite sample distribution always exceed 5.0, and for $m = 5$ the 5 percent critical value is even in double digits.

Additional Monte Carlo experiments along the lines of those described in Table III have been conducted for t-tests of $1 - \beta_m = 0$. They produce results that are quite close to those in Table III and are not reported here in order to conserve space.

GRADUATE SCHOOL OF BUSINESS, COLUMBIA UNIVERSITY,
AND NATIONAL BUREAU OF ECONOMIC RESEARCH

REFERENCES

Blanchard, Olivier, "The Lucas Critique and the Volcker Deflation," *American Economic Review*, LXXIV (1984), 211–15.

Clarida, Richard H., and Benjamin M. Friedman, "The Behavior of U. S. Short-Term Interest Rates Since October 1979," *Journal of Finance*, XXXIX (1984), 671–82.

Dornbusch, Rudiger, "Credibility, Debt and Unemployment: Ireland's Failed Stabilization," NBER Working Paper No. 2785, 1988.

Engle, Robert F., "Autoregressive Conditional Heteroscedasticity with Estimates of the Variance of the United Kingdom Inflation," *Econometrica*, L (1982), 987–1007.

Fama, Eugene F., "The Information in the Term Structure," *Journal of Financial Economics*, XIII (1984), 509–28.

____, "Term Structure Forecasts of Interest Rates, Inflation and Real Returns," *Journal of Monetary Economics*, XXV (1990), 59–76.

____, and Robert R. Bliss, "The Information in Long-Maturity Forward Rates," *American Economic Review*, LXXVII (1987), 680–92.

Hansen, Lars P., "Large Sample Properties of Generalized Method of Moments Estimators," *Econometrica*, L (1982), 1029–54.

____, and Robert Hodrick, "Forward Exchange Rates as Optimal Predictors of Future Spot Rates," *Journal of Political Economy*, LXXXVIII (1980), 829–53.

Huizinga, John, and Frederic S. Mishkin, "Inflation and Real Interest Rates on Assets with Different Risk Characteristics," *Journal of Finance*, XXXIX (1984), 699–712.

____, and ____, "Monetary Policy Regime Shifts and the Unusual Behavior of Real Interest Rates," *Carnegie-Rochester Conference Series on Public Policy*, XXIV (1986), 231–74.

Jones, David S., and V. Vance Roley, "Rational Expectations and the Expectations Model of the Term Structure: A Test Using Weekly Data," *Journal of Monetary Economics*, XII (1983), 453–65.

Mankiw, N. Gregory, and Lawrence H. Summers, "Do Long-Term Interest Rates Overreact to Short-Term Interest Rates?" *Brookings Papers on Economic Activity* (1984:1), 223–42.

Mankiw, N. Gregory, and Matthew D. Shapiro, "Do We Reject Too Often? Small Sample Properties of Tests of Rational Expectations Models," *Economics Letters*, XX (1986), 139–45.

McCulloch, J. Huston, "Appendix II: U. S. Term Structure Data, 1946–87," in Robert J. Shiller and J. Huston McCulloch, "The Term Structure of Interest Rates, NBER Working Paper No. 2341, 1987.

Mishkin, Frederic S., "The Real Rate of Interest: An Empirical Investigation," *The Cost and Consequences of Inflation*, Carnegie-Rochester Conference Series on Public Policy, XV (1981), 151–200.

____, "The Information in the Longer-Maturity Term Structure About Future Inflation," NBER Working Paper No. 3126, 1989.

____, "What Does the Term Structure Tell Us About Future Inflation," *Journal of Monetary Economics*, XXV (1990), 77–95.

Newey, W., and Kenneth West, "A Simple, Positive Definite, Heterocedasticity and Autocorrelation Consistent Covariance Matrix," *Econometrica*, LIII (1987), 703–08.

Roley, V. Vance, "The Response of Interest Rates to Money Announcements Under Alternative Operating Procedures and Reserve Retirement Systems," NBER Working Paper #1812, 1986.

Shiller, Robert J., John Y. Campbell, and Kermit L. Schoenholtz, "Forward Rates and Future Policy: Interpreting the Term Structure of Interest Rates," *Brookings Papers on Economic Activity* (1983:1), 173–217.

Stambaugh, Robert F., "Bias in Regressions with Lagged Stochastic Regressors," Graduate School of Business, University of Chicago, January 1986.

Startz, Richard, "Do Forecast Errors or Term Premia Really Make the Difference Between Long and Short Rates?" *Journal of Financial Economics*, X (1982), 323–29.

White, Halbert, "A Heterocedasticity-Consistent Covariance Matrix Estimator and Direct Tests for Heterocedasticity," *Econometrica*, XLVIII (1980), 817–38.

[14]

Journal of International Money and Finance (1991), **10**, 2–22

A multi-country study of the information in the shorter maturity term structure about future inflation

FREDERIC S. MISHKIN*

Graduate School of Business, Columbia University, Uris Hall 619, New York, New York 10027, USA
and National Bureau of Economic Research

Empirical analysis of data from ten OECD countries indicates that, except for France, the United Kingdom, and Germany, the shorter maturity term structure does not contain a great deal of information about the future path of inflation. On the other hand, except for the United Kingdom, there is a great deal of information in the term structure of *nominal* interest rates at shorter maturities about the term structure of *real* interest rates. These results are explained by differences in the relative variability of expected future inflation changes and real term structure slopes for the different countries.

In recent years, central banks of many countries have increasingly focused on the goal of price stability. In pursuing this goal, central banks need information on the degree of inflationary pressures in the economy, and one natural place to look for this information is the term structure of interest rates. Research beginning with Fama (1975) often finds that the level of interest rates helps forecast future inflation,[1] while recent research has focused on the information in the term structure about future interest rate movements.[2] These two lines of research suggest that the term structure of interest rates might contain information about the future path of inflation.

One reason why the information in the term structure about future inflation requires careful study is that it bears directly on whether central banks should use the term structure as a guide for monetary policy, as has recently been advocated by the Vice-Chairman of the Board of Governors of the Federal Reserve. A second reason is that empirical evidence on this topic can tell us

* Research support has been provided by the Faculty Research Fund of the Graduate School of Business, Columbia University. I thank Jae-Won Park for research assistance, David Backus, Vance Roley, Maury Obstfeld, anonymous referees, the editor of this journal, and participants in seminars at Columbia, Cornell, Princeton and the NBER for their helpful comments, and Robert Cumby for supplying me with a computer program. The research reported here is part of the NBER's research programs in Financial Markets and Monetary Economics and Economic Fluctuations. Any opinions expressed are those of the author and not those of the National Bureau of Economic Research. The data in this paper will be made available free of charge to any researcher who sends me a standard formatted $5\frac{1}{4}''$ 360 KB diskette with a stamped, self-addressed mailer.

whether movements in the term structure of *real* interest rates (which is not directly observable) are revealed by movements in the term structure of *nominal* interest rates (which is observable). The term structure of real interest rates has an important role in understanding asset pricing and in theories of the business cycle and so is of much concern to theorists. Finding out whether observable data on the nominal term structure provide information about the behavior of the *real* term structure can thus help guide theoretical research.

This paper examines empirically what the term structure of interest rates tells us about future inflation in the United States and in nine other OECD countries using Euro market data. Previous research has examined the information in the term structure about future inflation in the USA using Treasury bill rate data (Mishkin, 1990a). However, there are several reasons why a multi-country empirical analysis of the information in the term structure about future inflation is needed. Assessing future inflationary pressures in the economy is a concern of central banks in all the countries studied here. Thus learning about the ability of the term structure to forecast the future path of inflation in each of these countries is important knowledge for their central bankers to have because it will help them decide whether using the term structure as a guide for monetary policy is a sensible strategy. It is also worth examining what the term structure tells us about future inflation in other countries besides the USA because it will provide us with clues about how the information in the term structure might change with different monetary regimes. Different countries do provide different conclusions on the relationship between inflation and interest rates,[3] and so it is plausible that the information in the term structure might differ substantially across countries. A final reason for examining data in other countries is that it will provide further information on which results found in the United States are robust across countries. This is also important because the information in the term structure in the USA may be representative of only one type of monetary regime and a change in the regime may alter the information in the term structure. US policymakers should not be confident in conclusions derived from US data unless they are found to be generally true for other countries as well.

I. The methodology

This paper focuses on estimates of a forecasting equation that tell us whether the term structure helps to predict the future path of inflation. This equation, which will be referred to as the 'inflation change equation,' is a regression of the change in the future $\underline{m}$-period inflation rate from the $\underline{n}$-period inflation rate $(\pi_t^m - \pi_t^n)$ on the 'slope' of the term structure $(i_t^m - i_t^n)$.

$$\langle 1 \rangle \qquad \pi_t^m - \pi_t^n = \alpha_{m,n} + \beta_{m,n}[i_t^m - i_t^n] + \eta_t^{m,n}\,.$$

To understand this regression framework, we need to carefully examine the link between nominal interest rates, real interest rates and expected inflation in order to understand how to clearly interpret the results. According to the Fisher (1930) equation, expected inflation over m periods is equal to the m-period nominal interest rate minus the m-period real interest rate:

$$\langle 2 \rangle \qquad E_t\pi_t^m = i_t^m - rr_t^m\,,$$

where E_t = expectations at time t; π_t^m = the inflation rate from time t to $t+m$;

i_t^m = the m-period nominal interest rate at time t; rr_t^m = the m-period (*ex-ante*) real interest rate at time t, *i.e.*, the *ex-ante* real return on an m-period bond from t to $t+m$. The realized inflation rate over the next m periods can be written as the expected inflation rate plus the forecast error of inflation:

$$\langle 3\rangle \qquad \pi_t^m = E_t\pi_t^m + \varepsilon_t^m ,$$

where ε_t^m = the forecast error of inflation $= \pi_t^m - E_t\pi_t^m$. Substituting in for $E_t\pi_t^m$ from equation ⟨2⟩, we obtain,

$$\langle 4\rangle \qquad \pi_t^m = i_t^m - rr_t^m + \varepsilon_t^m .$$

In order to examine the information in the term structure about future changes in the inflation rate, we can subtract equation ⟨4⟩ above for the n-period inflation rate from equation ⟨4⟩ for the m-year inflation rate to obtain,

$$\langle 5\rangle \qquad \pi_t^m - \pi_t^n = i_t^m - i_t^n - rr_t^m + rr_t^n + \varepsilon_t^m - \varepsilon_t^n .$$

This equation can be rewritten in the form of the inflation change forecasting equation ⟨1⟩, which is the equation estimated in this paper, as follows:

$$\pi_t^m - \pi_t^n = \alpha_{m,n} + \beta_{m,n}[i_t^m - i_t^n] + \eta_t^{m,n} ,$$

where

$$\alpha_{m,n} = \overline{rr}^n - \overline{rr}^m ,$$
$$\beta_{m,n} = 1 ,$$
$$\eta_t^{m,n} = \varepsilon_t^m - \varepsilon_t^n - (u_t^m - u_t^n) ,$$
$$u_t^m = rr_t^m - \overline{rr}^m ,$$
$$u_t^n = rr_t^n - \overline{rr}^n .$$

If we assume that expectations are rational and the slope of the real term structure, $rr_t^m - rr_t^n$, remains constant over time, then ordinary least squares (OLS) estimates of the forecasting equation above produce a consistent estimate of $\beta_{m,n} = 1$. In other words, a test of $\hat{\beta}_{m,n} = 1$ is a valid test of the null hypothesis of rational expectations and a constant slope of the real term structure. We see this by first recognizing that rational expectations implies that the forecast errors of inflation, ε_t^m *and* ε_t^n, are orthogonal to the right-hand-side regressors because under rational expectations $E_t\varepsilon_t^m = E_t\varepsilon_t^n = 0$, *i.e.*, forecast errors of inflation must be unforecastable conditional on all available information at time t which includes i_t^m and i_t^n. Constancy of the slope of the real term structure then makes OLS estimates consistent because the $-(u_t^m - u_t^n)$ term disappears, leaving an error term for the forecasting equation of $\varepsilon_t^m - \varepsilon_t^n$, which is orthogonal to the right-hand-side regressors under rational expectations. In addition, since the error term, $\varepsilon_t^m - \varepsilon_t^n$, is a minimum variance error term under rational expectations, the slope of the nominal term structure adjusted by a constant is an optimal predictor of the change in the inflation rate.

If the slope of the real term structure is not constant, then the nominal term structure no longer is an optimal predictor because $-(u_t^m - u_t^n)$ is no longer equal to zero. Furthermore, if the slope of the nominal term structure is correlated with the slope of the real term structure, then $u_t^m - u_t^n$ and hence $\eta_t^{m,n}$ is correlated with $i_t^m - i_t^n$ and the OLS estimate of $\beta_{m,n}$ will have a probability limit different from one. In addition, correlation of $\eta_t^{m,n}$ and $i_t^m - i_t^n$ implies that the OLS estimate of $-\alpha_{m,n}$ will also not be a consistent estimate of the mean slope of the real term structure $(\overline{rr}^m - \overline{rr}^n)$. However, when the slope of the real term structure is not constant, we can still view the inflation change forecasting equation in ⟨1⟩ as a projection equation in which the statistical significance of the $\hat{\beta}_{m,n}$ coefficient tells us about the information in the nominal term structure about future inflation.

An alternative interpretation of tests on $\hat{\beta}_{m,n}$ is obtained by subtracting $i_t^m - i_t^n$ from both sides of the forecasting equation ⟨5⟩ and then multiplying both sides by -1 to obtain the following regression equation which involves the difference between m-period and n-period *ex-post* real interest rates:

$$\langle 6 \rangle \qquad eprr_t^m - eprr_t^n = -\alpha_{m,n} + [1 - \beta_{m,n}](i_t^m - i_t^n) - \eta_t^{m,n}.$$

where $eprr_t^m = i_t^m - \pi_t^m$, the *ex-post* real interest rate on a m-period at time t (*i.e.*, the realized real return from t to m periods in the future). Now we see that $\beta_{m,n} = 1$ implies that the coefficient $[1 - \beta_{m,n}]$ on the slope of the nominal term structure, $i_t^m - i_t^n$, equals zero in the *ex-post* real rate regression. Since the *ex-ante* real interest rate is just the conditional expectation at time t of the *ex-post* real interest rate, a rejection of $\beta_{m,n} = 1$ (or equivalently, $1 - \beta_{m,n} = 0$) in the inflation-change forecasting equation indicates that the slope of the term structure of nominal interest rates $(i_t^m - i_t^n)$ contains significant information about the slope of the term structure of *ex-ante* real interest rates $(rr_t^m - rr_t^n)$.[5] Using similar reasoning, a rejection of $\beta_{m,n} = 0$ (or equivalently, $1 - \beta_{m,n} = 1$) means that the null hypothesis that the slope of the term structure of real interest rates $(rr_t^m - rr_t^n)$ moves one-for-one with the slope of the nominal term structure $(i_t^m - i_t^n)$ is rejected.

To summarize: a statistical rejection of $\beta_{m,n} = 0$ provides evidence that (a) the term structure contains significant information about the future path of inflation, and (b) assuming rational expectations, the slopes of the term structures of real and nominal interest rates do not move one-for-one with each other. On the other hand, a statistical rejection of $\beta_{m,n} = 1$ provides evidence that, assuming rational expectations, (a) the slope of the real term structure is not constant over time,[6] and (b) the term structure of nominal interest rates provides information about the term structure of real interest rates.

Note that the phrase 'information in the term structure' is being used in this paper quite narrowly. Information in the term structure about the path of future inflation refers only to the ability of the slope, $i_t^m - i_t^n$ to predict the change in the inflation rate, $\pi_t^m - \pi_t^n$. This paper focuses on the predictive power of the slope term, $i_t^m - i_t^n$, because it is the most natural piece of information in the term structure to examine.

II. Some additional econometric issues

Before going on to a discussion of the data and the empirical results, several additional econometric issues that have important consequences for hypothesis testing need to be discussed. One important econometric consideration is that the regression error term $\eta_t^{m,n}$ exhibits serial correlation which renders OLS standard errors invalid. One source of the serial correlation arises from the use here of overlapping data in which $m > 1$, *i.e.*, the number of periods for the interest rate and the inflation rate are greater than the observation interval. As is well known, this leads to correlation of the error term ε_t^m with up to $m-1$ of its lagged values. However, the other component of the $\eta_t^{m,n}$ error term, $u_t^m - u_t^n$, the real rate slope relative to its mean, could be serially correlated, possibly resulting in serial correlation in $\eta_t^{m,n}$ for lags greater than $m-1$. Panel A of Table 1 conducts tests to determine whether there is serial correlation in the error term for the inflation-change forecasting equations studied in this paper at lags greater than $m-1$ using a test statistic developed by Cumby and Huizinga (1989).[7] The Cumby–Huizinga statistic in Panel A is distributed as $\chi^2(12)$ under the null hypothesis that the 12 autocorrelations of the regression error terms starting with the mth are all zero. The Panel A results indicate that when m is six or less, there is serial correlation in the regression error terms at lags beyond $m-1$ for several countries other than the USA. However, when $m=12$ the test statistics do not suggest the presence of serial correlation at lags of 12 or greater for any country. Panel B provides additional test statistics to see if there is serial correlation at lags of 12 or greater in the regressions in which m is less than 12. The Panel B results suggest that for these models there is no evidence of serial correlation beyond the 11th lag.

The Table 1 results suggest that the standard errors of the coefficients in the OLS regressions need to be constructed allowing for non-zero autocorrelations of the regression error terms at lags up to 11.[8] The standard errors reported in the following empirical analysis are generated using the method outlined by Hansen and Hodrick (1980), with a modification due to White (1980) and Hansen (1982) that allows for heteroscedasticity[9] and a modification by Newey and West (1987) that insures the variance–covariance matrix is positive by imposing linearly declining weights on autocovariance matrices.

TABLE 1. Tests for serial correlation of the regression error term.

m, n (*Months*)	Countries									
	US	C	UK	B	F	G	I	N	S	J
Panel A: Tests for serial correlation at lags > $m-1$										
3, 1	17.1	20.3	20.8	19.9	21.1*	22.9*	27.5**	51.1**	22.3*	27.5**
6, 1	14.9	14.3	17.2	22.8*	15.1	20.3	13.8	29.0**	19.1	24.4*
6, 3	14.1	12.8	13.5	13.8	13.2	17.3	14.3	27.2**	13.9	22.4*
12, 1	12.6	12.7	13.0	13.3	12.1	13.1	13.0	15.0	13.5	12.7
12, 3	10.6	10.9	11.9	11.3	12.7	13.9	11.3	14.8	10.8	18.3
12, 6	13.3	12.6	13.5	9.9	12.7	14.3	12.1	8.7	11.6	14.5
Panel B: Tests for serial correlation at lags > 11										
3, 1	14.6	13.2	13.5	13.0	12.9	14.6	11.4	15.1	12.8	14.0
6, 1	12.3	12.5	12.3	12.2	11.9	13.5	12.2	15.0	11.5	12.6
6, 3	10.5	11.4	12.1	10.9	10.2	13.4	14.4	14.0	10.7	15.9

Notes:
The countries are as follows: US = United States, C = Canada, UK = United Kingdom, B = Belgium, F = France, G = West Germany, I = Italy, N = Netherlands, S = Switzerland, J = Japan.
The tests statistics are described by Cumby and Huizinga (1989) and are distributed as $\chi^2(12)$ under the null hypothesis that the first 12 autocorrelations after q ($=m-1$ in Panel A and $=11$ in Panel B) are all zero.
* = Significant at the 5 per cent level.
** = Significant at the 1 per cent level.

Additional information is available in the term structure that is not being used in ordinary least squares estimation because contemporaneous errors in forecasting inflation for different horizons may be highly correlated. Therefore, seemingly unrelated regression (SUR) estimates of a system of equations with different horizons may produce substantial gains in efficiency.[10] The SUR standard error estimates will again be incorrect because of the serial correlation of the error terms. The Hansen–Hodrick–White–Newey–West estimate of the variance–covariance matrix allowing for conditional heteroscedasticity can be generalized to apply to a seemingly unrelated regression system of g equations as follows. The SUR estimation method assumes that the variance–covariance matrix of the residuals is $\Sigma \otimes I_T$, where Σ = variance–covariance matrix of the contemporaneous residuals from the g equations; and $I_T = T \times T$ identity matrix, where T is the number of observations. Using the Choleski decomposition $\Sigma^{-1} = P'P$, we get the GLS (*i.e.*, the SUR) estimates by premultiplying the system by $P \otimes I_T$ and then proceed with OLS estimation. Allowing for conditional heteroscedasticity, the Hansen–Hodrick variance–covariance matrix of the parameter estimates of the transformed system is then,

$$\langle 7 \rangle \qquad V = (\tilde{X}'\tilde{X})^{-1} E[\tilde{X}'\tilde{\eta}\tilde{\eta}'\tilde{X}](\tilde{X}'\tilde{X})^{-1},$$

where,

V = variance–covariance matrix of estimated coefficients,

$$X = \begin{bmatrix} X^1 & 0 & . & . & . & 0 \\ 0 & X^2 & 0 & . & . & 0 \\ . & & & & & \\ . & & & & & \\ 0 & . & . & . & 0 & X^g \end{bmatrix},$$

X^i = the matrix of explanatory variables for the ith equation,
$\tilde{X} = (P \otimes I_T)X$,
$\tilde{\eta} = (P \otimes I_T)\eta$, and
$E[\ldots]$ = the expectations operator.

Writing the variance–covariance matrix out results in

$$\langle 8 \rangle \qquad V = (X'(P' \otimes I_T)(P \otimes I_T)X)^{-1} E[X'(P' \otimes I_T)(P \otimes I_T)\eta\eta'(P' \otimes I_T)(P \otimes I_T)X] \times (X'(P' \otimes I_T)(P \otimes I_T)X)^{-1}.$$

Making use of the fact that $P'P = \Sigma^{-1}$, the variance–covariance matrix for the SUR estimates, which is corrected for serial correlation both within and across equations and allows for conditional heteroscedasticity, can be rewritten as,

$$\langle 9 \rangle \quad V = (X'(\Sigma^{-1} \otimes I_T)X)^{-1} E[X'(\Sigma^{-1} \otimes I_T)\eta\eta'(\Sigma^{-1} \otimes I_T)X](X'(\Sigma^{-1} \otimes I_T)X)^{-1}$$

with the j, k (where j and k reference equations) block of the $E[X'(\Sigma^{-1} \otimes I_T)\eta\eta'(\Sigma^{-1} \otimes I_T)X]$ matrix using the Newey–West procedure estimated as[11]

$$\sum_{i=-q}^{q} \sum_{t=1}^{T} [1 - i/(q+1)] X_t^{j\prime} \hat{\eta}_t^j \hat{\eta}_{t-i}^k X_{t-i}^k,$$

where q = the order of the MA process for the error terms in the system = 11.

Now that we have completed our discussion of the econometric details, we can go on to discuss the data used in the empirical analysis.

III. The data

The empirical analysis makes use of monthly data on inflation rates and one, three, six, and 12-month interest rates in the Euro deposit market for the following ten OECD countries: the United States, Canada, United Kingdom, Belgium, France, Germany, Italy, Netherlands, Switzerland, and Japan. For every country except Japan, the sample period extends from the beginning of the floating rate period, April 1973, to December 1986.[12] However, the data for Japan are unavailable until October 1975, so the sample period for Japan starts in October 1975. The inflation data for these countries are seasonally unadjusted CPI measures obtained from the International Financial Statistics (IFS) tape maintained by the International Monetary Fund with the exception of the US data. Because of the well known problems with the treatment of housing costs in the US CPI before 1983, the US inflation data are calculated from a CPI series which appropriately treats housing costs on a rental-equivalence basis throughout the sample period. For more details on this series see Huizinga and Mishkin (1984, 1986). The Euro market data have been obtained from the Harris Bank tape maintained at the NYU Business School and are used in this study for several reasons.[13] High quality data for domestic interest rates are not as readily available for other countries besides the United States and Canada. In some of the other countries, domestic Treasury bill rates are not always market clearing, so that these data, although sometimes available, do not reflect the true cost of credit. Euro rates, however, are market clearing. In addition, Euro deposits denominated in different currencies are issued by banks that have similar default risks,[14] and they are not subject to capital controls because they are offshore securities. This makes the term structures of different countries comparable because they will not have to be adjusted for differing default risks or non-comparability because of capital controls. Both the interest rate and inflation data are expressed on a continuously compounded basis at an annual rate in per cent.

The timing of the variables is as follows. A January interest rate observation uses the Euro rate data for the last Friday of December. A January observation for a one-month inflation rate is calculated from the December and January CPI data; a three-month inflation rate from the December and March CPI data: and so on.

IV. The empirical results

Table 2 contains the estimates of the inflation-change forecasting equations which regress the change in the future m-period inflation rate from the n-period inflation rate $(\pi_t^m - \pi_t^n)$ on the 'slope' of the term structure $(i_t^m - i_t^n)$. In contrast to previous research which has found that the level of interest rates contains a great deal of information about the level of future inflation, there is less evidence in Table 2 that the slope of the term structure provides information about the future path of inflation. The $\beta_{m,n}$ coefficients are statistically significant less than 25 per cent of the time and are not always positive (almost one-quarter of them are negative).

TABLE 2 Estimates of inflation change equations.[a]

$$\pi_t^m - \pi_t^n = \alpha_{m,n} + \beta_{m,n}[i_t^m - i_t^n] + \eta_t^{m,n}$$

m, n (Months)	$\alpha_{m,n}$	$\beta_{m,n}$	R^2	SE	t-Test of $\beta_{m,n}=0$	t-Test of $\beta_{m,n}=1$
Country: United States						
3, 1	0.0121	−0.3166	0.005	2.145	−1.08	4.49**
	(0.0788)	(0.2931)				
6, 1	−0.0522	0.0995	0.001	2.620	0.51	4.59**
	(0.1594)	(0.1963)				
6, 3	−0.0422	0.2547	0.006	1.359	0.77	2.26*
	(0.0971)	(0.3293)				
12, 1	−0.0679	0.3339	0.022	2.735	2.23*	4.45**
	(0.2481)	(0.1496)				
12, 3	−0.0075	0.4514	0.059	1.726	2.15*	2.61**
	(0.2001)	(0.2103)				
12, 6	0.0441	0.4316	0.057	1.054	2.47*	3.25**
	(0.1441)	(0.1748)				
Country: Canada						
3, 1	−0.0655	0.2881	0.001	3.114	0.65	1.60
	(0.0908)	(0.4453)				
6, 1	−0.1067	0.0035	0.000	3.379	0.01	3.70**
	(0.1547)	(0.2695)				
6, 3	−0.0569	−0.2710	0.006	1.473	−0.79	3.73**
	(0.0905)	(0.3410)				
12, 1	−0.1920	−0.0096	0.000	3.655	−0.04	4.16**
	(0.2699)	(0.2428)				
12, 3	−0.1850	−0.1547	0.004	1.940	−0.49	3.67**
	(0.2459)	(0.3147)				
12, 6	−0.1236	−0.1347	0.003	1.199	−0.39	3.27**
	(0.1983)	(0.3471)				
Country: United Kingdom						
3, 1	−0.0834	0.5229	0.002	6.491	0.63	0.58
	(0.1929)	(0.8246)				
6, 1	−0.0035	0.7434	0.010	7.763	1.01	0.35
	(0.4370)	(0.7327)				
6, 3	0.0817	0.7328	0.009	3.857	0.98	0.36
	(0.3116)	(0.7508)				
12, 1	0.2039	1.0072	0.031	8.224	1.92	−0.01
	(0.8047)	(0.5237)				
12, 3	0.2881	0.9934	0.039	5.141	2.34*	0.02
	(0.6377)	(0.4254)				
12, 6	0.1655	0.9798	0.042	3.053	2.27*	0.05
	(0.3264)	(0.4308)				
Country: Belgium						
3, 1	−0.0571	0.5829	0.006	3.041	0.62	0.44
	(0.1274)	(0.9383)				
6, 1	−0.0349	−0.0131	0.000	3.392	−0.03	1.97*
	(0.2080)	(0.5137)				
6, 3	−0.0340	−0.0846	0.001	1.653	−0.36	4.60**
	(0.1319)	(0.2356)				

TABLE 2—*continued*

m, n (Months)	$\alpha_{m,n}$	$\beta_{m,n}$	R^2	SE	t-Test of $\beta_{m,n}=0$	t-Test of $\beta_{m,n}=1$
12, 1	−0.1298	0.0353	0.000	3.793	0.10	2.70**
	(0.4001)	(0.3577)				
12, 3	−0.1143	0.0466	0.000	2.213	0.19	3.90**
	(0.3467)	(0.2444)				
12, 6	−0.1068	−0.0096	0.000	1.287	−0.03	3.41**
	(0.2265)	(0.2959)				
Country: France						
3, 1	−0.0816	0.3863	0.054	2.183	3.59**	5.70**
	(0.1006)	(0.1077)				
6, 1	−0.1150	0.3256	0.062	2.660	4.51**	9.34**
	(0.1773)	(0.0722)				
6, 3	−0.0462	0.2319	0.029	1.316	3.40**	11.26**
	(0.1023)	(0.0682)				
12, 1	−0.1377	0.2700	0.063	2.873	4.34**	11.73**
	(0.2837)	(0.0622)				
12, 3	−0.0913	0.2394	0.052	1.828	1.89	5.99**
	(0.2354)	(0.1270)				
12, 6	−0.0237	0.2910	0.057	1.117	1.76	4.28**
	(0.1631)	(0.1655)				
Country: Germany						
3, 1	−0.0649	0.5959	0.009	2.460	1.68	1.14
	(0.0811)	(0.3538)				
6, 1	−0.1062	0.3523	0.006	3.024	1.23	2.26*
	(0.1485)	(0.2864)				
6, 3	−0.0390	0.0414	0.000	1.596	0.11	2.43*
	(0.0867)	(0.3945)				
12, 1	−0.2122	0.3420	0.012	3.137	1.70	3.28**
	(0.2187)	(0.2008)				
12, 3	−0.1627	0.3071	0.011	2.093	1.24	2.80**
	(0.1737)	(0.2473)				
12, 6	−0.1116	0.5418	0.030	1.308	1.86	1.57
	(0.1151)	(0.2920)				
Country: Italy						
3, 1	−0.0589	−0.2659	0.007	4.443	−1.26	5.98**
	(0.1762)	(0.2118)				
6, 1	−0.1183	−0.0621	0.001	5.514	−0.37	6.36**
	(0.3911)	(0.1670)				
6, 3	−0.0009	0.1876	0.006	2.945	1.30	5.64**
	(0.2066)	(0.1440)				
12, 1	0.0131	0.1880	0.009	6.013	1.64	7.07**
	(0.6900)	(0.1149)				
12, 3	0.4276	0.5346	0.075	3.883	3.09**	2.69**
	(0.5245)	(0.1731)				
12, 6	0.5129	0.7635	0.118	2.267	2.94**	0.91
	(0.4020)	(0.2594)				

TABLE 2—*continued*

m, n (Months)	$\alpha_{m,n}$	$\beta_{m,n}$	R^2	SE	t-Test of $\beta_{m,n}=0$	t-Test of $\beta_{m,n}=1$
Country: Netherlands						
3, 1	−0.1752	0.0875	0.000	4.078	0.15	1.58
	(0.1115)	(0.5767)				
6, 1	−0.2086	−0.0179	0.000	4.619	−0.03	1.88
	(0.1735)	(0.5418)				
6, 3	−0.0416	0.0025	0.000	2.561	0.01	2.75**
	(0.0979)	(0.3625)				
12, 1	−0.3293	0.0275	0.000	4.739	0.07	2.65**
	(0.2408)	(0.3668)				
12, 3	−0.1588	0.1692	0.000	2.760	0.93	4.57**
	(0.2083)	(0.1816)				
12,6	−0.1109	0.1455	0.007	0.922	0.94	5.52**
	(0.1322)	(0.1548)				
Country: Switzerland						
3, 1	−0.0276	0.1184	0.000	3.813	0.24	1.81
	(0.1802)	(0.4883)				
6, 1	0.2670	−0.5338	0.006	4.728	−0.99	2.85**
	(0.3029)	(0.5373)				
6, 3	0.1647	−0.7804	0.016	2.412	−1.49	3.41**
	(0.1564)	(0.5224)				
12, 1	−0.0742	−0.2668	0.003	4.836	−0.74	3.51**
	(0.3730)	(0.3614)				
12, 3	−0.1631	−0.2588	0.005	2.957	−0.65	3.14**
	(0.2940)	(0.4003)				
12, 6	−0.1936	0.0767	0.000	1.722	0.20	2.36*
	(0.1800)	(0.3910)				
Country: Japan[b]						
3, 1	−0.7235	2.9616	0.056	6.923	2.33*	−1.55
	(0.3475)	(1.2692)				
6, 1	−0.6336	1.7293	0.044	7.212	2.45*	−1.04
	(0.3712)	(0.7046)				
6, 3	−0.0451	0.2564	0.001	3.204	0.61	1.77
	(0.1266)	(0.4190)				
12, 1	−0.5186	1.0314	0.028	7.647	1.98	−0.06
	(0.3508)	(0.5216)				
12, 3	−0.1938	0.1594	0.002	3.628	0.52	2.77**
	(0.2766)	(0.3039)				
12, 6	−0.1569	0.1523	0.002	1.702	0.43	2.41*
	(0.1842)	(0.3513)				

[a] $\pi_t^m - \pi_t^n =$ difference between the m-period inflation rate from time t to $t+m$ and the n-period inflation rate from t to $t+n$. $i_t^m - i_t^n =$ difference between the m-period nominal interest rate and the n-period nominal interest rate at time t. Standard errors of coefficients in parentheses. SE = standard error of the regression. * = Significant at the 5 per cent level. ** = Significant at the 1 per cent level.

[b] The sample period for Japan starts in October 1975, the first date that data are available.

The United States displays negative as well as positive $\beta_{m,n}$ coefficients for horizons less than 12 months and only for $m=12$ are the $\beta_{m,n}$ coefficients statistically significant. The US results thus suggest that the shortest end of the term structure (maturities of six months or less) provides no information about future inflation, while around maturities of 12 months, there is some information in the term structure about future changes in inflation. These results are consistent with those found with US Treasury bill data in Mishkin (1990a), although Treasury bill data indicate stronger forecasting ability for the spread between 12-month and six-month rates than do Euro rate data.

The somewhat stronger ability of Treasury bill rates to forecast future changes in inflation suggest that the Euro rate results in Table 2 may even understate somewhat the information in the term structure of domestic interest rates for the future path of inflation.[15] As is pointed out in Mishkin (1984), Euro rates bear a substantial risk premium over Treasury bill rates because, in contrast to Treasury securities, which are riskless in nominal terms, Euro deposits are subject to default risk since their issuing bank might fail. Indeed, this default risk premium is very variable and has at times exceeded five percentage points. Fluctuations in this risk premium in the Euro rates are likely to obscure some of the ability of the term structure of Euro rates to forecast the future path of inflation, and this is exactly what we find for US data.

Other countries also sometimes reveal that there is information about the future path of inflation in the term structure, but only in one case, France, is there quite strong evidence for significant forecasting ability of the term structure. For France, all the $\beta_{m,n}$ coefficients are positive, ranging from 0.23 to 0.39, and in four cases are statistically significant at the 1 per cent level.

Examination of the results on $[1-\beta_{m,n}]$ in Table 2 indicates that the nominal term structure contains substantial information about the term structure of real interest rates in most countries. With the exception of the United Kingdom and Japan, the $[1-\beta_{m,n}]$ estimates are always positive, are statistically significant 80 per cent of the time and are significant at the 1 per cent level 70 per cent of the time. For Japan, the evidence is somewhat mixed with two of the $[1-\beta_{m,n}]$ estimates positive and statistically significant, while three of the estimates are negative but statistically insignificant. The term structure for the United Kingdom, on the other hand, reveals absolutely no information about the term structure of real interest rates. All the $[1-\beta_{m,n}]$ estimates are statistically insignificant with t-statistics less than one in absolute value.

As was discussed in the methodology section, if equation residuals across different time horizons are correlated, more efficient estimates can be obtained by exploiting this information with seemingly unrelated regression (SUR) estimation. Table 3, which contains the SUR estimates of the same inflation change equations found in Table 2, indicates that SUR estimation often leads to large increases in efficiency—coefficient standard errors often decline by more than 50 per cent and in one case declines by 80 per cent.[16]

The increased efficiency of the SUR estimates tends to strengthen the conclusions reached before. All the $\beta_{m,n}$ coefficients for France are now statistically significant at the 1 per cent level, providing even stronger evidence that the term structure in France contains substantial information about the future path of inflation. The $\beta_{m,n}$ coefficients for the United Kingdom are also now all statistically significant at the 5 per cent level, while five out of six are significant for Germany.

TABLE 3. Seemingly unrelated regression (SUR) estimates of inflation change equations.[a]

$$\pi_t^m - \eta_t^n = \alpha_{m,n} + \beta_{m,n}[i_t^m - i_t^n] + \eta_t^{m,n}$$

m, n (Months)	$\alpha_{m,n}$	$\beta_{m,n}$	t-Test of $\beta_{m,n}=0$	t-Test of $\beta_{m,n}=1$
Country: United States				
3, 1	−0.0366	0.2940	1.04	2.49*
	(0.0871)	(0.2840)		
6, 1	−0.0841	0.3099	1.75	3.90**
	(0.1549)	(0.1767)		
6, 3	−0.0467	0.3160	1.91	4.14**
	(0.0896)	(0.1654)		
12, 1	−0.0695	0.3173	2.17*	4.66**
	(0.2530)	(0.1465)		
12, 3	−0.0304	0.3208	2.14*	4.52**
	(0.2069)	(0.1501)		
12, 6	0.0173	0.3239	2.23*	4.66**
	(0.1397)	(0.1451)		
Country: Canada				
3, 1	−0.0471	−0.1560	−0.48	3.53**
	(0.0866)	(0.3277)		
6, 1	−0.1023	−0.1570	−0.55	4.07**
	(0.1532)	(0.2844)		
6, 3	−0.0553	−0.1583	−0.57	4.17**
	(0.0901)	(0.2780)		
12, 1	−0.2327	−0.1570	−0.57	4.17**
	(0.2911)	(0.2776)		
12, 3	−0.1859	−0.1576	−0.58	4.28**
	(0.2444)	(0.2702)		
12, 6	−0.1305	−0.1572	−0.56	4.15**
	(0.1798)	(0.2791)		
Country: United Kingdom				
3, 1	−0.0882	0.8549	2.58**	0.44
	(0.1917)	(0.3317)		
6, 1	0.0112	0.8600	2.61**	0.43
	(0.4084)	(0.3289)		
6, 3	0.0995	0.8600	2.61**	0.42
	(0.2578)	(0.3294)		
12, 1	0.1412	0.8659	2.47*	0.38
	(0.7242)	(0.3503)		
12, 3	0.2296	0.8659	2.48*	0.38
	(0.6082)	(0.3498)		
12, 6	0.1299	0.8681	2.49*	0.38
	(0.3882)	(0.3480)		
Country: Belgium				
3, 1	−0.0095	0.0107	0.03	3.03**
	(0.1008)	(0.3268)		

TABLE 3—*continued*

m, n (Months)	$\alpha_{m,n}$	$\beta_{m,n}$	t-Test of $\beta_{m,n}=0$	t-Test of $\beta_{m,n}=1$
6, 1	−0.0349	−0.0169	−0.07	4.15**
	(0.2086)	(0.2452)		
6, 3	−0.0279	−0.0189	−0.07	4.00**
	(0.1339)	(0.2546)		
12, 1	−0.1431	−0.0151	−0.06	4.12**
	(0.3969)	(0.2464)		
12, 3	−0.1359	−0.0153	−0.06	4.02**
	(0.3374)	(0.2528)		
12, 6	−0.1082	−0.0149	−0.06	4.26**
	(0.2164)	(0.2380)		
Country: France				
3, 1	−0.0646	0.2967	2.91**	6.89**
	(0.0934)	(0.1021)		
6, 1	−0.1097	0.2951	3.17**	7.57**
	(0.1746)	(0.0931)		
6, 3	−0.0454	0.2931	3.57**	8.62**
	(0.1023)	(0.0820)		
12, 1	−0.1319	0.2941	3.66**	8.78**
	(0.2864)	(0.0804)		
12, 3	−0.0683	0.2929	3.78**	9.12**
	(0.2354)	(0.0775)		
12, 6	−0.0229	0.2930	3.88**	9.35**
	(0.1541)	(0.0756)		
Country: Germany				
3, 1	−0.0513	0.4072	2.09*	3.05**
	(0.0779)	(0.1944)		
6, 1	−0.1132	0.4035	2.28*	3.37**
	(0.1381)	(0.1768)		
6, 3	−0.0619	0.3992	1.87	2.82**
	(0.0803)	(0.2133)		
12, 1	−0.2219	0.4039	2.21*	3.27**
	(0.2151)	(0.1824)		
12, 3	−0.1707	0.4020	2.23*	3.32**
	(0.1716)	(0.1799)		
12, 6	−0.1087	0.4046	2.04*	3.01**
	(0.1152)	(0.1981)		
Country: Italy				
3, 1	−0.0089	0.2923	1.24	3.01**
	(0.1690)	(0.2349)		
6, 1	0.0301	0.3113	1.65	3.65**
	(0.3677)	(0.1887)		
6, 3	0.0431	0.3305	2.29*	4.63**
	(0.2179)	(0.1445)		
12, 1	0.2007	0.3402	2.39*	4.63**
	(0.6637)	(0.1425)		

TABLE 3—*continued*

m, n (Months)	$\alpha_{m,n}$	$\beta_{m,n}$	t-Test of $\beta_{m,n}=0$	t-Test of $\beta_{m,n}-1$
12, 3	0.2329	0.3643	2.56*	4.46**
	(0.5460)	(0.1424)		
12, 6	0.2099	0.4009	2.29*	3.43**
	(0.3884)	(0.1748)		
Country: Netherlands				
3, 1	−0.1775	0.1212	1.02	7.37**
	(0.1124)	(0.1193)		
6, 1	−0.2241	0.1191	0.90	6.68**
	(0.1501)	(0.1318)		
6, 3	−0.0466	0.1169	0.96	7.23**
	(0.0936)	(0.1221)		
12, 1	−0.3361	0.1194	0.96	7.10**
	(0.2292)	(0.1240)		
12, 3	−0.1587	0.1195	0.99	7.29**
	(0.2082)	(0.1208)		
12, 6	−0.1119	0.1206	0.99	7.26**
	(0.1303)	(0.1212)		
Country: Switzerland				
3, 1	0.0372	−0.0996	−0.35	3.87**
	(0.1499)	(0.2844)		
6, 1	0.0402	−0.1261	−0.42	3.75**
	(0.2856)	(0.3006)		
6, 3	0.0009	−0.1481	−0.45	3.49**
	(0.1593)	(0.3293)		
12, 1	−0.1601	−0.1131	−0.40	3.98**
	(0.3712)	(0.2797)		
12, 3	−0.1999	−0.1183	−0.42	4.01**
	(0.2830)	(0.2788)		
12, 6	−0.1932	−0.0944	−0.32	3.73**
	(0.1799)	(0.2931)		
Country: Japan[b]				
3, 1	−0.2111	0.4424	0.44	0.55
	(0.2928)	(1.0138)		
6, 1	−0.2565	0.3916	0.66	1.03
	(0.3219)	(0.5913)		
6, 3	−0.0518	0.3409	1.10	2.12*
	(0.1254)	(0.3103)		
12, 1	−0.3888	0.3704	0.94	1.60
	(0.3479)	(0.3925)		
12, 3	−0.1926	0.3379	1.07	2.10*
	(0.2767)	(0.3155)		
12, 6	−0.1412	0.3360	1.06	2.09*
	(0.1881)	(0.3175)		

[a] $\pi_t^m - \pi_t^n =$ difference between the m-period inflation rate from time t to $t+m$ and the n-period inflation rate from t to $t+n$. $i_t^m - i_t^n =$ difference between the m-period nominal interest rate and the n-period nominal interest rate at time t. Standard errors of coefficients in parentheses. SE = standard error of the regression. * = Significant at the 5 per cent level. ** = Significant at the 1 per cent level.

[b] The sample period for Japan starts in October 1975, the first date that data are available.

These countries' term structures display an ability to forecast future changes in inflation.

The statistical significance of the $[1-\beta_{m,n}]$ coefficients in the SUR estimates also increases dramatically, thus providing even stronger evidence that the nominal term structure contains substantial information about the term structure of real interest rates for most countries. With the exception of the United Kingdom and Japan, almost all of the $[1-\beta_{m,n}]$ estimates are significantly positive at the 1 per cent level. For Japan, all of the $[1-\beta_{m,n}]$ estimates are positive and half are statistically significant at the 5 per cent level. The evidence for these nine countries is thus quite strong that the term structure of nominal rates reveals a great deal of information about the term structure of real rates. The results for the United Kingdom continue to tell a different story. Despite much greater precision in the coefficient estimates—the standard errors of half the coefficients decline by over 50 per cent as a result of using SUR estimation—none of the $[1-\beta_{m,n}]$ coefficients is statistically significant; indeed, none even has a *t*-statistic exceeding one. The evidence is thus even stronger that the UK differs from other countries in an important respect: its term structure of nominal interest rates contains no information about its term structure of real interest rates.

IV.A. Interpretation

Under the assumption of rational expectations, the interpretation of the inflation-change, forecasting equation $\beta_{m,n}$ is quite straightforward. Following Fama (1984) and Hardouvelis (1988), $\beta_{m,n}$ can be derived to be:

$$\beta_{m,n} = \frac{\tilde{\sigma}^2 + \rho\tilde{\sigma}}{1 + \tilde{\sigma}^2 + 2\rho\tilde{\sigma}} \qquad \langle 10 \rangle$$

where $\tilde{\sigma} = \sigma[E_t(\pi_t^m - \pi_t^n)]/\sigma[rr_t^m - rr_t^n]$ = the ratio of the standard deviation of the expected inflation change to the standard deviation of the slope of the real term structure; and ρ = the correlation between the expected inflation change, $E_t(\pi_t^m - \pi_t^n)$, and the slope of the real term structure, $rr_t^m - rr_t^n$.[17] This expression is derived by writing down the standard formula for the projection equation coefficient $\beta_{m,n}$, and recognizing that the covariance of the inflation forecast error with $rr_t^m - rr_t^n$ equals zero given rational expectations.

The equation above indicates that $\beta_{m,n}$ is determined by how variable the expected inflation change is relative to the variability of the slope of the real term structure [represented by $\tilde{\sigma}$, the ratio of the standard deviations of $E_t(\pi_t^m - \pi_t^n)$ and $(rr_t^m - rr_t^n)$], as well as by the correlation of the expected inflation change with the real term structure slope (ρ). Differences in the correlation and relative variation of expected inflation and the real term structure slope in the ten countries, possibly the result of different monetary regimes, will thus produce different $\beta_{m,n}$ and hence different conclusions about the information in the term structure about the future path of inflation. Figure 1 shows how $\beta_{m,n}$ varies with $\tilde{\sigma}$ and ρ.

In order to understand why the $\hat{\beta}_{m,n}$ differ across countries, we can get some idea about the values of $\tilde{\sigma}$ and ρ using the procedure outlined in Mishkin (1981), in which estimates of the real term structure spreads, $rr_t^m - rr_t^n$, are obtained from fitted values of regressions of the *ex-post* real rate differentials on past inflation changes and past interest rate spreads.[18] Then the

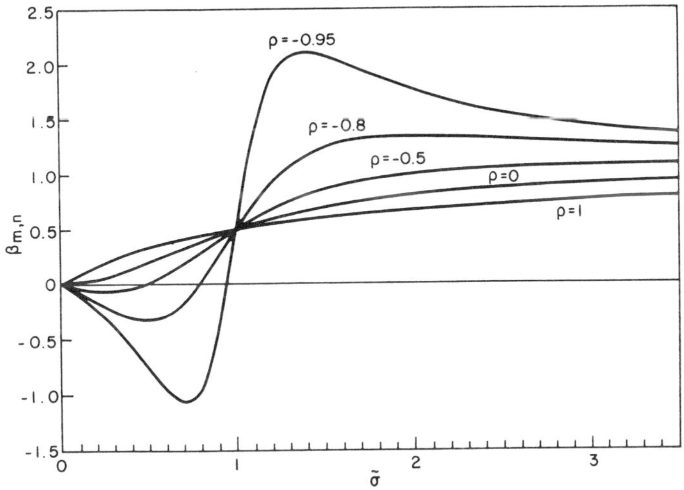

FIGURE 1.

estimated expected inflation change is calculated from the following definitional relationship.

$$\langle 11\rangle \qquad E_t(\pi_t^m - \pi_t^n) = i_t^m - i_t^m - (rr_t^m - rr_t^n).$$

Finally estimates of $\tilde{\sigma}$ and ρ are calculated from the estimated $E_t(\pi_t^m - \pi_t^n)$ and $(rr_t^m - rr_t^n)$. Note that, as is pointed out in Mishkin (1981), these estimates of $\tilde{\sigma}$ and ρ will only be accurate to the extent which the relevant information is included in the *ex-post* real rate regressions. Because the estimated values of $\tilde{\sigma}$ and ρ are found to be robust to different specifications of the real rate regressions, they are likely to be useful in interpreting the $\hat{\beta}_{m,n}$ coefficients using equation ⟨10⟩. However, since we can never be sure that all the relevant information has been included in the *ex-post* real rate regressions, we cannot use the estimated values of $\tilde{\sigma}$ and ρ to derive consistent estimates of $\beta_{m,n}$.

With the exception of France, the estimated values of ρ for the other countries in Table 1 were quite negative, averaging around -0.8 and typically ranging from -0.5 to -0.95. These values of ρ follow from the fact that with the exception of France, the variability of the slope of the nominal term structure, $i_t^m - i_t^n$, is very small relative to the variability of the slope of the real term structure, $rr_t^m - rr_t^n$, and thus, as is evident in equation ⟨11⟩ above, the correlation between $E_t(\pi_t^m - \pi_t^n)$ and $rr_t^m - rr_t^n$ must necessarily be quite negative. As can be seen in Figure 1, with estimates of ρ around -0.8, if the variability of expected inflation changes is sufficiently less than the variability of the real term structure slope so that $\tilde{\sigma}$ is less than 0.8, then $\beta_{m,n}$ will not be above zero.

Low estimated values of $\tilde{\sigma}$ which are less than 0.8 are exactly what we find for all the horizons in countries such as Canada, Belgium, Netherlands, and Switzerland. These low values of $\tilde{\sigma}$ and very negative values of ρ explain why we do not find significant positive $\hat{\beta}_{m,n}$ coefficients for these countries.

Research that suggests that term premiums undergo substantial fluctuations over time[19] provide a rationale for the low values of $\tilde{\sigma}$ and the resulting inability of the term structure to provide information about the future path of inflation. Variation in the slope of the real term structure can be attributed to the variation of term premiums over time as well as changes in the average of expected one-period real interest rates over the next m-periods versus the next n-periods. High variation in these term premiums will then produce high variation in the slope of the real term structure and make it more likely that the variation of the real term structure slope will dominate the variation of expected future inflation changes. The outcome of substantial time variation of term premiums will then be a low $\tilde{\sigma}$ and a low $\hat{\beta}_{m,n}$ estimate, so that the term structure will provide little information about future inflation changes. The flip side of this argument is that substantial variation in term premiums, which produces low $\hat{\beta}_{m,n}$ estimates, lead to the finding that the term structure of nominal interest rates contains a great deal of information about the term structure of real interest rates.[20]

In the case of Germany, the variability of expected future inflation changes is close to the variability of the real term structure slopes and this explains why the estimated $\hat{\beta}_{m,n}$ coefficients are positive and close to 0.5. In the case of the United States and Italy, for the short horizons in which m is less than 12 months, $\tilde{\sigma}$ is quite low; but as the m-horizon lengthens the variability of the real term structure slope declines relative to the variability of the expected inflation changes so that $\tilde{\sigma}$ rises above 0.9. The result is that the $\hat{\beta}_{m,n}$ coefficients get larger as m increases, and this is why results for both Italy and the USA suggest that there is an increase in the information in the term structure about future inflation changes as the maturity increases.

In Tables 2 and 3 the results for the United Kingdom stand out because it has the highest values of $\hat{\beta}_{m,n}$ and is the only country for which we cannot reject the null hypothesis that $\beta_{m,n}=1$. These findings are readily explained by the fact that the UK consistently has the highest variability of expected future inflation changes relative to the variability of the real term structure slopes. The estimated $\tilde{\sigma}$ which range from 1.0 to 1.1 interact with ρs which are around -0.9 to produce $\hat{\beta}_{m,n}$ coefficients close to 1.0.

The estimated values of ρ for France are quite different than for the other countries. In contrast to all the other countries studied here, France has greater variation in the slope of the nominal term structure than in the slope of the real term structure. The result is estimates of ρ that are generally around zero. Thus, even though the variability of expected future inflation changes for France are less than the variability of real term structure slopes, so that $\tilde{\sigma}$s are less than 0.85, Figure 1 shows us that the $\beta_{m,n}$ will be positive but less than 0.5, which is exactly what we find in Tables 2 and 3. The fact that France displays large variation in the nominal term structure slope (the explanatory variable) explains the statistical significance for the French $\hat{\beta}_{m,n}$ estimates because in the regressions it leads to high variability of the explanatory variable relative to the variability of the dependent variable.[21]

It is important to emphasize that the results for the ten countries studied here examine the information in the term structure only for short maturities of 12 months or less. Forecasting equations or forecast surveys often do better at longer horizons, and thus we might expect the inflation forecasting ability of the term structure to improve at longer maturities. This is exactly what is found using data from the United States in Mishkin (1990b). For maturities over a year, the variation in real term structure slopes in the USA appear to be substantially smaller than the variation in expected inflation changes. Hence, the $\hat{\beta}_{m,n}$ coefficients for the longer maturities are found to be well above zero and statistically significant. We might expect to find a similar result for other countries, and this is being studied in my ongoing research on this topic.

V. Conclusions

This paper provides evidence on what the term structure (for maturities of 12 months or less) tells us about future inflation in ten OECD countries. The empirical results on the information in the term structure contrast with those in previous research which find that the level of interest rates help forecast the future level of inflation. Instead they indicate that for the majority of the countries in the sample, the term structure does not contain a great deal of information about the future path of inflation. The results for France, and, to a lesser extent, the United Kingdom and Germany tell a different story, however. In the case of France, the term structure contains a highly significant amount of information about future changes in inflation, while the term structure in both Germany and the UK provide some significant information, but not as much.

It is worth mentioning again that the use of the phrase 'information in the term structure' is being used quite narrowly. Even if the slope of the real term structure has substantial variation so that the slope of the nominal term structure by itself has little predictive power for future inflation, it might be possible to extract useful predictions from the nominal term structure if changes in the real term structure slopes were modeled carefully. This is indeed the subject of research I am currently exploring.

The analysis in this paper suggests that central banks for most of the countries studied here should exercise some caution in using the term structure of interest rates as a guide for assessing inflationary pressures in the economy, as is currently under consideration by the US central bank. There are two reasons for this conclusion. First, the empirical evidence here indicates that although there is significant information in the term structure about the future path of inflation for a few of the countries, this is not a result that is true in general.

Second, as the interpretation of the results indicates, the β-regression coefficients are sensitive to the relative variability of expected future inflation changes and real term structure slopes, as well as to the correlation of these two variables. Any change in the method of conducting monetary policy, such as focusing on the term structure as a guide to monetary policy, is likely to change the correlation and relative variability of expected future inflation changes and real term structure slopes, thus causing the regression coefficients to change in the inflation-change forecasting equation. Thus the forecasting ability of the term structure for the path of future inflation could change dramatically, making the term structure a poor guide for monetary policy. This is, of course, just another example of the Lucas (1976) critique.

The empirical evidence does reveal, however, that for every country studied except the United Kingdom, there is a great deal of information in the term structure of *nominal* interest rates at shorter maturities about the term structure of *real* interest rates. This finding is an extremely useful one because it suggests that for most countries researchers can examine observable data on the nominal term structure to provide them with information about the behaviour of the *real* term structure.

Notes

1. For example, Nelson and Schwert (1977), Mishkin (1981, 1984), Fama and Gibbons (1982), and Huizinga and Mishkin (1986).
2. For example, Shiller *et al.* (1983) and Mankiw and Summers (1984) have questioned the value of the term structure in predicting future short-term interest rates, while recent evidence in Fama (1984), Fama and Bliss (1987), Campbell and Shiller (1987), Hardouvelis (1988), and Mishkin (1988) is more positive about the ability of the term structure to forecast future interest rates.
3. For example, see Mishkin (1984).
4. The discussion of the methodology in this section follows closely that in Mishkin (1990a). It can be skimmed briefly by readers already familiar with Mishkin (1990a).
5. For a more detailed demonstration that inferences from *ex-post* real rate regressions yield inferences about *ex-ante* real interest rates, see Mishkin (1981).
6. Note, however, that $\beta_{m,n}=1$ might not be rejected even asymptotically even if the slope of the real term structure is not constant. This could occur when the term $(u_t^m-u_t^n)$ is not zero if it is orthogonal to $i_t^m-i_t^n$.
7. The statistics in Table 1 have been calculated using the computer program described in Cumby and Huizinga (1988).
8. I also estimated the standard errors for each equation allowing for non-zero autocorrelations going back only $m-1$ periods and also going back 36 periods; the results are very similar to those reported in this paper and none of the conclusions is altered.
9. The Hansen (1982) modification is the same numerically as that proposed by White (1980). The Hansen modification applies when there is conditional heteroscedasticity while White's results are obtained with unconditional heteroscedasticity rather than conditional heteroscedasticity, but additional assumptions are required. The correction for heteroscedasticity is used here because Lagrange-multiplier tests outlined by Engle (1982) reject conditional homoscedasticity for the error term of the forecasting equation. The results were very similar to those reported in the text when a heteroscedasticity correction was not used in calculating the standard errors of the coefficient estimates.
10. There are two ways to think about the inflation change forecasting equation and hence about the consistency of SUR estimated coefficients. If the forecasting equation is just viewed as a projection equation in which the error term is by construction orthogonal to the $i_t^m-i_t^n$ regressor, then consistency of the SUR estimates requires an additional assumption that the $i_t^m-i_t^n$ in each equation is uncorrelated with all the error terms. An alternative way of viewing the inflation change equation is as a test for $\beta_{m,n}=1$. With this interpretation, the same conditions that produce consistency for OLS estimates of $\beta_{m,n}=1$—the constancy of the real rate differentials, $rr_t^m-rr_t^n$—also produce consistency of the SUR estimates. Constancy of the real rate differentials implies that the error terms just equal the difference between the forecast errors of inflation at the *m* and *n* horizon. Since under rational expectations these forecast errors are uncorrelated with all information available at time *t*, which includes i_t^m for all *m*, constancy of the real rate differentials implies the condition for consistency of the SUR estimates, that all of the explanatory variables in the equations are orthogonal to all the error terms.
11. Note that the presence of $\eta\eta'$ in the formula for the variance–covariance matrix in ⟨9⟩ takes account of serial correlation of the error terms both within an equation and across equations as well as for conditional heteroscedasticity in these covariances. Thus even though SUR estimation only takes account of contemporaneous correlation of error terms across equations, the variance–covariance matrix above is corrected for serial correlation both within and across equations as well as for conditional heteroscedasticity.
12. Note that with a sample period ending in December 1986, inflation data for the year 1987 are required.
13. In the few cases where Euro data were missing, the Euro rate was calculated from the interest parity condition. The rest of the data were checked by verifying that there were

no large deviations from interest parity. Several obvious errors in the tape were found in this manner and were corrected.

14. The Euro deposit rates are collected from quotes by the Harris Bank in the case of Euro dollars and by other banks that specialize in issuing Euro deposits in other currencies. The fact that interest parity holds fairly tightly in the data here indicates that the risk premiums are very similar for the different banks quoting the Euro deposit rates.
15. This might be less true if there are significant capital and exchange controls in the economy which result in greater time-variability of the risk premiums in domestic interest rates.
16. Note, however, that in several cases, the estimated standard errors are higher in Table 2 than they are in Table 1. Even though the SUR estimates are asymptotically more efficient than OLS estimates, in small samples estimated SUR standard errors can turn out to be larger than OLS standard errors.
17. Note that $\tilde{\sigma}$ and ρ are constructed from unconditional variances and covariances.
18. The estimates described in the text were generated from OLS regressions in which the *ex-post* real rate differential, $eprr_t^m - eprr_t^n$, was regressed on $i_t^m - i_t^n$; this differential lagged 12 months, 15 months, and 24 months, and on the inflation change $(\pi^m - \pi^n)$ lagged 12 months and 24 months. I also experimented with other choices of lags and the estimated values of $\tilde{\sigma}$ and ρ were robust to different specifications of the regression equations.
19. Jones and Roley (1983), Mankiw and Summers (1984), Shiller *et al.* (1983), and Startz (1982).
20. The same reasoning in this paragraph provides a more rigorous explanation of why results using Euro rates indicate that there is less information in the term structure about the path of future inflation than when *T*-bill data are used as in Mishkin (1990a). As explained in the text, Euro rates embody a default risk premium not found in *T*-bill rates. The additional risk premium in Euro rates can thus lead to greater variation in the real term structure slope which leads to smaller $\tilde{\sigma}$ and hence lower $\hat{\beta}_{m,n}$ estimates.
21. This fact also explains why the French regressions have the highest R^2s because R^2 equals β^2 times the ratio of the variance of the explanatory variable to the variance of the dependent variable.

References

CAMPBELL, JOHN Y., AND ROBERT J. SHILLER, 'Cointegration and Tests of Present Value Models,' *Journal of Political Economy*, October 1987, **95:** 1062–1088.

CUMBY, ROBERT E., AND JOHN HUIZINGA, 'Two Step Two Stage Least Squares User's Guide Personal Computer Version 2.1,' unpublished, Graduate School of Business, New York University, September 1988.

CUMBY, ROBERT E., AND JOHN HUIZINGA, 'Testing for Autocorrelation Structure of Disturbances in Ordinary Least Squares and Instrumental Variables Regressions, unpublished,' Graduate School of Business, New York University, January 1989, forthcoming *Econometrica.*

ENGLE, ROBERT F., 'Autoregressive Conditioned Heteroscedasticity with Estimates of the Variance of the United Kingdom – Inflation,' *Econometrica*, 1982, **50:** 987–1007.

FAMA, EUGENE F., 'Short Term Interest Rates as Predictors of Inflation,' *American Economic Review*, June 1975, **65:** 269–282.

FAMA, EUGENE F., 'The Information in the Term Structure,' *Journal of Financial Economics*, December 1984, **13:** 509–528.

FAMA, EUGENE F., AND ROBERT R. BLISS, 'The Information in Long-Maturity Forward Rates,' *American Economic Review*. September 1987, **77:** 680–692.

FAMA, EUGENE F., AND MICHAEL R. GIBBONS, 'Inflation, Real Returns and Capital Investment,' *Journal of Monetary Economics*, 1982, **9:** 297–324.

FISHER, IRVING, *The Theory of Interest*, New York: Macmillan, 1930.

HANSEN, LARS P., 'Large Sample Properties of Generalized Method of Moments Estimators,' *Econometrica*, 1982, **50:** 1029–1054.

HANSEN, LARS, AND ROBERT HODRICK, 'Forward Exchange Rates as Optimal Predictors of Future Spot Rates,' *Journal of Political Economy*, June 1980, **88:** 829–853.

HARDOUVELIS, GIKAS A., 'The Predictive Power of the Term Structure During Recent Monetary Regimes,' *Journal of Finance*, June 1988, **43:** 339–356.

HUIZINGA, JOHN, AND FREDERIC S. MISHKIN, 'Inflation and Real Interest Rates on Assets with Different Risk Characteristics,' *Journal of Finance*, 1984: **39:** 699–712.

HUIZINGA, JOHN, AND FREDERIC S. MISHKIN, 'Monetary Policy Regime Shifts and the Unusual Behavior of Real Interest Rates,' *Carnegie-Rochester Conference Series on Public Policy*, Spring 1986, **24:** 231–274.

JONES, DAVID S., AND V. VANCE ROLEY, 'Rational Expectations and the Expectations Model of the Term Structure: A Test Using Weekly Data,' *Journal of Monetary Economics*, September 1983, **12:** 453–465.

LUCAS, ROBERT E. JR., 'Econometric Policy Evaluation: A Critique,' in Karl Brunner and Allan H. Meltzer, eds, *The Phillips Curve and Labor Markets*, Carnegie-Rochester Conference Series on Public Policy, Amsterdam: North Holland, 1976, **1**, 19–46.

MANKIW, N. GREGORY, AND LAWRENCE H. SUMMERS, 'Do Long-Term Interest Rates Overreact to Short-Term Interest Rates?,' *Brookings Papers on Economic Activity*, 1984, **1:** 223–242.

MISHKIN, FREDERIC S., 'The Real Rate of Interest: An Empirical Investigation,' *The Cost and Consequences of Inflation*, Carnegie-Rochester Conference Series on Public Policy, Amsterdam: North Holland, 1981, **15:** 151–200.

MISHKIN, FREDERIC S., 'The Real Interest Rate: A Multi-Country Empirical Study,' *Canadian Journal of Economics*, May 1984, **17:** 283–311.

MISHKIN, FREDERIC S., 'The Information in the Term Structure: Some Further Results,' *Journal of Applied Econometrics*, October–December 1988, **3:** 307–314.

MISHKIN, FREDERIC S., 'What Does the Term Structure Tell Us About Future Inflation,' *Journal of Monetary Economics*, January 1990, **25:** 77–95 (1990a).

MISHKIN, FREDERIC S., 'The Information in the Longer-Maturity Term Structure About Future Inflation,' *Quarterly Journal of Economics*, August 1990, **55:** 815–828 (1990b).

NELSON, CHARLES R., AND G. WILLIAM SCHWERT, 'Short-Term Interest Rates as Predictors of Inflation: On Testing the Hypothesis that the Real Rate of Interest is Constant,' *American Economic Review*, June 1977, **67:** 478-486.

NEWEY, W., AND KENNETH WEST, 'A Simple, Positive Definite, Heteroscedasticity and Aurocorrelation Consistent Covariance Matrix,' *Econometrica*, 1987, **55:** 703–708.

SHILLER, ROBERT J., JOHN Y. CAMPBELL AND KERMIT L. SCHOENHOLTZ, 'Forward Rates and Future Policy: Interpreting the Term Structure of Interest Rates,' *Brookings Papers on Economic Activity*, 1983, **1:** 173–217.

STARTZ, RICHARD, 'Do Forecast Errors or Term Premia Really Make the Difference Between Long and Short Rates?,' *Journal of Financial Economics*, 1982, **10**, 323–329.

WHITE, HALBERT, 'A Heteroskedasticity-Consistent Covariance Matrix Estimator and Direct Tests for Heteroskedasticity,' *Econometrica*, 1980, **48:** 817–838.

[15]

Journal of Financial Economics 29 (1991) 59–80. North-Holland

A multicountry comparison of term-structure forecasts at long horizons*

Philippe Jorion
Columbia University, New York, NY 10027, USA

Frederic Mishkin
Columbia University, New York, NY 10027, USA
National Bureau of Economic Research, Boston, MA 02138, USA

Received August 1990, final version received October 1990

This paper extends previous work on the information in the U.S. term structure at longer maturities to Britain, West Germany, and Switzerland. We find strong evidence that the term structure does have significant ability to forecast changes in inflation, particularly at long maturities. On the other hand, the ability of the term structure to forecast changes in one-year interest rates is somewhat weaker; only at the very longest horizon (five years) is there significant forecasting ability for interest-rate changes.

1. Introduction

Evidence is accumulating that the term structure of interest rates in the U.S. contains substantial information about the future path of interest rates and of inflation rates. Work by Fama (1984) and Fama and Bliss (1987) shows that forward-spot spreads have significant power to forecast spot-rate changes, especially at long horizons. Fama (1990) and Mishkin (1990a, 1990b) also

*Research support has been provided by the Faculty Research Fund of the Graduate School of Business at Columbia University. We thank participants in the NBER Summer Institute for comments. Mr. Nijenhuis of Eurostat provided useful information on the construction of the consumer price indices in the European Community. This paper is part of NBER's research program in Financial Markets and Monetary Economics and Economic Fluctuations. Opinions expressed here are those of the authors and not necessarily those of the National Bureau of Economic Research. The data in this paper will be made available to any researcher who sends us a standard formatted $5\frac{1}{4}$ inch 360 KB diskette with a stamped, self-addressed envelope.

report that the slope of the term structure is correlated with future changes in inflation rates.

In most cases, the information content of the U.S. term structure is found to increase with the forecast horizon, which has been studied up to a length of five years. One problem with these studies is that they typically focus on monthly data observed over 30 years or less. Because of the overlapping nature of the sample, it is difficult to evaluate the stability of the results over shorter sample periods. An alternative procedure to assess the robustness of these findings is to analyze foreign term-structure data.

Although the information content of foreign term structures at short maturities has been studied with Eurocurrency data,[1] the information in longer maturities has not been studied because of the lack of foreign data. We have constructed a new data set for the one- to five-year interest rates from Britain, West Germany, and Switzerland. In addition, we do not rely on asymptotic distributions to conduct statistical inference; instead, we conduct inferences based on the small-sample distributions derived from Monte Carlo simulations. This allows us to analyze the information content of U.S., British, German, and Swiss term structures at longer horizons, where the greatest information content is usually found.

Such comparisons are bound to be informative because of the wide differences in inflation processes across these countries. Britain has experienced high inflation, while Germany and Switzerland have enjoyed relatively low inflation rates. In light of these differences, an important issue is whether the results found for the U.S. term structure carry over to foreign markets and, in particular, whether the nominal term structure reveals similar information about the term structure of *real* interest and inflation rates.

This research also bears directly on whether central banks should use the term structure as a guide for monetary policy. If the prevalent view that an upward-sloping spot-rate curve reflects expectations of higher future long-term inflation is supported, monetary policy could conceivably be guided by the slope of the term structure. Of course, such an interpretation is subject to caution, because changes in the conduct of monetary policy could affect the long-run relationship between the term structure and changes in inflation rates.

The paper is organized as follows. Section 2 presents the models we test and summarizes the econometric issues. Section 3 details our data sources and explains how foreign term-structure data have been obtained for long horizons. Empirical tests are reported in section 4 and interpreted in section 5. The last section contains some concluding remarks.

[1] Mishkin (1991) examines the information in the term structure about future inflation at short horizons (twelve months or less) for the U.S. and nine other OECD countries.

2. Methodology

We investigate the information content of the term structure by estimating several regression equations. As in Mishkin (1990a, 1990b, 1991), we test the information in the term structure about the future path of inflation by estimating the following inflation-change regression equation:

$$\pi_t^m - \pi_t^1 = \alpha^m + \beta^m\left(i_t^m - i_t^1\right) + \varepsilon_t^m, \tag{1}$$

where the future annualized m-year inflation rate (from year t to year $t+m$) minus the one-year inflation rate is regressed on the slope of the term structure, defined as the spread between the annualized m-year interest rate and the one-year interest rate, both measured at time t. Throughout the analysis, all inflation rates and interest rates are continuously compounded.

The slope coefficient β^m in this regression reveals information on the ability of the term structure to forecast inflation changes. As described in Mishkin (1990a), a value of β^m significantly different from zero suggests that the term structure contains information about the path of future inflation and that the slopes of the real and nominal term structures do not move one-for-one with each other. A value of β^m significantly different from one indicates that the slope of the term structure of *real* interest rates is not constant over time and that the nominal term structure contains information about the term structure of real interest rates.

Alternatively, as in Fama (1984) and Fama and Bliss (1987), the information content of the term structure can be analyzed in terms of future changes in the one-year spot rate:

$$i_{t+m-1}^1 - i_t^1 = \gamma^m + \delta^m\left(f_t^m - i_t^1\right) + \varepsilon_t^m, \tag{2}$$

where f_t^m is the one-year forward rate derived from spot rates for maturities of $m-1$ and m. A value of δ^m significantly different from zero indicates that the term structure contains information about future spot-rate changes, whereas a value of δ^m significantly different from one indicates a rejection of the expectations hypothesis of the term structure.

The approach above can be related to (1) by noting that the one-year spot rate i_{t+m-1}^1, observed at time $t+m-1$, can be decomposed into an 'ex post' one-year inflation rate component π_{t+m}^1 plus an 'ex post' one-year real interest rate component rr_{t+m}^1, both observed at time $t+m$. Thus, as in Fama (1990), the equation above can be separated into

$$\pi_{t+m}^1 - \pi_t^1 = \gamma'^m + \delta'^m\left(f_t^m - i_t^1\right) + \varepsilon_t'^m \tag{3}$$

and

$$rr^1_{t+m} - rr^1_t = \gamma''^m + \delta''^m(f^m_t - i^1_t) + \varepsilon''^m_t. \tag{4}$$

Since adding (3) and (4) together produces (2), the coefficients γ'^m and γ''^m must sum to γ^m and δ'^m and δ''^m to δ^m.[2]

The specification in terms of multiyear inflation changes in relation to one-year inflation changes in (1) is clearly linked to the model analyzing changes in the one-year inflation rates in (3). For example, with $m = 2$, we have $\pi^m_t = (\pi^1_{t+1} + \pi^1_t)/2$, and $i^m_t = (i^1_t + f^2_t)/2$, so that β^2 must be identical to δ'^2. In general, for m greater than 2, the coefficient β^m will be a weighted average of the coefficients $\delta'^2, \ldots, \delta'^m$.

Before discussing the data and empirical results, we need to address several important econometric issues. An essential consideration is that the regression error terms are likely to exhibit serial correlation, which renders the usual Ordinary Least Squares standard errors invalid. One source of serial correlation arises from the use of overlapping forecasts with a monthly observation interval that is shorter than the forecast horizon. For instance, with $m = 5$ years, the overlapping forecasts in (2) induce an MA($12(m-1)-1$) = MA(47) process in ε^m_t. Because the error terms in (1), (3), and (4) are realized one year later, they follow an MA($12m - 1$) process, which is for instance an MA(59) for $m = 5$ years.

Another possible source of serial correlation, however, could be serial correlation in such variables as term premiums. Serial correlation beyond the lag lengths arising from overlapping forecasts is thus a possibility. We test for serial correlation beyond that arising from overlapping forecasts using a statistic developed by Cumby and Huizinga (1989) that extends the usual portmanteau statistic to account properly for the fact that lower-order terms are not zero. To test whether 12 lags beyond those resulting from overlapping forecasts should be included for each regression, we compute the 'L-statistic', distributed as $\chi^2(12)$. None of the reported statistics indicates that additional lags are required. Therefore, the standard errors need to be corrected only for the moving-average process induced by overlapping forecasts. The standard-error corrections are computed using the method proposed by Hansen and Hodrick (1980), in which the autocovariances are estimated from the data, with a modification due to White (1980) and Hansen (1982) that allows for conditional heteroskedasticity, and a modification suggested by Newey and West (1987) that ensures that the variance–covariance matrix is positive definite.

[2] In these regressions, the hypothesis that δ'^m and δ''^m equal one has no natural interpretation. Hence in the following empirical analysis, we only test for the statistical significance of δ'^m and δ''^m.

As Mishkin (1990b) has pointed out, although the corrected standard errors are valid asymptotically, they can produce misleading inferences in small samples. This bias can be especially serious when five-year forecasts measured over a fifteen-year period are examined. Monte Carlo simulations demonstrate that the small-sample bias is indeed severe. Using a standard 5% critical value from the asymptotic distribution, the test statistics reject far too often under the null, typically around 20% of the time for $m = 2$ years and often as high as 50% of the time when $m = 5$ years. We find that the 5% critical values from the simulation are of the order of 3.5 for $m = 2$ years and 5.0 for $m = 5$ years. As a result, all the critical values and p-values for every test statistic reported in the following empirical analysis have been obtained from the finite-sampling distributions generated by Monte Carlo simulations.[3]

3. Data

Our empirical analysis is based on monthly observations from August 1973 to June 1989 for the U.S., Britain, Germany, and Switzerland. We chose the August 1973 starting point because it is after exchange rates began to float and also because it is the first date for which data are available for all four countries. All interest-rate and inflation-rate data are continuously compounded and expressed in percent per annum.

The spot rates for the U.S. government bond market are taken from Shiller and McCulloch (1987) until February 1987. These data are updated to June 1989 using the same method, which involves fitting splines to the discount function for each month of the sample. The same methodology is applied to the gilt (British government bond) market and is explained in more detail in the appendix. The procedure involves fitting discount functions to bond-price data as reported by the *Financial Times*. For the bund (German government bond) market, spot rates are inferred from constant-maturity yield data provided by Bundesbank.

Government bond rates for Switzerland are not available,[4] so the interest rates used are Euro Swiss franc rates obtained from *Data Resources Incorporated*. Euromarket interest rates are also available for the U.S. dollar and the German mark, and we verified that the conclusions from the empirical

[3]These simulations are carried out as follows. First, ARMA models are fitted for all time series, under each null hypothesis examined. Next, error terms are drawn from a multivariate normal distribution and transformed so as to follow ARCH processes. Finally, empirical p-values are calculated from the number of times that the test statistics were exceeded in one thousand trials. Further details on simulations are available in the appendix to the working-paper version of this paper; see Jorion and Mishkin (1990).

[4]The Swiss government bond market is very small since Switzerland has recently been running a moderate budget surplus. At year-end 1989, outstanding issues amounted to about $7 billion in the Swiss government bond market versus approximately $1,530 billion for the U.S. Treasury market, $200 billion for the gilt market, and $220 billion for the bond market.

Table 1

Summary statistics for inflation rates and changes, August 1973 to June 1989.

Means, standard deviations, autocorrelations (for the number of lags between parentheses), contemporaneous correlations with U.S. data. The inflation-rate and inflation-change series, annualized and continuously compounded, are: (1) one-month rate (multiplied by 12 for comparison with annual data), (2) one-year rate, (3) two-year minus one-year rate, (4) three-year minus one-year rate, (5) four-year minus one-year rate, (6) five-year minus one-year rate. Series (2) to (6) are measured with overlapping data. Data are sampled monthly.

Period	Series	Mean	Std. dev.	Autocorrelations (1)[a]	(12)	(60)	Correlation with U.S.
			U.S.				
August 1973–May 1989	1 month	6.01	3.55	0.696	0.465	−0.016	1.000
August 1973–June 1988	1 year	5.97	2.57	0.993	0.738	−0.081	1.000
August 1973–June 1987	2 − 1 year	−0.17	0.93	0.969	0.253	−0.298	1.000
August 1973–June 1986	3 − 1 year	−0.32	1.53	0.984	0.483	−0.366	1.000
August 1973–June 1985	4 − 1 year	−0.57	1.88	0.988	0.565	−0.331	1.000
August 1973–June 1984	5 − 1 year	−0.79	2.12	0.992	0.614	−0.271	1.000
			Britain				
August 1973–May 1989	1 month	9.97	9.36	0.453	0.525	0.489	0.335
August 1973–June 1988	1 year	9.82	5.69	0.991	0.659	0.680	0.734
August 1973–June 1987	2 − 1 year	−0.43	2.31	0.959	−0.364	0.443	0.444
August 1973–June 1986	3 − 1 year	−1.09	2.91	0.971	−0.013	0.433	0.542
August 1973–June 1985	4 − 1 year	−1.78	3.36	0.974	0.029	0.464	0.543
August 1973–June 1984	5 − 1 year	−2.36	3.41	0.973	0.032	0.499	0.513
			Germany				
August 1973–May 1989	1 month	3.49	3.68	0.481	0.483	0.162	0.490
August 1973–June 1988	1 year	3.35	2.01	0.988	0.729	−0.162	0.824
August 1973–June 1987	2 − 1 year	−0.15	0.73	0.940	0.012	−0.476	0.636
August 1973–June 1986	3 − 1 year	−0.35	1.09	0.972	0.377	−0.569	0.656
August 1973–June 1985	4 − 1 year	−0.63	1.30	0.976	0.512	−0.526	0.624
August 1973–June 1984	5 − 1 year	−0.80	1.47	0.982	0.615	−0.522	0.627
			Switzerland				
August 1973–May 1989	1 month	3.49	5.29	0.295	0.330	−0.128	0.286
August 1973–June 1988	1 year	3.23	2.22	0.977	0.383	−0.337	0.609
August 1973–June 1987	2 − 1 year	−0.22	1.14	0.947	−0.012	−0.388	0.610
August 1973–June 1986	3 − 1 year	−0.36	1.69	0.972	0.323	−0.557	0.613
August 1973–June 1985	4 − 1 year	−0.52	2.04	0.977	0.437	−0.571	0.592
August 1973–June 1984	5 − 1 year	−0.55	2.32	0.981	0.452	−0.496	0.566

[a]Number of lags.

analysis are not affected by the use of government bond data rather than Euromarket data.

Finally, consumer price levels are taken from the International Monetary Fund's *International Financial Statistics*. For the U.S., the series before December 1983 is that used by Huizinga and Mishkin (1984), which appropriately treats housing costs on a rental-equivalent basis.

Table 2

Summary statistics for the term structure, July 1973 to June 1989.

Means, standard deviations, autocorrelations (lags between parentheses), contemporaneous correlations with U.S. data. Term-structure data for the U.S., Britain, and Germany measured from government bond data; for Switzerland, the series are based on Eurocurrency data. The data, sampled monthly and continuously compounded, are: (1) the one-year spot rate, (2) the two-year minus the one-year spot rate (which is also the 1-to-2-year forward rate), (3) the three-year minus the one-year spot rate, (4) the four-year minus the one-year spot rate, (5) the five-year minus the one-year spot rate. Data are sampled monthly.

Period	Series	Mean	Std. dev.	Autocorrelations (1)[a]	(12)	(60)	Correlation with U.S.
			U.S.				
August 1973–June 1988	1 year	8.85	2.68	0.956	0.643	−0.733	1.000
August 1973–June 1987	2 − 1 year	0.21	0.50	0.909	0.514	−0.232	1.000
August 1973–June 1986	3 − 1 year	0.29	0.79	0.916	0.513	−0.318	1.000
August 1973–June 1985	4 − 1 year	0.30	0.95	0.911	0.496	−0.368	1.000
August 1973–June 1984	5 − 1 year	0.25	1.04	0.900	0.420	−0.186	1.000
			Britain				
August 1973–June 1988	1 year	10.58	1.81	0.911	0.248	−0.016	0.598
August 1973–June 1987	2 − 1 year	0.44	0.57	0.823	0.187	−0.068	0.140
August 1973–June 1986	3 − 1 year	0.74	0.82	0.859	0.137	−0.005	0.168
August 1973–June 1985	4 − 1 year	0.96	0.85	0.872	0.108	−0.115	0.273
August 1973–June 1984	5 − 1 year	1.15	0.90	0.875	0.172	−0.245	0.372
			Germany				
August 1973–June 1988	1 year	6.38	2.22	0.985	0.612	−0.527	0.710
August 1973–June 1987	2 − 1 year	0.43	0.44	0.958	0.427	−0.619	0.573
August 1973–June 1986	3 − 1 year	0.63	0.69	0.962	0.436	−0.610	0.579
August 1973–June 1985	4 − 1 year	0.75	0.88	0.965	0.446	−0.586	0.569
August 1973–June 1984	5 − 1 year	0.82	1.05	0.969	0.462	−0.598	0.591
			Switzerland				
August 1973–June 1988	1 year	4.64	2.16	0.966	0.402	−0.441	0.517
August 1973–June 1987	2 − 1 year	0.32	0.61	0.676	0.184	−0.326	0.320
August 1973–June 1986	3 − 1 year	0.60	0.86	0.836	0.264	−0.498	0.350
August 1973–June 1985	4 − 1 year	0.82	1.11	0.893	0.333	−0.598	0.403
August 1973–June 1984	5 − 1 year	0.97	1.27	0.911	0.377	−0.713	0.469

[a]Number of lags.

Table 1 provides summary statistics for the inflation rates and inflation changes for the four countries under consideration, sampled on a monthly basis. Over the period 1973–1989, the U.S. inflation rate averages 6%; Germany and Switzerland have a lower rate of about 3.5%; and the British inflation rate, of around 10%, is not only much higher, it is highly volatile as well.[5]

[5]Part of the volatility can be attributed to distortions in the British index due to various factors. For instance, the gradual imposition of the value-added tax in 1973 and a substantial VAT increase in 1979 are reflected in the British retail price index. In addition, the official index

Term-structure statistics for the four countries are presented in table 2. As expected, the ranking of average one-year spot rates corresponds to the ranking of average inflation rates: Switzerland and Germany display the lowest average nominal interest rates, while the United States and Britain have higher interest rates. For all countries, the term structure has been on average positively sloped, and the standard deviation of the slope is similar across countries.

4. Empirical results

Table 3 displays estimates of the inflation-change regression (1) for the U.S., British, and German government bond markets and the Swiss Euromarket at maturities of two, three, four, and five years. Underneath each t-statistic is the p-value, reported in parentheses, calculated from the small-sample distribution obtained from the Monte Carlo simulations. The results for the U.S. indicate that the slope of the U.S. term structure for long maturities has substantial power to forecast U.S. inflation changes. Two of the four β^m slope coefficients are statistically significant at the 5% level and the third, for $m = 4$, is nearly so (with a p-value of 0.08). In addition, the explanatory power of the regression increases substantially with the maturity: the R^2's rise from 26% to 53%. Further, none of the β^m coefficients is significantly different from one, indicating that we cannot reject the hypothesis that the slope of the real term structure is constant over time for maturities greater than one year: the implication is that the nominal term structure contains no information about the slope of the real term structure.

The U.S. results presented here are very similar to those found in Mishkin (1990b), which are estimated for a sample period (data from 1953 to 1987) that is less current but substantially longer than the one we look at. The estimated β^m coefficients have a similar rising pattern as m increases and are of a similar magnitude. Further, the percentage of variation explained by the U.S. regressions in table 3 is also similar in magnitude to that in Mishkin (1990b), but the R^2's are actually slightly higher here. One difference from previous results is that the β^m coefficients are not quite as statistically significant. This is readily explained by the fact that our sample is half the size of Mishkin's (1990b).

---

in Britain includes mortgage-interest payments as the main element of owner-occupied housing cost, and local taxation, as measured by real-estate taxes ('rates') or the recently imposed poll tax. Other countries in this sample measure housing costs on a more appropriate rental-equivalent basis, and thus have CPIs that are more comparable to the series used in the U.S. The British CPI, therefore, may have distortions not found in the CPI of other countries. The Institute for Fiscal Studies, for instance, has recently compiled a different measure of the British CPI that attempts to correct the treatment of housing costs, and reports that, for the year ending April 1990, the British inflation rate was 3% below the official measure of 9.4%. Further information on the construction of the British and German price indices can be found for instance in Teekens (1989).

Table 3

Estimates of inflation-change regressions.

$$\pi_t^m - \pi_t^1 = \alpha^m + \beta^m\left(i_t^m - i_t^1\right) + \varepsilon_t^m$$

The annualized m-year inflation rate minus the one-year inflation rate is regressed against the slope of the term structure $i_t^m - i_t^1$, defined as the spread between the annualized m-year interest rate and the one year interest rate. Data are sampled monthly.

Period	Series	α^m (s.e.)[a]	β^m (s.e.)	R^2	t-test of $\beta^m = 0$ [simulation	t-test of $1 - \beta^m = 0$ p-values][b]
		U.S.				
August 1973–June 1987	2 – 1 year	−0.385 (0.203)	0.948 (0.246)	0.260	3.85[c] [0.03]	0.21 [0.88]
August 1973–June 1986	3 – 1 year	−0.702 (0.307)	1.220 (0.257)	0.392	4.75[c] [0.03]	−0.86 [0.61]
August 1973–June 1985	4 – 1 year	−1.034 (0.363)	1.372 (0.351)	0.483	3.91 [0.08]	−1.06 [0.61]
August 1973–June 1984	5 – 1 year	−1.210 (0.446)	1.491 (0.377)	0.535	3.96 [0.12]	−1.30 [0.55]
		Britain				
August 1973–June 1987	2 – 1 year	−0.812 (0.517)	0.913 (0.845)	0.050	1.08 [0.43]	0.10 [0.94]
August 1973–June 1986	3 – 1 year	−1.772 (0.893)	0.931 (0.940)	0.069	0.99 [0.51]	0.07 [0.96]
August 1973–June 1985	4 – 1 year	−3.194 (0.879)	1.464 (0.811)	0.138	1.81 [0.29]	−0.57 [0.72]
August 1973–June 1984	5 – 1 year	−4.168 (0.597)	1.585 (0.560)	0.175	2.83 [0.17]	−1.04 [0.60]
		Germany				
August 1973–June 1987	2 – 1 year	−0.273 (0.205)	0.276 (0.279)	0.027	0.99 [0.54]	2.59 [0.16]
August 1973–June 1986	3 – 1 year	−0.664 (0.282)	0.473 (0.201)	0.091	2.35 [0.25]	2.62 [0.21]
August 1973–June 1985	4 – 1 year	−1.120 (0.298)	0.636 (0.127)	0.189	5.01 [0.09]	2.87 [0.19]
August 1973–June 1984	5 – 1 year	−1.522 (0.273)	0.876 (0.099)	0.385	8.82[c] [0.03]	1.25 [0.61]
		Switzerland				
August 1973–June 1987	2 – 1 year	−0.454 (0.289)	0.689 (0.267)	0.133	2.58 [0.07]	1.16 [0.35]
August 1973–June 1986	3 – 1 year	−0.996 (0.460)	1.019 (0.244)	0.263	4.17[c] [0.03]	−0.08 [0.96]
August 1973–June 1985	4 – 1 year	−1.555 (0.510)	1.223 (0.204)	0.432	6.00[c] [0.03]	−1.09 [0.56]
August 1973–June 1984	5 – 1 year	−1.900 (0.473)	1.362 (0.184)	0.539	7.41[c] [0.03]	−1.97 [0.37]

[a]Asymptotic standard errors between parentheses.
[b]Simulation p-values between brackets.
[c]Significant at 5% level, using critical values from simulations.

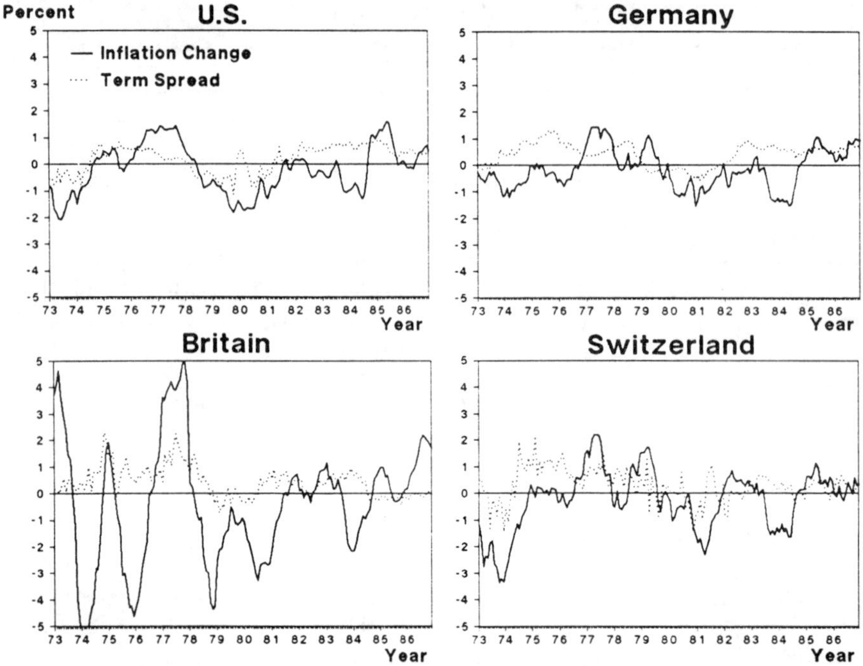

Fig. 1. 2-to-1-year inflation change and term spread. Time series of the annualized two-year inflation rate minus the one-year inflation rate $\pi_t^2 - \pi_t^1$ ('inflation change') and of the slope of the term structure $i_t^2 - i_t^1$ ('term spread'), defined as the spread between the annualized two-year interest rate and the one-year interest rate.

The results for Germany and Switzerland also show significant ability of the term structure to forecast the path of inflation. The Swiss β^m coefficients for maturities of three, four, and five years are significant at the 5% level, and the remaining β^m coefficient for $m = 2$ is significant at 10%. The German β^m coefficient for $m = 5$ is significant at the 5% level, and for $m = 4$ it is significant at 10%. For shorter horizons, however, the German β^m coefficients are small and are not statistically significant. The British data indicate that, although most of the slope coefficients are close to one, the standard deviations of the estimates are much higher than for other countries. The null hypothesis of $\beta^m = 1$ cannot be rejected in any country, so we cannot reject the hypothesis that for these maturities the slope of the real term structure is constant over time.

Some of these results can be interpreted in terms of fig. 1, which displays the relationship between the 2-to-1-year slope of the term structure and 2-to-1-year inflation change for the four countries under study. For comparability, the vertical scale has been kept the same for all countries. The figures dramatically illustrate the volatility of the British inflation rate and the stability of German inflation in comparison with other countries. The fit of the U.S. term structure seems quite good, whereas the results for the pound

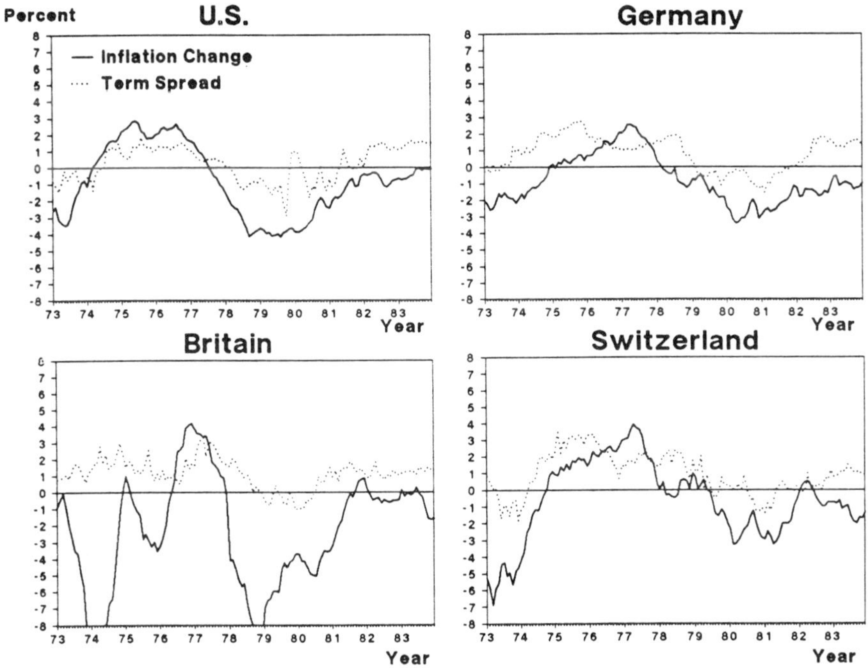

Fig. 2. 5-to-1-year inflation change and term spread. Time series of the annualized five-year inflation rate minus the one-year inflation rate $\pi_t^5 - \pi_t^1$ ('inflation change') and of the slope of the term structure $i_t^5 - i_t^1$ ('term spread'), defined as the spread between the annualized five-year interest rate and the one-year interest rate.

are erratic. Changes in the German inflation rate, however, are not adequately captured by the 2-to-1-year slope of the term structure.

The results are more clear-cut in fig. 2, which reports 5-to-1-year changes in inflation rates, which have longer swings than shorter-term changes. As a result, the fit of the U.S. term structure is quite good, and the fit for Germany improves considerably.

A comparison of these results with those for shorter maturities in Mishkin (1991) provides an additional perspective on the results. At maturities of twelve months or less in the U.S., Germany, and Switzerland, the ability of the term structure to forecast the path of inflation is quite low: the β^m coefficients are small and typically not statistically significant, and the R^2's of the inflation-change regressions are well below 0.10. In addition, the β^m coefficients are typically significantly less than 1.0, so that there does appear to be information in the nominal term structure about the real term structure. The results at the shorter maturities are thus quite different from those in table 3, which indicate that at longer maturities there is significant information in the nominal term structure about future inflation but not about the real term structure. This result is further confirmed by the pattern of increasing R^2 as m increases in table 3.

In contrast to the other countries, the results on the British inflation-change regressions are similar for both shorter and longer maturities: the β^m coefficients for maturities of twelve months or less are much closer to 1.0 than to zero, and have magnitudes similar to those in table 3. The β^m coefficients are typically statistically significant at the shorter maturities, however, whereas they aren't here. The findings for the shorter maturities suggest that a likely explanation for the lack of statistical significance for the longer-term British results is the low power of the test, caused by more data overlap, with forecast horizons much greater than the observation interval. Indeed, the longer-maturity regressions for Britain do display higher R^2's than are found in the shorter-maturity results in Mishkin (1991). The R^2's also increase with maturity.

In view of these results, a natural question is whether the results differ across countries. In table 3, the slope coefficients are not all that different in magnitude and therefore it is entirely possible that differences are due simply to sampling variation. To explore this possibility, we test for the equality of the β^m coefficients across countries, using a chi-square test statistic for which the p-value is calculated from the small-sample distribution obtained from the Monte Carlo simulations. Not one of the statistics is statistically significant.[6] Thus we cannot reject the null hypothesis that the information in the term structure is similar for these four countries. A reasonable conclusion, then, is that in all four countries the term structure has some ability to forecast long-term changes in inflation rates.

The information in the term structure about future interest-rate changes is analyzed in table 4, which displays estimates of (2). These regressions of the changes in the one-year spot rates on the forward-spot spread are comparable to Fama and Bliss's (1987) results. A surprising finding is that, in contrast to Fama and Bliss's (1987) results, the forward-spot spread has no significant power to forecast changes in U.S. interest rates: none of the δ^m coefficients is statistically significant, and only one of the t-statistics is above 2.0. One possible explanation for the difference is the shorter sample period used here,[7] although the additional two and a half years of data at the end of our sample seem a more like cause. When we estimate these regressions over the period August 1973 to December 1986, the results are very similar to those in Fama and Bliss (1987).[8] The t-statistic on δ^m is below 2.0 for $m = 2$ and 3, but rises to above 4.0 for $m = 4$ and above 10.0 for $m = 5$. Figs. 3 and 4 present plots of 2-to-1-year and 5-to-1-year changes in the one-year spot rate, along with the forward-spot spreads, for the four countries. In fig. 4, it is particularly clear that the relationship between spot-rate changes and the

[6] These results, as well as similar tests for the other regressions, are reported in an appendix to the working-paper version of this paper; see Jorion and Mishkin (1990).

[7] For example, when $m = 5$, Fama and Bliss have 216 observations versus 131 in our sample.

[8] Indeed, Mishkin (1990b) finds that the Fama–Bliss and McCulloch data sets produce almost identical results.

Table 4

Estimates of spot-change regressions.

$$i^1_{t-m-1} - i^1_t = \gamma^m + \delta^m(f^m_t - i^1_t) + \varepsilon^m_t$$

The change in the one-year spot rate from t to $t+m-1$ is regressed on the forward-spot spread, defined as the spread between the annualized one-year forward rate derived from the $(m-1)$-year and m-year spot rates, and the one-year interest rate. Data are sampled monthly.

Period	Series	γ^m (s.e.)[a]	δ^m (s.e.)	R^2	t-test of $\delta^m = 0$ [simulation p-values][b]	t-test of $1-\delta^m = 0$ [simulation p-values][b]
		U.S.				
August 1973–June 1987	2 − 1 year	0.008 (0.486)	−0.156 (0.322)	0.005	−0.48 [0.76]	3.59 [0.06]
August 1973–June 1986	3 − 1 year	−0.136 (1.107)	−0.036 (0.586)	0.000	−0.06 [0.97]	1.77 [0.29]
August 1973–June 1985	4 − 1 year	−0.334 (0.651)	0.469 (0.652)	0.029	0.72 [0.69]	0.81 [0.66]
August 1973–June 1984	5 − 1 year	−0.303 (1.716)	1.395 (0.688)	0.192	2.03 [0.31]	−0.57 [0.78]
		Britain				
August 1973–June 1987	2 − 1 year	−0.716 (0.357)	0.667 (0.284)	0.115	2.34 [0.09]	1.17 [0.39]
August 1973–June 1986	3 − 1 year	−1.485 (0.458)	1.056 (0.439)	0.270	2.40 [0.14]	−0.13 [0.91]
August 1973–June 1985	4 − 1 year	−1.595 (0.567)	1.068 (0.445)	0.202	2.40 [0.15]	−0.15 [0.92]
August 1973–June 1984	5 − 1 year	−2.121 (0.527)	1.195 (0.375)	0.256	3.19 [0.11]	−0.52 [0.75]
		Germany				
August 1973–June 1987	2 − 1 year	−0.764 (0.720)	0.408 (0.521)	0.035	0.78 [0.64]	1.14 [0.53]
August 1973–June 1986	3 − 1 year	−1.520 (0.993)	0.737 (0.440)	0.094	1.67 [0.38]	0.60 [0.76]
August 1973–June 1985	4 − 1 year	−2.329 (0.837)	1.271 (0.372)	0.246	3.41 [0.15]	−0.73 [0.71]
August 1973–June 1984	5 − 1 year	−2.924 (0.910)	1.705 (0.248)	0.447	6.88[c] [0.03]	−2.84 [0.31]
		Switzerland				
August 1973–June 1987	2 − 1 year	−0.539 (0.509)	0.322 (0.297)	0.029	1.08 [0.43]	2.28 [0.11]
August 1973–June 1986	3 − 1 year	−1.590 (0.844)	0.836 (0.535)	0.151	1.56 [0.39]	0.31 [0.87]
August 1973–June 1985	4 − 1 year	−2.193 (0.714)	1.062 (0.437)	0.305	2.43 [0.27]	−0.14 [0.94]
August 1973–June 1984	5 − 1 year	−2.500 (0.951)	1.366 (0.194)	0.443	7.11[c] [0.01]	−1.95 [0.36]

[a]Asymptotic standard errors between parentheses.
[b]Simulation p-values between brackets.
[c]Significant at 5% level, using critical values from simulations.

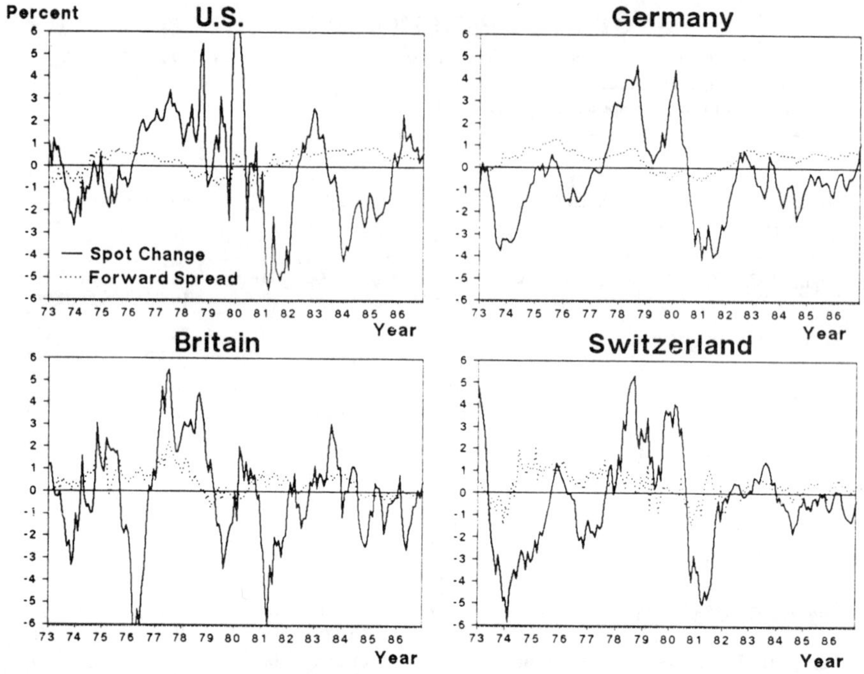

Fig. 3. 2-to-1-year spot change and forward-spot spread. Time series of the difference between the annualized one-year spot rates $i^1_{t-1} - i^1_t$ ('spot change') and of $f^2_t - i^1_t$ ('forward-spot spread'), defined as the spread between the annualized one-year forward rate derived from the one-year and two-year spot rates, and the one-year interest rate.

forward spread breaks down, and is even reversed, in the last three years of the sample for the U.S. The conclusion in Fama and Bliss that there is substantial information in the term structure about future changes in interest rates at longer horizons, particularly when $m = 4$ and 5,[9] is greatly weakened by the addition of another two and a half years of data.

The results for the other countries do not reveal a great deal of information in the term structure about future spot-interest-rate changes. Only in Germany and Switzerland are there significant δ^m coefficients, and these occur only at the longest horizon of $m = 5$. These tests are likely to have low power, however, because as the last column in table 4 reveals, we are also unable to reject that $\delta^m = 1$ for any country or horizon. We also conduct tests of the equality of the δ^m coefficients across countries using chi-square tests. These statistics suggest that there are no major differences in the results among the four countries: the null hypothesis that the δ^m are equal is

[9]Although Fama and Bliss (1987) find a t-statistic of 2.65 for $m = 3$, the Monte Carlo results here indicate that this statistic is unlikely to be statistically significant. Only in the $m = 4$ and 5 regressions, when the t-statistics are above 5.0, it is likely that the estimates of the δ^m coefficients are statistically significant.

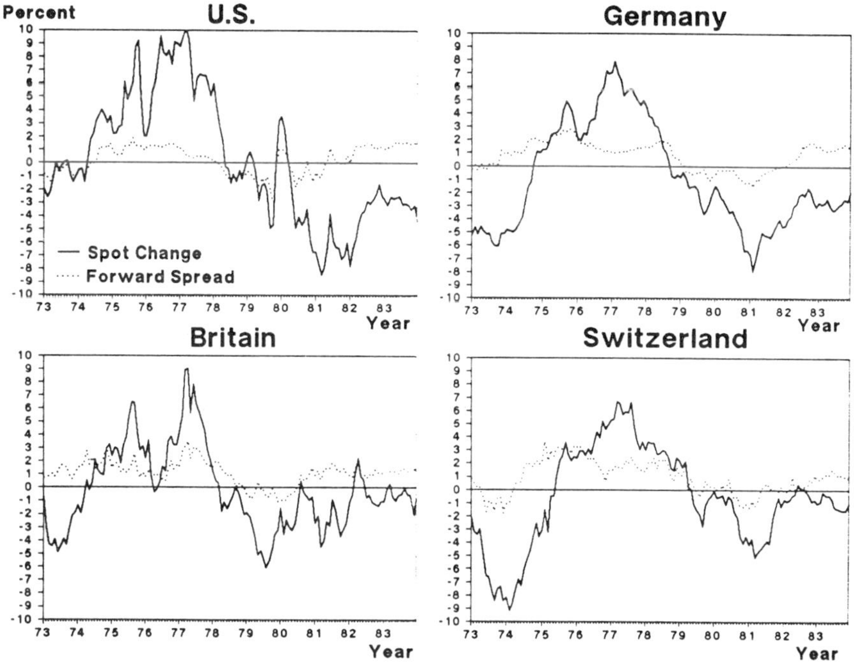

Fig. 4. 5-to-1-year spot change and forward-spot spread. Time series of the difference between the annualized one-year spot rates $i_{t+1}^1 - i_t^1$ ('spot change') and of $f_t^2 - i_t^1$ ('forward-spot spread'), defined as the spread between the annualized one-year forward rate derived from the four-year and five-year spot rates, and the one-year interest rate.

never rejected. Given the low power of the tests and the fact that there are significant δ^m in two cases, the following conclusion seems to be warranted: there does seem to be some evidence that the term structure can forecast changes in spot interest rates, but only when the horizon is quite long.

The decomposition of the spot-change regressions is found in table 5, which displays estimates of (3) and (4). The ability of the term structure to forecast inflation changes is again quite evident in this table. In all the countries except Britain, most of the δ'^m coefficients are significant at the 5% level. For the estimated δ''^m coefficients for the U.S., which tell us about the ability of the term structure to forecast changes in one-year real rates, we find a result already reported by Fama (1990): the δ''^m coefficients are in opposite sign to the δ'^m coefficients, with the δ''^m coefficient for $m = 1$ statistically significant at the 5% level. Further, at maturities of less than five years the δ''^m coefficients almost exactly offset the δ'^m coefficients. This explains why the δ^m coefficients are so near zero for maturities of less than five years and hence why the term structure at these maturities has so little ability to forecast changes in spot rates. For the other countries, however, the δ''^m coefficients are not typically negative and none of the δ''^m coefficients are

Table 5

Decomposition of spot-change regressions.

Inflation-rate change: $\pi^1_{t+m} - \pi^1_t = \gamma'^m + \delta'^m(f^m_t - i^1_t) + \varepsilon'^m_t$

Real rate change: $rr^1_{t+m} - rr^1_t = \gamma''^m + \delta''^m(f^m_t - i^1_t) + \varepsilon''^m_t$

The variables are regressed on the forward-spot spread, defined as the spread between the annualized one-year forward rate derived from the $(m-1)$-year and m-year spot rates, and the one-year interest rate. Data are sampled monthly.

Period	Series	γ'^m (s.e.)[a]	δ'^m (s.e.)	R^2	t-test of $\delta'^m = 0$ [p-value][b]	γ''^m (s.e.)	δ''^m (s.e.)	R^2	t-test of $\delta''^m = 0$ [p-value]
				U.S.					
August 1973–June 1987	2 − 1 year	−0.769 (0.407)	0.948 (0.246)	0.260	3.85[c] [0.03]	0.777 (0.430)	−1.104 (0.269)	0.152	−4.10[c] [0.02]
August 1973–June 1986	3 − 1 year	−1.298 (0.526)	1.404 (0.315)	0.428	4.46[c] [0.04]	1.163 (0.904)	−1.439 (0.562)	0.240	−2.56 [0.16]
August 1973–June 1985	4 − 1 year	−1.857 (0.629)	1.734 (0.408)	0.536	4.25 [0.07]	1.523 (1.397)	−1.265 (0.456)	0.167	−2.77 [0.17]
August 1973–June 1984	5 − 1 year	−2.005 (1.047)	1.570 (0.264)	0.411	5.95[c] [0.04]	1.702 (1.684)	−0.175 (0.525)	0.003	−0.33 [0.88]
				Britain					
August 1973–June 1987	2 − 1 year	−1.624 (1.03)	0.913 (0.845)	0.050	1.08 [0.43]	0.908 (1.135)	−2.45 (0.706)	0.004	−0.35 [0.79]
August 1973–June 1986	3 − 1 year	−2.955 (1.874)	0.624 (1.073)	0.028	0.58 [0.73]	1.471 (1.968)	0.431 (0.903)	0.013	0.48 [0.76]
August 1973–June 1985	4 − 1 year	−4.187 (2.060)	0.649 (1.169)	0.020	0.56 [0.77]	2.592 (2.010)	0.419 (0.834)	0.010	0.50 [0.78]
August 1973–June 1984	5 − 1 year	−5.519 (1.165)	0.826 (0.469)	0.056	1.76 [0.39]	3.398 (1.190)	0.369 (0.330)	0.012	1.12 [0.60]

Table 5 (continued)

Period	Series	γ'^m (s.e.)[a]	δ'^m (s.e.)	R^2	t-test of $\delta'^m = 0$ [p-value][b]	γ''^m (s.e.)	δ''^m (s.e.)	R^2	t-test of $\delta''^m = 0$ [p-value]
				Germany					
August 1973–June 1987	2 − 1 year	−0.546 (0.410)	0.276 (0.279)	0.027	0.99 [0.56]	−0.218 (0.604)	0.132 (0.424)	0.003	0.31 [0.81]
August 1973–June 1986	3 − 1 year	−1.405 (0.449)	0.676 (0.240)	0.149	2.82 [0.20]	−0.115 (0.765)	0.061 (0.298)	0.001	0.20 [0.89]
August 1973–June 1985	4 − 1 year	−2.272 (0.355)	1.018 (0.155)	0.329	6.57[c] [0.05]	−0.056 (0.592)	0.252 (0.288)	0.017	0.88 [0.66]
August 1973–June 1984	5 − 1 year	−3.015 (0.211)	1.370 (0.111)	0.657	12.34[c] [0.01]	0.091 (0.753)	0.335 (0.196)	0.040	1.71 [0.47]
				Switzerland					
August 1973–June 1987	2 − 1 year	−0.908 (0.578)	0.689 (0.267)	0.133	2.58 [0.10]	0.369 (0.464)	−0.367 (0.224)	0.027	−1.64 [0.24]
August 1973–June 1986	3 − 1 year	−2.048 (0.752)	1.228 (0.257)	0.336	4.78[c] [0.03]	0.458 (0.483)	−0.393 (0.290)	0.036	−1.36 [0.45]
August 1973–June 1985	4 − 1 year	−2.708 (0.612)	1.356 (0.205)	0.545	6.61[c] [0.03]	0.516 (0.299)	−0.294 (0.439)	0.025	−0.67 [0.73]
August 1973–June 1984	5 − 1 year	−2.934 (0.271)	1.549 (0.163)	0.589	9.50[c] [0.01]	0.434 (0.854)	−0.172 (0.183)	0.009	−0.94 [0.67]

[a]Asymptotic standard errors between parentheses.
[b]Simulation p-values between brackets.

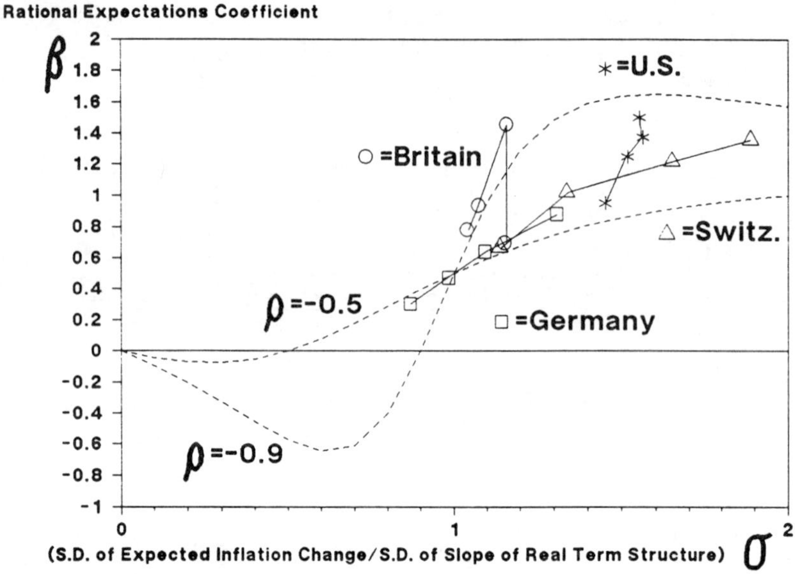

Fig. 5. Interpretation of inflation-change regressions. The dashed lines represent the implied coefficients β of the regression of the inflation change on the slope of the term structure $\pi_t^m - \pi_t^1 = \alpha^m + \beta^m(i_t^m - i_t^1) + \varepsilon_t^m$ for typical values of ρ ($\rho = -0.5$ and $\rho = -0.9$) under rational expectations: ρ is the correlation between the expected inflation change and the slope of the real term structure and σ is the ratio of the standard deviation of the expected inflation change to the standard deviation of the slope of the real term structure. Each marker on the graph plots the implied regression coefficients β that correspond to the estimated values of ρ and σ for four maturities. The coefficient for $m = 2$ is always represented by the leftmost marker, and a line is connected to the next higher m coefficient.

statistically significant. We thus see that for these countries, if forward-spot spreads can forecast spot-interest-rate changes, this is because the term structure can forecast inflation changes. Not surprisingly considering the earlier results, the chi-square tests indicate that there is no evidence that the δ' and δ'' slope coefficients differ across countries.

We can obtain an even better understanding of the information in the term structure about both future inflation and future interest-rate changes by using the assumption of rational expectations, as is done in Fama (1984), Hardouvelis (1988), and Mishkin (1990a). Given rational expectations, the slope coefficients β^m or δ^m can be written as $(\sigma^2 + \rho\sigma)/(1 + \sigma^2 + 2\rho\sigma)$, where σ is the ratio of the standard deviation of the expected inflation change (or spot-rate change) to the standard deviation of the slope of the real term structure (or the forward premium) and ρ is the correlation between the expected inflation (spot-rate) change and the slope of the real term structure (forward premium). The dashed lines in figs. 5 and 6 show the theoretical relationship between σ and the slope coefficients for $\rho = -0.5$ or -0.9, which is the typical range of ρ values found in the data. The dashed lines indicate that high σ's result in slope coefficients that are substantially

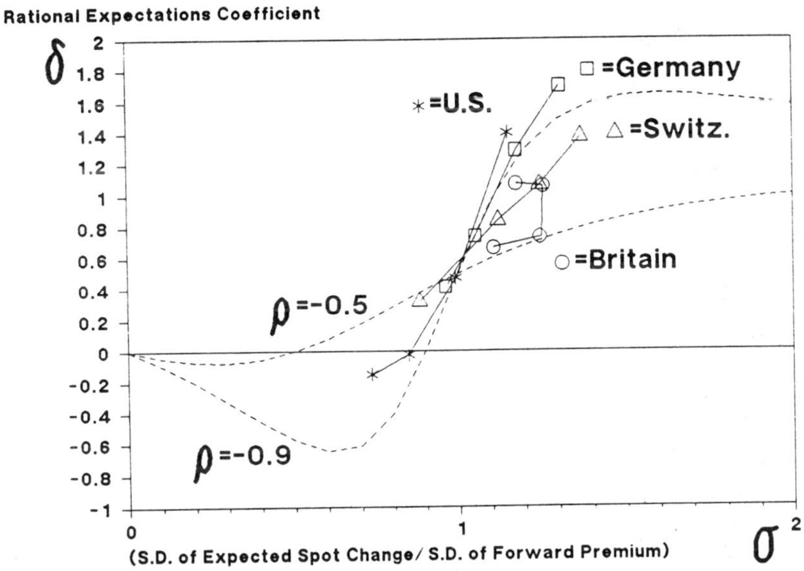

Fig. 6. Interpretation of spot-change regressions. The dashed lines represent the implied coefficients δ of the regression of the spot-rate change on the forward premium $i^1_{t-m-1} - i^1_t = \gamma^m + \delta^m(f^m_t - i^1_t) + \varepsilon^m_t$ for typical values of ρ ($\rho = -0.5$ and $\rho = -0.9$) under rational expectations; ρ is the correlation between the expected spot change and the forward premium and σ is the ratio of the standard deviation of the spot-rate change to the standard deviation of the forward premium. Each marker on the graph plots the implied regression coefficients δ that correspond to the estimated values of ρ and σ for four maturities. The coefficient for $m = 2$ is always represented by the leftmost marker, and a line is connected to the next higher m coefficient.

above zero, which means that the term structure has informational content. The σ are best thought of as akin to signal-to-noise ratios where the noise is either variation in the real-term-structure slope or in forward premiums, which obscures the information in the term structure about expected changes in inflation or interest rates.

Estimated values of the σ and ρ can be computed using a procedure outlined in Mishkin (1990a); the resulting implied β^m and δ^m slope coefficients are plotted in figs. 5 and 6. The coefficient for $m = 2$ is always the leftmost coefficient and a line is connected to the next higher m coefficient. The estimated implied coefficients in fig. 5 reveal why the β^m coefficients tend to be high for all countries, which means that the term structure does reveal information about future inflation changes. Except at the shorter horizons for Germany, the σ are always above one, leading to β^m coefficients that exceed 0.5. Further, the pattern of β^m coefficients rising with m in table 3 results from an increase in σ as the maturity lengthens. At longer horizons the variability of expected inflation changes increases in relation to the variability in the real-term-structure slope, which produces more information in the term structure about future inflation.

Fig. 6 shows a similar pattern of σ and implied δ^m coefficients increasing as m increases, except for Britain. The rise in σ with increasing m in both figures is not coincidental, because variation in the real-term-structure slope can be in part attributed to variation in the forward premium. In addition, the presence of a Fisher effect – the positive correlation between nominal interest rates and expected inflation – might link expected inflation changes to expected interest-rate changes. Thus when σ in fig. 6 rises, we might also expect the σ in fig. 5 to rise. The major difference between the two figures is that the σ are more likely to be below 1.0 in fig. 6 when the m-horizon is short. This is what produces the low δ^m coefficients at the shorter horizons. This helps explain the empirical results that, for shorter horizons, there is more information in the term structure about future inflation changes than about future interest-rate changes.

5. Conclusions

This paper extends previous work on the information in the term structure at longer maturities to countries besides the U.S. Results for these countries are similar to those found for the U.S. There is strong evidence that the term structure does have significant ability to forecast changes in inflation, particularly at long maturities. On the other hand, the ability to forecast changes in one-year interest rates is somewhat weaker; only at the very longest horizon (five years) is there significant forecasting ability for interest-rate changes.

The evidence in this paper does suggest that for countries besides the U.S. the term structure can be used to help assess long-run inflationary pressures: a steepening of the slope of the longer-maturity term structure indicates that the inflation rate will rise several years in the future and, conversely, a negative slope indicates reduced inflationary pressures. We need to be cautious about this interpretation, however, because changes in the conduct of monetary policy could affect the variation of expected inflation changes relative to variation in the real term structure and thus alter the relationship between the term structure and changes in inflation rates.

Appendix: Data construction

The spot rates for the U.S. market are taken from Shiller and McCulloch (1987) until February 1987. These data are updated to December 1988 using the same method, which involves fitting splines to the discount function for each month of the sample. Since the same methodology is applied to the gilt (British government bond) market, it is worth explaining in some detail.

A.1. Spline estimation

First, a functional form for the discount function is postulated. The discount function is formally defined as the present value of a dollar paid at time t, and will be used to price any bond. For computational ease, the discount function is assumed to take the shape of a cubic spline:

$$D(t)=a_{i0}+a_{i1}t+a_{i2}t^2+a_{i3}t^3, \qquad t_i<t<t_{i+1},$$

where the values of the parameter a_{ij} are allowed to differ across knot points t_i, $i=1,\dots,N$. To ensure continuity and smoothness of the spline curve, the function value and its first and second derivatives are restricted to be the same at the knot points. In addition, the discount function is set equal to one at time zero. For N knot points, this yields $3+N$ parameters to estimate.

Second, the theoretical prices of the sample of selected bonds are computed from this discount function. For instance, if a bond pays the cash flows c_k, $k=1,\dots,K$, at respective times t_k, the model price is set at the present value of the future cash flows,

$$\hat{P}=\sum_k c_k D(t_k),$$

which can be written as a linear function of the spline parameters,

$$\hat{P}=a_0 f_0(c_k)+a_1 f_1(c_k)+a_2 f_2(c_k)+\cdots.$$

The parameter $\{a\}$ are estimated by comparing the theoretical prices $\hat{P}$ with the market prices P for the selected bonds. Minimizing the square of the discrepancies amounts to running a simple linear regression of the market prices on the model prices expressed as a linear function of the parameters of interest.

Once the discount function is found from market data, annualized spot rates can be derived as $D(t)=\exp(-i(t)*t)$, where t is expressed in years.

A.2. Data sources

For the gilt market, discount functions are estimated from bond-price data as reported by the *Financial Times*. All bonds with maturities up to fifteen years are included in the sample. Because of the presence of tax effects, reported, for instance, by Litzenberger and Rolfo (1984), low-coupon bonds were discarded.

For the bund market, spot rates are inferred from data provided by the Bundesbank. The Bundesbank reports monthly bond yields for maturities of one to five years. These yields are then assumed to correspond to par instruments with annual coupons. The spot rates are recovered from the bond-equivalent yields by using the shorter spot rates to account for intermediate coupon payments. For instance, the two-year spot rate is found by subtracting from the value of the bond, which is assumed at par, the present value of the first interest payment, using the one-year spot rate.

Euromarket interest rates are obtained from DRI for the U.S. dollar, German mark (DM), and Swiss franc (SF) from June 1973 to December 1988. The end-of-month quotes consist of one-, two-, three, four-, and five-year rates on Eurocurrency deposits, reported at the close of the London market. These deposits are essentially equivalent to par bonds paying an annual coupon equal to the Eurocurrency rate. Spot rates are recovered from the Eurocurrency rates by forward substitution, as performed above for DM government bonds.

Results with Eurocurrency data are not reported for the U.S., Britain, and Germany, but estimates are similar to those in the text. Tests for the equality of the slope coefficients across the Eurocurrency and government data sets were conducted and in no case was the hypothesis of equal coefficients rejected.

References

Cumby, Robert and John Huizinga, 1989, Testing for autocorrelation structure of disturbances in ordinary least squares and instrumental variables regressions, Unpublished paper (New York University, New York, NY).

Engle, Robert, 1982, Autoregressive conditional heteroskedasticity with estimates of the variance of United Kingdom inflation, Econometrica 50, 987–1007.

Fama, Eugene F., 1984, The information in the term structure, Journal of Financial Economics 13, 509–528.

Fama, Eugene F., 1990, Term structure forecasts of interest rates, inflation and real returns, Journal of Monetary Economics 25, 59–76.

Fama, Eugene F. and Robert Bliss, 1987. The information in long-maturity forward rates, American Economic Review 77, 680–692.

Hansen, Lars, 1982, Large sample properties of generalized method of moments estimators, Econometrica 50, 1029–1054.

Hansen, Lars and Robert Hodrick, 1980, Forward exchange rates as optimal predictors of future spot rates, Journal of Political Economy 88, 829–853.

Hardouvelis, Gikas, 1988, The predictive power of the term structure during recent monetary regimes. Journal of Finance 43, 339–356.

Huizinga, John and Frederic S. Mishkin, 1984, Inflation and real interest rates on assets with different risk characteristics, Journal of Finance 39, 699–712.

Jorion, Philippe and Frederic S. Mishkin, 1990, A multi-country comparison of term structure forecasts at long horizons, Working paper (National Bureau of Economic Research, Boston, MA).

Litzenberger, Robert and Jacques Rolfo, 1984, An international study of tax effects on government bonds, Journal of Finance 39, 1–22.

Mishkin, Frederic S., 1981, The real rate of interest, an empirical investigation, The cost and consequences of inflation, Carnegie–Rochester Conference Series on Public Policy 15, 151–200.

Mishkin, Frederic S., 1984, The real interest rate: A multi-country empirical study, Canadian Journal of Economics 17, 283–311.

Mishkin, Frederic S., 1990a, What does the term structure tell us about future inflation?, Journal of Monetary Economics 25, 77–95.

Mishkin, Frederic S., 1990b, The information in the longer-maturity term structure about future inflation, Quarterly Journal of Economics 55, 815–828.

Mishkin, Frederic S., 1991, A multi-country study of the information in the term structure about future inflation, Journal of International Money and Finance, forthcoming.

Newey, W. and Kenneth West, 1987, A simple, positive definite, heteroskedasticity and autocorrelation consistent covariance matrix, Econometrica 55, 703–708.

Shiller, Robert and J. Huston McCulloch, 1987, The term structure of interest rates, Working paper (National Bureau of Economic Research, Boston, MA).

Teeken, Rudolf, 1989, Consumer price indices in the European Community (Office of Official Publication of the European Communities, Eurostat, Luxembourg).

White, Halbert, 1980, A heteroskedasticity-consistent covariance matrix estimator and direct tests for heteroskedasticity, Econometrica 48, 817–838.

Index

Economists of the Twentieth Century

Monetarism and Macroeconomic Policy
Thomas Mayer

Studies in Fiscal Federalism
Wallace E. Oates

The World Economy in Perspective
Essays in International Trade and European Integration
Herbert Giersch

Towards a New Economics
Critical Essays on Ecology, Distribution and Other Themes
Kenneth E. Boulding

Studies in Positive and Normative Economics
Martin J. Bailey

The Collected Essays of Richard E. Quandt (2 volumes)
Richard E. Quandt

International Trade Theory and Policy
Selected Essays of W. Max Corden
W. Max Corden

Organization and Technology in Capitalist Development
William Lazonick

Studies in Human Capital
Collected Essays of Jacob Mincer, Volume 1
Jacob Mincer

Studies in Labor Supply
Collected Essays of Jacob Mincer, Volume 2
Jacob Mincer

Macroeconomics and Economic Policy
The Selected Essays of Assar Lindbeck, Volume I
Assar Lindbeck

The Welfare State
The Selected Essays of Assar Lindbeck, Volume II
Assar Lindbeck

Classical Economics, Public Expenditure and Growth
Walter Eltis

Money, Interest Rates and Inflation
Frederic S. Mishkin

The Public Choice Approach to Politics
Dennis C. Mueller

The Liberal Economic Order
Volume I Essays on International Economics
Volume II Money, Cycles and Related Themes
Gottfried Haberler
Edited by Anthony Y.C. Koo

Economic Growth and Business Cycles
Prices and the Process of Cyclical Development
Paolo Sylos Labini